LATIN AMERICAN POPULATION AND URBANIZATION ANALYSIS

Statistical Abstract of Latin America Supplement Series

Supplement 8

James W. Wilkie, *Series Editor*

Latin American Population and Urbanization Analysis

MAPS AND STATISTICS, 1950-1982

RICHARD W. WILKIE

UCLA Latin American Center Publications
University of California
Los Angeles, California

UCLA Latin American Center Publications
University of California
Los Angeles, California 90024

Library of Congress Cataloging in Publication Data

Wilkie, Richard W., 1938–
    Latin American population and urbanization analysis.

    (Statistical abstract of Latin America, supplement
series ; suppl. 8)
    Bibliography: p.
    1. Latin America--Population--Statistics. 2. Urbaniza-
tion--Latin America--Statistics. 3. Latin America--
Population--Maps. 4. Urbanization--Latin America--Maps.
I. Title. II. Series.
HB3530.5.W54   1984   312'.098   83-620019
ISBN 0-87903-242-1 (alk. paper)

All photos by Richard W. Wilkie, unless otherwise noted.

To my parents,
Lucile Likins Wilkie and Waldo W. Wilkie,
whose Idaho spirit extended to Latin America

Contents

Illustrations

PHOTOS

MAPS

PART ONE   OVERVIEW

PART TWO   COUNTRY DATA

FIGURES

PART ONE   OVERVIEW

PART TWO   COUNTRY DATA

Tables

Acknowledgments

The preparation of the maps, cartograms, and graphs in this volume, as well as much of the data collection, involved the cooperation of many people. Although all cannot be named here, I would like to note the individual contributions of an outstanding few. James W. Wilkie originally approached me with the idea of compiling a map supplement to the *Statistical Abstract of Latin America* (SALA), to consist of maps I had prepared for the annual SALA since 1969. I agreed to write the book and decided to build it from population and settlement data that I had been gathering and analyzing for several years.

The production of maps is extremely time consuming. This book could not have been completed without the help of many students at the University of Massachusetts, Amherst (UMA) who worked on the project over the years. In addition to these students, who are named below, other individuals contributed ideas and useful comments about the study of population and urbanization in Latin America. Special thanks go to Jane R. Wilkie, Armin K. Ludwig, Nicolas Chrisman, Oriol Pi-Sunyer, Robert Potash, Kenneth Erickson, Robert N. Thomas, Barry Lentnek, Gene Martin, Richard C. Jones, and Brad Benedict. Pauline Collins, the Latin American Bibliographer at UMA, never failed to alert me to the latest census materials or books to arrive from Latin America on population and urbanization.

Mrs. Erwin Raisz, Cambridge, Massachusetts, gave me permission to use her husband's physiographic maps showing the landscapes of Mexico, Central America, and the Caribbean. The maps of South America, drawn by Guy Harold-Smith, are published with permission from the Hammond Publishing Company.

Research was conducted under the auspices of the Historical Research Foundation, to which I am greatly indebted. The detailed original planning of the content of the volume took place at Warm Lake, Idaho, in the summer of 1972, at a series of research seminars sponsored by the Foundation, which has continued to support my research on the analysis of population in Latin America.

Financial support came from the UCLA Latin American Center for cartographic and darkroom supplies; from the Department of Geology and Geography at UMA for darkroom materials, office supplies, and secretarial assistance; and from the UMA Computer Center for the 78 three-dimensional computer maps. Robert Gonter, Associate Director of the Computer Center, was especially helpful in arranging support for the plotting time. Mary Richards and Thomas Gallagher guided the maps through the Computer Center to completion. Darkroom assistance throughout the project was provided by Michael Mow and Michael Leonard.

I alone am responsible for the finished volume, including whatever strengths and weaknesses it may contain. There would have been no book at all had it not been for the assistance of the following students at UMA:

W. R. Alcott	Kristy Maxwell
Richard Ashenfelter	William McElhiney
John Bye	Jock Montgomery
Chris Coffin	Steve Morgan
Steven Connor	Michael Mow
Douglas Cotton	William Nechamen
John Creaven, Jr.	Vanesa Nii
John Crowe	Robert Nordstrom
Patricia Cutts	Alexander Paine
David M. Feinberg	Kathy Price
Chris Fraser	Gerald Quigley
Beverly Garside	Mary Richards
Thomas Gallagher	Melody Seawell
Howard Glassman	Peter Serafino
Jeffrey Grell	Frank Shear
Daniel Harbacevich	Douglas Smith
Jack F. Hunter	Kenneth Stuart
Rosanne Hynes	Claire Sweeney
Janet Jewett	Jerry Tisser
Steven Kocur	Michael Voutselas
Wilfred LaCroix	Lee R. Warren
Michael Leonard	Lee Wicks
Tucker Lindquist	Jenny Wood
Jane Lundquist	David Zuckerman
John E. Mart	

R. W. W.

University of Massachusetts, Amherst
December 1982

Part One: Overview

1

Introduction

Those who have attempted to understand population and urbanization changes in Latin America have discovered the difficulty of finding relevant up-to-date information in the available sources. This volume of Latin American population data and maps attempts to assemble the most recent population data on the twenty Latin American republics. In addition to offering an analysis of levels in the urban-rural hierarchy of settlements, the work is also a source book for the study of the population dynamics of Latin America.

Organization

Part One consists of four overview chapters which provide varying regional scales of analyses and map coverage. Following the discussion of the conceptual framework for examining population change in the introductory chapter, Chapters 2, 3, and 4 provide data and maps for Latin America as a whole, for Middle America, which encompasses Mexico, Central America, and the Caribbean, and for South America.

The twenty chapters comprising Part Two present detailed data and maps for each Latin American country. Population data for each country includes the latest census results by civil division, population of the major urban centers, a breakdown of the population into five levels in the urban-rural hierarchy of settlements for the 1950s, 1960s, and 1970s, and a table of selected indicators of population change since the 1940s. Maps for each country include both political and physical base maps, population cartograms showing political units by population size, and three-dimensional computer maps of total population, population density, and population change between the two most recent censuses.

The remainder of this chapter discusses the rapid acceleration of change in Latin America and the methodology for the analysis of urban and rural data on population. Emphasis is placed on the development over time of a population living in each of five levels in the settlement settlement hierarchy of cities and the proportion of the hierarchy for each country—rural dispersed population, rural villages of up to 2,000 inhabitants, simple urban cen-

ters of up to 20,000 population, complex urban centers of up to 500,000 population, and metropolitan centers of more than half a million inhabitants.

Acceleration of Population Change in Latin America

A most striking aspect for many who traveled in Latin America before the 1970s, and who return there today, is the very rapid change that has taken place over the last decade or more. Not only is it difficult to recognize most of the major cities one came to know in the 1950s and 1960s, but also the forces of change seem to have accelerated and to have filtered far down the settlement hierarchy, reaching the most remote villages and previously untouched landscapes. The impact of the automobile, electricity, refrigeration, television and the media, and other aspects of modernization can be seen everywhere.

Of the many examples of rapid change, an image comes to mind of Asunción, Paraguay, in 1966 when it was still a relatively sleepy provincial city with a moderate assortment of motorized vehicles, many of which were of pre-World War II vintage. At the ragtag parade celebrating the 450th anniversary of its founding (see Photo 21-3), I was able to walk right up to President Stroessner with a camera and take his picture at a distance of two feet from the reviewing stand. Three body guards of slight build glanced at me, but they were more interested in the parade than in verifying my intentions. The entire event was extremely casual, with Stroessner and his family seated on a small wooden reviewing stand elevated not more than two feet above street level. The laissez-faire attitude that surrounded the Presidential party could be observed everywhere in the country in 1966. I remember that we virtually checked ourselves into Paraguay upon arrival at Puente Stroessner. After crossing the new bridge from Brazil, we came to the two-room wooden shed that served as the customs post, and found no one on duty. We looked about and finally found an old woman in a nearby house who said the guards had all gone to lunch, but to go ahead into Paraguay as nobody really cared. We thanked her but explained that we needed an entrance stamp in order to be able to leave the country with no problem, and asked where we could find the guards. Sure enough, they were having lunch in a run-down one-room wooden restaurant about 200 yards down the road. They too gave us the same advice—"Go on into Paraguay as nobody cares whether you are stamped into the country or not." Again we gave our reasons for not wanting to enter according to that procedure. They found our concern about potential exit problems worth a good laugh. Since the guards wanted to take their full lunch break, they explained which two rubber stamps, of the three they had, we could use, and told us to stop by the restaurant on the way out to have the entrance visas signed. After virtually admitting ourselves into the country, we proceeded to Asunción and its anniversary celebration. As we left Paraguay several days later from a tiny run-down airport, where nobody looked at the entrance stamp, we felt that Paraguay truly fit the description of a charming undeveloped backwater.

In 1974 I again entered Paraguay over the same route via Iguazú Falls from Argentina and Brazil. The changes that had occurred in Paraguay during the eight years were astounding. On both sides of the border at the Puente Stroessner stood cities approaching 20,000 population. The two-room customs post had been replaced by a three-story concrete building swarming with efficient officials who made us open all our bags and searched the car with care. It was hard to believe an entirely modern town stood where only a few wooden shacks had existed eight years before. Asunción was even more difficult to recognize. No longer a backwater, it was a dynamic, booming trade center with new automobiles and traffic jams, and businesses and people everywhere. Although the new road and commercial linkages to Brazil were greatly responsible for the changes in Paraguay, similar processes of change were under way elsewhere in Latin America as well.

Is it possible to qualitatively and quantitatively document this kind of rapid change? What are the patterns of rapid development and urbanization and how do they relate to human settlement patterns? The data presented here, based on the most recent census materials available at the time of the analysis, will, it is hoped, document these changes over time.

Classification of Settlement Hierarchy

Traditionally, an urban versus rural classification has been used to show relative urbanization. This classification, however, does not provide a picture of the sizes of communities and the types of settlement hierarchies that exist, nor does it indicate the stages of settlement change

that regions or nations go through. The following typology,[1] which isolates five levels in the rural-urban continuum, has been developed to better examine the urbanization process (see R. Wilkie 1976, 1980a, 1980b, 1981).

0   DISPERSED SETTLEMENT: less than 100 inhabitants
1   VILLAGE: rural centers between 100 and 2,500 inhabitants
2   SIMPLE URBAN: centers between 2,501 and 20,000 inhabitants
3   COMPLEX URBAN: centers between 20,001 and 500,000 inhabitants
4   METROPOLITAN: centers over 500,000 inhabitants

In addition, a sixth category can be used for more recent census results:

5   MEGALOPOLIS: centers over 10 million inhabitants.

The division of this urban-rural classification corresponds to break points in common usage (e.g., 2,500 or 2,000 dividing urban from rural populations and 500,000 designating the metropolitan category) and to even incremental breaks between the five categories taken from a straight line drawn on a semilogarithmic graph (see R. Wilkie, 1976:106). The two approaches for determining the upper and lower limits of each of these five categories produce nearly identical results.

Dispersed Settlement (0)

The division between dispersed and village populations falls between 100 and 167 individuals and closely approximates the figure currently in use in most Latin American countries. Mexico, for example, has census categories of under 100 and 100 to 500 for small villages, while Argentina stops listing village populations between 100 and 200 in size.

Village (1)

The common break point between rural villages and an urban classification falls in the range of 2000 to 2,500 inhabitants. According to Doherty and Ball (1971:20−28), 2,500 inhabitants in Mexico appears to be a quite accurate threshold for the maintenance of many basic services. With the exceptions of a primary school and a physician (with population thresholds of 960 and 2,133), the crucial size to support most basic services was as follows: health center (2,498), pharmacy (2,512), gasoline station (2,596), sec-

---

[1] Portions of this settlement classification have been presented previously in R. Wilkie (1976 and 1981). The most recent calculations of population, however, are based on data presented here.

ondary school (2,696), cinema (2,860), auto repair shop (2,912), and restaurant (2,933). While the authors recognized that these figures from a sample of 30 villages around Mexico can only be approximate, they feel that "the thresholds generally do reflect the high population requirements for the appearance of urban functions and reveal the order of occurrence of functions." Argentina, with a somewhat more mobil rural population, uses the figure of 2,000 population as the break between rural villages and the urban classification.

Simple Urban (2)

The division between simple and complex urban centers at 20,000 inhabitants is compatible with international units of measurement. Ducoff (1965:199) and Elizaga (1965:145) feel that a population of 20,000 inhabitants clearly marks the beginning of a more complex urban category in the Latin American context. This figure is also used by the United Nations (1969:19) for international comparative purposes, as well as by other scholars (Ginsburg 1961:34).

Complex Urban (3)

The figure of 500,000 is often used in census volumes as a tabular break, but it is also about the size at which a city moves out of a complex urban level to become a true metropolitan center. Complex urban cities are clearly distinguished from simple urban centers, but usually serve as regional rather than national centers.

Metropolitan (4)

Between half a million and about 10 million inhabitants designates those cities that often dominate an entire country or at least a very large region within a nation. The lower figure seems to be the minimum requirement to truly maintain the metropolitan atmosphere of cities in the category which are for the most part at least several million in size.

Megalopolis (5, Not used in this study)

At about 10 million population, metropolitan centers begin to move into a new category which Gottman [1961] notes is "more the size of a nation than that of metropolis." Megalopolis units so completely dominate the landscape that most centers in the hierarchy begin to merge into one huge urban agglomeration. By 1980, Latin America has at least four megalopolis regions approaching or surpassing that population threshold—Mexico City with 15 million, São Paulo with 13.5 million, Rio de Janeiro with 10.7 million, and Buenos Aires with 10.1 million (United Nations:1980). Thus all four currently surpass fourteen of the twenty largest countries in Latin America, and only one country

(Colombia) not associated with those cities has a larger national population than the Mexico City and São Paulo/Rio de Janeiro megalopolis regions.

By identifying the sizes of communities in which various proportions of the population live, this classification permits detailed analysis of the changing spatial settlement hierarchy of a nation over time.

Typology for Classifying Settlement Hierarchies

Whereas in most countries population resides at each of the five community size levels, in virtually every case a substantial majority of the population (more than three-fifths) lives in only two of the five levels. The two levels with the highest percentage of population are used to classify countries and subregions on the settlement typology presented in Figure 1-1. For example, Colombia in 1964 would be classified as dispersed–complex urban (0–3). The dispersed level with 40.5 percent of the Colombian population was the highest ranking category followed by the complex urban level with 19.2 percent of the population. Together these two settlement levels accounted for three-fifths of the Colombian population in 1964. Of the remaining population, 17 percent resided in metropolitan centers, 15 percent in simple urban communities, and 8 percent in villages.

Data for the settlement hierarchies of all twenty Latin American countries are presented in Tables 1-1A, 1-2A, 1-1B, 1-2B, 1-1C, and 1-2C for the 1950s, 1960s, and 1970s. The resulting settlement classifications are given in Map 1-1 and countries are grouped by classification level over time in Figure 1-2. Rather than analyzing all countries individually, a case study of Mexico for the period 1910 to 1970 is used to illustrate how these settlement hierarchies evolve over time. In addition, the five examples below show the range of settlement hierarchy types existing in Latin America:

a. *Dispersed Rural Type:* Between 1910 and 1970, but especially in 1950, Haiti was overwhelmingly a dispersed settlement pattern with small villages. Nearly nine out of ten Haitians (88 percent) lived in either of these two most rural settlement levels, thus classified as 0–1.

b. *Village–Simple Urban Type:* For most of the twentieth century more than half of the Mexican population lived in villages of between 100 and 2,500 inhabitants and about a fifth of the population lived in lower order urban centers under 20,000 in size. In 1950, for example, seven out of ten Mexicans lived in these two lower order urban types of communities.

Photo 1-1

DISPERSED SETTLEMENT LANDSCAPE NEAR COCHABAMBA, BOLIVIA (1977)

Photo 1-2

SETTLEMENT PATTERN OF A SMALL BOLIVIAN MOUNTAIN VILLAGE
BETWEEN COCHABAMBA AND POTOSÍ (1977)

Figure 1-1

A MATRIX TYPOLOGY OF URBAN-RURAL HIERARCHIES

(PERCENT OF POPULATION IN HIGHEST TWO CATEGORIES)*

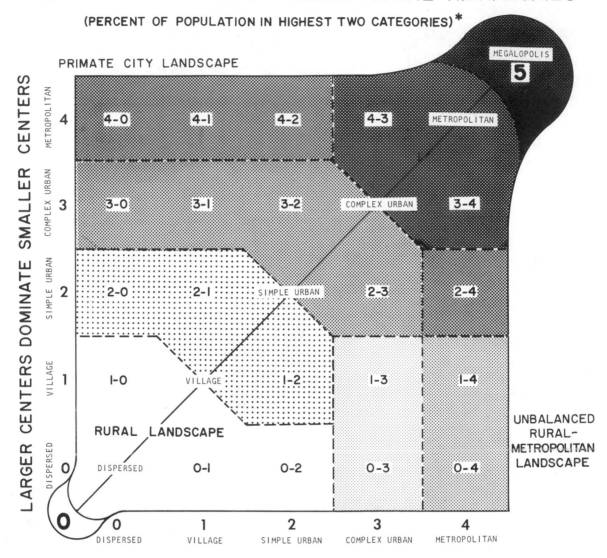

SMALLER CENTERS DOMINATE LARGER CENTERS

*The two urban-rural levels with the largest percentages usually
have between 55 and 80 percent of the total population of the region.

	CODE		SETTLEMENT TYPE	POPULATION SIZE
RURAL	0	=	Dispersed Settlement	under 200[a]
	1	=	Village	200 to 2,000[b]
URBAN	2	=	Simple Urban	2,001 to 20,000[c]
	3	=	Complex Urban	20,0001 to 500,000
	4	=	Metropolitan	over 500,000
	5	=	Megalopolis	over 10 million

[a]varies between countries (range 50 to 250 upper limit)
[b]varies between countries (range 1500 to 2500)
[c]varies between countries (range 20,000 to 35,000)

Photo 1-3

GUATEMALAN VILLAGE SETTLEMENT PATTERN, SAN ANTONIO PALOPO (1979)

Table 1-1A

TOTAL POPULATION IN EACH OF FIVE LEVELS IN THE SETTLEMENT HIERARCHY OF LATIN AMERICA, 1950s, 1960s, AND 1970s

COUNTRIES Grouped Regionally (North to South)	YEAR OF CENSUS	TOTAL POPULATION	0 DISPERSED Population 1–99	1 VILLAGE 100– 1,900	2 SIMPLE URBAN 2,000– 19,999	3 COMPLEX URBAN 20,000– 500,000	4 METRO- POLITAN Over 500,000
MEXICO	1950	25,791,017	1,772,256	13,018,043	4,795,348	3,609,477	2,604,893
	1960	34,923,129	1,571,541	15,645,561	6,181,394	5,517,855	6,006,778
	1970	48,225,238	1,446,757	18,518,491	7,548,675	7,830,211	12,881,102
	1980	67,405,700	- -	- -	- -	- -	- -
CENTRAL AMERICA (Total Region)	1950s	8,678,391	.... 6,274,303		1,265,327	1,138,761	0
	1960s	12,627,894	.... 8,179,394		2,103,477	1,772,086	572,937
	1970s	17,276,369	.... 10,450,905		2,412,680	2,339,041	2,073,743
	1980s	- -		- -	- -	- -	- -
GUATEMALA	1950	2,790,686	.... 2,082,947		385,723	322,016	0
	1964	4,284,473	.... 2,827,752		791,781	92,269	572,937
	1973	5,879,700	.... 3,527,820		1,182,280	180,500	989,100
EL SALVADOR	1950	1,855,917	.... 1,341,562		274,000	240,355	0
	1961	2,510,984	.... 1,491,418		535,887	483,679	0
	1971	3,549,260	.... 2,165,049		585,611	233,600	565,000
HONDURAS	1950	1,368,605	.... 1,109,939		165,142	93,524	0
	1961	1,884,765	.... 1,449,760		197,078	237,927	0
	1967	2,495,000	1,703,278	163,997	281,693	346,032	0
	1974	2,653,857	.... 1,963,854		96,813	593,190	0
NICARAGUA	1950	1,057,023	.... 687,774		208,318	160,931	0
	1963	1,535,588	.... 905,997		275,648	353,946	0
	1971	1,894,690	.... 994,002		287,874	612,814	0
COSTA RICA	1950	800,875	.... 536,586		122,432	141,857	0
	1963	1,336,274	.... 875,774		107,724	352,776	0
	1973	1,871,780	.... 1,110,680		207,925	552,175	0
PANAMA	1950	805,285	214,318	301,177	109,712	180,078	0
	1960	1,075,541	255,523	373,213	90,843	355,962	0
	1970	1,428,082	.... 689,500		52,177	166,762	519,643
	1980	1,788,748		- -	- -	- -	- -
CARIBBEAN (Total Region)	1950s	11,062,123	.... 7,237,257		1,185,940	1,398,557	1,240,369
	1960s	14,158,190	.... 8,826,744		1,570,670	2,166,776	1,594,000
	1970s	16,879,612	.... 9,268,539		2,011,434	3,149,423	2,450,216
	1980s	- -		- -	- -	- -	- -
CUBA	1953	5,829,029	2,541,440	347,000	838,280	1,003,722	1,098,587
	1964	7,434,200	.... 3,568,416		1,051,784	1,220,000	1,594,000
	1970	8,553,395	.... 3,461,307		1,407,381	1,933,491	1,751,216

Table 1-2A

PERCENT OF POPULATION IN EACH OF FIVE LEVELS IN THE SETTLEMENT HIERARCHY OF LATIN AMERICA, 1950s, 1960s, AND 1970s

COUNTRIES Grouped Regionally (North to South)	YEAR OF CENSUS	0 DISPERSED Population 1–99	1 VILLAGE 100–1,999	2 SIMPLE URBAN 2,000–19,999	3 COMPLEX URBAN 20,000–500,000	4 METRO-POLITAN Over 500,000	SETTLEMENT HIERARCHY Classification	SETTLEMENT HIERARCHY PERCENT in Top 2 Levels
MEXICO	1950	6.9	50.5	18.6	13.9	10.1	1-2	69.1
	1960	4.5	44.8	17.7	15.8	17.2	1-2	62.5
	1970	3.0	38.4	15.7	16.2	26.7	1-4	65.1
	1980	- -	- -	- -	- -	- -	- -	- -
CENTRAL AMERICA (Total Region)	1950s	....	72.3	14.6	13.1	0	0-2	70 to 75
	1960s	....	64.8	16.7	14.0	4.5	0-2	65 to 70
	1970s	....	60.5	14.0	13.5	12.0	0-2	60 to 66
	1980s	- -	- -	- -	- -	- -	- -	- -
GUATEMALA	1950	....	74.6	13.8	11.5	0	0-1	74.6
	1964	....	66.0	18.4	2.2	13.4	0-2	66 to 70
	1973	....	60.0	20.1	3.1	16.8	0-2	66 to 70
EL SALVADOR	1950	....	72.2	14.8	13.0	0	0-1	72.2
	1961	....	59.4	21.3	19.3	0	0-2	61 to 65
	1971	....	61.0	16.5	6.6	15.9	0-2	61 to 65
HONDURAS	1950	....	81.1	11.2	6.8	0	0-2	80 to 86
	1961	....	76.9	10.5	12.6	0	0-3	82.7
	1967	68.2	6.6	11.3	13.9	0	0-3	82.1
	1974	....	74.0	3.6	22.4	0	0-3	84 to 90
NICARAGUA	1950	....	65.1	19.7	15.2	0	0-2	68 to 75
	1963	....	59.0	18.0	23.0	0	0-3	68 to 75
	1971	....	52.0	15.2	32.3	0	0-3	65 to 75
COSTA RICA	1950	....	66.5	15.8	17.7	0	0-3	67 to 72
	1963	....	65.5	8.1	26.4	0	0-3	67 to 72
	1973	....	59.4	11.1	29.5	0	0-3	68 to 75
PANAMA	1950	26.6	37.5	13.5	22.4	0	1-0	64.1
	1960	23.8	34.7	8.4	33.1	0	1-3	67.8
	1970	....	48.3	3.6	11.7	36.4	4-1	66 to 69
	1980	- -	- -	- -	- -	- -	- -	- -
CARIBBEAN (Total Region)	1950s	....	65.4	10.7	12.6	11.2	0-3	62 to 68
	1960s	....	62.3	11.1	15.3	11.3	0-3	60 to 66
	1970s	....	54.9	11.9	18.7	14.5	0-3	58 to 63
	1980s	- -	- -	- -	- -	- -	- -	- -
CUBA	1953	43.6	6.0	14.4	17.2	18.8	0-4	62.4
	1964	....	48.0	14.1	16.4	21.4	0-4	62 to 64
	1970	....	40.5	16.4	22.6	20.5	0-3	60 to 65

Table 1-1B

TOTAL POPULATION IN EACH OF FIVE LEVELS IN THE SETTLEMENT HIERARCHY OF LATIN AMERICA, 1950s, 1960s, AND 1970s

COUNTRIES Grouped Regionally (North to South)	YEAR OF CENSUS	TOTAL POPULATION	0 DISPERSED Population 1–99	1 VILLAGE 100– 1,900	2 SIMPLE URBAN 2,000– 19,999	3 COMPLEX URBAN 20,000– 500,000	4 METRO- POLITAN Over 500,000
DOMINICAN REP.	1950	2,135,872	....	1,623,263	216,587	296,022	0
	1960	3.047,070	....	2,132,949	238,401	675,720	0
	1970	4,011,589	....	2,312,383	375,206	625,000	699,000
	1981	5,621,985		- -	- -	- -	1,318,000
HAITI	1950	3,097,220	....	2,725,554	131,073	240,593	0
	1960	3,676,938	....	3,125,397	280,485	271,056	0
	1971	4,314,628	....	3,494,849	228,847	590,932	0
GRAN COLOMBIA (Total Region)	1950s	16,583,010	....	9,977,036	2,273,210	2,827,058	1,505,852
	1960s	25,008,507	....	11,251,385	3,827,184	5,404,169	4,525,769
	1970s	31,791,637	....	10,349,902	4,039,818	8,755,107	8,646,810
	1980s	- -		- -	- -	- -	- -
VENEZUELA	1950	5,034,838	1,988,578	597,628	771,987	886,189	790,602
	1961	7,523,999	....	2,783,880	1,203,813	2,043,928	1,492,378
	1971	10,721,522	....	2,680,380	1,544,529	3,668,874	2,827,739
	1981	14,602,480		- -	- -	- -	- -
COLOMBIA	1951	11,548,172	....	7,390,830	1,501,223	1,940,869	715,250
	1964	17,484,508	7,083,593	1,383,912	2,623,371	3,360,241	3,033,391
	1973	21,070,115	....	7,669,522	2,495,289	5,086,233	5,819,071
CENTRAL ANDES (Total Region)	1950s	14,136,788	....	9,209,918	2,081,603	1,633,515	1,211,752
	1960s	18,270,222	....	10,943,580	2,135,450	2,834,497	2,356,695
	1970s	25,045,795	....	11,751,883	2,947,374	4,467,334	5,879,131
	1980s	- -		- -	- -	- -	- -
ECUADOR	1950	3,202,757	....	2,305,985	326,749	570,023	0
	1962	4,476,000	....	2,932,145	397,518	741,028	510,785
	1974	6,829,967	....	3,782,174	562,601	919,755	1,565,437
	1982	8,072,702	....	3,676,606	770,950	1,348,136	2,277,010
PERU	1950	7,915,000	....	4,669,850	1,493,462	539,936	1,211,752
	1961	9,906,746	....	5,250,575	1,582,870	1,227,391	1,845,910
	1972	13,567,939	....	5,427,176	2,148,673	2,373,962	3,618,128
BOLIVIA	1950	3,019,031	....	2,234,083	261,392	523,556	0
	1960	3,782,000	....	2,760,860	155,062	866,078	0
	1976	4,647,816	....	2,542,533	236,100	1,173,617	695,566

Table 1-2B

PERCENT OF POPULATION IN EACH OF FIVE LEVELS IN THE SETTLEMENT HIERARCHY OF LATIN AMERICA, 1950s, 1960s, AND 1970s

COUNTRIES Grouped Regionally (North to South)	YEAR OF CENSUS	0 DISPERSED Population 1–99	1 VILLAGE 100– 1,999	2 SIMPLE URBAN 2,000– 19,999	3 COMPLEX URBAN 20,000– 500,000	4 METRO- POLITAN Over 500,000	SETTLEMENT HIERARCHY Classifi- cation	PERCENT in Top 2 Levels
DOMINICAN REP.	1950	.... 76.0		10.1	13.9	0	0-1	76.0
	1960	.... 70.0		7.8	22.2	0	0-3	72 to 80
	1970	.... 57.6		9.4	15.6	17.4	0-4	60 to 70
	1981	- -	- -	- -	- -	23.4	- -	- -
HAITI	1950	.... 88.0		4.2	7.8	0	0-1	88.0
	1960	.... 85.0		7.6	7.4	0	0-1	85.0
	1971	.... 81.0		5.3	13.7	0	0-1	81.0
GRAN COLOMBIA (Total Region)	1950s	.... 60.2		13.7	17.1	9.0	0-3	55 to 60
	1960s	.... 45.0		15.3	21.6	18.1	0-3	50 to 55
	1970s	.... 32.6		12.7	27.5	27.2	3-4	54.7
VENEZUELA	1950	39.5	11.9	15.3	17.6	15.7	0-3	57.1
	1961	.... 37.0		16.0	27.2	19.8	0-3	55 to 60
	1971	.... 25.0		14.4	34.2	26.4	3-4	60.6
	1981	- -	- -	- -	- -	- -	- -	- -
COLOMBIA	1951	.... 64.0		13.0	16.8	6.2	0-3	65 to 70
	1964	40.5	7.9	15.0	19.2	17.3	0-3	59.7
	1973	.... 36.4		11.8	24.2	27.6	0-4	56 to 58
CENTRAL ANDES (Total Region)	1950s	.... 65.1		14.7	11.6	8.6	0-2	62 to 68
	1960s	.... 59.9		11.7	15.5	12.9	0-3	60 to 66
	1970s	.... 46.9		11.8	17.8	23.5	0-4	60 to 66
	1980s	- -	- -	- -	- -	- -	- -	- -
ECUADOR	1950	.... 72.0		10.2	17.8	0	0-3	73 to 80
	1962	.... 64.0		8.7	16.2	11.1	0-3	65 to 75
	1974	.... 55.4		8.2	13.5	22.9	0-4	68 to 74
	1982	.... 45.5		9.6	16.7	28.2	0-4	65 to 73
PERU	1950	.... 59.0		18.9	6.8	15.3	0-2	60 to 68
	1961	.... 53.0		16.0	12.4	18.6	0-4	58 to 64
	1972	.... 40.0		15.8	17.5	26.7	0-4	54 to 60
BOLIVIA	1950	.... 74.0		8.7	17.3	0	0-1	74.0
	1960	.... 73.0		4.1	22.9	0	0-3	74 to 84
	1976	.... 54.7		5.0	25.3	15.0	0-3	70 to 80

Table 1-1C

TOTAL POPULATION IN EACH OF FIVE LEVELS IN THE SETTLEMENT HIERARCHY
OF LATIN AMERICA, 1950s, 1960s, AND 1970s

			0	1	2	3	4
COUNTRIES					SIMPLE	COMPLEX	
Grouped	YEAR		DISPERSED	VILLAGE	URBAN	URBAN	METRO-
Regionally	OF	TOTAL	Population	100—	2,000—	20,000—	POLITAN
(North to South)	CENSUS	POPULATION	1—99	1,900	19,999	500,000	Over 500,000
BRAZIL	1950	51,944,397	30,930,373	2,781,534	5,518,286	6,620,756	6,193,448
	1960	70,992,343	35,693,970	3,293,556	8,775,192	10,093,242	13,136,383
	1970	94,508,554	41,603,810	3,591,325	11,938,792	13,022,966	24,351,661
	1980	121,113,084	- -	- -	- -	- -	37,029,235
SOUTHERN SOUTH							
AMERICA	1950s	25,347,733	.... 10,127,061		3,489,527	4,675,522	7,055,623
(Total Region)	1960s	31,799,864	.... 9,433,768		5,037,753	6,117,341	11,211,002
	1970s	37,318,689	.... 7,591,140		4,664,260	7,190,362	17,872,927
	1980s	- -	- -		- -	- -	- -
PARAGUAY	1950	1,328,452	.... 863,494		258,324	206,634	0
	1962	1,819,103	.... 1,164,226		349,717	305,160	0
	1972	2,354,071	.... 540,071		569,775	678,862	565,363
URUGUAY	1950	1,328,452	.... 943,420		54,038	286,923	909,619
	1963	2,595,510	.... 726,743		274,205	435,477	1,159,085
	1975	2,763,964	470,066	89,970	316,278	500,452	1,387,198
ARGENTINA	1947	15,897,127	4,740,892	1,219,255	2,254,414	2,955,344	4,722,381
	1960	20,010,539	3,497,250	1,754,948	3,212,431	3,438,741	8,067,972
	1970	23,364,431	3,906,503	1,087,950	2,836,673	4,501,608	11,031,697
	1980	27,949,840	- -	- -	- -	6,046,832	13,532,907
CHILE	1952	5,932,995	.... 2,360,000		922,751	1,226,621	1,423,623
	1960	7,374,712	.... 2,485,000		967,804	1,937,963	1,983,945
	1970	8,836,223	.... 1,496,580		941,534	1,509,440	4,888,669
	1982	11,275,440	- -		- -	- -	- -
LATIN AMERICA	1950s	153,543,459	.... 90,777,380		23,347,907	20,934,503	18,483,815
Totals	1960s	207,780,149	....104,839,499		29,631,120	33,905,966	39,403,564
	1970s	271,045,821	....114,572,752		35,563,033	46,754,444	74,155,590
LATIN AMERICA	1950s	100.0	.... 59.2		15.2	13.6	12.0
Percentages	1960s	100.0	.... 50.4		14.3	16.3	19.0
	1970s	100.0	.... 42.3		13.1	17.2	27.4

Table 1-2C

PERCENT OF POPULATION IN EACH OF FIVE LEVELS IN THE SETTLEMENT HIERARCHY OF LATIN AMERICA, 1950s, 1960s, AND 1970s

COUNTRIES Grouped Regionally (North to South)	YEAR OF CENSUS	0 DISPERSED Population 1—99	1 VILLAGE 100—1,999	2 SIMPLE URBAN 2,000—19,999	3 COMPLEX URBAN 20,000—500,000	4 METRO-POLITAN Over 500,000	SETTLEMENT HIERARCHY Classification	SETTLEMENT HIERARCHY PERCENT in Top 2 Levels
BRAZIL	1950	59.5	5.3	10.6	12.6	11.9	0-3	72.1
	1960	50.3	4.6	12.4	14.2	18.5	0-4	68.8
	1970	44.0	3.8	12.6	13.8	25.8	0-4	69.8
	1980	- -	- -	- -	- -	31.1	- -	- -
SOUTHERN SOUTH AMERICA (Total Region)	1950s	.... 40.0		13.8	18.4	27.8	0-4	58 to 63
	1960s	.... 29.7		15.8	19.2	35.3	4-3	55 to 60
	1970s	.... 20.3		12.5	19.3	47.9	4-3	65 to 68
	1980s	- -	- -	- -	- -	- -	- -	- -
PARAGUAY	1950	.... 65.0		19.4	15.6	0	0-2	68 to 75
	1962	.... 64.0		19.2	16.8	0	0-2	68 to 75
	1972	.... 22.9		24.2	28.9	24.0	3-2	53.1
URUGUAY	1950	.... 43.0		2.4	13.1	41.5	4-0	67 to 73
	1963	.... 28.0		10.5	16.8	44.7	4-2	64.3
	1975	17.0	3.3	11.5	18.1	50.1	4-3	68.2
ARGENTINA	1947	29.6	7.7	14.3	18.6	29.8	4-0	59.4
	1960	17.5	8.7	16.0	17.6	40.2	4-3	57.8
	1970	16.7	4.7	12.2	19.2	47.2	4-3	66.4
	1980	- -	- -	- -	21.6	48.4	4-3	70.0
CHILE	1952	.... 39.8		15.5	20.7	24.0	4-0	50 to 55
	1960	.... 33.7		13.1	26.3	26.9	4-3	53.2
	1970	.... 16.9		10.7	17.1	55.3	4-3	72.4
	1982	- -	- -	- -	- -	- -	- -	- -
LATIN AMERICA Totals	1950s	...90,777,380 ..		23,347,907	20,934,503	18,483,815		
	1960s	..104,839,499 ..		29,631,120	33,905,966	39,403,564		
	1970s	..114,572,752 ..		35,563,033	46,754,444	74,155,590		
LATIN AMERICA Percentages	1950s	.... 59.2		15.2	13.6	12.0	0-2	
	1960s	.... 50.4		14.3	16.3	19.0	0-4	
	1970s	.... 42.3		13.1	17.2	27.4	0-4	

Figure 1-2

SETTLEMENT CLASSIFICATION BY COUNTRY, 1950s, 1960s, and 1970s

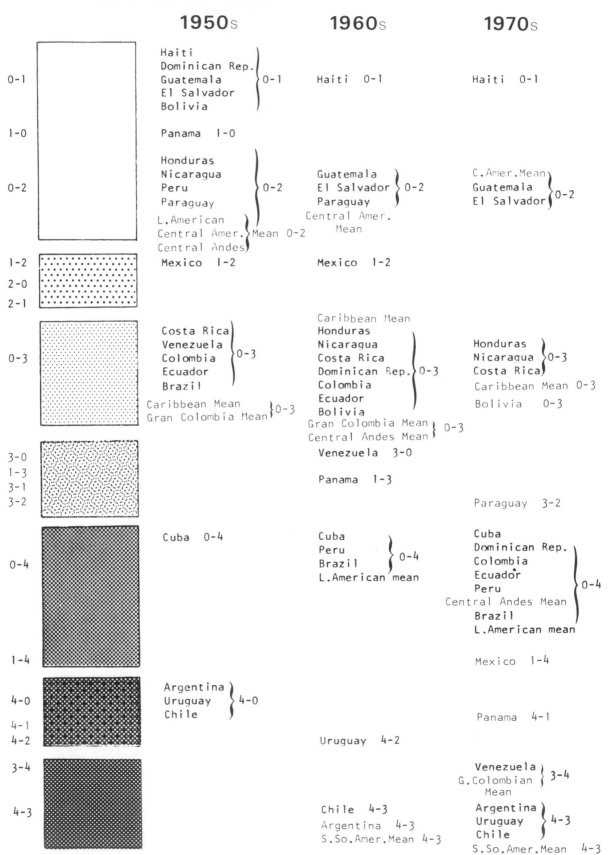

Map 1-1

SETTLEMENT HIERARCHIES OF LATIN AMERICA

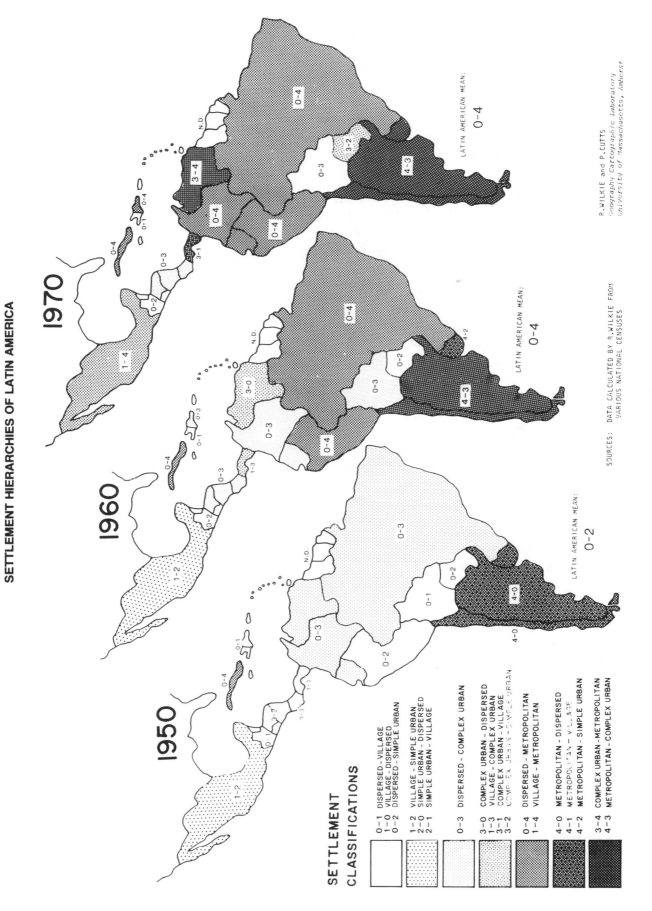

1950   1960   1970

LATIN AMERICAN MEAN:
0-2

LATIN AMERICAN MEAN:
0-4

LATIN AMERICAN MEAN:
0-4

SETTLEMENT
CLASSIFICATIONS

0-1	DISPERSED-VILLAGE	
1-0	VILLAGE-DISPERSED	
0-2	DISPERSED-SIMPLE URBAN	
1-2	VILLAGE - SIMPLE URBAN	
2-0	SIMPLE URBAN - DISPERSED	
2-1	SIMPLE URBAN - VILLAGE	
0-3	DISPERSED - COMPLEX URBAN	
3-0	COMPLEX URBAN - DISPERSED	
1-3	VILLAGE - COMPLEX URBAN	
3-1	COMPLEX URBAN - VILLAGE	
3-2	COMPLEX URBAN - SIMPLE URBAN	
0-4	DISPERSED - METROPOLITAN	
1-4	VILLAGE - METROPOLITAN	
4-0	METROPOLITAN - DISPERSED	
4-1	METROPOLITAN - VILLAGE	
4-2	METROPOLITAN - SIMPLE URBAN	
3-4	COMPLEX URBAN - METROPOLITAN	
4-3	METROPOLITAN - COMPLEX URBAN	

P. WILKIE and P. CUTTS
Geographic Cartographic Laboratory
University of Massachusetts, Amherst

SOURCES: DATA CALCULATED BY R. WILKIE FROM
VARIOUS NATIONAL CENSUSES

c. *Imbalanced Type:* Argentina has traditionally been split between a large dispersed population and a large metropolitan population, with few intermediate-sized communities available to citizens. In 1947, for example, nearly a third of the population lived in metropolitan Buenos Aires, while nearly another third lived totally dispersed in isolated clusters of under 100 individuals. Together these two extremely contrasting settlement levels accounted for two-thirds of the Argentine population.

d. *Primate Urban Type:* Uruguay is a classic case of primate city dominance of a nation. By 1970 half the citizens of the country lived in metropolitan Montevideo and another fifth lived in complex urban centers. Thus, seven out of ten Uruguayans lived in urban centers of more than 20,000 population.

e. *Balanced Type:* Chile in 1960 was one of the few countries in Latin America to have a relative balance among the five urban-rural levels. At that time Chile had a quarter of the population in each of three levels—metropolitan, complex urban, and dispersed, and a quarter of the population was divided between the simple urban and village levels.

Mexico, 1910 to 1970

Data on the settlement hierarchy of Mexico from 1910 to 1970 illustrate the urbanization process over time. The settlement hierarchy of Mexico was consistently at the village—simple urban level (1–2) from 1910 to 1970 when it finally reached village—complex urban (1–3). In spite of such overall stability, significant regional patterns began to evolve about 1930. Maps 1-2A, 1-2B, 1-2C, and 1-2D show four time periods and the consolidation of regional patterns over time. Without going into great detail here,[2] several observations can be made:

1. Mexico in 1910 was overwhelmingly rural in character. Three out of five Mexicans lived in rural villages of between 100 and 2,500 inhabitants, and the village level was the predominant category in every Mexican state and region including the Mexico City area. In the states where the revolution began, rural villages and dispersed population accounted for between two-thirds and four-fifths of the population of those areas. The settlement patterns over larger regions were still broken into pockets of village—dispersed (1–0) or

[2]For more complete data and discussion of Mexican population growth between 1910 and 1970, see Wilkie (1976:99–134).

village—simple urban (1–2) rather than being uniform.

2. By 1930 Mexico's eleven distinct pockets of village—dispersed and village—simple urban areas had evolved into six more homogeneous regions. Nearly all of the central two-thirds of Mexico, with the exception of the Mexico City area and Querétaro, had become a village—simple urban (1–2) settlement hierarchy. The north of Mexico and Yucatán were still varied and ranged from a growing metropolitan category around Monterrey to very rural dispersed—village zones.

3. Mexico in 1960 still maintained a village—simple urban (1–2) hierarchy, but considerable growth had taken place in the metropolitan and complex urban levels (metropolitan had gone from 6.5 percent in 1930 to 17.2 percent in 1960 and complex urban from 9.4 percent to 15.8 percent). In addition to three highly metropolitan dominated regions (4–1) around Mexico City, Guadalajara, and Monterrey, and a more urban dominated region in the north, it was still possible to identify the old Mesoamierican cultural border between northern and central Mexico (where the 1–3 hierarcy borders the 1–2 hierarchy). Virtually all of the old Mesoamerican cultural region was still a village—simple urban (1–2) settlement classification.

4. Ten years is a relatively short period of time, yet between 1960 and 1970 the population of Mexico grew from nearly 35 million to more than 48 million, a 38.5 percent increase. This ten-year growth nearly equaled the entire population of Mexico in 1920, some 14.3 million inhabitants. Rapid growth puts tremendous stress on the expanding urban network. But in spite of this sizable increment, the settlement size classification changed in only nine of the thirty-two political units (see Map 1-28). The Mexico City hinterland, which by 1970 included the states of Mexico, Morelos, Tlaxcala, and parts of Puebla and Hidalgo, had become metropolitan—simple urban (4–2), as had most of the state of Jalisco around Guadalajara. These were the first two regions in Mexico where the village level dropped below second position. The rest of Mexico remained relatively unchanged, except growth of higher order urban centers took place earlier in the north of Mexico than in the south. Thus zone 3–1 occurred first in the north and then slowly expanded southward into the 1–3 zone, which in turn expanded southward into the 1–2 zone. The results of the 1980 census will probably show that much of Mexico's old settlement pattern of village—simple

urban (1–2) will have evolved into a higher order urban hierarchy.

Population and settlement changes have been tremendous since 1910 when the Mexican Revolution began. Not only has the overall population grown more than eightfold since then, but also more than 26,000 new settlements had been started on the landscape between 1910 and 1970. Although the basic framework of settlement location was well established by 1910, the filling in of the urban-rural hierarchy in more uniform patterns did not become evident until the 1930 census. It is likely that by 1980, Mexico will have one of the most evenly balanced settlement hierarchies among the five settlement size levels of any country in Latin America.

Understanding these patterns of the urban settlement systems in Latin America is only a first step. More detailed studies, such as that presented on Mexico between 1910 and 1970, show that much more complicated development of the urban system takes place within nations. In the case of Mexico it was possible to see that the evolution of higher order settlement hierarchies started in the north and formed homogeneous zones that moved to the south in waves. Mexico City and Guadalajara are exceptions, but neither metropolitan area appears to have strongly influenced the settlement hierarchy classification outside its immediate hinterland in the way it has occurred in the north of Mexico.

These different settlement hierarchies have implications for the types of urban and rural problems found in Latin American countries and their subregions. Activities that interconnect and channel the flow of people, ideas, and services throughout the various urban-rural levels are affected by the types of hierarchies that exist. In settlement hierarchies dominated by primate cities, migrants have few options except to go to the largest metropolitan areas where jobs and services have been concentrated. When small regional urban centers are capable of serving the dispersed population with basic economic and social services such as schools, medical facilities, meeting houses, and movie theaters, and perhaps more importantly, small factory and service sector jobs that will hold people in an area, the quality of rural life in many regions throughout Latin America will be enhanced. Without numerous focal points for economic and social activities distributed on the landscape, the rural population is forced to maintain these relationships with more distant regional centers or national capitals. Although an ideal urban-rural settlement hierarchy most likely varies for individual countries and at different points in time based on the level of development, available resources and technology, and national priorities, in general it appears that a balanced hierarchy, perhaps

with decreasing proportions of population descending the hierarchy, provides a more even flow and interconnection within modern urban networks.

One way to assure a more balanced distribution of settlement sizes is to strengthen middle and lower level regional centers. Unfortunately, stimulating growth in regional centers outside the dominant national capitals has not been easy. Industrial and commercial expansion of small and middle range centers provides options that will attract and hold population in the areas of origin.[3] Clearly the more that is known about the evolution of settlement hierarchies, the more readily development or nondevelopment decisions can be made to help alleviate many urban and rural problems before they arrive or are compounded.

Policy decisions, along with the developmental process in general, have major impact at the individual level. Forces that appear to help the situation for some groups may contribute heavily to the problems for other groups. For example, improved transportation in the rural areas of Latin America has not increased access to services, goods, and ideas for all segments of the population. With the rapid rise in the 1970s of the ownership of automobiles and trucks in the rural sectors of many countries in Latin America, the distances between the villages and the regional centers have been reduced, at least for the upper- and middle-class rural families. However, auto travel tends to bypass the lowest order urban centers to reach higher order urban centers with a greater range of services, thus further weakening villages and simple urban centers. When this occurs, as it has in Brazil, Argentina, and other countries, lower class rural populations are even more isolated from economic and social options and are more likely to be forced out of the rural areas in search of work, adding to the concentration of population in larger communities.

Studies such as those outlined above will provide some guidelines for social and economic planners. Those planning for a more rational distribution of population on the landscape need to know more about the internal processes or forces that shape communities of all sizes in the urban-rural hierarchy. If the developmental needs of intermediate level cities are ignored in favor of primate cities, the urban system may in time begin to break down, thus resulting in greater imbalances of population and opportunities. Urban systems that have a relative balance in population and development at all levels of the urban hierarchy will provide

---

[3]See B. Lentnek (1980) for an excellent analysis of five basic strategies for regional development, and E. A. J. Johnson (1970) for a lengthy discussion of the need to develop these middle level centers in the urban hierarchy.

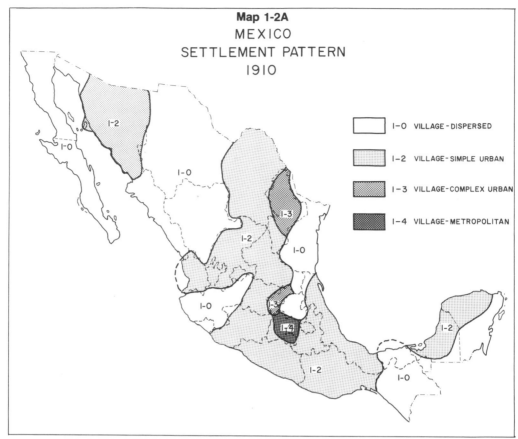

Map 1-2A

MEXICO
SETTLEMENT PATTERN
1910

☐	I-0 VILLAGE-DISPERSED
▨	I-2 VILLAGE-SIMPLE URBAN
▩	I-3 VILLAGE-COMPLEX URBAN
■	I-4 VILLAGE-METROPOLITAN

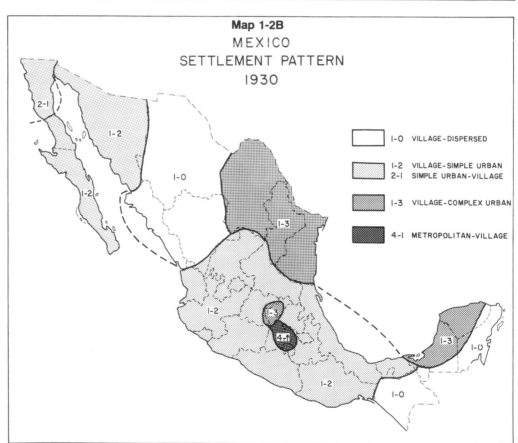

Map 1-2B

MEXICO
SETTLEMENT PATTERN
1930

☐	I-0 VILLAGE-DISPERSED
▨	I-2 VILLAGE-SIMPLE URBAN 2-1 SIMPLE URBAN-VILLAGE
▩	I-3 VILLAGE-COMPLEX URBAN
■	4-1 METROPOLITAN-VILLAGE

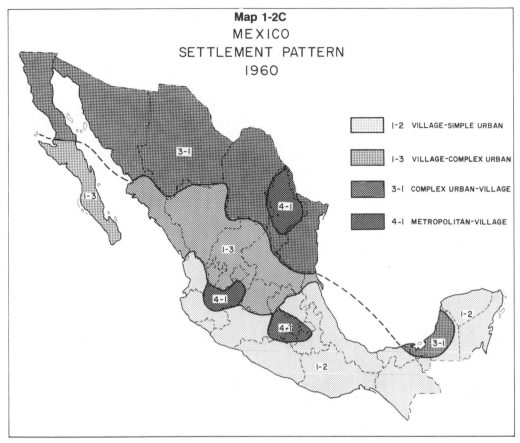

Map 1-2C
MEXICO
SETTLEMENT PATTERN
1960

1-2	VILLAGE-SIMPLE URBAN
1-3	VILLAGE-COMPLEX URBAN
3-1	COMPLEX URBAN-VILLAGE
4-1	METROPOLITAN-VILLAGE

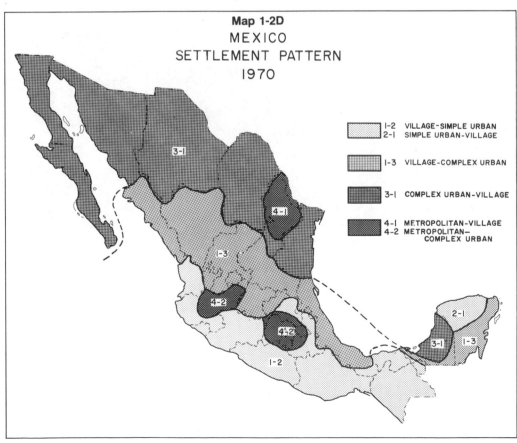

Map 1-2D
MEXICO
SETTLEMENT PATTERN
1970

1-2	VILLAGE-SIMPLE URBAN
2-1	SIMPLE URBAN-VILLAGE
1-3	VILLAGE-COMPLEX URBAN
3-1	COMPLEX URBAN-VILLAGE
4-1	METROPOLITAN-VILLAGE
4-2	METROPOLITAN—COMPLEX URBAN

Photo 1-4

RELIGIOUS FESTIVAL IN A SIMPLE URBAN CENTER, MEXICO (1974)

Photo 1-5

COMPLEX URBAN REGIONAL CENTER, POTOSÍ, BOLIVIA (1977)

an expanded series of options for citizens at all levels. Understanding how settlement hierarchies develop in these countries may lead to the development of options for the rural populations, the migrants, and to the creation of situations leading to a greater sense of satisfaction for those living in communities of all population sizes.

References

Ball, J.
1971   *Migration and the Rural Municipio in Mexico.* Atlanta: Georgia State University, Bureau of Business and Economic Research.

Doherty, P., and J. Ball
1971   "Central Functions of Small Mexican Towns." *Southeastern Geographer* 11:20−28.

Ducoff, L. E.
1965   "The Role of Migration in the Demographic Development of Latin America." *Milbank Memorial Fund Quarterly* 43:197−210.

Elizaga, J.
1965   "International Migration in Latin America." *Milbank Memorial Fund Quarterly* 43:144−161.

Ginsburg, N.
1961   *Atlas of Economic Development.* Chicago: University of Chicago Press.

Gottman, J.
1970   *Megalopolis: The Urbanized Northeastern Seaboard of the United States.* Cambridge, Mass.: Harvard University Press.

Johnson, E. A. J.
1970   *The Organization of Space in Developing Countries.* Cambridge, Mass.: Harvard University Press.

Lentnek, B.
1980   "Regional Development and Urbanization in Latin America: The Relationship of National Policy to Spatial Strategies." In R. Thomas and J. Hunter, eds., *International Migration Systems in the Developing World, With Special Reference to Latin America.* Cambridge, Mass.: Schenkman.

Luna, G.
1969   "Megalopolis Trends in Mexico." *Ekistics* 24:15−20.

United Nations
1969   "World Urbanization Trends as Measured in Agglomerations, 1920−1960." *Growth of the World's Urban and Rural Populations, 1920−2000.* Population Studies, No. 44. New York: United Nations.
1980   *Annual Report of Population Trends.* New York: United Nations Fund for Population Activities.

Wilkie J., and P. Reich
1977   *Statistical Abstract of Latin America,* Vol. 18. Los Angeles: UCLA Latin American Center Publications, University of California.
1978   *Statistical Abstract of Latin America,* Vol. 19. Los Angeles: UCLA Latin American Center Publications, University of California.

Wilkie, R. W.
1973a   "Toward a Behavioral Model of Peasant Migration: An Argentine Case of Spatial Behavior by Social Class Level." In R. N. Thomas, ed., *Population Dynamics of Latin America: Proceedings of the Conference of Latin Americanist Geographers,* vol. 2. East Lansing, Mich.: CLAG Publications.
1973b   "Selectivity in Peasant Spatial Behavior: Regional Interaction in Entre Ríos, Argentina." *Proceedings of the New England−St. Lawrence Valley Geographical Society* 11:10−20.
1974   "The Process Method Versus the Hypothesis Method: A Nonlinear Example of Peasant Spatial Perception and Behavior." In Maurice Yeates, ed., *Proceedings of the 1972 International Geographical Union Commission on Quantitative Geography.* Montreal and London: McGill−Queen's University Press. Pp. 1−31.
1976   "Urban Growth and the Transformation of the Settlement Landscape of Mexico: 1910−1970." In J. W. Wilkie, M. Meyer, and E. Monzón de Wilkie, eds., *Contemporary Mexico: Papers of the IV International Congress of Mexican History.* Berkeley and Mexico: University of California Press and El Colegio de México. Pp. 99−134.
1977   "Population Cartograms and Political Subdivisions: Latin American Populations in the 1970s." In J. Wilkie and P. Reich, eds., *Statistical Abstract of Latin America,* Vol. 18. Los Angeles: UCLA Latin American Center Publications, University of California. Pp. 1−26.
1980a   "Migration and Population Imbalance in the Settlement Hierarchy of Argentina." In D. Preston, ed., *Environment, Society and Rural Change in Latin America: The Past, Present and Future in the Countryside.* New York: Wiley. Pp. 157−184.
1980b   "The Rural Population of Argentina to 1970." In J. Wilkie and P. Reich, eds., *Statistical Abstract of Latin America,* Vol. 20. Los Angeles: UCLA Latin American Center Publications, University of California. Pp. 561−580.
1981   "The Dynamics of Human Settlement and Migration." In T. Martinson and G. Elbow, eds., *Geographic Research on Latin America: Benchmark 1980.* Muncie, Ind.: Conference of Latin Americanist Geographers. Pp. 66−89.

Wilkie, R. W., and J. R. Wilkie
1980a   "Environmental Perception and Migration Behavior: A Case Study in Rural Argentina." In R. Thomas and J. Hunter, eds., *Internal Migration Systems in the Developing World, with Special Reference to Latin America.* Cambridge, Mass.: Schenkman. Pp. 135−151.
1980b   *Migration and an Argentine Rural Community in Transition.* Latin American Studies Center Occasional Paper Series. Amherst, Mass.: University of Massachusetts.

Wolfe, M.
1966   "Rural Settlement Patterns and Social Change in Latin America." *Latin American Research Review* 1:5−50.

Photo 1-6

**AERIAL VIEW OF NEIGHBORHOOD OF MIXED RESIDENTIAL AND SMALL BUSINESSES,
BELEM, BRAZIL (1967)**

Photo 1-7

DENSELY SETTLED FAVELAS, RIO DE JANEIRO, BRAZIL (1974)

Photo 1-8

APARTMENT BUILDING, RIO DE JANEIRO, BRAZIL

Map 2-1

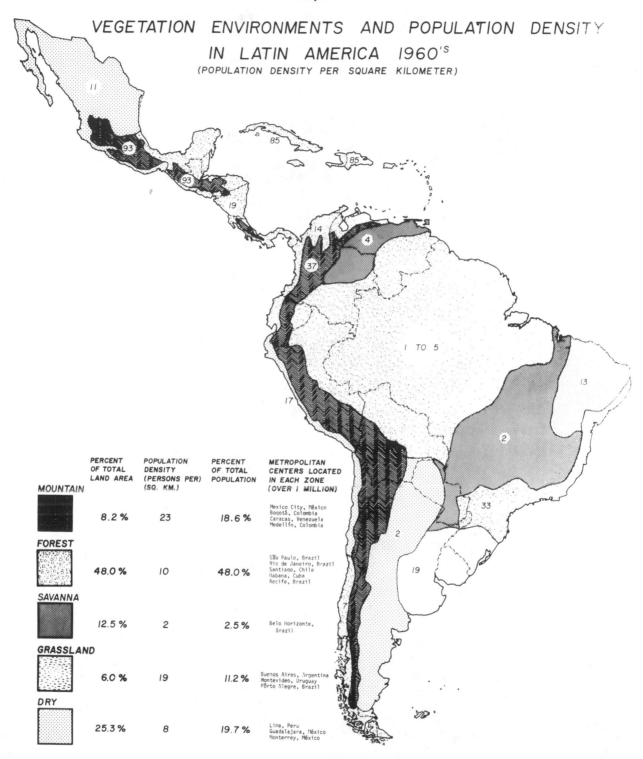

VEGETATION ENVIRONMENTS AND POPULATION DENSITY
IN LATIN AMERICA 1960'S
(POPULATION DENSITY PER SQUARE KILOMETER)

	PERCENT OF TOTAL LAND AREA	POPULATION DENSITY (PERSONS PER) (SQ. KM.)	PERCENT OF TOTAL POPULATION	METROPOLITAN CENTERS LOCATED IN EACH ZONE (OVER 1 MILLION)
MOUNTAIN	8.2 %	23	18.6 %	Mexico City, México Bogotá, Colombia Caracas, Venezuela Medellín, Colombia
FOREST	48.0 %	10	48.0 %	São Paulo, Brazil Rio de Janeiro, Brazil Santiago, Chile Habana, Cuba Recife, Brazil
SAVANNA	12.5 %	2	2.5 %	Belo Horizonte, Brazil
GRASSLAND	6.0 %	19	11.2 %	Buenos Aires, Argentina Montevideo, Uruguay Pôrto Alegre, Brazil
DRY	25.3 %	8	19.7 %	Lima, Peru Guadalajara, México Monterrey, México

2

Latin America

Several kinds of overview data for Latin America as a whole are presented. Included are twelve maps, seven tables, five figures, and two photographs. The kinds of information presented are grouped into the categories below.

POPULATION TABLES

Table 2-1　Population Data and Density by Country, 1980

Table 2-2　Metropolitan Centers with More Than One Million Population, About 1980

Table 2-3　National Self-Perception of Rural Population, 1940–1970

Table 2-7　Percent of Intercensal Urban Growth Attributable to Internal Migration and Reclassification

BASE MAPS

Five simple outline maps of political boundaries through the state, province, or departmental levels, including one each of all of Latin America (Map 2-2), Mexico (Map 2-5A), Central America (Map 2-5B), the Caribbean (Map 2-5C), and South America (Map 2-5D).

POPULATION DENSITY MAPS

Four maps of population density in the early 1960s for each region—Mexico (Map 2-4A), Central America (Map 2-4B), the Caribbean (Map 2-4C), and South America (Map 2-4D).

CARTOGRAMS

Two cartograms show the population of Latin America in 1972 (Map 2-3B) and 1980 (Map 2-3A)

PHYSICAL DATA

Map 2-1　Relates five zones to human settlement— mountain, forest, savana, grassland, and dry.

Figure 2-5　Presents a physical elements diagram of Latin America which shows how the various elements of the physical environment (wind patterns, rainfall, vegetation, and soils) relate to human settlement by latitude from 30° north to 60° south.

Figure 2-6　Presents the geographical size and percent of land area by region and country.

AGRICULTURAL DATA

Figure 2-1　Percent of agricultural population in 1960 and 1970 and the change in each country.

Figure 2-2　Breakdown of land tenure types for each country.

Figure 2-4　Precise data on the systems of land tenure.

LAND REFORM DATA

One table (2-5) and one figure (2-3) show the cumulative land reform data for hectares and families benefited through 1969 for the fifteen countries that have had land reform projects.

RACIAL CLASSIFICATION

Figure 2-4　Breakdown of the approximate percentage of population in each country except Brazil in each racial group in the early 1950s.

Table 2-1

LATIN AMERICA: POPULATION DATA AND DENSITY BY COUNTRY, 1980

Rank	Country	1980 Population	1980 Percent	Percent Change 1970-1980	Population Density 1980 (km^2)	Population Density Rank 1980
1	BRAZIL	119,061,470[a]	34.7	+24.4	14.1	16
2	MEXICO	67,383,000	19.6	+39.7	34.3	7
3	ARGENTINA	27,949,480	8.7	+17.6	10.0	18
4	COLOMBIA	25,614,000	7.5	+19.6	22.5	12
5	PERU	16,821,000	4.9	+24.6	13.1	17
6	VENEZUELA	14,200,000	4.1	+30.6	15.8	14
7	CHILE	11,084,000	3.2	+25.4	14.6	15
8	CUBA	9,718,000	2.8	+13.7	8.9	4
9	ECUADOR	7,543,000	2.2	+26.6	27.9	9
10	GUATEMALA	6,839,000	2.0	+30.0	62.8	5
11	BOLIVIA	5,825,000	1.7	+40.7	5.3	20
12	DOMINICAN REP.	5,600,000	1.7	+30.3	116.0	3
13	HAITI	5,534,000	1.6	+20.8	199.4	2
14	EL SALVADOR	4,524,000	1.3	+26.3	216.1	1
15	HONDURAS	3,439,000	1.0	+28.8	30.7	8
16	PARAGUAY	2,888,000	.8	+16.6	7.1	19
17	URUGUAY	2,886,000	.8	+ 2.2	16.3	13
18	NICARAGUA	2,559,000	.7	+34.1	21.6	11
19	COSTA RICA	2,111,000	.6	+21.6	41.5	6
20	PANAMA	1,788,748	.5	+22.2	23.2	10
	Total	343,368,000	100.0	+25.0	16.8	

a. Resident population only.

SOURCES: 1980 census reports from Brazil, Argentina, Mexico, and Panama; 1981 census reports from Chile, Dominican Republic, and Venezuela; 1980 estimates for the other 13 countries from CEPAL (Comisión Económica para América Latina). Percent change and population density were calculated by the author from SALA, 20-Map 1 and SALA, 20-301.

Table 2-2

LATIN AMERICA: METROPOLITAN CENTERS WITH MORE THAN ONE MILLION POPULATION, ABOUT 1980

Approximate Rank	Greater Metropolitan Cities	Population	1980 or Year of Record
1	Mexico City (Mexico)	13,993,866	1978
2	São Paulo (Brazil)	12,578,045	
3	Buenos Aires (Argentina)	9,942,232	
4	Rio de Janeiro (Brazil)	9,018,961	
5	Santiago (Chile)	4,294,938	1982
6	Lima (Peru)	3,618,128	1972
7	Bogotá (Colombia)	2,870,594	1973
8	Caracas (Venezuela)	2,576,000	1976
9	Belo Horizonte (Brazil)	2,534,576	
10	Recife (Brazil)	2,346,196	
11	Guadalajara (Mexico)	2,343,034	1978
12	Pôrto Alegre (Brazil)	2,232,370	
13	Habana (Cuba)	1,986,000	1978
14	Monterrey (Mexico)	1,923,402	1978
15	Salvador da Bahia (Brazil)	1,766,075	
16	Fortaleza (Brazil)	1,581,457	
17	Ritiba/Curitiba (Brazil)	1,441,743	
18	Medellín (Colombia)	1,410,154	1973
19	Montevideo (Uruguay)	1,387,198	1975
20	Santo Domingo (Dominican Rep.)	1,318,172	1981
21	Brasília (Brazil)	1,176,748	
22	Guayaquil (Ecuador)	1,022,010	1978
23	Belém (Brazil)	1,000,357	
	Total	84,362,256	

SOURCES: Table 2 in corresponding chapters herein.

Map 2-2

POLITICAL BASE MAP OF LATIN AMERICA WITH ALL MAJOR CIVIL DIVISIONS, 1980

Jock Montgomery & R.Wilkie, 1981

Map 2-3A

POPULATION CARTOGRAM OF LATIN AMERICA, 1980

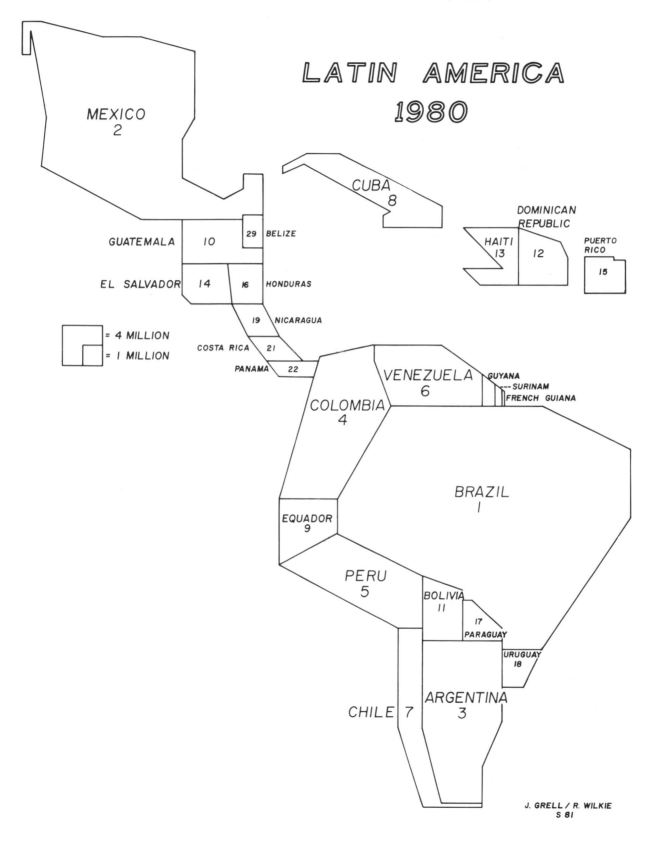

*LATIN AMERICA
1980*

MEXICO
2

CUBA
8

DOMINICAN
REPUBLIC

HAITI
13

12

PUERTO
RICO

15

GUATEMALA 10 29 BELIZE

EL SALVADOR 14 16 HONDURAS

19 NICARAGUA

= 4 MILLION
= 1 MILLION

COSTA RICA 21

PANAMA 22

VENEZUELA
6

GUYANA
---SURINAM
FRENCH GUIANA

COLOMBIA
4

BRAZIL
1

EQUADOR
9

PERU
5

BOLIVIA
11

17
PARAGUAY

URUGUAY
18

CHILE 7

ARGENTINA
3

J. GRELL / R. WILKIE
S 81

Map 2-3B

POPULATION CARTOGRAM OF LATIN AMERICA, 1972

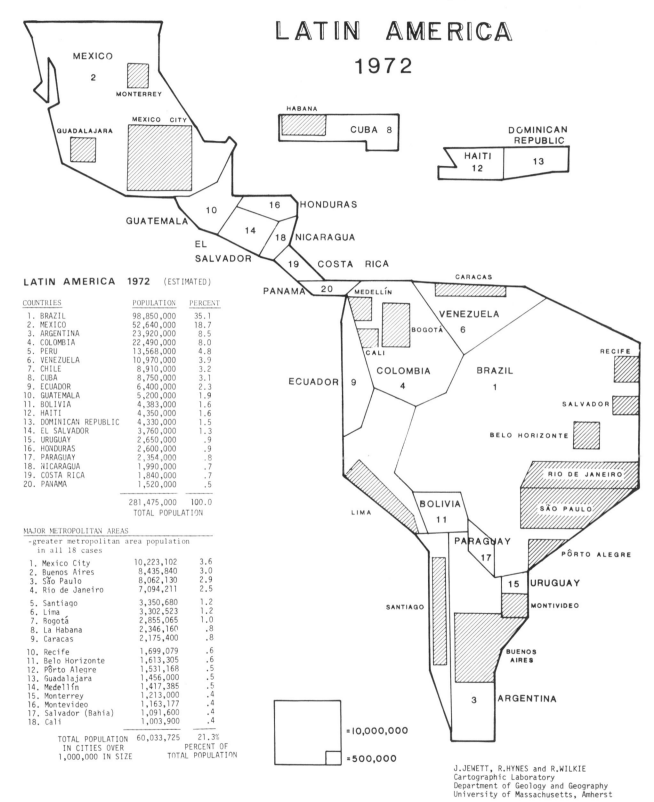

LATIN AMERICA 1972 (ESTIMATED)

COUNTRIES	POPULATION	PERCENT
1. BRAZIL	98,850,000	35.1
2. MEXICO	52,640,000	18.7
3. ARGENTINA	23,920,000	8.5
4. COLOMBIA	22,490,000	8.0
5. PERU	13,568,000	4.8
6. VENEZUELA	10,970,000	3.9
7. CHILE	8,910,000	3.2
8. CUBA	8,750,000	3.1
9. ECUADOR	6,400,000	2.3
10. GUATEMALA	5,200,000	1.9
11. BOLIVIA	4,383,000	1.6
12. HAITI	4,350,000	1.6
13. DOMINICAN REPUBLIC	4,330,000	1.5
14. EL SALVADOR	3,760,000	1.3
15. URUGUAY	2,650,000	.9
16. HONDURAS	2,600,000	.9
17. PARAGUAY	2,354,000	.8
18. NICARAGUA	1,990,000	.7
19. COSTA RICA	1,840,000	.7
20. PANAMA	1,520,000	.5
	281,475,000	100.0
	TOTAL POPULATION	

MAJOR METROPOLITAN AREAS
-greater metropolitan area population
 in all 18 cases

1. Mexico City	10,223,102	3.6
2. Buenos Aires	8,435,840	3.0
3. São Paulo	8,062,130	2.9
4. Rio de Janeiro	7,094,211	2.5
5. Santiago	3,350,680	1.2
6. Lima	3,302,523	1.2
7. Bogotá	2,855,065	1.0
8. La Habana	2,346,160	.8
9. Caracas	2,175,400	.8
10. Recife	1,699,079	.6
11. Belo Horizonte	1,613,305	.6
12. Pôrto Alegre	1,531,168	.5
13. Guadalajara	1,456,000	.5
14. Medellín	1,417,385	.5
15. Monterrey	1,213,000	.4
16. Montevideo	1,163,177	.4
17. Salvador (Bahia)	1,091,600	.4
18. Cali	1,003,900	.4

TOTAL POPULATION 60,033,725   21.3%
IN CITIES OVER   PERCENT OF
1,000,000 IN SIZE   TOTAL POPULATION

=10,000,000

=500,000

J.JEWETT, R.HYNES and R.WILKIE
Cartographic Laboratory
Department of Geology and Geography
University of Massachusetts, Amherst

Photo 2-1

ANDEAN URBAN PATTERNS, POTOSÍ, BOLIVIA (1977)

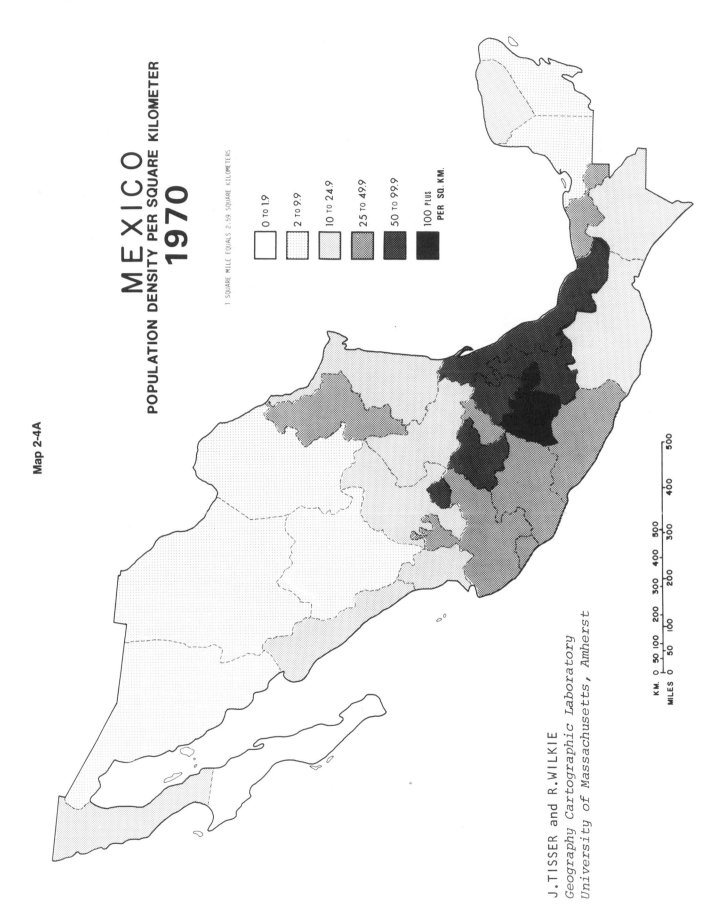

Map 2-4A

MEXICO
POPULATION DENSITY PER SQUARE KILOMETER
1970

1 SQUARE MILE EQUALS 2.59 SQUARE KILOMETERS

0 TO 1.9
2 TO 9.9
10 TO 24.9
25 TO 49.9
50 TO 99.9
100 PLUS
PER SQ. KM.

J.TISSER and R.WILKIE
Geography Cartographic Laboratory
University of Massachusetts, Amherst

K.M. 0 50 100   200   300   400   500
MILES 0   50   100   200   300   400   500

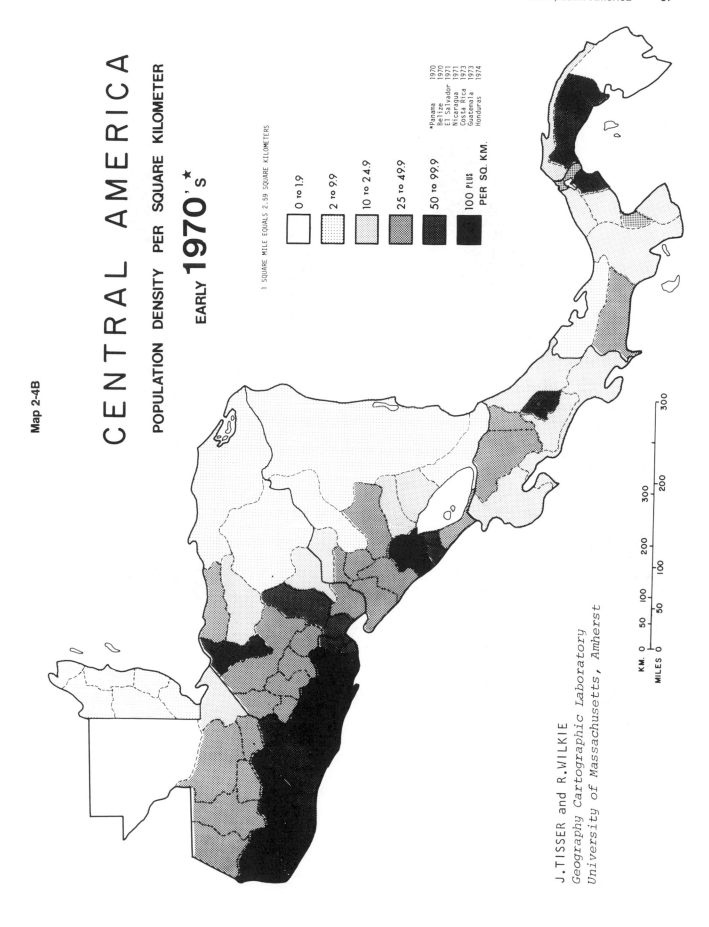

Map 2-4B

CENTRAL AMERICA

POPULATION DENSITY PER SQUARE KILOMETER

EARLY 1970's ★

1 SQUARE MILE EQUALS 2.59 SQUARE KILOMETERS

0 TO 1.9

2 TO 9.9

10 TO 24.9

25 TO 49.9

50 TO 99.9

100 PLUS
PER SQ. KM.

*Panama	1970
Belize	1970
El Salvador	1971
Nicaragua	1971
Costa Rica	1973
Guatemala	1973
Honduras	1974

J.TISSER and R.WILKIE
Geography Cartographic Laboratory
University of Massachusetts, Amherst

KM. 0   0   50   100   200   300

MILES 0   50   100   200   300

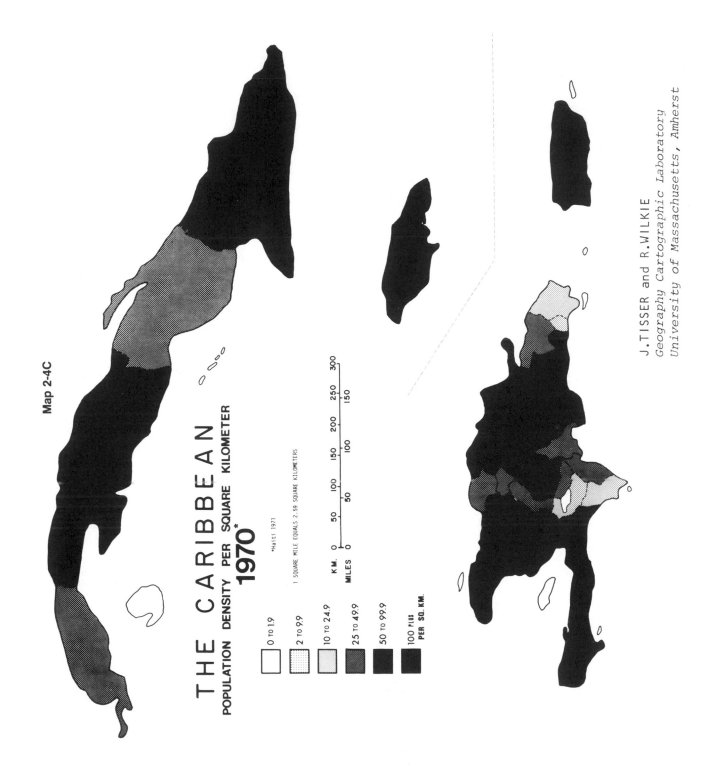

Map 2-4C

THE CARIBBEAN
POPULATION DENSITY PER SQUARE KILOMETER
1970*

*Haiti 1971

1 SQUARE MILE EQUALS 2.59 SQUARE KILOMETERS

K.M. 0   50   100   150   200   250   300
MILES 0   50   100   150

0 TO 1.9
2 TO 9.9
10 TO 24.9
25 TO 49.9
50 TO 99.9
100 PLUS PER SQ. KM.

J.TISSER and R.WILKIE
Geography Cartographic Laboratory,
University of Massachusetts, Amherst

Map 2-4D

SOUTH AMERICA

POPULATION DENSITY PER
SQUARE KILOMETER

EARLY 1970's★

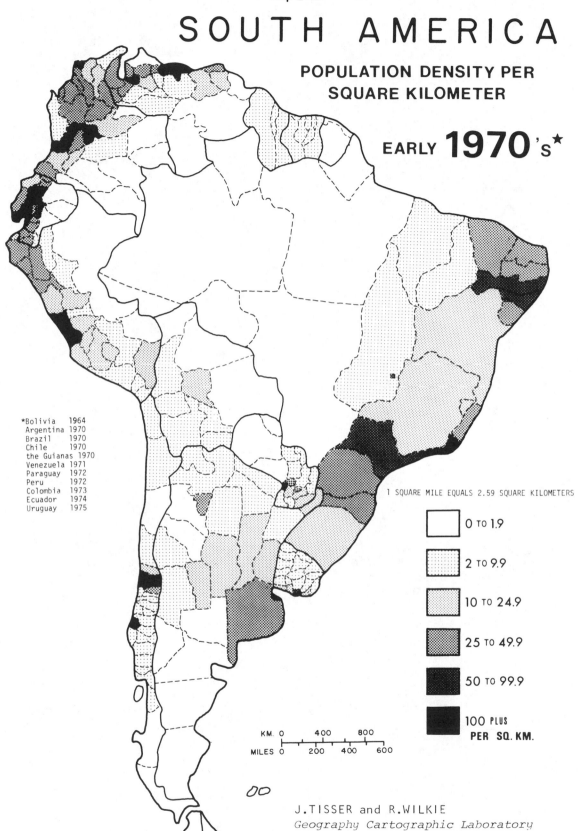

*Bolivia   1964
Argentina 1970
Brazil   1970
Chile   1970
the Guianas 1970
Venezuela 1971
Paraguay   1972
Peru   1972
Colombia   1973
Ecuador   1974
Uruguay   1975

1 SQUARE MILE EQUALS 2.59 SQUARE KILOMETERS

☐	0 TO 1.9
☐	2 TO 9.9
☐	10 TO 24.9
☐	25 TO 49.9
■	50 TO 99.9
■	100 PLUS PER SQ. KM.

KM. 0   400   800
MILES 0   200   400   600

J.TISSER and R.WILKIE
Geography Cartographic Laboratory
University of Massachusetts, Amherst

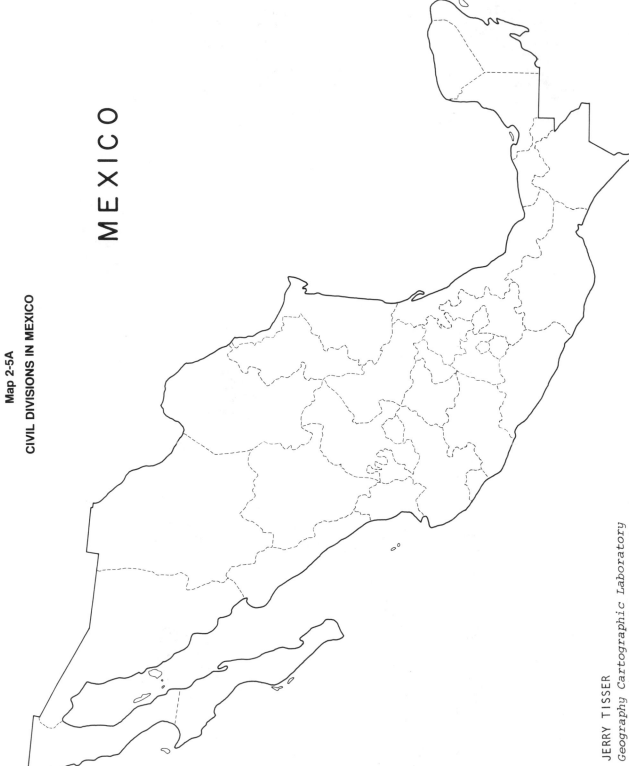

MEXICO

Map 2-5A
CIVIL DIVISIONS IN MEXICO

JERRY TISSER
Geography Cartographic Laboratory
University of Massachusetts, Amherst

Map 2-5B

CIVIL DIVISIONS IN CENTRAL AMERICA

CENTRAL AMERICA

JERRY TISSER
Geography Cartographic Laboratory
University of Massachusetts, Amherst

Map 2-5C

CIVIL DIVISIONS IN THE CARIBBEAN

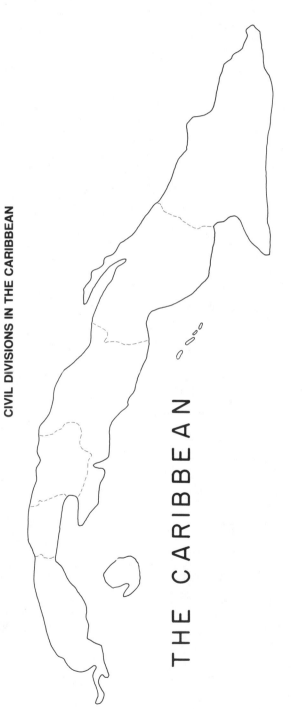

THE CARIBBEAN

JERRY TISSER
Geography Cartographic Laboratory
University of Massachusetts, Amherst

Map 2-5D

CIVIL DIVISIONS IN SOUTH AMERICA

SOUTH AMERICA

JERRY TISSER
Geography Cartographic Laboratory
University of Massachusetts, Amherst

Figure 2-1

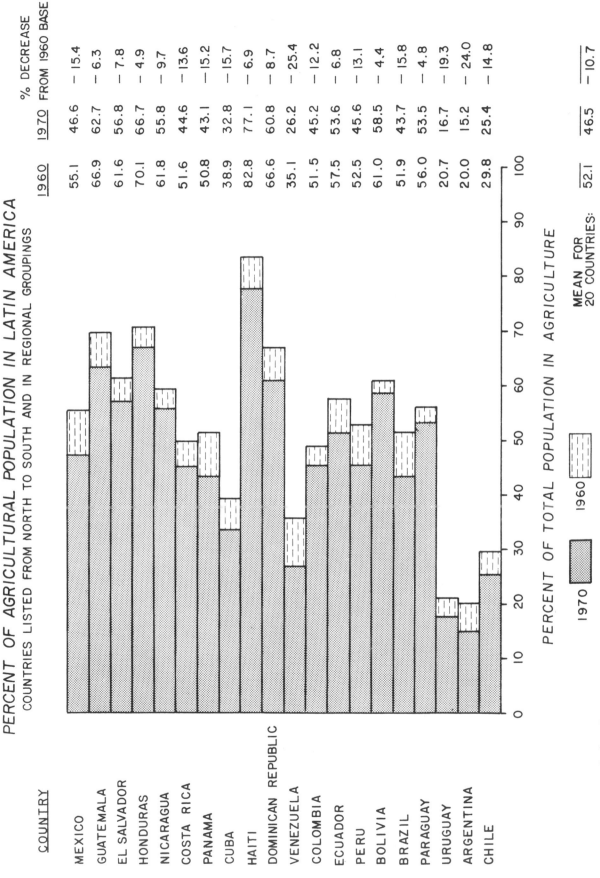

PERCENT OF AGRICULTURAL POPULATION IN LATIN AMERICA
COUNTRIES LISTED FROM NORTH TO SOUTH AND IN REGIONAL GROUPINGS

COUNTRY	1960	1970	% DECREASE FROM 1960 BASE
MEXICO	55.1	46.6	− 15.4
GUATEMALA	66.9	62.7	− 6.3
EL SALVADOR	61.6	56.8	− 7.8
HONDURAS	70.1	66.7	− 4.9
NICARAGUA	61.8	55.8	− 9.7
COSTA RICA	51.6	44.6	− 13.6
PANAMA	50.8	43.1	− 15.2
CUBA	38.9	32.8	− 15.7
HAITI	82.8	77.1	− 6.9
DOMINICAN REPUBLIC	66.6	60.8	− 8.7
VENEZUELA	35.1	26.2	− 25.4
COLOMBIA	51.5	45.2	− 12.2
ECUADOR	57.5	53.6	− 6.8
PERU	52.5	45.6	− 13.1
BOLIVIA	61.0	58.5	− 4.4
BRAZIL	51.9	43.7	− 15.8
PARAGUAY	56.0	53.5	− 4.8
URUGUAY	20.7	16.7	− 19.3
ARGENTINA	20.0	15.2	− 24.0
CHILE	29.8	25.4	− 14.8
MEAN FOR 20 COUNTRIES:	52.1	46.5	− 10.7

PERCENT OF TOTAL POPULATION IN AGRICULTURE

1970   1960

Source: Calculated and graphed by the author
from SALA 19-402.

Table 2-3

NATIONAL SELF-PERCEPTION OF RURAL POPULATION, 20 LRC, 1940-1980[a]

(%)

	Country	Data Years	ca. 1940	ca. 1950	ca. 1960	ca. 1970	ca. 1980	Rural Defined as Population Clusters Which Are:
A.	ARGENTINA	1947, 1960, 1970, 1980	?	38	26	21	17	Less than 2,000 persons
B.	BOLIVIA	1950, 1960, 1970, 1980	?	74	76	72	67	Less than 2,000 persons
C.	BRAZIL	1940, 1950, 1960, 1970, 1980	69	64	54	44	36	Non-administrative centers
D.	CHILE	1940, 1952, 1960, 1970, 1980	48	40	32	24	19	Lack of certain public services
E.	COLOMBIA	1938, 1951, 1964, 1973, 1980	71	61	47	40	32	Less than 1,500 persons
F.	COSTA RICA	1950, 1963, 1973, 1980	?	67	65	59	54	Non-administrative centers
G.	CUBA	1943, 1953, 1960, 1970, 1980	54	49	45	40	35	Less than 2,000 persons (adjusted by source)
H.	DOMINICAN REP.	1935, 1950, 1960, 1970, 1980	82	76	70	60	53	Non-administrative centers
I.	ECUADOR	1950, 1962, 1974, 1980	?	72	64	59	56	Non-administrative centers
J.	EL SALVADOR	1930, 1950, 1961, 1971, 1980	62	64	61	60	56	Lightly populated
K.	GUATEMALA	1940, 1950, 1964, 1973, 1980	74	75	66	66	62	Varies[1]
L.	HAITI	1950, 1960, 1971, 1980	?	88	85[†]	80	75	Non-administrative centers
M.	HONDURAS	1950, 1960, 1974, 1980	?	82[†]	77	69	51	Less than 1,000-2,000 persons
N.	MEXICO	1940, 1950, 1960, 1970, 1980	65	57	49	42	34	Less than 2,500 persons
O.	NICARAGUA	1950, 1963, 1971, 1980	?	65	59	52	46	Non-administrative centers
P.	PANAMA	1940, 1950, 1960, 1970, 1980	63	64	58	52	46	Less than 1,500 persons
Q.	PARAGUAY	1950, 1962, 1972, 1980	?	65	64	62	58	Non-administrative centers
R.	PERU	1940, 1950, 1961, 1972, 1980	65	59[†]	53	40	35	Non-administrative centers and/or lack of certain public services
S.	URUGUAY	1950, 1960, 1970, 1980	?	43[†]	28[†]	16[†]	15	Not cities[2]
T.	VENEZUELA	1941, 1950, 1961, 1971, 1980	69	52	37	25	21	Less than 2,500 persons
	LATIN AMERICA	20 countries	67[b]	63	56	42	36	Average of above, weighted by population
	UNITED STATES	1940, 1950, 1960, 1970, 1980	39	36	30	27	23	"Current Definition"[3]

1. In 1940: hamlets, small settlements, and farms; since 1950: less than 2,000 except 1,500 if running water.
2. In 1963 census definition gave 19%.
3. Less than 2,500 persons except for urbanized unincorporated areas; data for 1940 adjusted for consistency.

a. Self-definitions vary according to national circumstances.
b. Calculated from population-weighted data for 11 countries which had 80% of Latin America's population.

SOURCE: See SALA, 23-651.

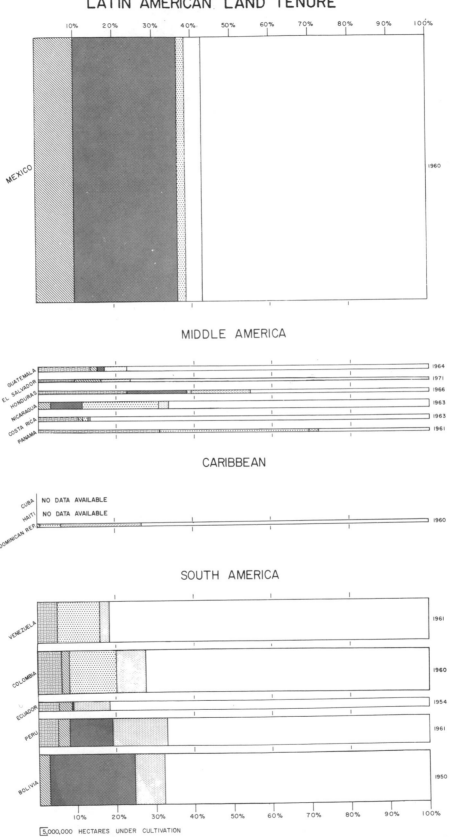

Figure 2-2

LATIN AMERICAN LAND TENURE

Figure 2-2 (Continued)

PERCENTAGE OF HECTARES IN CULTIVATION IN EACH OWNERSHIP CATEGORY

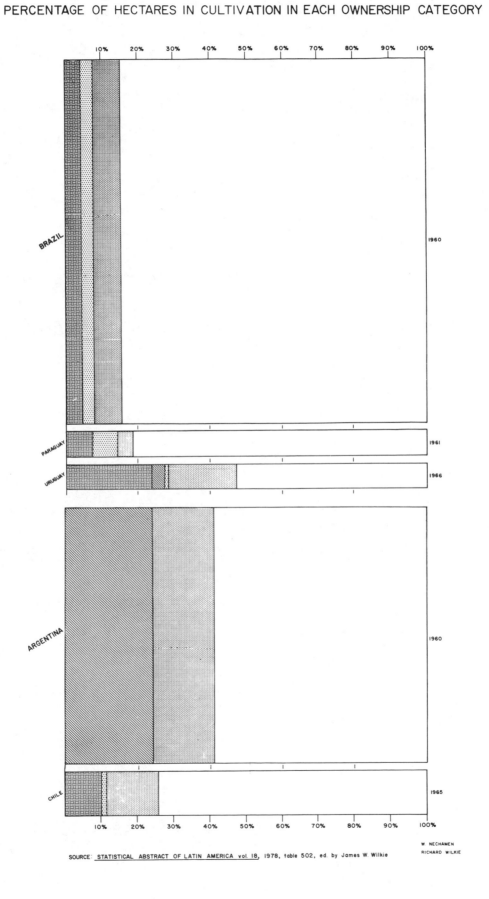

SOURCE: STATISTICAL ABSTRACT OF LATIN AMERICA vol. 18, 1978, table 502, ed. by James W. Wilkie

W. NECHAMEN
RICHARD WILKIE

Table 2–4

SYSTEMS OF LAND TENURE, PERCENTAGE DATA, 18 LC

(N and Ha.)

| Country | Year | Total | Operated Under Single Tenurial Systems | | | Rented from Others | | | | | | | | |
			Total	Operated by Owner	Total	Payment in Cash/Kind	Partnerships or Similar Forms	Payment by Services	Other Arrangements	Occupied Without Title	Operated Under Collective System	Operated Under Other Simple Systems	Operated Under Mixed Systems
ARGENTINA[1,2]	1960												
N		100.0	100.0	~	~	~	~	~	#	#	#	~	#
Ha.		100.0	100.0	58.9	16.9	12.9	1.2a	#	2.8b	#	#	24.2c	#
BOLIVIA[3]	1950u												
N		100.0	100.0	74.6d	20.0	15.8	3.5	.7e	#	#	4.4f	1.1g	#
Ha.		100.0	100.0	67.9d	7.5	6.0	1.2	.3e	#	#	21.9f	2.79	#
BRAZIL	1970												
N		100.0	97.3	60.4	20.4	~	~	~	~	16.5	~	~	2.7
Ha.		100.0	95.9	82.6	6.1	~	~	~	~	7.2	~	~	4.1
CHILE[6]	1965												
N		100.0	89.0	47.2	41.8	4.9	7.1	21.3	6.1	2.4	#	#	11.0
Ha.		100.0	89.8	74.0	14.2	11.5	.9	.3	1.5	1.6	#	#	10.2
COLOMBIA[4]	1960												
N		100.0	91.8	62.4	23.3	~	~	~	~	3.9	#	2.1	8.2
Ha.		100.0	93.9	72.4	7.3	~	~	~	~	12.1	#	2.0	6.1
COSTA RICA[5]	1973												
N		100.0	90.1	85.4	4.7b	1.8	.4j	..	.3k	-l	9.7	.2	..
Ha.		100.0	92.0	90.8	1.2b	.8	.1j	..	.1k	-l	7.8	.2	..
DOMINICAN REP.	1960												
N		100.0	~	58.8	30.8	3.7	6.9	1.9r	18.3jj	8.9jj	~	1.5	~
Ha.		100.0ii	~	73.1	20.6	4.5	4.2	1.7r	10.3jj	5.3jj	~	1.0	~
ECUADOR	1954												
N		100.0	91.1	67.9	14.6	5.0	3.9n	5.7o	#	#	1.7f	6.9p	8.9
Ha.		100.0	94.5	81.5	9.2	7.1	1.1n	1.0o	#	#	.4f	3.4p	5.5
EL SALVADOR	1961												
N		100.0	86.9	39.6	43.7	19.2	~	24.6q	~	#	#	3.5	13.1i
Ha.		100.0	92.2	77.5	7.8	5.0	~	2.8q	~	#	#	7.0	7.8i

Table 2-4 (Continued)

SYSTEMS OF LAND TENURE, PERCENTAGE DATA, 18 LC

(N and Ha.)

Country	Year	Total	Operated Under Single Tenurial Systems		Rented from Others					Occupied Without Title	Operated Under Collective System	Operated Under Other Simple Systems	Operated Under Mixed Systems
			Total	Operated by Owner	Total	Payment in Cash/Kind	Partnerships or Similar Forms	Payment by Services	Other Arrangements				
EL SALVADOR	1971												
N		100.0	85.9	39.4	46.5	29.6	~	~	~	#	#	16.9[r]	14.1[i]
Ha.		100.0	90.6	76.4	14.2	7.4	~	~	~	#	#	6.8[r]	9.4[i]
GUATEMALA	1964												
N		100.0	88.9	57.9	22.9	11.3	~[v]	11.6[q]	#	~	4.9[f]	3.2[x]	11.1
Ha.		100.0	86.5	77.4	5.7	3.1	~[v]	2.6[q]	#	~	1.7[f]	1.7[x]	13.5
HONDURAS	1966												
N		100.0	83.3	22.4	33.8	22.5	~	~	11.3[v]	2.4	24.7[aa]	#	16.7
Ha.		100.0	77.3	45.8	15.0	5.1	~	~	10.0[v]	1.2	15.3[aa]	#	22.7
MEXICO	1970												
N[7]		100.0	97.8	~	~	~	~[bb]	~	~[cc]	~[dd]	~	~	2.2
Ha.		100.0	50.2	44.5	2.6	2.2	.4[bb]	~	~[cc]	1.2[dd]	~	1.8	49.8
NICARAGUA	1963												
N		100.0	86.3	38.6	12.6	4.7	2.8	1.2	3.9	15.7	8.0[aa]	11.4[ee]	13.7
Ha.		100.0	100.0	66.7	2.6	1.4	.4	.1	.7	19.2	8.1[aa]	3.3[ee]	~[ff]
PANAMA[8]	1971												
N		100.0	88.3	12.3	4.4	~	~	~	~	71.6	..	..	11.7
Ha.		100.0	74.0	26.0	3.5	~	~	~	~	44.5	..	..	26.0
PARAGUAY[9]	1961												
N		100.0	86.2	37.3	7.5	7.5	#	#	#	41.5	#	#	13.8
Ha.		100.0	92.5	81.3	4.2	4.2	#	#	#	7.1	#	#	7.5
PERU	1961												
N		100.0[jj]	89.8	66.0	15.2	9.7	5.6[gg]	#	#	#	5.2[hh]	3.3	10.2
Ha.		100.0	94.9	67.0	13.9	12.7	1.2[gg]	#	#	#	10.9[hh]	3.1	5.1
URUGUAY[8]	1966												
N		100.0	90.9	55.1	27.9	24.2	3.6[2]	#	#	5.2	#	2.6	9.1
Ha.		100.0	76.9	49.6	23.3	22.3	1.0[2]	#	#	1.0	#	3.0	23.1

Table 2-4 (Continued)

SYSTEMS OF LAND TENURE, PERCENTAGE DATA, 18 LC

(N and Ha.)

Country	Year	Total	Operated Under Single Tenurial Systems									Operated Under Mixed Systems
			Total	Operated by Owner	Rented from Others — Total	Payment in Cash/Kind	Partnerships or Similar Forms	Payment by Services	Other Arrangements	Occupied Without Title	Operated Under Collective System	Operated Under Other Simple Systems	
URUGUAY[g]	1970												
N		100.0	90.1	58.6	22.6	19.6	3.0[2]	#	#	5.5	#	3.4	9.9
Ha.		100.0	76.1	52.7	18.6	17.7	.9[2]	#	#	1.1	#	3.7	23.9
VENEZUELA	1961[w]												
N		100.0[s]	90.9	39.2	12.9	8.1	4.8	#	#	38.8	#	#	7.7
Ha.		100.0[m]	94.7	81.5	2.4	1.9	.5	#	#	10.9	#	#	5.3
UNITED STATES	1969												
N		100.0	75.4	62.5	12.9	?	?[t]	?	?	- -	- -	—[h]	24.6[i]
Ha.		100.0	48.2	35.3	12.9	?	?[t]	?	?	- -	- -	—[h]	51.8[i]

1. Details on the number of holdings were not obtained.
2. Excluding 14,583 holdings, the area of which is unknown.
3. For data on Bolivian and Venezuelan land reform, see James W. Wilkie, *Measuring Land Reform,* Statistical Abstract of Latin America Supplement 5 (Los Angeles: UCLA Latin American Center, University of California, 1974).
4. Excluding *Intendencias and Comisarías.*
5. Data obtained by sampling.
6. Excluding 5,125 properties without lands.
7. The data refer to the type of producer.
8. Excluding holdings with an area of less than 1 ha.

a. "Medieros y Tanteros."
b. Free occupancy.
c. Comprises 29,477,389 ha. operated in the *Tierras Fiscales* and 12,833,619 ha. operated under "Other Forms of Tenancy."
d. Comprises holdings worked by proprietors alone, properties with settlers, day laborers, etc.
e. "Tolerados."
f. Communal lands.
g. Comprises 818 properties (439,264 ha.) operated by possessors of *Tierras Fiscales* and 136 properties (433,334 ha.) operated by *Granjas Cooperativas y Sociedades Agrícolas.*
h. Holdings operated by administrators.
i. Holdings operating by proprietors lesses.
j. Product-sharing arrangements.
k. Holdings operated without payment.
l. Holdings operated illegally.
m. For data on Venezuelan land reform, see Wilkie, *Measuring Land Reform.*

n. Holdings operated by "*Partidarios.*"
o. Holdings operated by "*Huasipungueros.*"
p. Data obtained by sampling.
q. Properties operated by settlers.
r. Holdings operated by "*Colonos.*"
s. Including 4,617 holdings without agricultural land.
t. Holdings operated by sharecroppers and livestock-sharers.
u. See note 3.
v. Excluding 14,583 holdings, the area of which is unknown.
w. See note 3.
x. Comprises those lands not included in preceding categories. Such lands include those in legal usufruct at time of census; those continuously and pacifically occupied without owner's permission by squatters who do not pay rent; lands in judicial process of transfer.
y. Agricultural holdings in National Lands.
z. Holdings operated by "*Medianeros.*"
aa. Agricultural holdings in Ejidal Lands.
bb. "*Aparcero*" only.
cc. "*Arrendatario.*"
dd. "*Ocupantes.*"
ee. Including 7,543 properties (93,716 ha.) operated by usufructurarios.
ff. Farms operated under mixed tenure systems are included in the category of those operated under single systems.
gg. Comprises partnership and bound-service by Amerinds (*Yanaconaje*).
hh. Including communal lands.
ii. Excluding 188,544 ha. in sugar cane.
jj. Concessionaire.

SOURCE: *América en Cifras,* 1974, table 311-03; 1977, table 311-03.

Table 2–5

CUMULATIVE LAND REFORM DATA,[1] 15 L

(Through 1969)

Country	Initiation of Program	Number of Families Benefitted	Number of Hectares Distributed or Confirmed
BOLIVIA	1955	208,181	9,740,681
BRAZIL	1964	46,457	957,106
CHILE	1965	15,800	2,093,300
COLOMBIA	1961	91,937	2,832,312
COSTA RICA	1963	3,889	60,055
DOMINICAN REP.	1963	9,717	46,082
ECUADOR	1964	27,857	152,115
GUATEMALA	1955	26,500	166,734
HONDURAS	1963	5,843	90,642
MEXICO	1916	2,525,811	59,413,656
NICARAGUA	1964	8,117	357,989
PANAMA	1963	2,594	37,339
PARAGUAY	1963	#	#
PERU	1961	31,600	850,522
VENEZUELA	1959	117,286	4,605,594

1. Excludes colonization and land settlement.

SOURCE: James W. Wilkie, *Measuring Land Reform*, Statistical Abstract of Latin
America, Supplement 5, (Los Angeles: UCLA Latin American Center Publications,
University of California, 1974, p. 3, from which this table is adapted.

Figure 2-3

CUMULATIVE LAND REFORM DATA
IN LATIN AMERICA
1916 – 1969

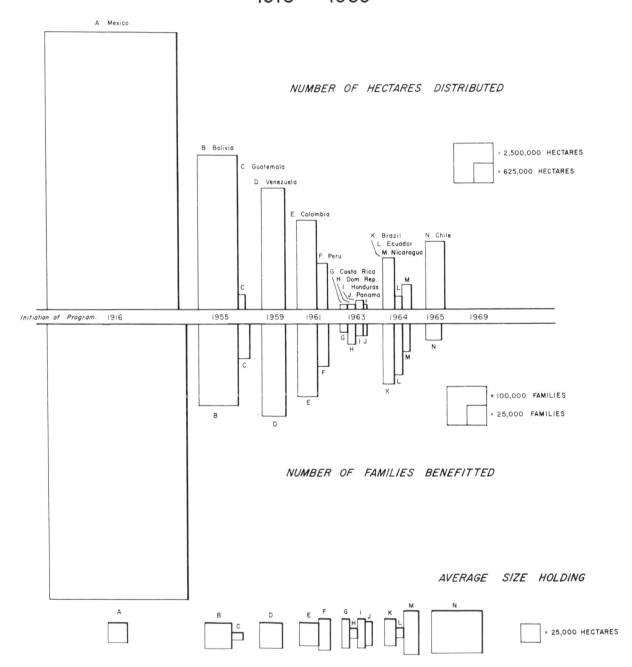

SOURCE James W. Wilkie, *Measuring Land Reform*, Statistical Abstract of Latin
America, Supplement 5 (Los Angeles UCLA Latin American Center Publications,
University of California, 1974), p. 3, from which this table is adapted.

J. DONZÉ / RICHARD WILKIE

Figure 2-4

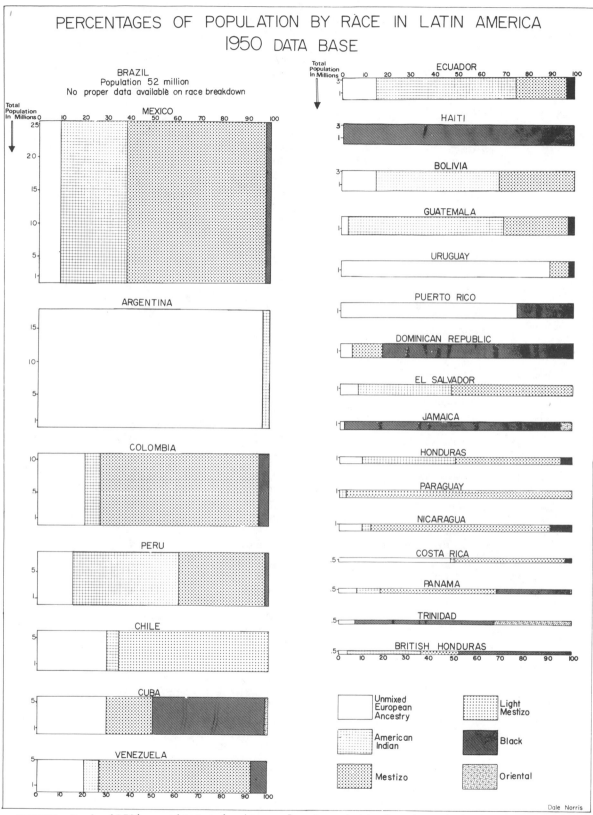

PERCENTAGES OF POPULATION BY RACE IN LATIN AMERICA
1950 DATA BASE

SOURCE: Early 1950's estimates in James, Preston, <u>Latin America</u>, 2nd Edition, 1956.

Table 2-6

ECONOMIC REGIONS OF LATIN AMERICA BY GEOGRAPHICAL SIZE AND PERCENT OF LAND AREA

WORLD REGIONS and Countries	Area in Square Kilometers	Percent of Land Area
World		
World Total	134,329,736	100.0
Africa	30,317,845	22.6
Americas[1]	41,004,512	30.5
Asia[2]	27,159,202	20.2
Europe	4,936,473	3.7
Oceania	8,509,704	6.3
USSR	22,402,000	16.7
Americas		
Americas Total	41,004,512	100.0
Latin America	19,898,644	48.5
United States	9,160,412	22.3
Other Western Hemisphere	11,945,456	29.2
Latin America		
Latin America Total	19,898,644	100.0
CACM	411,170	2.1
Costa Rica	50,900	.3
El Salvador	20,935	.1
Guatemala	108,889	.5
Honduras	112,088	.6
Nicaragua	118,358	.6[a]
ALALC	19,219,670	96.6
Argentina	2,776,889	14.0[b]
Brazil	8,456,508	42.5[c]
Mexico	1,958,201	9.8
Paraguay	406,752	2.0
Uruguay	177,508	.9
Andean Pact Total	5,443,818	27.4
Bolivia	1,098,581	5.5
Colombia	1,138,914	5.7
Chile	756,629	3.8[d]
Ecuador	270,670	1.4
Peru	1,280,219	6.4[e]
Venezuela	898,805	4.5
OTHER	267,798	1.3
Cuba	114,524	.6
Dominican Republic	48,442	.2
Haiti	27,750	.1
Panama	75,650	.4
Panama Canal Zone	1,432	

1. Latin America, 19,898,644; other Americas, 21,105,868.
2. Excludes USSR.

a. Excludes lakes.
b. Excludes Antarctica and Islas Malvinas.
c. Includes zones in litigation (8,511,965).
d. Excludes Antarctica.
e. Excludes Lake Titicaca.

SOURCE: Calculated from SALA, 21–300 and other tables.

Table 2-7

LATIN AMERICA: PERCENT OF INTERCENSAL URBAN GROWTH ATTRIBUTABLE TO INTERNAL MIGRATION AND RECLASSIFICATION

Country	Intercensal Period	Estimated Percent of Urban Growth Attributable to Internal Migration
ARGENTINA	1947–1960	50.8
BOLIVIA	- -	- -
BRAZIL	1950–1960	49.6
	1960–1970	44.9
CHILE	1952–1960	36.6
	1960–1970	37.4
COLOMBIA	1951–1964	36.6
COSTA RICA	- -	- -
CUBA	- -	- -
DOMINICAN REPUBLIC	1950–1960	35.9
	1960–1970	43.5
ECUADOR	1950–1962	37.6
	1962–1974	29.6
EL SALVADOR	1950–1961	23.1
	1961–1971	22.1
GUATEMALA	1964–1973	33.9
HAITI	- -	- -
HONDURAS	- -	- -
MEXICO	1960–1970	31.7
NICARAGUA	1950–1963	30.2
PANAMA	1950–1960	31.2
Puerto Rico	1960–1970	64.2
PARAGUAY	1962–1972	34.9
PERU	1961–1972	41.6
United States	1950–1960	35.4
	1960–1970	29.2
URUGUAY	1963–1975	7.3
VENEZUELA	1950–1961	36.7
	1961–1971	27.8

SOURCE: United Nations, *World Population Trends and Policies: 1979 Monitoring Report,* Vol. I: *Population Trends* (New York: United Nations, 1980), table 59, pp. 129–130.

Figure 2-5

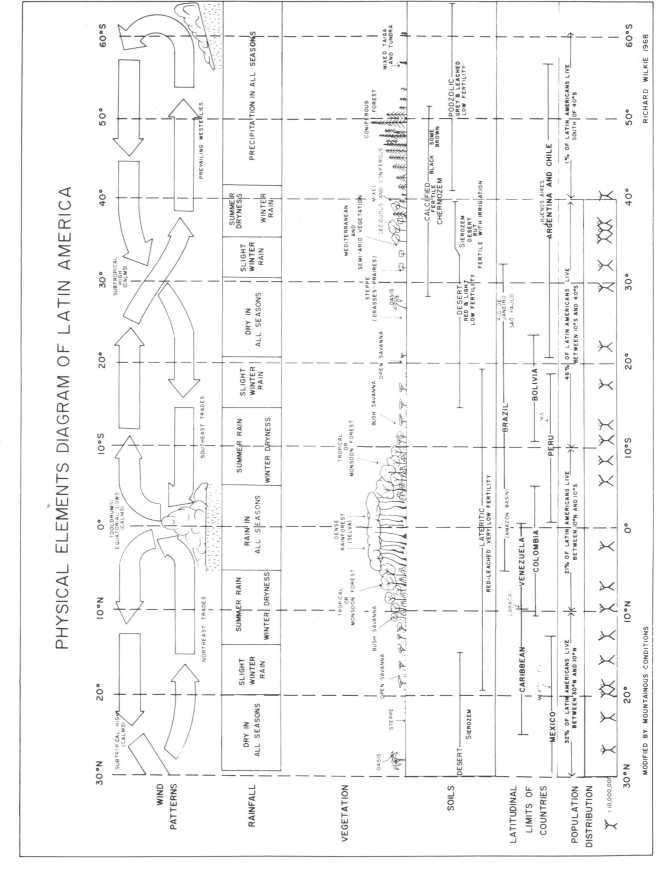

PHYSICAL ELEMENTS DIAGRAM OF LATIN AMERICA

RICHARD WILKIE 1968

Photo 2-2
BOY IN AN ALTIPLANO TOWN, PUCARANI, BOLIVIA (1966)

Map 3-1

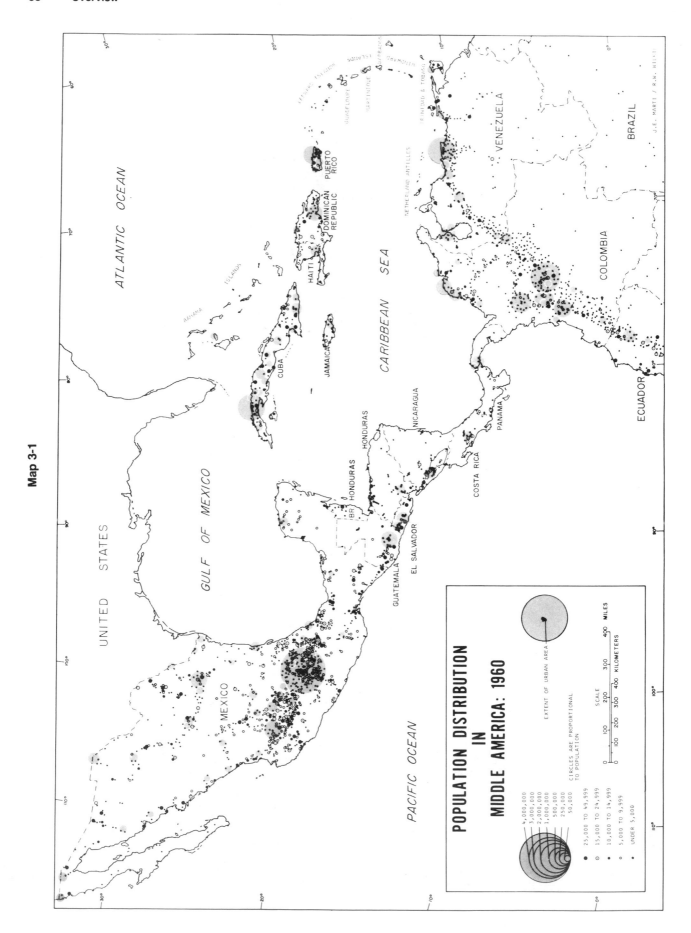

POPULATION DISTRIBUTION
IN
MIDDLE AMERICA: 1960

3

Middle America

A total of thirteen items are presented in the Middle America overview, including two tables, nine maps, and two photographs. The kinds of information are grouped into the categories below.

POPULATION

Table 3-1   Population data and density by country in 1980

Table 3-2   Metropolitan centers with more than 500,000 population

Map 3-1   Population dot map of Middle America in 1960

BASE MAP

Political boundaries and the location of major urban centers (Map 3-2).

CARTOGRAM

Size of the populations of the countries of the region and the urban population of cities with more than 500,000 population (Map 3-3).

THREE-DIMENSIONAL MAPS

Views of total population (Map 3-4), population density (Map 3-5), and population change between 1965 and 1975 (Map 3-6).

PHYSICAL MAPS

Three subregions of Middle America are presented on physiographic diagram drawings of the landscape (by Erwin Raisz): northern Central America (Map 3-7A), southern Central America (Map 3-7B), and the island of Hispaniola (Map 3-7C) in the Caribbean.

PHOTOGRAPHS

Two photographs.

Table 3-1

MIDDLE AMERICA: POPULATION DATA AND CHANGE
BY COUNTRY, 1970 AND 1980

1980 Rank	Country	1970 Population	1970 Percent	1980 Population	1980 Percent	Percent Change 1970-1980
1	MEXICO	50,078,000	55.0	67,383,000	57.4	+34.6
2	CUBA	8,551,000	9.4	9,718,000	8.3	+13.7
3	GUATEMALA	5,262,000	5.7	6,839,000	5.8	+30.0
4	DOMINICAN REP.	4,343,000	4.7	5,658,000	4.8	+30.3
5	HAITI	4,605,000	5.0	5,534,000	4.7	+20.8
6	EL SALVADOR	3,582,000	4.0	4,524,000	3.9	+26.3
7	HONDURAS	2,683,000	2.9	3,439,000	2.9	+28.8
8	Puerto Rico	2,718,000	3.0	3,395,000	2.9	+24.9
9	NICARAGUA	1,908,000	2.1	2,559,000	2.2	+34.1
10	Jamaica	1,944,000	2.1	2,215,000	1.8	+13.9
11	COSTA RICA	1,736,000	1.9	2,111,000	1.9	+21.6
12	PANAMA	1,497,000	1.6	1,789,000	1.5	+19.5
13	Trinidad and Tobago	1,027,000	1.1	1,150,000	1.0	+11.9
14	Guadeloupe	320,000	.4	312,000	.3	-2.5
15	Martinique	325,000	.4	310,000	.3	-4.6
16	Barbados	239,000	.3	279,000	.2	+16.7
17	Belize	122,000	.1	155,000	.1	+27.0
	Total	90,940,000	100.00	117,370,000	100.0	+29.1

SOURCES: 1980 census reports from Mexico and Panama; 1981 census report from the Dominican Republic; other estimates from CEPAL (Comisión Económica para América Latina). Percent and percent change were calculated by the author.

Table 3-2

MIDDLE AMERICA: METROPOLITAN CENTERS WITH MORE THAN 500,000 POPULATION, ABOUT 1980

Approximate Rank	Greater Metropolitan Cities	Population	1980 or Year of Record
1	✪ Mexico City (Mexico)	13,993,866	1978
2	● Guadalajara (Mexico)	2,343,034	1978
3	Habana (Cuba)	1,986,000	1978
4	Monterrey (Mexico)	1,923,402	1978
5	● Santo Domingo (Dominican Rep.)	1,318,172	1981
6	San Juan (Puerto Rico)	1,084,000	
7	● Guatemala City (Guatemala)	989,100	1973
8	Port-au-Prince (Haiti)	745,700	1978
9	Puebla (Mexico)	677,959	1978
10	Panama City (Panama)	650,796	1978
11	Ciudad Juárez (Mexico)	597,096	1978
12	León (Mexico)	589,950	1978
13	San Salvador (El Salvador)	565,000	1971
14	Tijuana (Mexico)	534,993	1978
15	Tampico/Ciudad Madero (Mexico)	510,000	1978
16	San José (Costa Rica)	480,938	1973
	Total	28,990,006	

SOURCES: Table 2 in each of the ten Middle American country chapters (chapters 10-12, 14-20) herein.

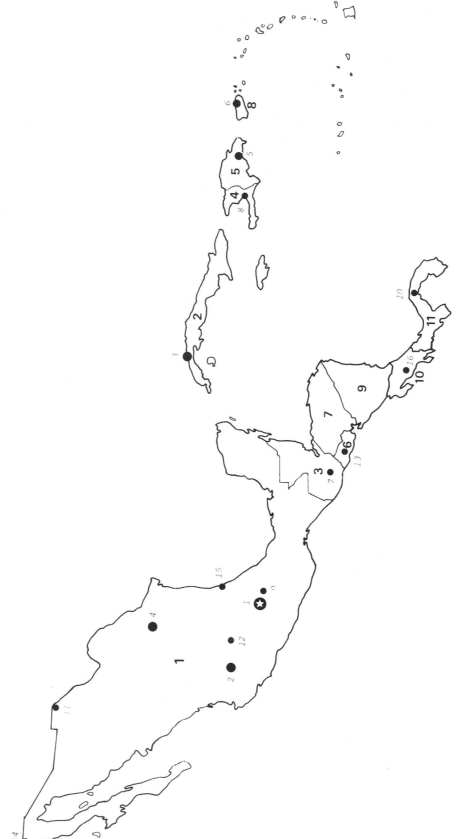

Map 3-2

**BASE MAP OF COUNTRIES IN MIDDLE AMERICA AND LOCATION OF
MAJOR URBAN CENTERS**

Note: Country numbers are rank ordered according
to 1980 population data listed on Table 3-1.

Map 3-3

POPULATION CARTOGRAM OF MIDDLE AMERICA, 1980

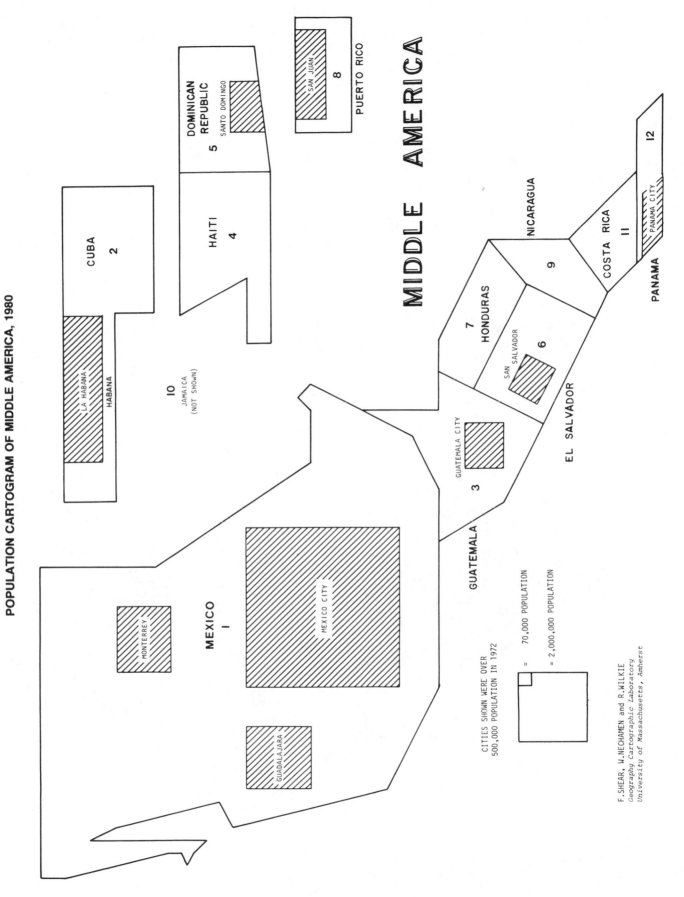

MIDDLE AMERICA

CUBA
2

LA HABANA
HABANA

DOMINICAN
REPUBLIC
5

SANTO DOMINGO

HAITI
4

PUERTO RICO

SAN JUAN
8

IO
JAMAICA
(NOT SHOWN)

NICARAGUA

COSTA RICA
II

HONDURAS
7

9

PANAMA
12

PANAMA CITY

SAN SALVADOR
6

EL SALVADOR

GUATEMALA CITY

GUATEMALA
3

MEXICO
I

MEXICO CITY

MONTERREY

GUADALAJARA

CITIES SHOWN WERE OVER
500,000 POPULATION IN 1972

=   70,000 POPULATION

= 2,000,000 POPULATION

F.SHEAR, W.NECHAMEN and R.WILKIE
Geography Cartographic Laboratory
University of Massachusetts, Amherst

Map 3-4

**THREE-DIMENSIONAL CHOROPLETH MAP OF TOTAL POPULATION
BY COUNTRY IN MIDDLE AMERICA, 1975**
(By Major Civil Division)

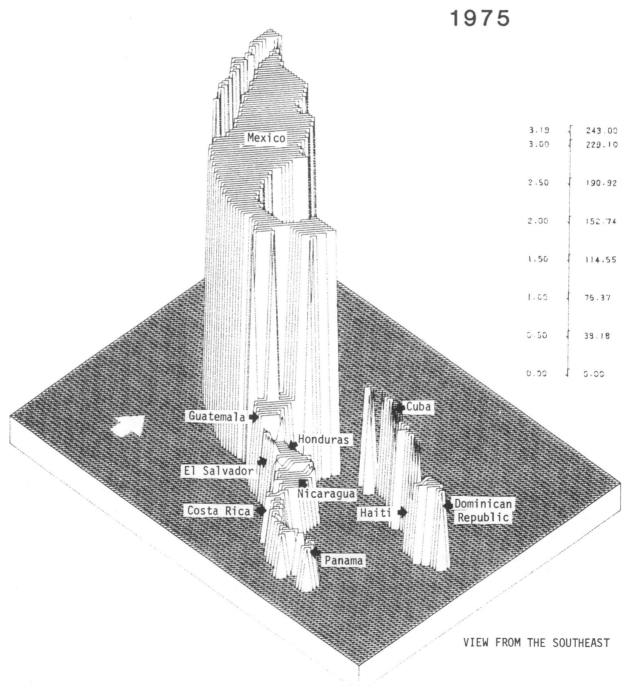

MIDDLE AMERICA
TOTAL POPULATION
(BY MAJOR CIVIL DIVISION)
1975

3.19	243.00
3.00	229.10
2.50	190.92
2.00	152.74
1.50	114.55
1.00	76.37
0.50	39.18
0.00	0.00

VIEW FROM THE SOUTHEAST

M.RICHARDS, S.KOCUR, and R.WILKIE, 1980
Geography Cartographic Laboratory, University of Massachusetts, Amherst
using the SYMVU program from the Harvard Univ. Center for Computer Graphics

Map 3-5

**THREE-DIMENSIONAL CHOROPLETH MAP OF POPULATION DENSITY
IN MIDDLE AMERICA, 1975
(Persons per km²)**

MIDDLE AMERICA
POPULATION DENSITY
(PERSONS PER KM²)
1975

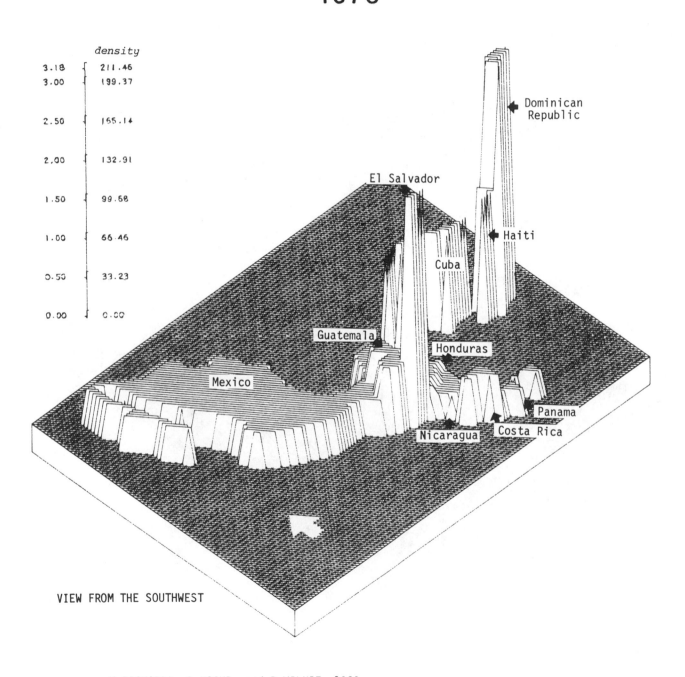

VIEW FROM THE SOUTHWEST

M.RICHARDS, S.KOCUR, and R.WILKIE, 1980
Geography Cartographic Laboratory, University of Massachusetts, Amherst
using the SYMVU program from the Harvard Univ. Center for Computer Graphics

Map 3-6

**THREE-DIMENSIONAL CHOROPLETH MAP OF POPULATION CHANGE
IN MIDDLE AMERICA, 1965–1975
(%)**

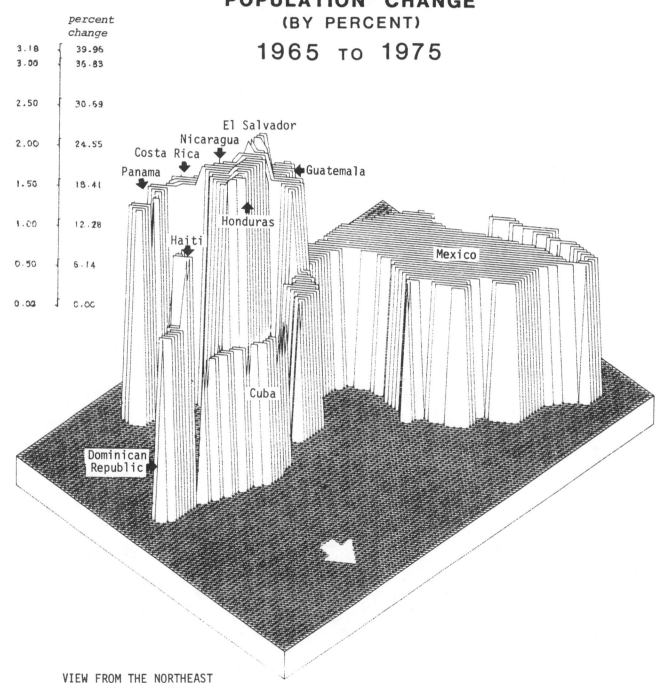

MIDDLE AMERICA
POPULATION CHANGE
(BY PERCENT)
1965 to 1975

VIEW FROM THE NORTHEAST

M.RICHARDS, S.KOCUR, and R.WILKIE, 1980
Geography Cartographic Laboratory, University of Massachusetts, Amherst
using the SYMVU program from the Harvard Univ. Center for Computer Graphics

Photo 3-1

**SIX-YEAR-OLD BOY CARRYING WHEAT WITH HIS FATHER,
NEAR NAHUALÁ, GUATEMALA (1979)**

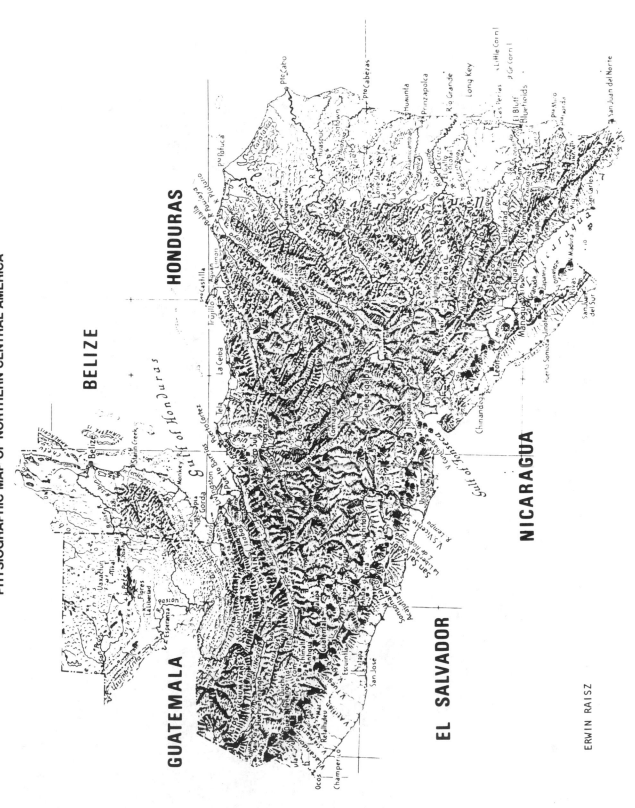

Map 3-7A

PHYSIOGRAPHIC MAP OF NORTHERN CENTRAL AMERICA

ERWIN RAISZ

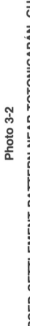

Photo 3-2

DISPERSED SETTLEMENT PATTERN NEAR TOTONICAPÁN, GUATEMALA (1979)

Map 3-7B

PHYSIOGRAPHIC MAP OF SOUTHERN CENTRAL AMERICA

PANAMA AND COSTA RICA

ERWIN RAISZ

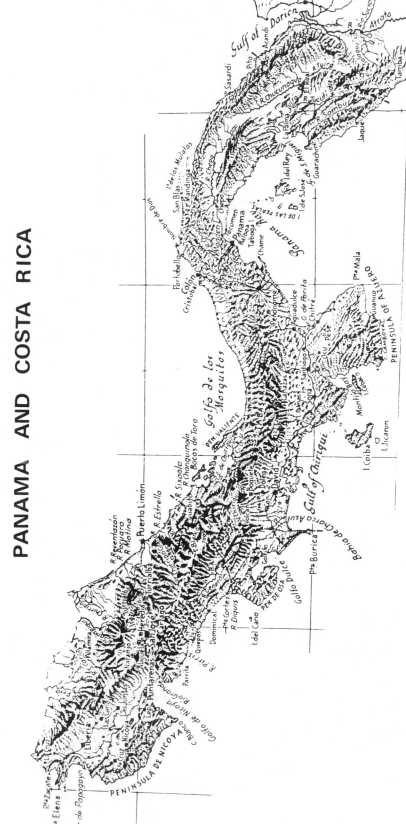

Map 3-7C

PHYSIOGRAPHIC MAP OF HISPANIOLA

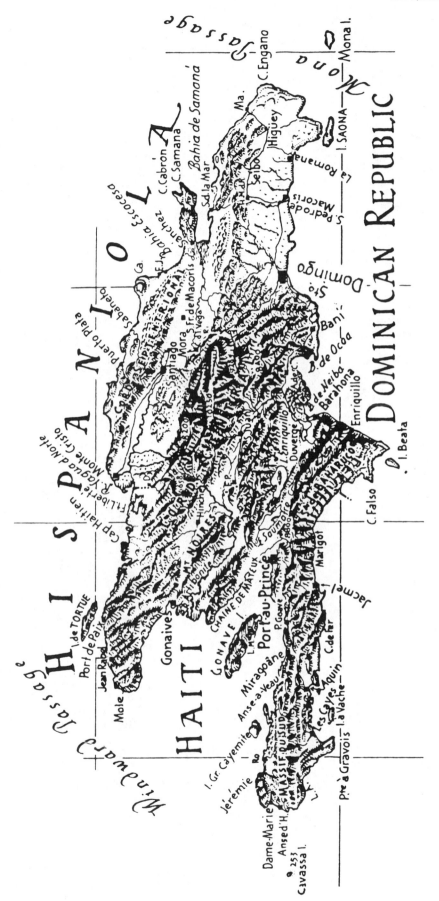

ERWIN RAISZ

Map 4-1

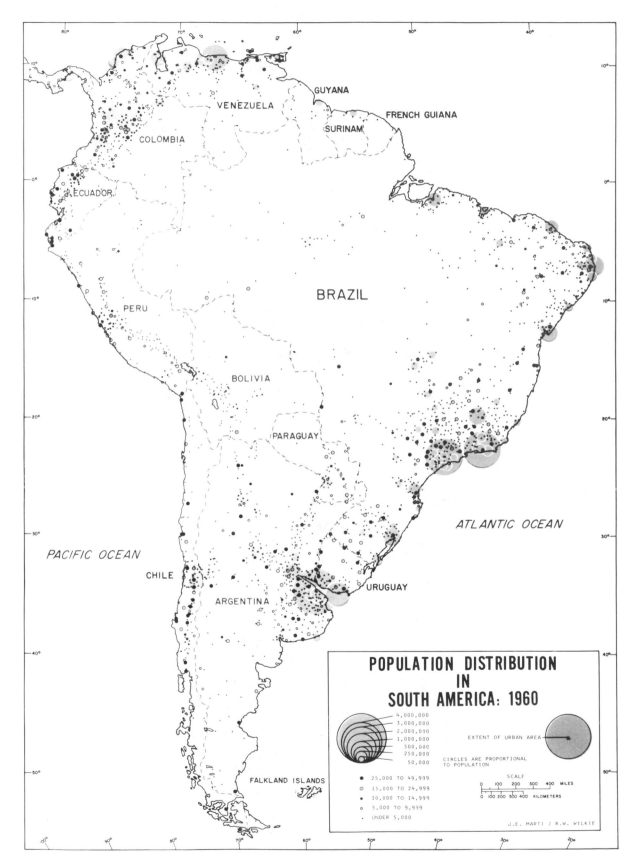

POPULATION DISTRIBUTION
IN
SOUTH AMERICA: 1960

4,000,000
3,000,000
2,000,000
1,000,000
500,000
250,000
50,000

EXTENT OF URBAN AREA

CIRCLES ARE PROPORTIONAL
TO POPULATION

● 25,000 TO 49,999
◉ 15,000 TO 24,999
• 10,000 TO 14,999
○ 5,000 TO 9,999
· UNDER 5,000

SCALE
0 100 200 300 400 MILES
0 100 200 300 400 KILOMETERS

J.E. MARTI / R.W. WILKIE

4

South America

A total of twenty items are presented in the South American overview, including two tables, fifteen maps, and three photographs. The kinds of information presented are grouped into the categories below.

POPULATION

Table 4-1   Population data and density by country in 1980

Table 4-2   Metropolitan centers with more than 500,000 population

Map 4-1   Population dot map of South America in 1960

BASE MAP

Political boundaries and the location of major urban centers (Map 4-2).

CARTOGRAM

Size of the populations of the countries and the major urban centers over 500,000 population (Map 4-3).

THREE DIMENSIONAL MAPS

Views of total population (Map 4-4), population density (Map 4-5), and population change between 1965 and 1975 (Map 4-6A and Map 4-6B).

PHYSICAL MAPS

Eight subregions of South America shown in physiographic landscape drawings (by Guy Harold-Smith):

Map 4-7A   Northern South America and the Amazon Basin

Map 4-7B   The Orinoco River Basin and the Guiana highlands of northern South America

Map 4-7C   Northern Andes and western Gran Colombia

Map 4-7D   The central Andes

Map 4-7E   South-central South America

Map 4-7F   Patagonia and southern Chile

Map 4-7G   Central Parana river region and the Gran Chaco

Map 4-7H   Uruguay, Rio Grande do Sul, and northeast Argentina

PHOTOGRAPHS

Three photographs.

Table 4-1

SOUTH AMERICA: POPULATION DATA AND CHANGE BY COUNTRY, 1970 AND 1980

1980 Rank	Country	1970 Population	1970 Percent	1980 Population	1980 Percent	Percent Change 1970-1980
1	BRAZIL	95,684,000	50.0	119,061,470[a]	50.8	+24.4
2	ARGENTINA	23,758,000	12.4	27,949,480	11.9	+17.6
3	COLOMBIA	21,430,000	11.2	25,614,000	10.9	+19.6
4	PERU	13,504,000	7.0	16,821,000	7.2	+24.6
5	VENEZUELA	10,709,000	5.6	13,989,000	6.0	+30.6
6	CHILE	9,369,000	5.0	10,732,000	4.6	+14.6
7	ECUADOR	5,958,000	3.1	7,543,000	3.2	+26.6
8	BOLIVIA	4,140,000	2.1	5,825,000	2.5	+40.7
9	PARAGUAY	2,477,000	1.3	2,888,000	1.2	+16.6
10	URUGUAY	2,824,000	1.3	2,886,000	1.2	+2.2
11	Guyana	715,000	.4	832,000	.4	+16.4
12	Suriname	373,000	.2	404,00	.2	+8.3
13	French Guiana	48,000	.02	63,000	.02	+31.3
	Total	190,989,000	100.0	234,359,000	100.0	+22.7

a. Resident population only.

SOURCES: 1980 census reports from Brazil and Argentina; 1981 census reports from Chile and Venezuela; other estimates for 1980 from CEPAL (Comisión Económica para América Latina). Percent and percent change were calculated by the author.

Table 4-2

SOUTH AMERICA: METROPOLITAN CENTERS WITH MORE THAN
500,000 POPULATION, ABOUT 1980

Approximate Rank	Greater Metropolitan Cities	Population	1980 or Year of Record
1	✪ São Paulo (Brazil)	12,578,045	
2	Buenos Aires (Argentina)	9,942,232	
3	Rio de Janeiro (Brazil)	9,018,961	
4	● Santiago (Chile)	4,294,938	1982
5	Lima (Peru)	3,618,128	1972
6	Bogotá (Colombia)	2,870,594	1973
7	Caracas (Venezuela)	2,576,000	1976
8	Belo Horizonte (Brazil)	2,534,576	
9	Recife (Brazil)	2,346,196	
10	Pôrto Alegre (Brazil)	2,232,370	
11	◉ Salvador da Bahia (Brazil)	1,766,075	
12	Fortaleza (Brazil)	1,581,457	
13	Ritiba/Curitiba (Brazil)	1,441,743	
14	Medellín (Colombia)	1,410,154	1973
15	Montevideo (Uruguay)	1,387,198	1975
16	Brasília (Brazil)	1,176,748	
17	Guayaquil (Ecuador)	1,022,010	1978
18	Belém (Brazil)	1,000,357	
19	● Córdoba (Argentina)	982,018	
20	Rosario (Argentina)	954,606	
21	Cali (Colombia)	926,264	1973
22	Valparaíso (Chile)	882,280	1982
23	Maracaibo (Venezuela)	792,000	1976
24	Quito (Ecuador)	742,858	1978
25	Barranquilla (Colombia)	728,533	1982
26	Concepción (Chile)	723,050	1982
27	Goiânia (Brazil)	717,948	
28	La Paz (Bolivia)	695,566	1976
29	Manaus (Brazil)	634,759	
30	Mendoza (Argentina)	596,796	
31	Asunción (Paraguay)	565,363	1974
32	La Plata (Argentina)	560,341	
33	Tucumán (Argentina)	496,914	
34	Rondônia/Pôrto Velho (Brazil)	492,744	
35	Valencia (Venezuela)	481,000	1976
	Total	74,770,822	

SOURCES: Table 2 in each of the 10 South American country chapters (chapters 5-9, 13, 21-24) herein.

Map 4-2

BASE MAP OF COUNTRIES IN SOUTH AMERICA AND LOCATION OF MAJOR URBAN CENTERS

Note: Country numbers are rank ordered
        according to 1980 population
        data listed in Table 4-1.

Map 4-3

POPULATION CARTOGRAM OF SOUTH AMERICA, 1980

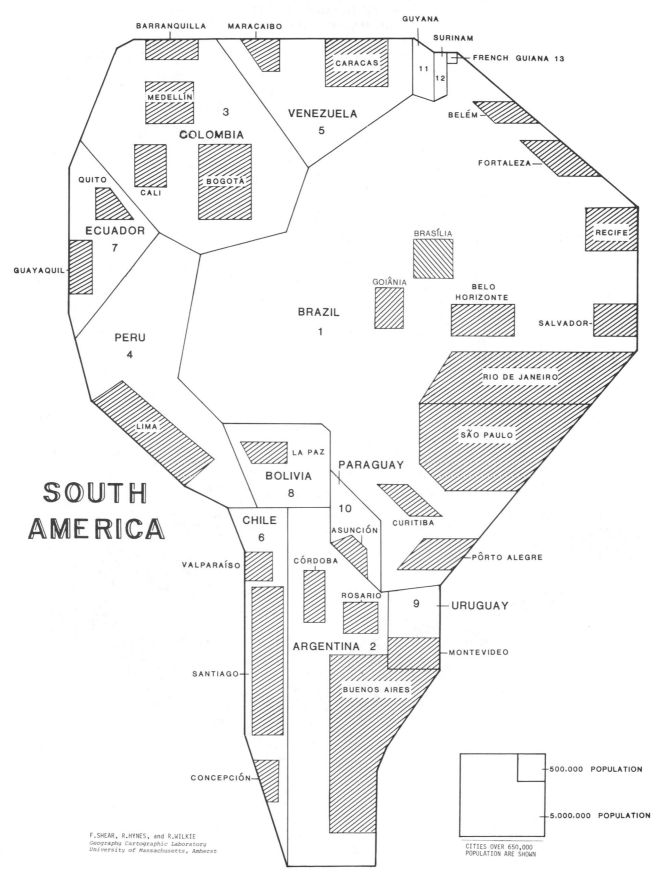

F.SHEAR, R.HYNES, and R.WILKIE
Geography Cartographic Laboratory
University of Massachusetts, Amherst

CITIES OVER 650,000
POPULATION ARE SHOWN

500,000 POPULATION

5,000,000 POPULATION

Map 4-4

**THREE-DIMENSIONAL CHOROPLETH MAP OF TOTAL POPULATION BY COUNTRY
IN SOUTH AMERICA, 1975
(By Major Civil Division)**

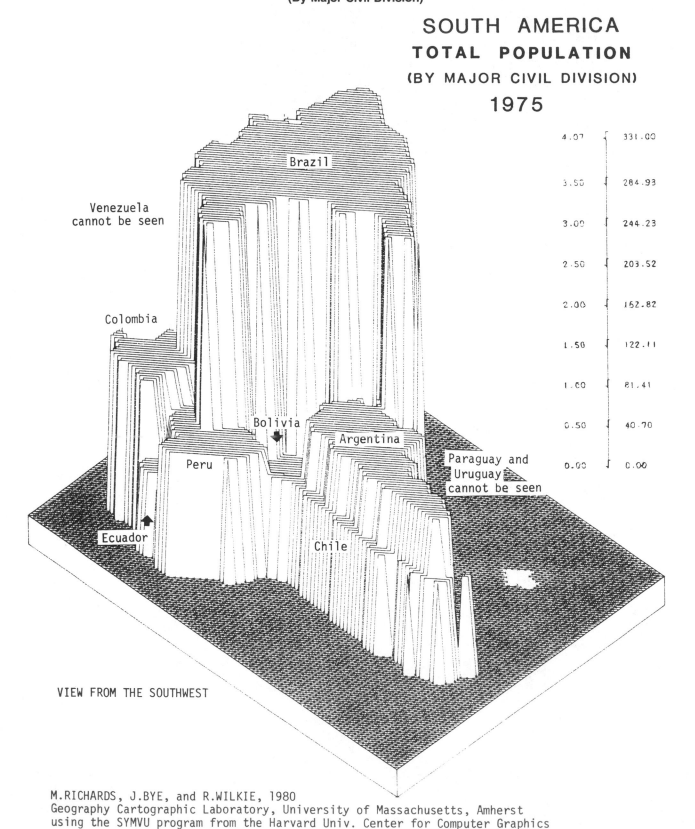

SOUTH AMERICA
TOTAL POPULATION
(BY MAJOR CIVIL DIVISION)
1975

4.07	331.00
3.50	284.93
3.00	244.23
2.50	203.52
2.00	162.82
1.50	122.11
1.00	81.41
0.50	40.70
0.00	0.00

Brazil

Venezuela
cannot be seen

Colombia

Bolivia

Argentina

Peru

Paraguay and
Uruguay
cannot be seen

Ecuador

Chile

VIEW FROM THE SOUTHWEST

M.RICHARDS, J.BYE, and R.WILKIE, 1980
Geography Cartographic Laboratory, University of Massachusetts, Amherst
using the SYMVU program from the Harvard Univ. Center for Computer Graphics

Map 4-5

**THREE-DIMENSIONAL CHOROPLETH MAP OF POPULATION DENSITY
IN SOUTH AMERICA, 1975
(Persons per km²)**

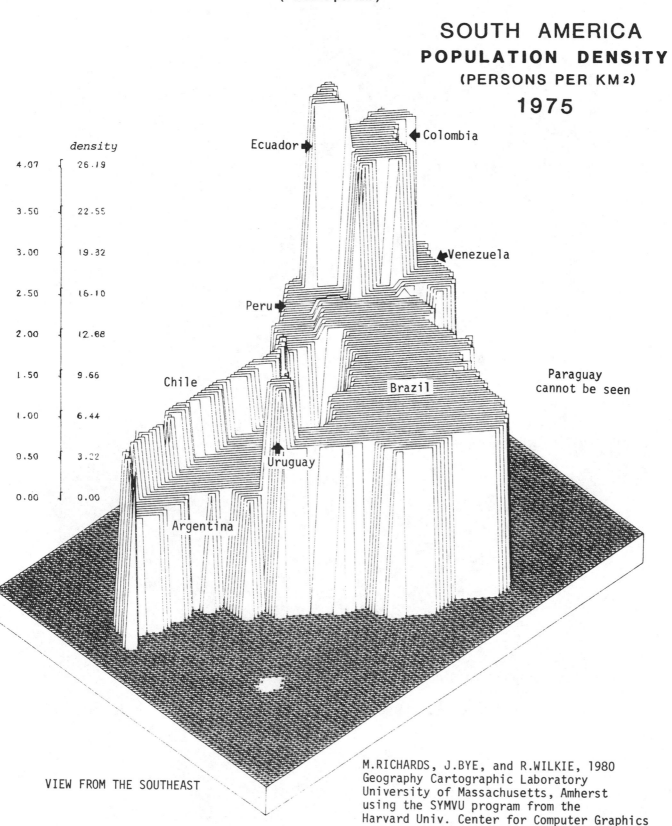

SOUTH AMERICA
POPULATION DENSITY
(PERSONS PER KM²)
1975

density

4.07	26.19
3.50	22.55
3.00	19.32
2.50	16.10
2.00	12.88
1.50	9.66
1.00	6.44
0.50	3.22
0.00	0.00

Ecuador

Colombia

Venezuela

Peru

Chile

Brazil

Paraguay
cannot be seen

Uruguay

Argentina

VIEW FROM THE SOUTHEAST

M.RICHARDS, J.BYE, and R.WILKIE, 1980
Geography Cartographic Laboratory
University of Massachusetts, Amherst
using the SYMVU program from the
Harvard Univ. Center for Computer Graphics

Map 4-6A

THREE-DIMENSIONAL CHOROPLETH MAP OF POPULATION CHANGE
IN SOUTH AMERICA, 1965–1975
(%)

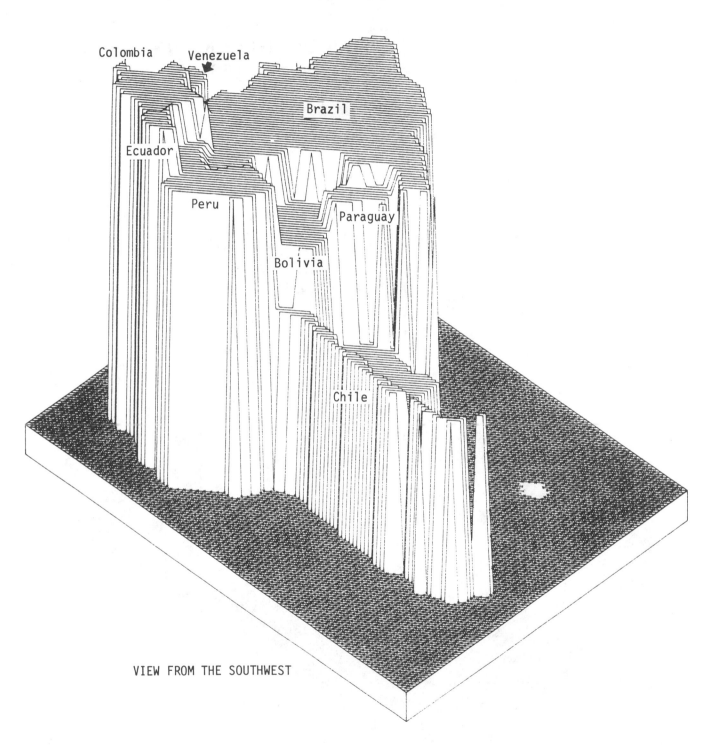

VIEW FROM THE SOUTHWEST

Map 4-6B

THREE-DIMENSIONAL CHOROPLETH MAP OF POPULATION CHANGE
IN SOUTH AMERICA, 1965–1975

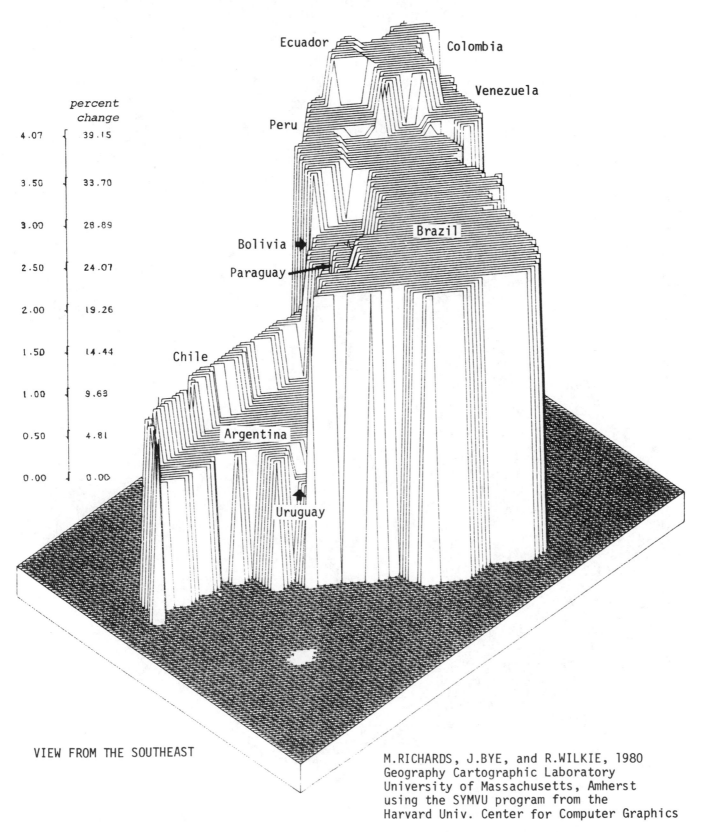

VIEW FROM THE SOUTHEAST

M.RICHARDS, J.BYE, and R.WILKIE, 1980
Geography Cartographic Laboratory
University of Massachusetts, Amherst
using the SYMVU program from the
Harvard Univ. Center for Computer Graphics

Map 4-7A

PHYSIOGRAPHIC MAP OF NORTHERN SOUTH AMERICA AND THE AMAZON BASIN

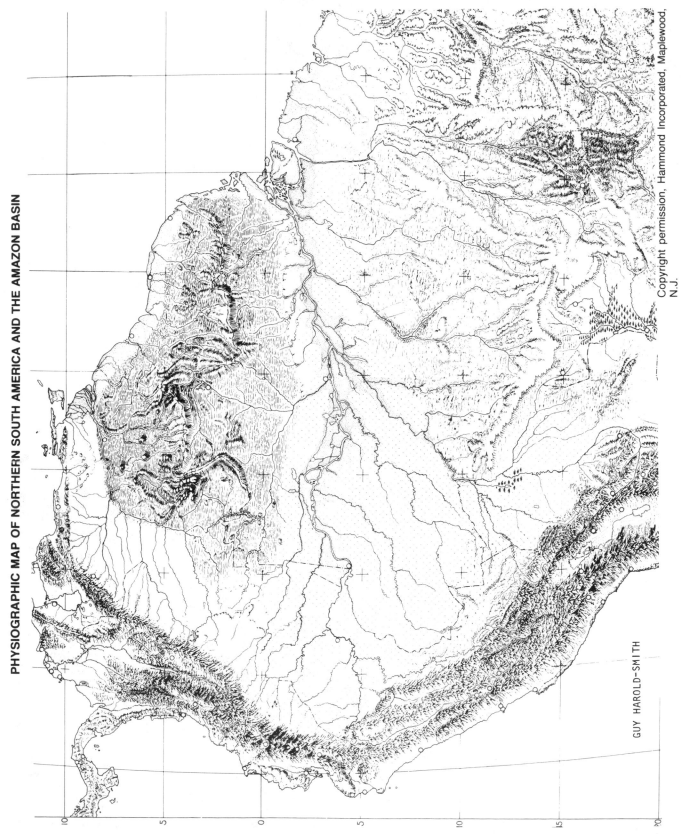

GUY HAROLD-SMITH

Map 4-7B

PHYSIOGRAPHIC MAP OF THE ORINOCO RIVER BASIN AND THE
GUIANA HIGHLANDS

GUY HAROLD-SMITH

Map 4-7C

PHYSIOGRAPHIC MAP OF THE NORTHERN ANDES
AND WESTERN GRAN COLOMBIA

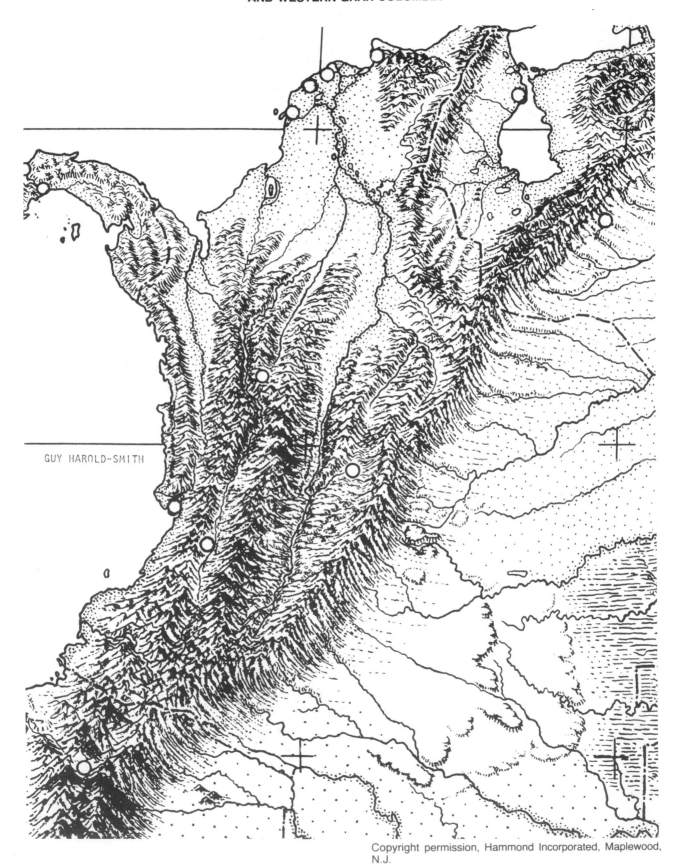

GUY HAROLD-SMITH

Photo 4-1

PATTERNS ON THE BOLIVIAN RURAL LANDSCAPE (1966)

Photo 4-2

PATTERNS ON THE PERUVIAN URBAN LANDSCAPE OF CUZCO (1966)

Map 4-7D

PHYSIOGRAPHIC MAP OF THE CENTRAL ANDES

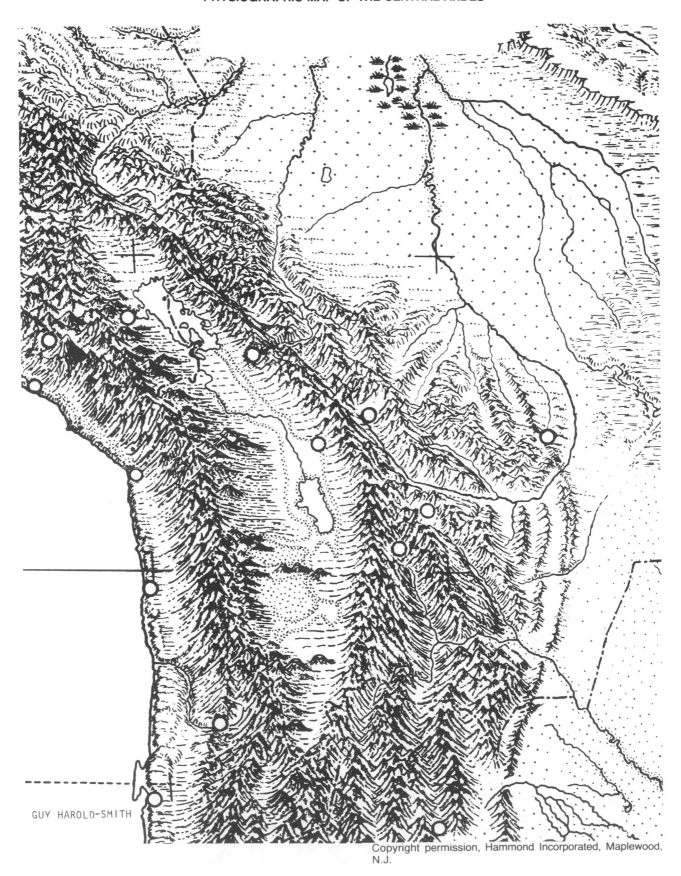

GUY HAROLD-SMITH

Photo 4-3

BOATING TO MARKET IN PUNO, PERU (1966)

Map 4-7E

PHYSIOGRAPHIC MAP OF SOUTH-CENTRAL SOUTH AMERICA

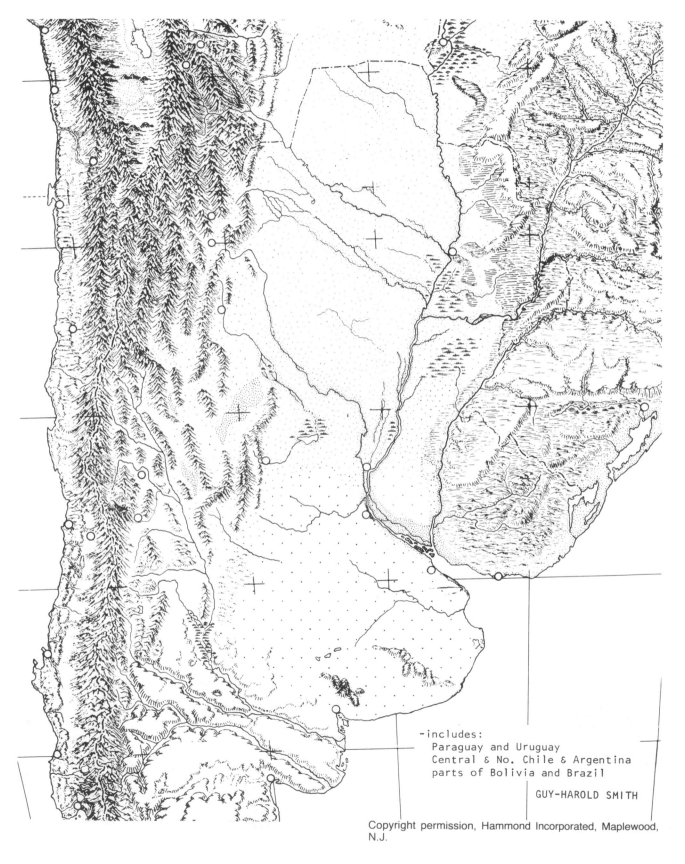

-includes:
  Paraguay and Uruguay
  Central & No. Chile & Argentina
  parts of Bolivia and Brazil

  GUY-HAROLD SMITH

Map 4-7F

PHYSIOGRAPHIC MAP OF PATAGONIA AND SOUTHERN CHILE

GUY HAROLD-SMITH

Map 4-7G

**PHYSIOGRAPHIC MAP OF THE CENTRAL PARANÁ RIVER REGION
AND THE GRAN CHACO**

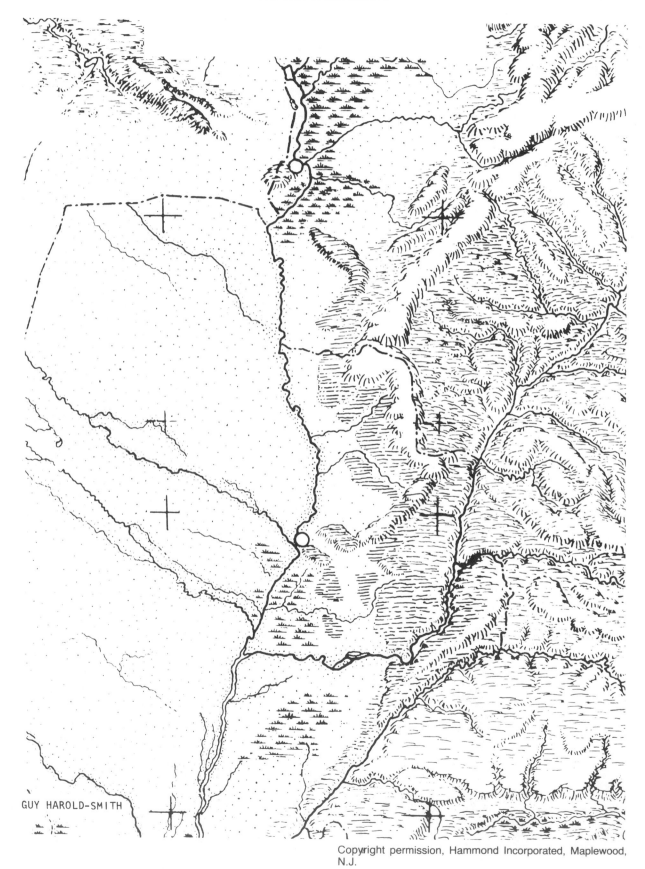

GUY HAROLD-SMITH

Map 4-7H

PHYSIOGRAPHIC MAP OF URUGUAY, RIO GRANDE DO SUL, AND NORTHEAST ARGENTINA

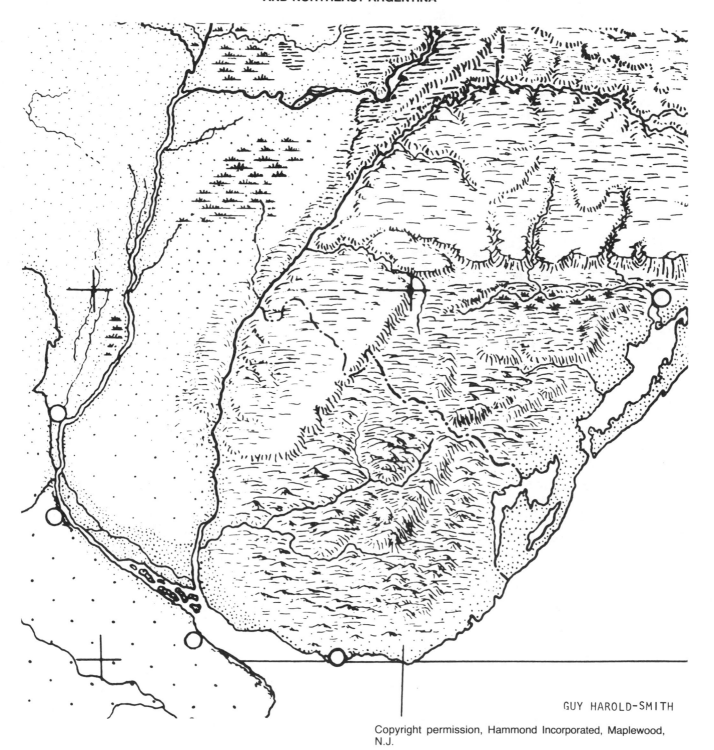

GUY HAROLD-SMITH

Part Two: Country Data

Introduction

With slight variations, the data on the twenty Latin American countries are presented in the sequence below.

MAP 1   Physiographic map showing the landforms of the country. (Drawn by Erwin Raisz or Guy Harold-Smith.)

TEXT   Brief introduction to each country, focusing on a historical examination of the national censuses, urban and rural trends at present, the settlement hierarchy of the country, and a summary of other selected demographic data.

TABLE 1   Most recent population of each political unit along with the percentage of the national total. The units are rank ordered by population size rather than alphabetically and the numbers are keyed to the political base map (map 2).

TABLE 2   Population of the major urban centers along with the percentage of the national total. The cities are rank ordered by population size and the largest ones are also located on the political base map (map 2).

MAP 2   Base map of the major civil divisions and the location of major urban cities. The numbers are rank ordered by size of population and are keyed to table 1.

MAP 3   Population cartogram showing in comparative terms the population size of each political unit found on map 2. State numbers are also keyed by size to table 1. States and cities are located as closely as possible to neighboring states so that the country is recognizable. Emphasis is on population size, however, and not on geographical size.

MAP 4   Three-dimensional map of total population by province for the most recent census period. The taller the unit, the greater its population.

MAP 5   Three-dimensional map of population density by province.

MAP 6   Three-dimensional map of population change between the two most recent censuses by province. As in maps 4 and 5, the taller the unit, the greater the volume (in this case growth of population by percent).

TABLE 3   List of all national censuses taken in the country.

TABLE 4   Breakdown of the population into five levels in the urban-rural settlement hierarchy for the 1950s, 1960s, and 1970s.

TABLE 5   Selected indicators of population change and per capita GNP between 1940 and 1982. Included are the following items: births and deaths per 1,000 population, rate of natural increase in percent per year, number of years to double the population, percent of population under the age of fifteen, life expectancy at birth, and per capita GNP in U.S. dollars each year.

TABLE 6   Major geographical units by square kilometers and number of geographical units in each province.

PHOTOGRAPHS   Depictions of urbanization, settlement landscapes, and the people of Latin America.

Map 5-1

PHYSIOGRAPHIC MAP OF ARGENTINA

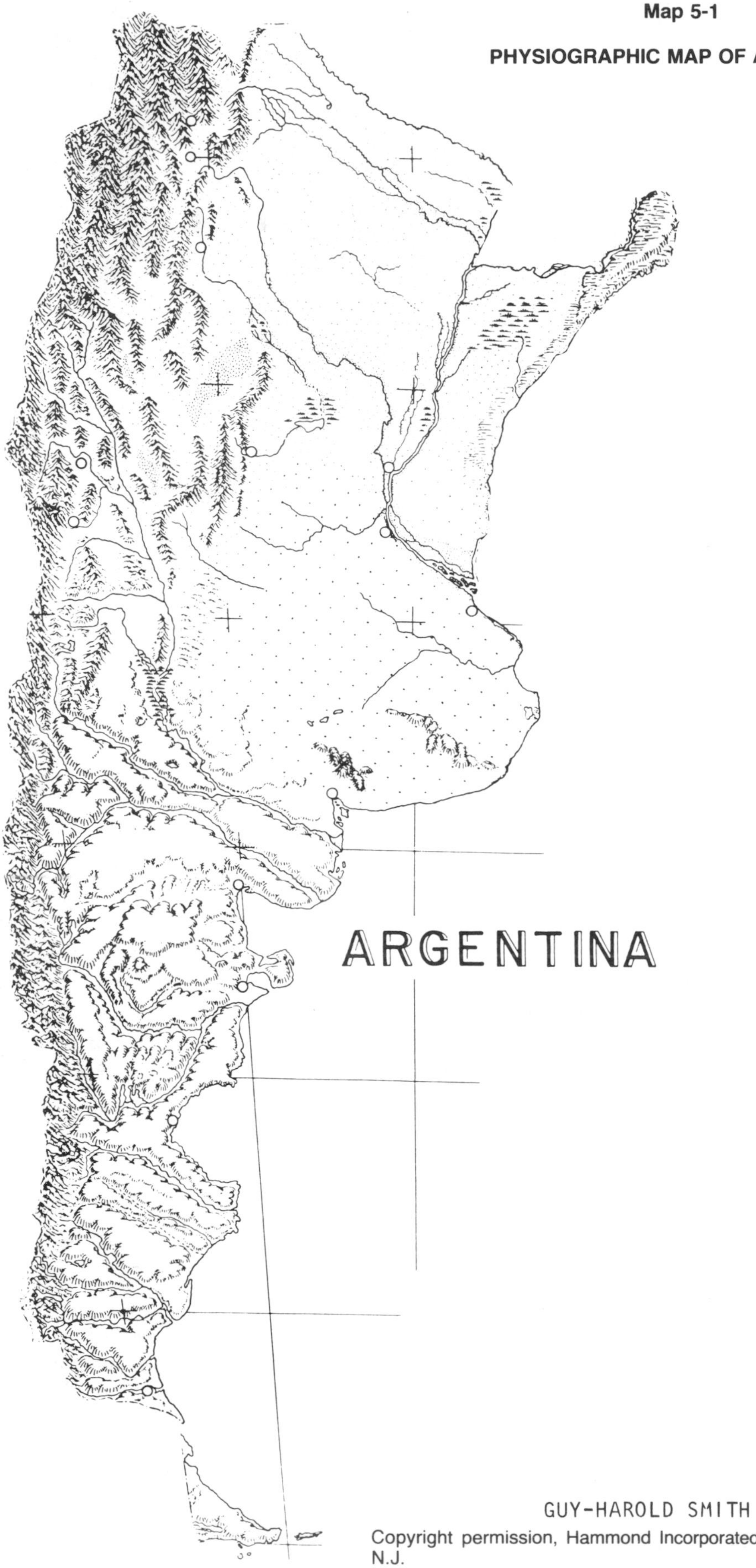
ARGENTINA
GUY-HAROLD SMITH

Copyright permission, Hammond Incorporated, Maplewood, N.J.

5

Argentina

Argentina has had seven official censuses over a 114-year period. The first census (1869) counted 1,737,076 inhabitants. By the second census, only twenty-six years later in 1895, the population had more than doubled to just under 4 million. The population nearly doubled again by 1914, and slightly more than doubled to just under 16 million by 1947. The seventh census in 1980 enumerated 27,862,771 inhabitants.

The population totals, trends, and characteristics of Argentina are presented in ten tables, nine maps, and two figures. Some of the findings concerning Argentina include those outlined below.

URBAN TRENDS

Argentina in 1970 had five urban centers that could be classified as metropolitan centers. Greater Buenos Aires with 8,435,840 represented 36 percent of the nation's population, while Gran Rosario (806,942), Gran Córdoba (790,508), Gran La Plata (478,666), and Gran Mendoza (470,896) together accounted for another 11 percent. In the census of 1980, Gran Buenos Aires had grown 15 percent to 9,710,223 inhabitants. Beyond these five metropolitan centers which accounted for nearly half of the population in 1970, there were ten regional centers with between 100,000 and 400,000, and sixteen regional centers between 50,000 and 100,000

population. Fewer than 3 million people lived in simple urban centers between 2,000 and 20,000 in size, and they accounted for only 12.4 percent of the nation's population.

RURAL TRENDS

The rural population of Argentina has remained between 5 and 6 million since 1947, but the percentage of the total population living in rural areas has declined from 37.3 percent to 21.4 percent.

SETTLEMENT HIERARCHY

Since 1947 when Argentina could be classified as an unbalanced metropolitan–dispersed settlement landscape (4–0), it has gradually become a metropolitan–complex urban settlement (4–3) with two-thirds of its citizens living in cities of more than 20,000 population.

OTHER DEMOGRAPHIC DATA

The annual rate of population growth in Argentina has remained between 1.3 and 1.6 percent since the late 1950s. Life expectancy in the early 1980s was 69 years and 27 percent of the population was under fifteen years of age. Per capita GNP in 1982 of $2,390 was up by only 85 percent from $1,290 in 1975, but Argentina still ranked number 3 among the twenty Latin American republics in that category.

Table 5-1

POPULATION DATA AND DENSITY BY PROVINCE IN ARGENTINA, 1970 AND 1980

1980 Rank	Province	1970 Population	1980 Population	1980 Percent	Percent Change 1970-1980	Population Density 1980 (km^2)
1	Buenos Aires Province	8,774,529	10,865,408	38.9	+23.8	35
2	Capital Federal	2,972,453	2,922,829	10.4	−1.7	14,614
3	Santa Fé	2,135,583	2,465,546	8.8	+15.5	19
4	Córdoba	2,073,991	2,407,754	8.6	+16.1	14
5	Mendoza	973,075	1,196,228	4.3	+22.9	8
6	Tucumán	765,962	972,655	3.5	+27.0	43
7	Entre Ríos	811,691	908,313	3.2	+11.9	12
8	Chaco	566,613	701,392	2.5	+23.8	7
9	Salta	509,803	662,870	2.4	+30.0	4
10	Corrientes	564,147	661,454	2.4	+17.2	7
11	Santiago del Estero	496,419	594,920	2.1	+19,8	4
12	Misiones	443,020	588,977	2.1	+32.9	20
13	San Juan	384,284	465,976	1.7	+21.3	5
14	Jujuy	302,436	410,008	1.7	+35.6	8
15	Río Negro	262,622	383,354	1.4	+46.0	2
16	Formosa	234,075	295,887	1.0	+26.4	4
17	Chubut	189,920	263,116	.9	+38.5	1
18	Neuquén	154,570	243,850	.9	+57.8	3
19	San Luis	183,460	214,416	.8	+16.9	3
20	La Pampa	172,029	208,260	.7	+21.1	1
21	Catamarca	172,323	207,717	.7	+20.5	2
22	La Rioja	136,237	164,217	.6	+20.5	2
23	Santa Cruz	84,457	114,941	.4	+36.0	0.5
24	Tierra del Fuego and territories	15,658	29,392	.1	+87.7	1
	Total	23,364,431	27,949,480	100.0	+19.6	10.1

SOURCES: República Argentina, *Censo Nacional de Población y Vivienda, 1980* (Capital Federal: Instituto Nacional de Estadística y Censos, Ministerio de Economía, July 1982), revised 1980 figures for each state in 22 volumes. Density and percent figures were calculated by the author.

Table 5-2

MAJOR URBAN CENTERS IN ARGENTINA, 1970 AND 1980

1980 Rank	Major Urban Centers	1980 Population	1980 Percent	1970 Population	1970 Percent	Percent Change
1	✪ Gran Buenos Aires (1 and 2)	9,942,232	35.6	8,461,955	36.2	+17
	Capital Federal (2)	2,922,829	10.5	2,972,453	12.7	–2
	Buenos Aires Province (1)	7,019,403	25.1	5,489,502	23.5	+28
2	◉ Gran Córdoba (4)	982,018	3.5	792,925	3.4	+24
3	Gran Rosario (3)	954,606	3.4	813,068	3.5	+17
4	Gran Mendoza (5)	596,796	2.1	477.810	2.0	+25
5	Gran La Plata (1)	560,341	2.0	485,939	2.1	+15
6	Gran Tucumán (6)	496,914	1.8	366,392	1.6	+36
7	● Mar del Plata (1)	407,024	1.5	302,282	1.3	+35
8	Gran San Juan (13)	290,479	1.0	222,601	1.0	+30
9	Santa Fé (3)	287,240	1.0	244,655	1.0	+17
10	Salta (9)	260,323	.9	176,216	.8	+48
11	Gran Bahía Blanca (1)	220,765	.8	182,158	.8	+21
12	Gran Resistencia (8)	218,438	.8	142,848	.6	+53
13	● Corrientes (10)	179,590	.6	136,924	.6	+31
14	Paraná (7)	159,581	.6	127,635	.5	+25
15	Santiago del Estero (11)	148,357	.5	105,127	.4	+41
16	Posadas (12)	139,941	.5	97,514	51.6	+44
17	S. Salvador de Jujuy (14)	124,487	.4	82,638		+51
18	Río Cuarto (4)	110,148	.4	88,852		+36
19	o Comodoro Rivadavia (17)	96,865	57.4	72,906		+33
20	San Nicolás (1)	96,313		64,730		+49
21	Formosa (16)	95,067		61,071		+56
22	Concordia (7)	93,618		72,136		+30
23	Neuquén (18)	90,037		43,070		+109
24	Gran Catamarca, S.F. del Valle (21)	88,432		64,410		+37
25	Tandil (1)	78,821		65,876		+20
26	San Luis (19)	70,632		50,771		+39
27	San Rafael (5)	70,477		58,237		+21
28	Pergamino (1)	68,989		56,078		+23
29	Gran Villa Maria (4)	67,490		56,087		+20
30	La Rioja (22)	66,826		46,090		+45
31	Zárate (1)	65,504		54,772		+20
32	Olavarría (1)	63,686		52,453		+21
33	Junín (1)	62,080		59,020		+5
34	Gran San Francisco (4)	58,616		48,896		+20
35	Punta Alta (C. Rosales/P. Belg. '70) (1)	54,375		36,805		n.a.
36	Rafaela (3)	53,152		43,695		+22
37	Trelew (17)	52,073		24,214		+115
38	Santa Rosa (20)	51,698		33,649		+54
39	Campana (1)	51,489		33,919		+52
40	Gualeguaychú (7)	51,057		40,661		+26
41	Necochea (1)	50,939		39,868		+28
42	Mercedes (19)	50,856		40,052		+27

Table 5-2 (Continued)

1980 Rank	Major Urban Centers	1980 Population	1970 Population	Percent Change 1970-1980
43	Presidente Roque Sáenz Peña (8)	49,261	38,620	+28
44	San Carlos de Bariloche (15)	48,222	26,799	+80
45	Goya (9)	47,357	39,367	+20
46	La Banda (11)	46,994	33,032	+42
47	Venado Tuerto (3)	46,775	35,677	+31
48	Mercedes (1)	46,581	39,760	+20
49	Concepción del Uruguay (7)	46,065	38,967	+18
50	Chivilcoy (1)	43,779	37,190	+18
51	Azul (1)	43,582	36,023	+21
52	Río Gallegos (23)	43,479	27,833	+56
53	Tres Arroyas (1)	42,118	37,991	+11
54	Cipolletti (15)	40,123	23,768	+69
55	Luján (1)	38,919	38,393	+1
56	General Roca (15)	38,296	29,320	+31
57	San Salvador de Jujuy (14)	36,907	25,265	+46
58	Villa Constitución (3)	36,157	25,148	+44
59	Santo Tomé (3)	35,363	23,572	+50
60	Río Tercero (4)	34,735	21,907	+59
61	San R. de la N. Orán (9)	32,955	20,212	+63
62	Reconquista (3)	32,442	25,333	+28
63	Tartagal (9)	31,367	23,696	+32
64	Libertador San Martin (14)	30,814	10,643	+190
65	Alta Gracia (4)	30,628	24,371	+26
66	General Pico (20)	30,180	21,897	+38
67	San Martin (5)	29,746	29,746	+22
68	Villa Carlos Paz (4)	29,553	20,056	+47
69	Concepción (6)	29,359	20,694	+42
70	Balcarce (1)	28,985	26,461	+10
71	Palpala (14)	27,857	15,879	+75
72	Oberá (12)	27,311	16,994	+61
73	Bragado (1)	27,101	23,366	+16
74	San Pedro (1)	27,058	23,365	+16
75	Tafí Viejo (6)	26,625	21,897	+23
76	9 de Julio (1)	26,608	19,762	+35
77	Bell Ville (4)	26,559	22,528	+18
78	Chacabuco (1)	26,492	23,660	+12
79	Cuatral-Có (18)	25,870	19,404	+33
80	Pehuajó (1)	25,613	21,078	21
81	Villa Angela (8)	25,586	17,091	+50
82	Curuzú Cuatia (10)	24,955	20,636	+21
83	Gualeguay (7)	24,883	24,883	+22
84	Cañada de Gómez (3)	24,706	20,611	+20
85	Viedma (15)	24,338	12,888	+89
86	Paso de los Libres (9)	24,112	17,341	+39
87	Casilda (3)	23,492	19,240	+22
88	Cruz del Eje (4)	23,473	23,401	0
89	Esperanza (3)	22,838	17,636	+29
90	Eldorado (12)	22,821	14,057	+62
91	Trenque Lauquen (1)	22,504	18,169	+24
92	Chascomús (1)	21,864	17,103	+28
93	Villa Dolores (4)	21,508	19,010	+13
94	General Alvear (5)	21,250	17,277	+23
95	Clorinda (16)	21,008	16,125	+30
96	Frías (11)	20,901	12,421	+68
97	Lobos (1)	20,798	13,677	+52
98	Puerto Madryn (17)	20,709	6,115	+239
99	Termas de Río Hondo (11)	20,652	10,917	+89
100	Mercedes (10)	20,603	18,476	+12
101	Aguilares/Villa Nueva de Monte Rico (6)	20,286	13,105	+55
102	Caleta Olivia (23)	20,141	13,366	+51
103	Baradero (1)	20,103	16,026	+25

Photo 5-1

**HORSE-DRAWN TAXIS WAITING OUTSIDE CENTRAL MARKET,
SALTA, ARGENTINA (1966)**

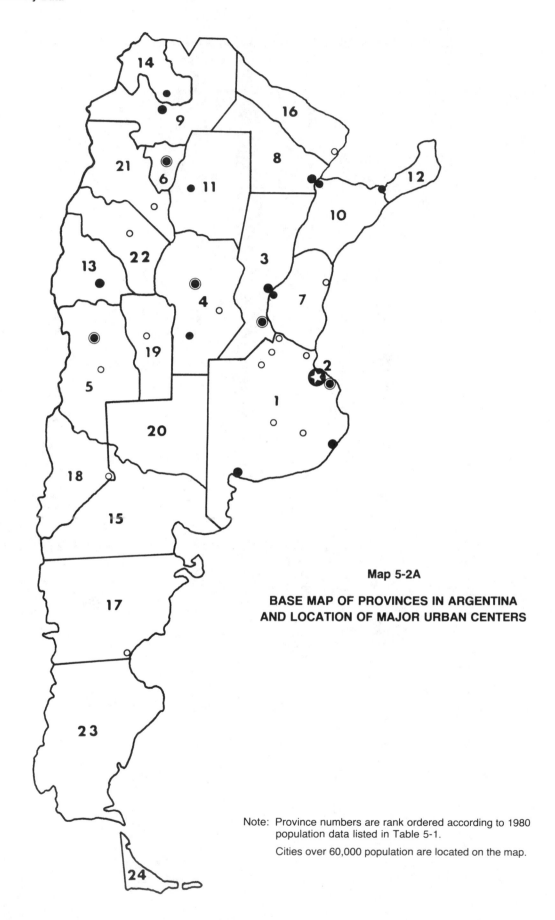

Map 5-2A

**BASE MAP OF PROVINCES IN ARGENTINA
AND LOCATION OF MAJOR URBAN CENTERS**

Note: Province numbers are rank ordered according to 1980
population data listed in Table 5-1.

Cities over 60,000 population are located on the map.

Map 5-2B

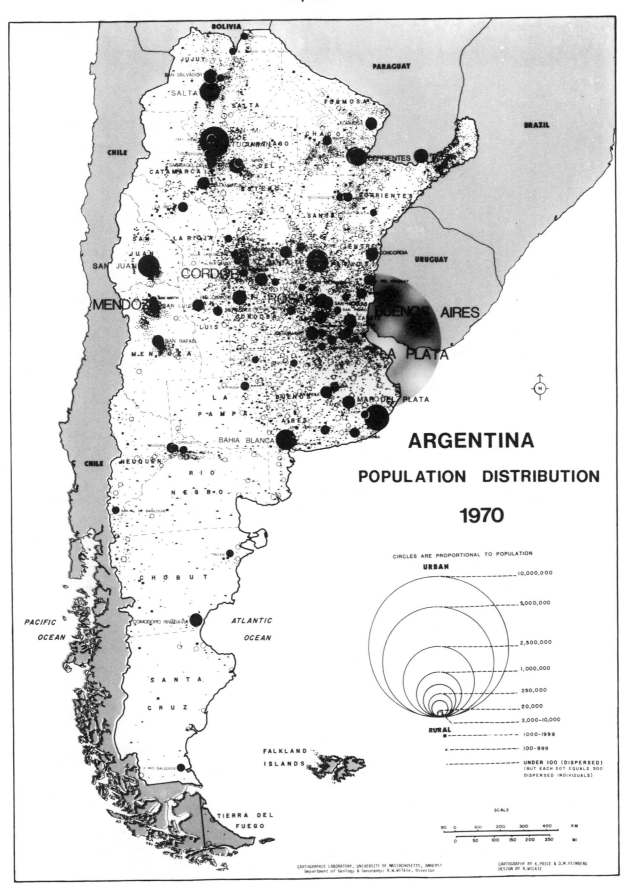

ARGENTINA

POPULATION DISTRIBUTION

1970

CIRCLES ARE PROPORTIONAL TO POPULATION

URBAN

— — — 10,000,000

— — — 5,000,000

— — — 2,500,000

— — — 1,000,000

— — — 250,000

— — — 20,000

— — — 2,000–10,000

RURAL

— — — 1000–1999

— — — 100–999

— — — UNDER 100 (DISPERSED)
(BUT EACH DOT EQUALS 500
DISPERSED INDIVIDUALS)

SCALE

50 0   100   200   300   400   KM

0   50   100 150 200 250   MI

CARTOGRAPHIC LABORATORY, UNIVERSITY OF MASSACHUSETTS, AMHERST
Department of Geology & Geography: R.W.Wilkie, Director

CARTOGRAPHY BY K.PRICE & D.M.FEINBERG
DESIGN BY R.WILKIE

Map 5-3A

POPULATION CARTOGRAM OF ARGENTINA, 1980

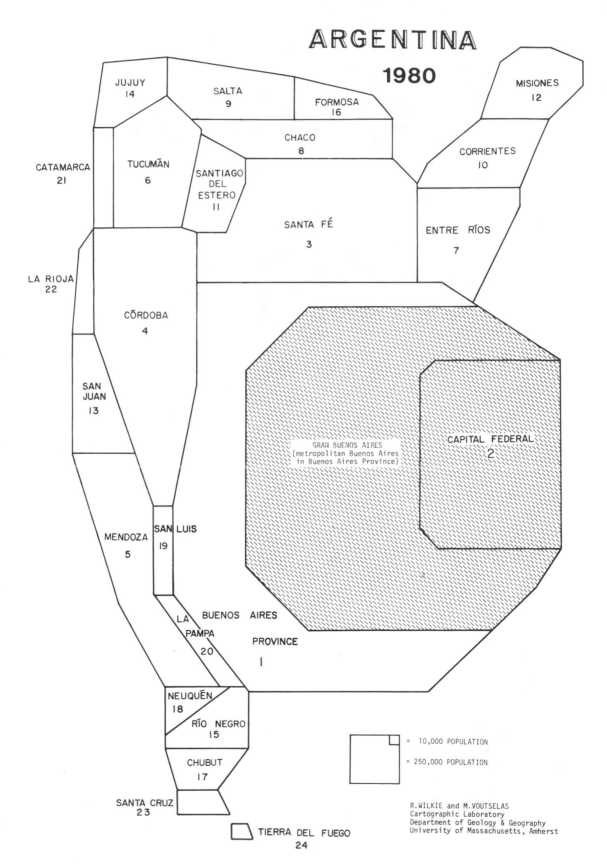

ARGENTINA
1980

| | = 10,000 POPULATION |
| | = 250,000 POPULATION |

R.WILKIE and M.VOUTSELAS
Cartographic Laboratory
Department of Geology & Geography
University of Massachusetts, Amherst

Map 5-3B

POPULATION CARTOGRAM OF ARGENTINA, 1970

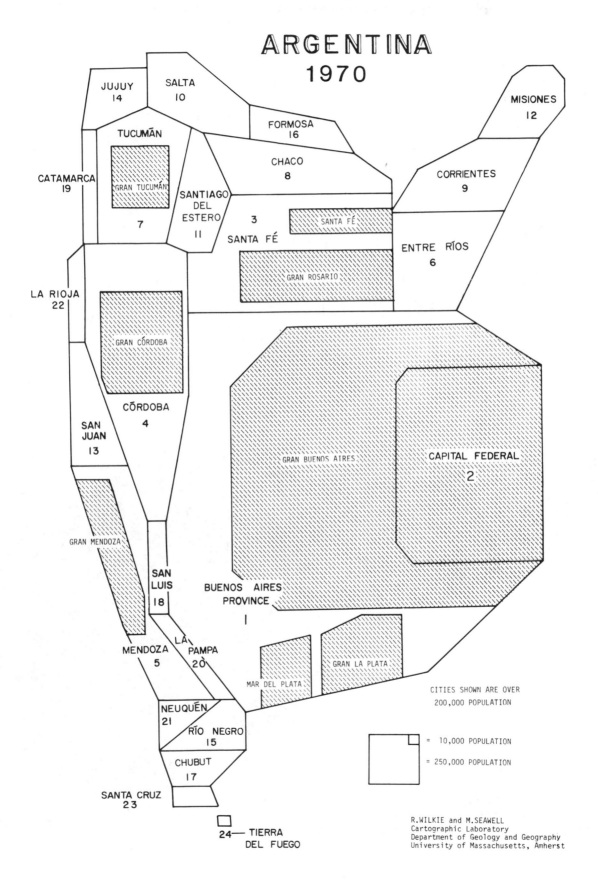

ARGENTINA
1970

JUJUY 14

SALTA 10

MISIONES 12

TUCUMÁN

FORMOSA 16

CHACO 8

CATAMARCA 19

GRAN TUCUMÁN

SANTIAGO DEL ESTERO 11

CORRIENTES 9

SANTA FÉ

7

3

SANTA FÉ

ENTRE RÍOS 6

LA RIOJA 22

GRAN ROSARIO

GRAN CÓRDOBA

CÓRDOBA 4

GRAN BUENOS AIRES

CAPITAL FEDERAL 2

SAN JUAN 13

GRAN MENDOZA

SAN LUIS 18

BUENOS AIRES PROVINCE

1

MENDOZA 5

LA PAMPA 20

GRAN LA PLATA

MAR DEL PLATA

CITIES SHOWN ARE OVER 200,000 POPULATION

NEUQUÉN 21

RÍO NEGRO 15

= 10,000 POPULATION

CHUBUT 17

= 250,000 POPULATION

SANTA CRUZ 23

24 — TIERRA DEL FUEGO

R.WILKIE and M.SEAWELL
Cartographic Laboratory
Department of Geology and Geography
University of Massachusetts, Amherst

Map 5-4A

**THREE-DIMENSIONAL CHOROPLETH MAP OF TOTAL POPULATION
BY PROVINCE IN ARGENTINA, SOUTHWEST VIEW, 1980**

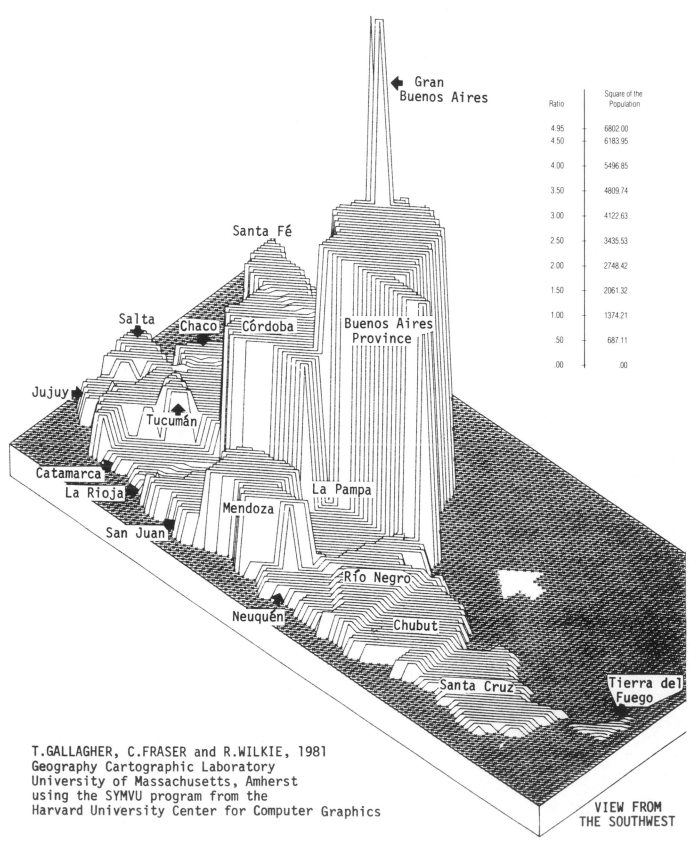

Ratio	Square of the Population
4.95	6802.00
4.50	6183.95
4.00	5496.85
3.50	4809.74
3.00	4122.63
2.50	3435.53
2.00	2748.42
1.50	2061.32
1.00	1374.21
.50	687.11
.00	.00

T.GALLAGHER, C.FRASER and R.WILKIE, 1981
Geography Cartographic Laboratory
University of Massachusetts, Amherst
using the SYMVU program from the
Harvard University Center for Computer Graphics

VIEW FROM
THE SOUTHWEST

Map 5-4B

THREE-DIMENSIONAL CHOROPLETH MAP OF TOTAL POPULATION
BY PROVINCE IN ARGENTINA, NORTHEAST VIEW, 1980

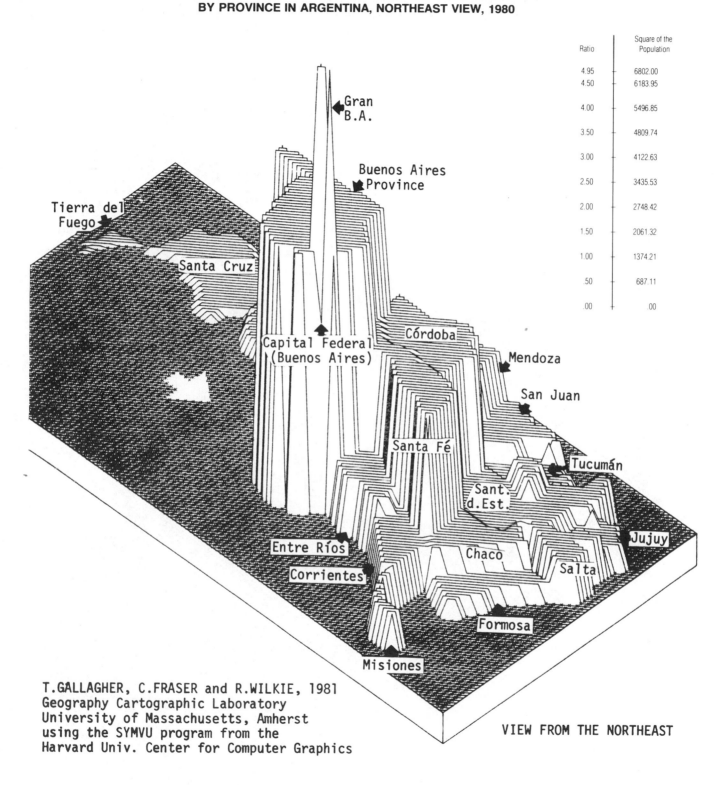

Ratio	Square of the Population
4.95	6802.00
4.50	6183.95
4.00	5496.85
3.50	4809.74
3.00	4122.63
2.50	3435.53
2.00	2748.42
1.50	2061.32
1.00	1374.21
.50	687.11
.00	.00

T.GALLAGHER, C.FRASER and R.WILKIE, 1981
Geography Cartographic Laboratory
University of Massachusetts, Amherst
using the SYMVU program from the
Harvard Univ. Center for Computer Graphics

VIEW FROM THE NORTHEAST

Map 5-5A

THREE-DIMENSIONAL CHOROPLETH MAP OF POPULATION DENSITY
IN ARGENTINA, 1980
(Persons per km²)

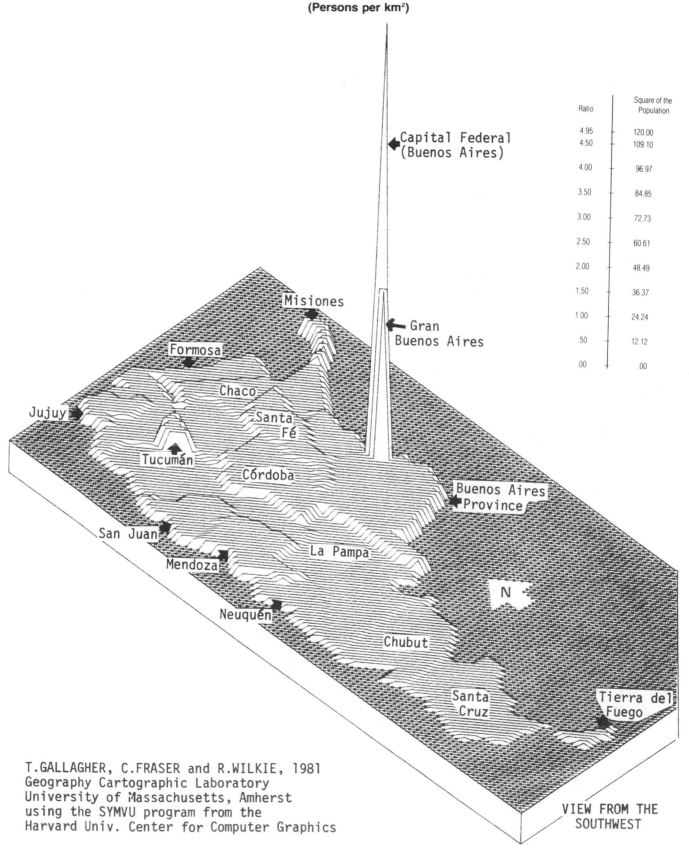

Ratio	Square of the Population
4.95	120.00
4.50	109.10
4.00	96.97
3.50	84.85
3.00	72.73
2.50	60.61
2.00	48.49
1.50	36.37
1.00	24.24
.50	12.12
.00	.00

Capital Federal
(Buenos Aires)

Gran
Buenos Aires

Misiones

Formosa

Chaco

Santa Fé

Jujuy

Tucumán

Córdoba

Buenos Aires Province

San Juan

Mendoza

La Pampa

N

Neuquén

Chubut

Santa Cruz

Tierra del Fuego

T.GALLAGHER, C.FRASER and R.WILKIE, 1981
Geography Cartographic Laboratory
University of Massachusetts, Amherst
using the SYMVU program from the
Harvard Univ. Center for Computer Graphics

VIEW FROM THE
SOUTHWEST

Map 5-5B

THREE-DIMENSIONAL ISOPLETH MAP OF POPULATION DENSITY
IN ARGENTINA, 1980
(Persons per km²)

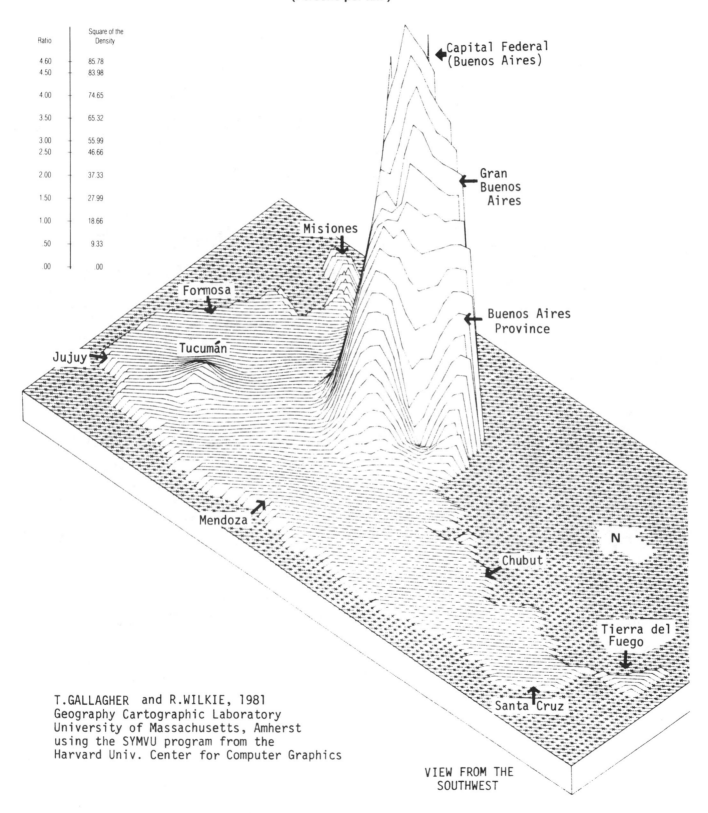

Ratio	Square of the Density
4.60	85.78
4.50	83.98
4.00	74.65
3.50	65.32
3.00	55.99
2.50	46.66
2.00	37.33
1.50	27.99
1.00	18.66
.50	9.33
.00	.00

Capital Federal
(Buenos Aires)

Gran
Buenos
Aires

Buenos Aires
Province

Misiones

Formosa

Tucumán

Jujuy

Mendoza

N

Chubut

Tierra del
Fuego

Santa Cruz

T.GALLAGHER and R.WILKIE, 1981
Geography Cartographic Laboratory
University of Massachusetts, Amherst
using the SYMVU program from the
Harvard Univ. Center for Computer Graphics

VIEW FROM THE
SOUTHWEST

Map 5-6A

THREE-DIMENSIONAL CHOROPLETH MAP OF POPULATION CHANGE
IN ARGENTINA, 1970–1980
(%)

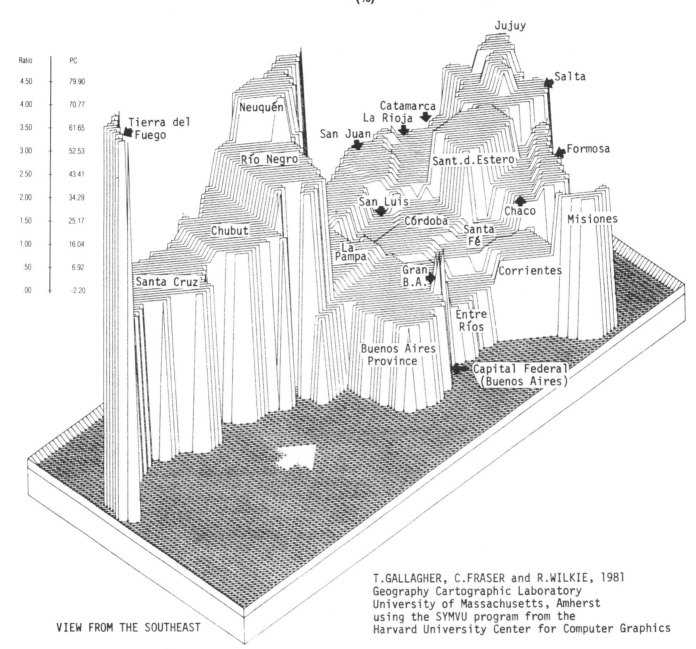

VIEW FROM THE SOUTHEAST

T.GALLAGHER, C.FRASER and R.WILKIE, 1981
Geography Cartographic Laboratory
University of Massachusetts, Amherst
using the SYMVU program from the
Harvard University Center for Computer Graphics

Map 5-6B

THREE-DIMENSIONAL ISOPLETH MAP OF POPULATION CHANGE
IN ARGENTINA, 1970–1980
(%)

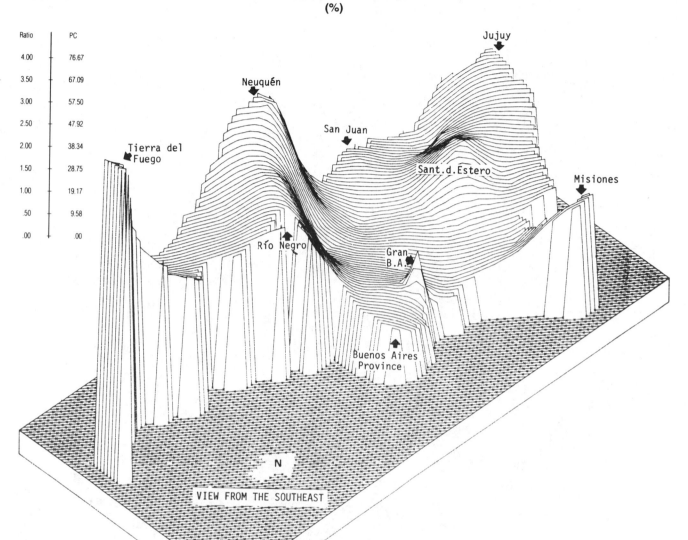

T.GALLAGHER and R.WILKIE, 1981
Geography Cartographic Laboratory
University of Massachusetts, Amherst
using the SYMVU program from the
Harvard University Center for Computer Graphics

Map 5-7

THREE-DIMENSIONAL CHOROPLETH MAP OF POPULATION CHANGE
IN ARGENTINA, 1960–1970
(%)

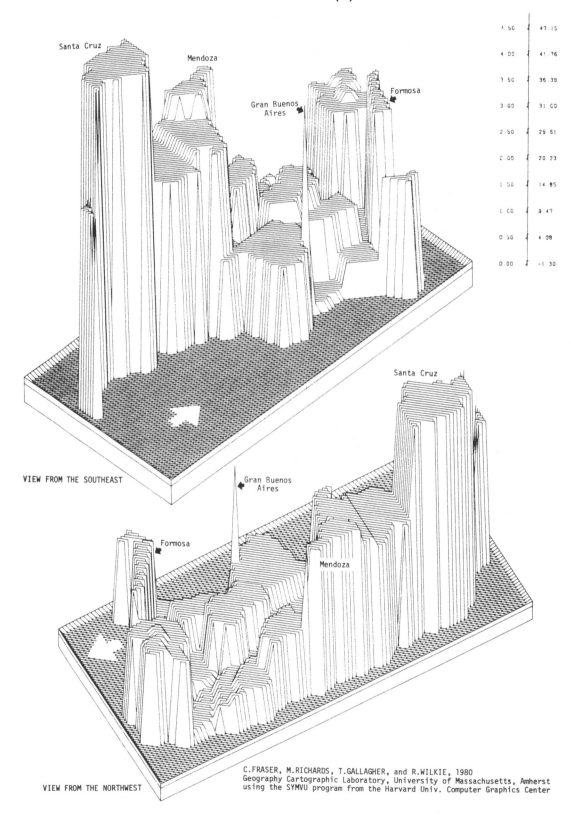

VIEW FROM THE SOUTHEAST

VIEW FROM THE NORTHWEST

C.FRASER, M.RICHARDS, T.GALLAGHER, and R.WILKIE, 1980
Geography Cartographic Laboratory, University of Massachusetts, Amherst
using the SYMVU program from the Harvard Univ. Computer Graphics Center

Photo 5-2

COMMERCIAL BUILDING ARCHITECTURE WITH APARTMENTS AND BALCONIES
ON UPPER STORIES, BUENOS AIRES, ARGENTINA (1977)

Table 5-3

POPULATION FOR EACH NATIONAL CENSUS IN
ARGENTINA, 1869–1980

Census Year	Population
1869	1,737,076
1895	3,954,911
1914	7,885,237
1947	15,897,127
1960	20,010,539
1970	23,364,431
1980	27,949,840

Table 5-4

TOTAL AND PERCENT POPULATION IN FIVE LEVELS OF THE URBAN-RURAL
SETTLEMENT HIERARCHY OF ARGENTINA SINCE 1950

	0	1	2	3	4	SETTLEMENT HIERARCHY	
CENSUS YEAR	DISPERSED Population 1 to 99	VILLAGE 100 to 2,500	SIMPLE URBAN 2,501– 20,000	COMPLEX URBAN 20,001– 500,000	METROPOLITAN over 500,000	Classification	PERCENT in top 2 levels
TOTAL							
1947	4,740,892	1,219,255	2,254,414	2,955,344	4,722,381		
1960	3,536,447	1,754,948	3,212,431	3,438,741	8,067,972		
1970	3,906,503	1,087,950	2,836,673	4,501,608[a]	11,031,697[a]		
1980	- -	- -	- -	6,046,832[a]	13,532,907[a]		
PERCENT							
1869	66.9	4.5	16.7	12.4	- -	0-2	83.6
1895	.... 62.5		13.2	7.5	16.8	0-4	71 to 75
1914	.... 47.3		17.1	15.6	20.0	0-4	59 to 63
1947	29.6	7.7	14.3	18.6	29.8	4-0	59.4
1960	17.7	8.8	16.0	17.2	40.3	4-3	58.0
1970	16.7	4.7	12.2	19.2[a]	47.2[a]	4-3	66.4
1980	- -	- -	- -	21.6[a]	48.4[a]	4-3	70.0

a. La Plata and Mendoza in 1970 and Tucumán in 1980 were just under half a million population, but were counted as metropolitan since they were well above other cities in the complex urban category.

SOURCE: Calculated from various Argentine national censuses since 1950, and from SALA, 20 tables 631, 632, 634, 635, 636, 637, and 638.

Table 5-5

SELECTED INDICATORS OF POPULATION CHANGE AND PER CAPITA GNP IN ARGENTINA

Years	Per 1000 Population		Rate of Natural Increase (Annual %)	Number of Years to Double Population	Percent Population Under Age 15	Life Expectancy at Birth	Per Capita GNP (US)
	Births	Deaths					
1940–45	24	10	1.7	- -	- -	- -	- -
1945–50	25	10	2.1	- -	- -	- -	- -
1950–55	25	9	2.1	- -	- -	- -	- -
1955–60	24	9	2.0	- -	- -	- -	374[a]
1960–65	23	9	1.6	- -	- -	66[b]	- -
1965–70	22	9	1.6	- -	- -	- -	- -
1970–74	23	9	1.3	47[c]	29[c]	- -	800[c]
1975	22	9	1.3	53	28	68	1,290
1976	22	9	1.4	50	29	68	1,900
1977	26	9	1.3	53	29	68	1,590
1978	23	9	1.3	53	29	68	1,550
1979	22	9	1.3	53	28	68	1,730
1980	26	9	1.6	43	28	69	1,910
1981	25	9	1.6	43	28	69	2,280
1982	25	9	1.6	43	27	69	2,390

a. 1955.
b. 1959–61.
c. 1970

MAJOR SOURCES:

Births: SALA, 19-204; SALA, 20-705 through 1977.

Deaths: SALA, 18-703d and 706 through 1970.

Life expectancy: SALA, 19-700 through 1970.

Per capita GNP: 1955 data from Ginsburg, *Atlas of Economic Development* (Chicago: University of Chicago Press, 1961).

Rate of natural increase: SALA, 22-626 from CELADE-BD 10 (1972) through 1970.

All other data: Population Reference Bureau, Washington, D.C., annual world population data sheets.

Table 5-6

ARGENTINA PROVINCES BY GEOGRAPHICAL SIZE AND SUBDIVISION, 1970

Province	Civil Subdivision (N)	Area km^2	%
Total	482[a]	2,776,656[b]	100.0
Capital	* *	200	#
Provinces and Territories			
Buenos Aires	119	307,571	11.1
Catamarca	16	99,818	3.6
Córdoba	26	168,766	6.1
Corrientes	25	88,199	3.2
Chaco	24	99,633	3.6
Chubut	15	224,686	8.1
Entre Ríos	14	76,216	2.7
Formosa	9	72,066	2.6
Jujuy	15	53,219	1.9
La Pampa	22	143,440	5.2
La Rioja	18	92,331	3.3
Mendoza	18	150,839	5.4
Misiones	17	29,801	1.1
Neuquén	16	94,078	3.4
Río Negro	13	203,013	7.3
Salta	23	154,775	5.6
San Juan	19	86,137	3.1
San Luis	9	76,748	2.8
Santa Cruz	7	243,943	8.8
Santa Fé	19	133,007	4.8
Santiago del Estero	27	135,254	4.9
Territorio Nacional de Tierra del Fuego, Antártida e Islas del Atlántico Sur			
Sector Continental	* *	20,392	.7
Sector Antártico, Islas Malvinas and other islands	* *	1,247,803	~
Tucumán	11	22,524	.8

a. Composed of 363 departments and 119 partidos.
b. Excludes 1,247,803 km^2 of the Antarctica, Islas Malvinas, and other islands of the South Atlantic.

SOURCE: SALA, 21-301.

Table 5-7

POPULATION CHANGE BY REGION IN ARGENTINA, 1970–1980

Region	1970 Total Population	1970 Percent	Change, 1970 to 1980 Total Growth	Change, 1970 to 1980 Percent Increase	Change, 1970 to 1980 Percent of All Growth	1980 Total Population	1980 Percent
CORE REGION 3 provinces and Federal Capital	15,942,630	68.23	2,625,730	16.5	58.4	18,568,360	66.6
CORE FRINGE 10 provinces	4,658,627	19.94	968,507	20.8	21.5	5,627,134	20.2
PERIPHERY (Frontier) 9 provinces and 1 territory	2,763,174	11.83	904,103	32.7	20.1	3,667,277	13.2
Total	23,364,431	100.0	4,498,340	19.3	100.0	27,862,771	100.0

Table 5-8

NUMBER OF CENTERS, TOTAL POPULATION, AND PERCENT OF POPULATION LIVING IN EACH OF FIVE SETTLEMENT SIZE LEVELS IN ARGENTINA, 1970 AND 1980

Level in the Urban-Rural Settlment Hierarchy	1970 Number Urban Centers	1970 Population	1970 Percent	1980 Number Urban Centers	1980 Population	1980 Percent
METROPOLITAN	5	11,031,697	47.2	6	13,532,907	48.4
Over 1,000,000	1	8,461,955	36.2	1	9,942,232	35.6
475,000 to 999,999	4	2,569,742	11.0	5	3,590,675	12.8
COMPLEX URBAN	74	4,501,608	19.2	97	6,046,832	21.6
250,000 to 475,000	2	668,674	2.9	4	1,245,066	4.5
100,000 to 250,000	8	1,338,164	5.7	8	1,301,307	4.7
75,000 to 100,000	3	269,004	1.2	7	639,153	2.3
60,000 to 75,000	6	401,129	1.7	8	535,684	1.9
50,000 to 60,000	7	387,418	1.7	9	474,255	1.7
40,000 to 50,000	6	262,464	1.1	12	544,336	1.9
30,000 to 40,000	14	519,261	2.2	12	408,763	1.5
20,000 to 30,000	28	655,494	2.8	37	898,268	3.2
SIMPLE URBAN	- -	2,836,673	12.2	- -	- -	- -
15,000 to 19,999	25	432,304	1.9			
10,000 to 15,000	61	704,177	3.0			
2,000 to 10,000	- -	1,700,192	7.3			
VILLAGE (100 to 1,999)	- -	1,087,950	4.7	- -	- -	- -
DISPERSED (1 to 99)	- -	3,906,503	16.7	- -	- -	- -

Map 5-8

SETTLEMENT LANDSCAPES OF ARGENTINA

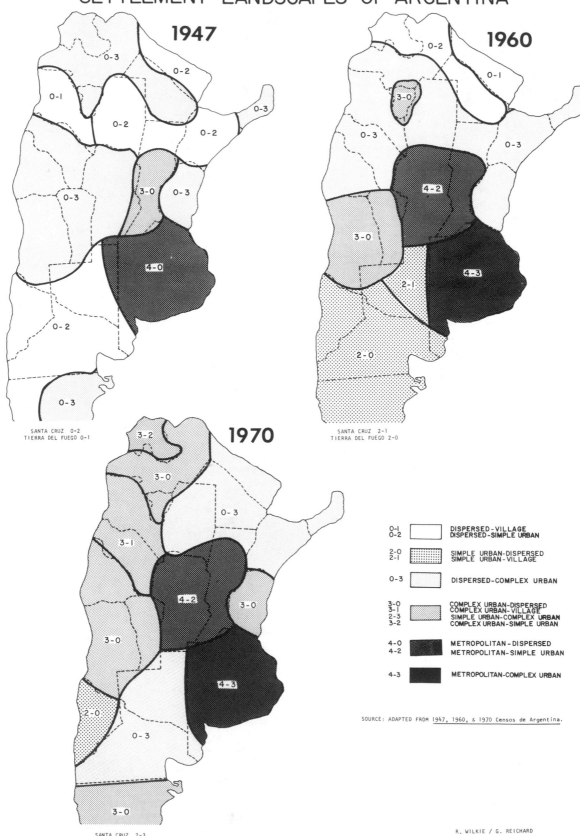

1947

SANTA CRUZ 0-2
TIERRA DEL FUEGO 0-1

1960

SANTA CRUZ 2-1
TIERRA DEL FUEGO 2-0

1970

SANTA CRUZ 2-3
TIERRA DEL FUEGO 2-0

0-1	DISPERSED-VILLAGE
0-2	DISPERSED-SIMPLE URBAN
2-0	SIMPLE URBAN-DISPERSED
2-1	SIMPLE URBAN-VILLAGE
0-3	DISPERSED-COMPLEX URBAN
3-0	COMPLEX URBAN-DISPERSED
3-1	COMPLEX URBAN-VILLAGE
2-3	SIMPLE URBAN-COMPLEX URBAN
3-2	COMPLEX URBAN-SIMPLE URBAN
4-0	METROPOLITAN-DISPERSED
4-2	METROPOLITAN-SIMPLE URBAN
4-3	METROPOLITAN-COMPLEX URBAN

SOURCE: ADAPTED FROM 1947, 1960, & 1970 Censos de Argentina.

R. WILKIE / G. REICHARD

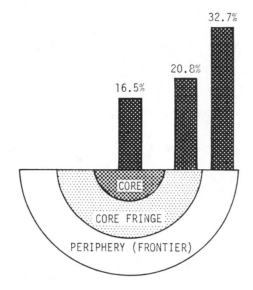

Figure 5-1

ARGENTINA POPULATION INCREASE BY REGION, 1970-1980

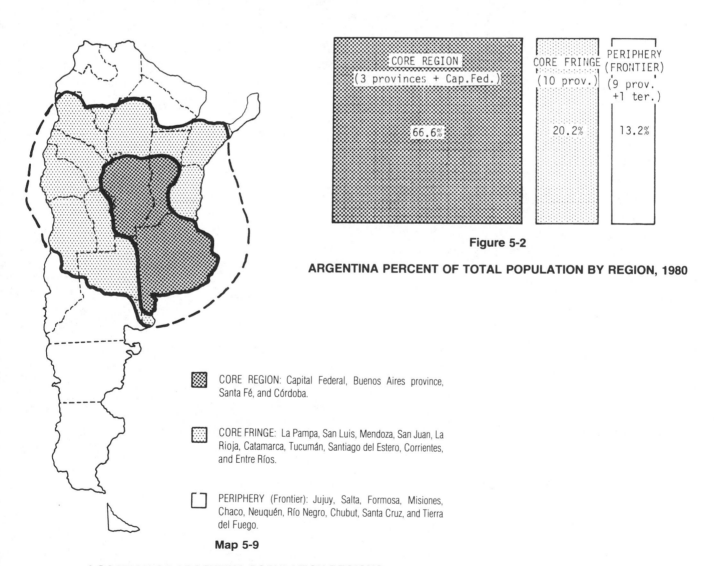

Figure 5-2

ARGENTINA PERCENT OF TOTAL POPULATION BY REGION, 1980

CORE REGION: Capital Federal, Buenos Aires province, Santa Fé, and Córdoba.

CORE FRINGE: La Pampa, San Luis, Mendoza, San Juan, La Rioja, Catamarca, Tucumán, Santiago del Estero, Corrientes, and Entre Ríos.

PERIPHERY (Frontier): Jujuy, Salta, Formosa, Misiones, Chaco, Neuquén, Río Negro, Chubut, Santa Cruz, and Tierra del Fuego.

Map 5-9

LOCATION OF ARGENTINA POPULATION REGIONS

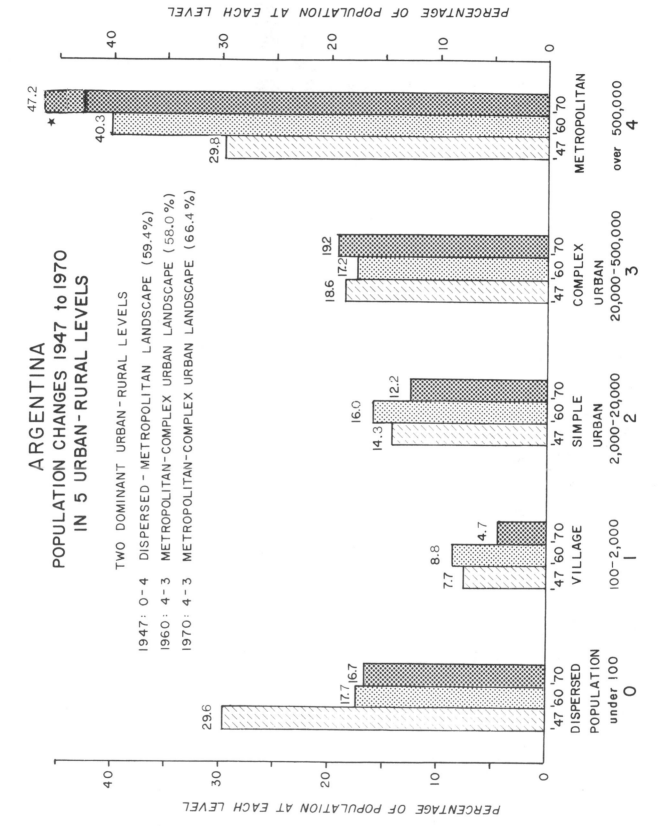

Figure 5-3

ARGENTINA
POPULATION CHANGES 1947 to 1970
IN 5 URBAN-RURAL LEVELS

TWO DOMINANT URBAN-RURAL LEVELS

1947: 0-4   DISPERSED-METROPOLITAN LANDSCAPE (59.4%)
1960: 4-3   METROPOLITAN-COMPLEX URBAN LANDSCAPE (58.0%)
1970: 4-3   METROPOLITAN-COMPLEX URBAN LANDSCAPE (66.4%)

Figure 5-4

ARGENTINA CHANGE IN AVERAGE SIZE OF AGRICULTURAL LANDHOLDINGS NORTH OF THE RÍO COLORADO, 1960–1969

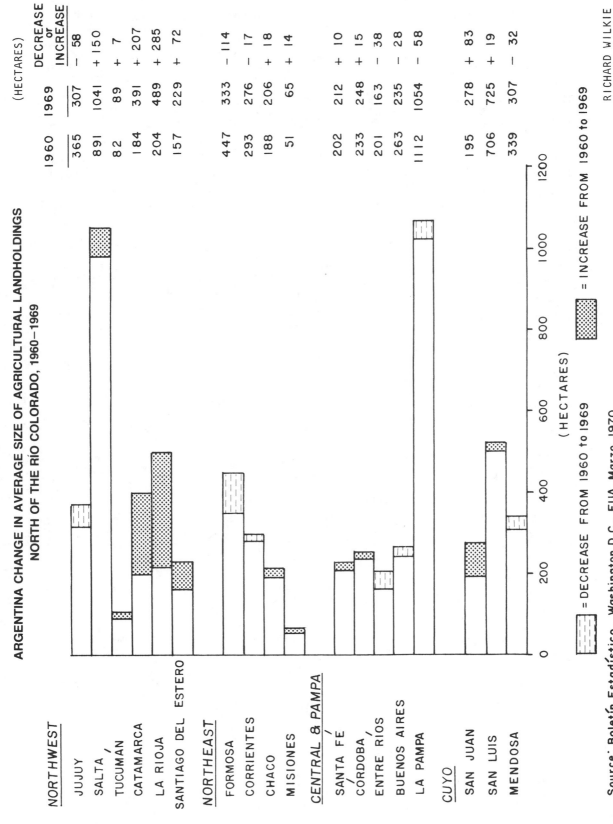

	1960	1969	DECREASE or INCREASE
NORTHWEST			(HECTARES)
JUJUY	365	307	− 58
SALTA	891	1041	+ 150
TUCUMAN	82	89	+ 7
CATAMARCA	184	391	+ 207
LA RIOJA	204	489	+ 285
SANTIAGO DEL ESTERO	157	229	+ 72
NORTHEAST			
FORMOSA	447	333	− 114
CORRIENTES	293	276	− 17
CHACO	188	206	+ 18
MISIONES	51	65	+ 14
CENTRAL & PAMPA			
SANTA FE	202	212	+ 10
CORDOBA	233	248	+ 15
ENTRE RIOS	201	163	− 38
BUENOS AIRES	263	235	− 28
LA PAMPA	1112	1054	− 58
CUYO			
SAN JUAN	195	278	+ 83
SAN LUIS	706	725	+ 19
MENDOSA	339	307	− 32

(HECTARES)

= DECREASE FROM 1960 to 1969

= INCREASE FROM 1960 to 1969

RICHARD WILKIE

Source: Boletín Estadístico, Washington D.C., EUA, Marzo, 1970

Table 5-9

DISPERSED RURAL POPULATION IN ARGENTINA: 1947, 1960, AND 1970

(All population in settlements less than 100 inhabitants by nation, region, and province)

Regions and Provinces	Total Population			Percent		
	1947	1960	1970	1947	1960	1970
TOTAL	4,740,892	3,488,250	3,906,503	29.6	17.5	16.7
NORTHWEST	906,245	832,568	750,538	50.7	37.8	31.5
Jujuy	85,118	92,528	75,457	51.1	38.3	24.9
Salta	147,291	129,986	147,161	50.6	31.5	28.9
Tucumán	245,455	281,811	226,702	41.4	36.4	29.6
Santiago del Estero	309,153	231,864	229,687	64.5	48.7	46.4
Catamarca	62,135	57,960	39,090	42.2	34.5	22.7
La Rioja	57,093	38,419	32,441	51.6	30.0	23.8
NORTHEAST	1,127,021	1,116,009	1,112,960	53.6	46.1	42.5
Formosa	68,777	78,221	123,320	60.5	43.3	52.7
Chaco	270,308	282,021	265,351	62.8	51.9	46.8
Misiones	172,835	180,508	249,701	70.1	49.9	56.4
Corrientes	305,401	232,661	206,081	58.1	43.6	36.5
Entre Ríos	309,700	342,598	268,507	39.3	42.5	33.1
CENTRAL	1,981,242	987,394	1,323,519	34.6	14.9	17.4
Córdoba	513,531	298,354	343,920	34.3	17.0	16.7
Santa Fé	522,198	194,925	320,723	30.7	10.3	15.0
Buenos Aires Province[1]	945,513	494,115	658,876	37.3	16.5	19.4
WEST CENTRAL	527,428	427,362	536,091	44.5	28.3	31.3
La Pampa	81,201	13,675	68,270	47.9	8.6	39.7
San Luis	76,120	50,676	54,792	46.0	29.1	29.9
San Juan	126,144	119,385	107,348	48.3	33.9	27.9
Mendoza	243,963	243,626	305,681	41.5	29.6	31.4
PATAGONIA	198,956	133,917	183,395	55.0	26.4	25.9
Neuquén	56,337	42,589	44,200	64.9	38.8	28.6
Río Negro	79,049	38,015	83,355	58.8	19.7	31.7
Chubut	42,211	41,072	39,446	45.6	28.8	20.8
Santa Cruz	19,632	11,350	12,298	45.8	21.5	14.6
Tierra del Fuego	1,727	891	4,096	34.2	11.2	26.2

1. Excludes metropolitan Greater Buenos Aires and the Capital Federal which would lower the percentages for Buenos Aires Province and the region to 13.0% and 15.3% for 1947, 5.1% and 6.0% for 1960, and 5.6% and 6.8% for 1970.

Table 5-10

VILLAGE POPULATION IN ARGENTINA: 1947, 1960, AND 1970

(All population in settlements between 100 and 2,000 inhabitants by nation, region, and province)

Regions and Provinces	Total Population			Percent		
	1947	1960	1970	1947	1960	1970
TOTAL	1,219,255	1,754,947	1,087,950	7.7	8.7	4.6
NORTHWEST	200,546	309,100	244,896	11.2	14.0	10.3
Jujuy	20,311	30,269	30,566	12.2	12.5	10.1
Salta	28,247	55,969	42,416	9.7	13.6	8.3
Tucumán	48,533	71,324	43,773	8.2	9.2	5.7
Santiago del Estero	46,799	76,695	52,534	9.8	16.1	10.6
Catamarca	37,766	39,701	42,011	25.7	23.6	24.4
La Rioja	18,890	35,143	33,596	17.0	27.4	24.7
NORTHEAST	173,877	279,713	163,331	8.3	11.5	6.2
Formosa	19,036	40,357	16,412	16.7	22.6	7.0
Chaco	30,618	55,847	34,774	7.1	10.3	6.2
Misiones	27,765	65,836	27,347	11.3	18.2	6.2
Corrientes	40,110	53,228	35,212	7.7	10.0	6.2
Entre Ríos	56,348	64,445	49,586	7.2	8.0	6.1
CENTRAL	670,981	900,488	517,226	11.7	13.6	6.8
Córdoba	197,161	259,296	170,337	13.1	14.8	8.3
Santa Fé	196,178	253,194	155,188	11.5	13.4	7.3
Buenos Aires Province[1]	277,642	387,998	191,701	11.0	13.0	5.6
WEST CENTRAL	123,601	181,517	105,418	10.4	12.0	6.2
La Pampa	36,180	53,506	18,088	21.3	33.7	10.5
San Luis	24,757	33,408	23,582	15.0	19.2	12.9
San Juan	14,971	41,614	37,275	5.7	11.8	9.7
Mendoza	47,693	52,989	26,473	8.1	6.4	2.7
PATAGONIA	50,250	84,129	57,079	13.9	16.6	8.1
Neuquén	10,796	14,505	8,382	12.4	13.2	5.4
Río Negro	19,169	32,579	22,693	14.3	16.8	8.7
Chubut	10,217	23,840	18,294	11.1	16.7	9.6
Santa Cruz	6,750	13.205	7,710	15.7	25.0	9.1
Tierra del Fuego	3,318	~	~	65.8	~	~

1. Excludes metropolitan Greater Buenos Aires and the Capital Federal which would lower the percentages for Buenos Aires Province and the region to 3.8% and 5.2% for 1947, 4.0% and 5.5% for 1960, and 1.6% and 2.7% for 1970.

Map 5-10A

RATIO OF OUT- TO IN-MIGRATION IN ARGENTINA, BY PROVINCE, 1947

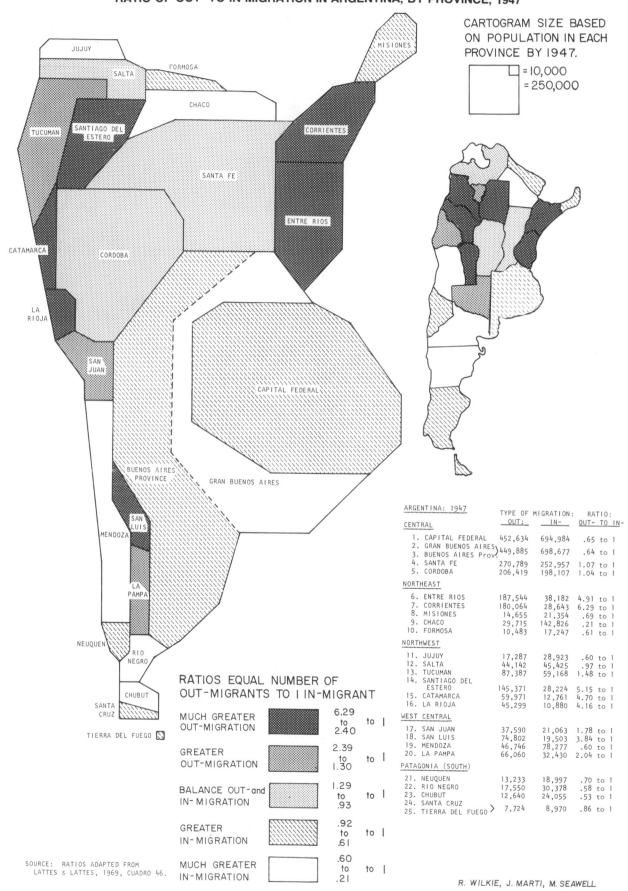

CARTOGRAM SIZE BASED
ON POPULATION IN EACH
PROVINCE BY 1947.

□ = 10,000
  = 250,000

RATIOS EQUAL NUMBER OF
OUT-MIGRANTS TO 1 IN-MIGRANT

MUCH GREATER OUT-MIGRATION		6.29 to 2.40 to 1
GREATER OUT-MIGRATION		2.39 to 1.30 to 1
BALANCE OUT- and IN-MIGRATION		1.29 to .93 to 1
GREATER IN-MIGRATION		.92 to .61 to 1
MUCH GREATER IN-MIGRATION		.60 to .21 to 1

SOURCE: RATIOS ADAPTED FROM
LATTES & LATTES, 1969, CUADRO 46.

ARGENTINA: 1947	TYPE OF MIGRATION:		RATIO:
CENTRAL	OUT:	IN-	OUT- TO IN-
1. CAPITAL FEDERAL	452,634	694,984	.65 to 1
2. GRAN BUENOS AIRES	449,885	698,677	.64 to 1
3. BUENOS AIRES Prov.			
4. SANTA FE	270,789	252,957	1.07 to 1
5. CORDOBA	206,419	198,107	1.04 to 1
NORTHEAST			
6. ENTRE RIOS	187,544	38,182	4.91 to 1
7. CORRIENTES	180,064	28,643	6.29 to 1
8. MISIONES	14,655	21,354	.69 to 1
9. CHACO	29,715	142,826	.21 to 1
10. FORMOSA	10,483	17,247	.61 to 1
NORTHWEST			
11. JUJUY	17,287	28,923	.60 to 1
12. SALTA	44,142	45,425	.97 to 1
13. TUCUMAN	87,387	59,168	1.48 to 1
14. SANTIAGO DEL ESTERO	145,371	28,224	5.15 to 1
15. CATAMARCA	59,971	12,761	4.70 to 1
16. LA RIOJA	45,299	10,880	4.16 to 1
WEST CENTRAL			
17. SAN JUAN	37,590	21,063	1.78 to 1
18. SAN LUIS	74,802	19,503	3.84 to 1
19. MENDOZA	46,746	78,277	.60 to 1
20. LA PAMPA	66,060	32,430	2.04 to 1
PATAGONIA (SOUTH)			
21. NEUQUEN	13,233	18,997	.70 to 1
22. RIO NEGRO	17,550	30,378	.58 to 1
23. CHUBUT	12,640	24,055	.53 to 1
24. SANTA CRUZ	7,724	8,970	.86 to 1
25. TIERRA DEL FUEGO			

R. WILKIE, J. MARTI, M. SEAWELL

Map 5-10B

RATIO OF OUT- TO IN-MIGRATION IN ARGENTINA, BY PROVINCE, 1960

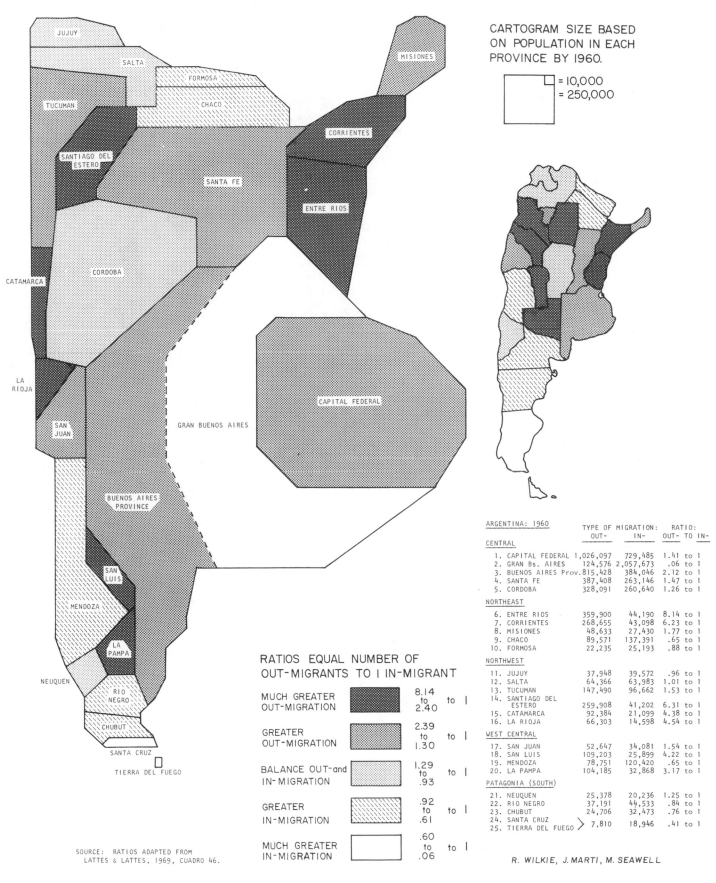

CARTOGRAM SIZE BASED
ON POPULATION IN EACH
PROVINCE BY 1960.

☐ = 10,000
■ = 250,000

**RATIOS EQUAL NUMBER OF
OUT-MIGRANTS TO 1 IN-MIGRANT**

MUCH GREATER OUT-MIGRATION	■	8.14 to to 1 2.40
GREATER OUT-MIGRATION	▒	2.39 to to 1 1.30
BALANCE OUT- and IN-MIGRATION	░	1.29 to to 1 .93
GREATER IN-MIGRATION	╱	.92 to to 1 .61
MUCH GREATER IN-MIGRATION	☐	.60 to to 1 .06

SOURCE: RATIOS ADAPTED FROM
LATTES & LATTES, 1969, CUADRO 46.

ARGENTINA: 1960

	TYPE OF MIGRATION: OUT-	IN-	RATIO: OUT- TO IN-
CENTRAL			
1. CAPITAL FEDERAL	1,026,097	729,485	1.41 to 1
2. GRAN Bs. AIRES	124,576	2,057,673	.06 to 1
3. BUENOS AIRES Prov.	815,428	384,046	2.12 to 1
4. SANTA FE	387,408	263,146	1.47 to 1
5. CORDOBA	328,091	260,640	1.26 to 1
NORTHEAST			
6. ENTRE RIOS	359,900	44,190	8.14 to 1
7. CORRIENTES	268,655	43,098	6.23 to 1
8. MISIONES	48,633	27,430	1.77 to 1
9. CHACO	89,571	137,391	.65 to 1
10. FORMOSA	22,235	25,193	.88 to 1
NORTHWEST			
11. JUJUY	37,948	39,572	.96 to 1
12. SALTA	64,366	63,983	1.01 to 1
13. TUCUMAN	147,490	96,662	1.53 to 1
14. SANTIAGO DEL ESTERO	259,908	41,202	6.31 to 1
15. CATAMARCA	92,384	21,099	4.38 to 1
16. LA RIOJA	66,303	14,598	4.54 to 1
WEST CENTRAL			
17. SAN JUAN	52,647	34,081	1.54 to 1
18. SAN LUIS	109,203	25,899	4.22 to 1
19. MENDOZA	78,751	120,420	.65 to 1
20. LA PAMPA	104,185	32,868	3.17 to 1
PATAGONIA (SOUTH)			
21. NEUQUEN	25,378	20,236	1.25 to 1
22. RIO NEGRO	37,191	44,533	.84 to 1
23. CHUBUT	24,706	32,473	.76 to 1
24. SANTA CRUZ	7,810	18,946	.41 to 1
25. TIERRA DEL FUEGO			

R. WILKIE, J. MARTI, M. SEAWELL

Map 5-10C

RATIO OF OUT- TO IN-MIGRATION IN ARGENTINA, BY PROVINCE, 1970

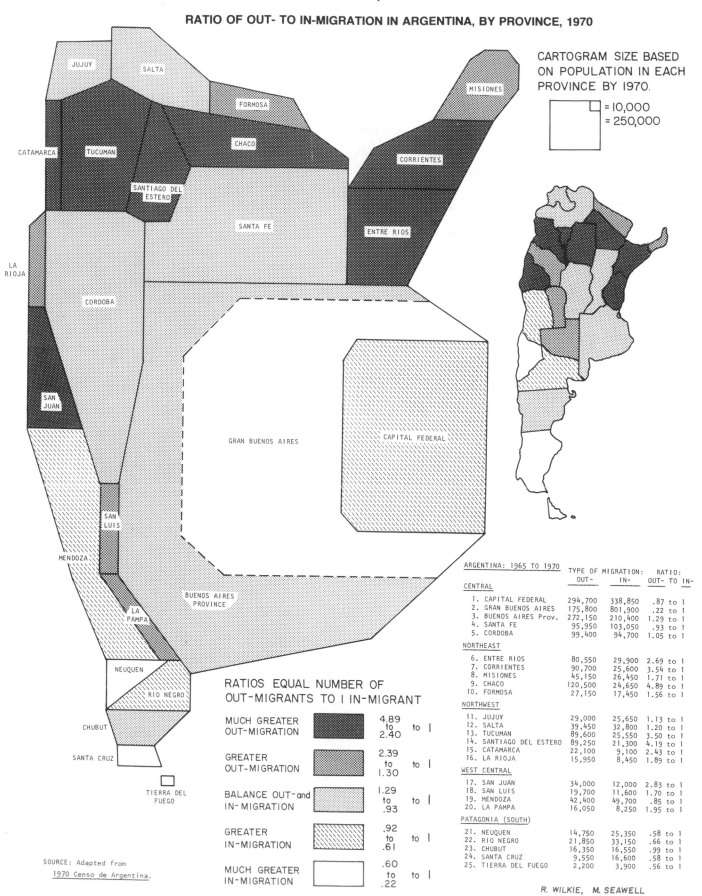

CARTOGRAM SIZE BASED
ON POPULATION IN EACH
PROVINCE BY 1970.

☐ = 10,000
= 250,000

RATIOS EQUAL NUMBER OF
OUT-MIGRANTS TO 1 IN-MIGRANT

MUCH GREATER OUT-MIGRATION		4.89 to 2.40 to 1
GREATER OUT-MIGRATION		2.39 to 1.30 to 1
BALANCE OUT-and IN-MIGRATION		1.29 to .93 to 1
GREATER IN-MIGRATION		.92 to .61 to 1
MUCH GREATER IN-MIGRATION		.60 to .22 to 1

SOURCE: Adapted from
1970 Censo de Argentina.

ARGENTINA: 1965 TO 1970	TYPE OF MIGRATION:		RATIO:
	OUT-	IN-	OUT- TO IN-
CENTRAL			
1. CAPITAL FEDERAL	294,700	338,850	.87 to 1
2. GRAN BUENOS AIRES	175,800	801,900	.22 to 1
3. BUENOS AIRES Prov.	272,150	210,400	1.29 to 1
4. SANTA FE	95,950	103,050	.93 to 1
5. CORDOBA	99,400	94,700	1.05 to 1
NORTHEAST			
6. ENTRE RIOS	80,550	29,900	2.69 to 1
7. CORRIENTES	90,700	25,600	3.54 to 1
8. MISIONES	45,150	26,450	1.71 to 1
9. CHACO	120,500	24,650	4.89 to 1
10. FORMOSA	27,150	17,450	1.56 to 1
NORTHWEST			
11. JUJUY	29,000	25,650	1.13 to 1
12. SALTA	39,450	32,800	1.20 to 1
13. TUCUMAN	89,600	25,550	3.50 to 1
14. SANTIAGO DEL ESTERO	89,250	21,300	4.19 to 1
15. CATAMARCA	22,100	9,100	2.43 to 1
16. LA RIOJA	15,950	8,450	1.89 to 1
WEST CENTRAL			
17. SAN JUAN	34,000	12,000	2.83 to 1
18. SAN LUIS	19,700	11,600	1.70 to 1
19. MENDOZA	42,400	49,700	.85 to 1
20. LA PAMPA	16,050	8,250	1.95 to 1
PATAGONIA (SOUTH)			
21. NEUQUEN	14,750	25,350	.58 to 1
22. RIO NEGRO	21,850	33,150	.66 to 1
23. CHUBUT	16,350	16,550	.99 to 1
24. SANTA CRUZ	9,550	16,600	.58 to 1
25. TIERRA DEL FUEGO	2,200	3,900	.56 to 1

R. WILKIE, M. SEAWELL

Figure 5-5

MIGRATION IN ARGENTINA: RATIO OF OUT- TO IN-MIGRATION, 1947, 1960, 1970

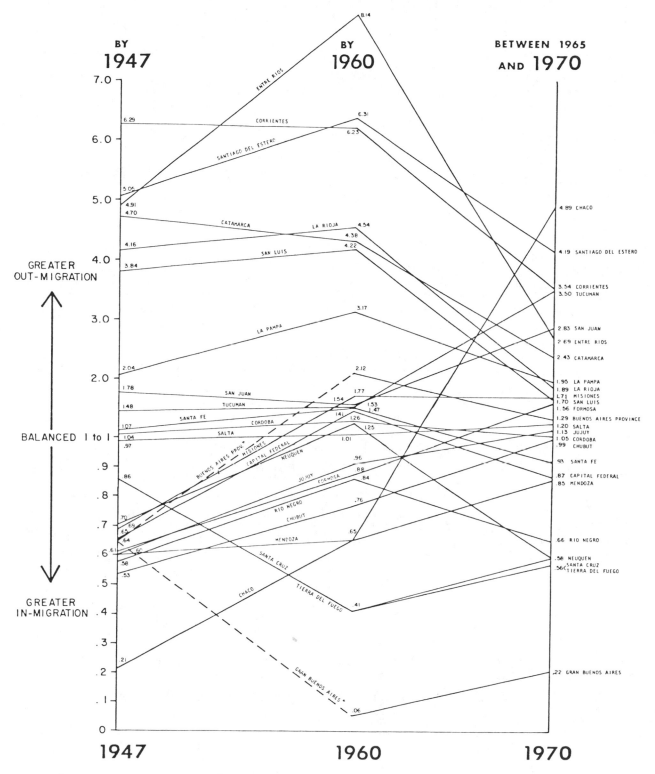

Data on Gran Buenos Aires and Buenos Aires Province were not kept separately in 1947, so both are connected to the 1947 ratio with dashed lines.

SOURCE: Map 5-10A, Map 5-10B, and Map 5-10C.

Figure 5-6

ARGENTINA PROVINCES GROUPED BY MIGRATION RATIOS, 1947, 1960, 1970

```
┌─────────────────────────────────────────┐
│   GENERALLY CONSISTENT PATTERNS*         │
└─────────────────────────────────────────┘
```

EXCESS OUT-MIGRATION

EXTREME OUT-MIGRATION

> Santiago del Estero
> Corrientes
> Entre Ríos

CONSIDERABLE OUT-MIGRATION

> Tucumán
> La Rioja
> Catamarca
> San Luis

MODERATE OUT-MIGRATION

> La Pampa
> San Juan

BALANCED

> Salta
> Córdoba
> Santa Fé
> Capital Federal
> Buenos Aires
>   Province

EXCESS IN-MIGRATION

EXTREME IN-MIGRATION

> Gran Buenos Aires
> Santa Cruz
> Tierra del Fuego

CONSIDERABLE IN-MIGRATION

> Mendoza
> Río Negro
> Chubut

MODERATE IN-MIGRATION

> Jujuy
> Neuquén

```
┌─────────────────────────────────────────┐
│   GENERALLY VARIED PATTERNS              │
└─────────────────────────────────────────┘
```

EXCESS IN- CHANGING TO EXCESS OUT-MIGRATION

> Formosa
> Misiones

EXTREME IN- CHANGING TO EXTREME OUT-MIGRATION

> Chaco

---

*Nearly all patterns show some rises or drops,
 so the word consistent is used in general terms
 and relates to overall trends shown graphically
 in Figure 9.

PUBLICATION SOURCE: The preceeding series of three maps (5-10A, 5-10B, and 5-10C)
 and two figures (5-5 and 5-6) were published in: Wilkie, Richard, "Migration
 and Population Imbalance in the settlement hierarchy of Argentina," in David
 Preston (Ed.), Environment, Society, and Rural Change in Latin America (New York:
 John Wiley and Sons, 1980), pp. 157-184.

Photo 5-3

PORT FACILITIES IN LA BOCA DISTRICT, BUENOS AIRES, ARGENTINA (1966)

Map 5-11

VILLAGE AND SETTLEMENT LANDSCAPE OF 300 INHABITANTS, ALDEA SPATZENKUTTER, ENTRE RÍOS, ARGENTINA

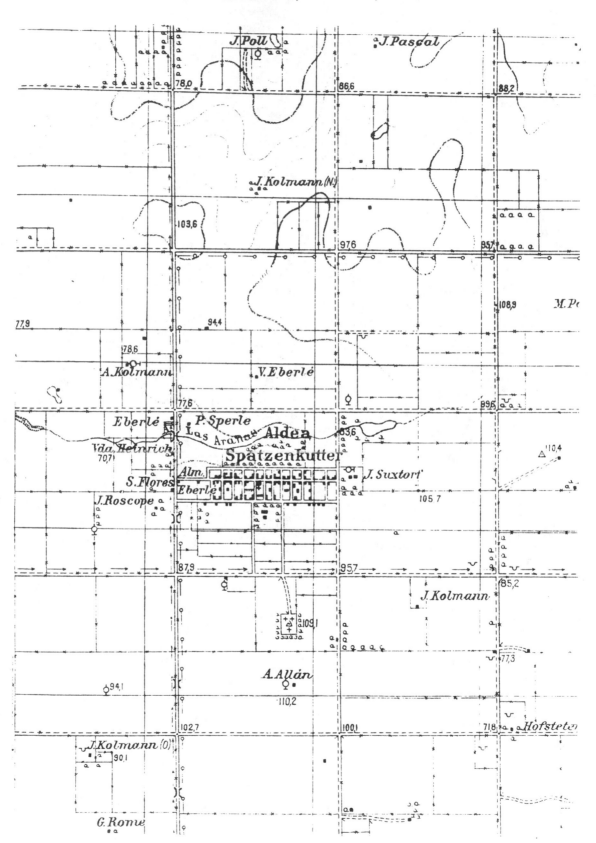

Photo 5-4

**MID-AFTERNOON BREAK FROM HERDING CATTLE AND HORSES,
GENERAL ALVEAR, ENTRE RÍOS, ARGENTINA (1974)**

Map 6-1

PHYSIOGRAPHIC MAP OF BOLIVIA

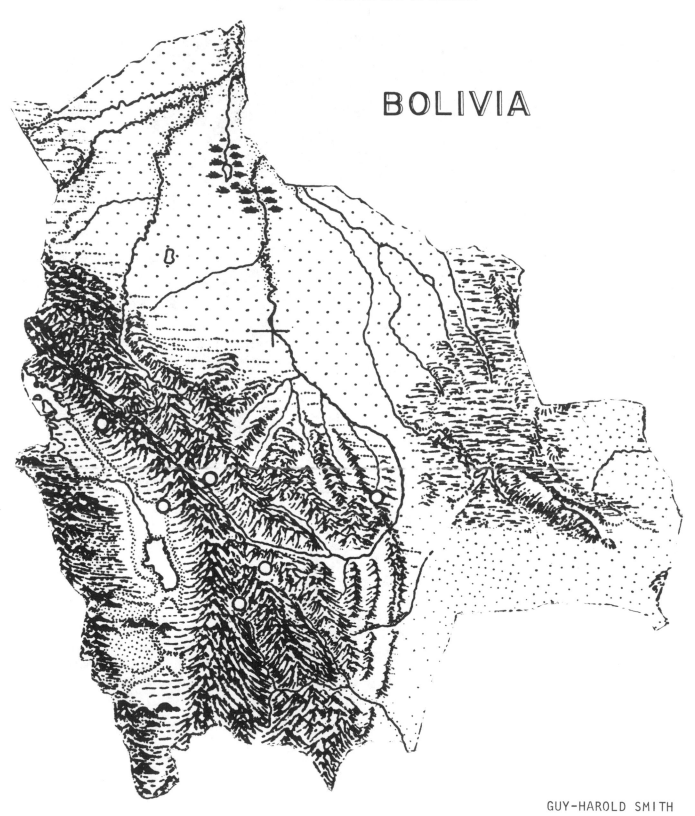

BOLIVIA

GUY-HAROLD SMITH

6

Bolivia

Bolivia has had eight official censuses over a 152-year period. The first census (1831) counted 1,018,900 inhabitants. By the sixth census (1900) there were 1,696,400 Bolivians, and by 1950 the number had nearly doubled to 3,019,031. The last census (1976) documented a rise of 54 percent to 4,647,816 inhabitants. Problems of under-enumeration exist in Bolivia and the U.S. Bureau of the Census (1978) estimated that 4.2 percent of the population was not counted, thus giving Bolivia approximately 4,850,000 inhabitants in 1976. In 1980 the population was estimated by the Latin American Economic Commission to be 5,825,000 inhabitants.

The population totals, trends, and characteristics of Bolivia are presented in six tables and six maps. Some of the findings concerning Bolivia include those outlined below.

URBAN TRENDS

Greater La Paz in 1976, with nearly 700,000 population representing 15 percent of the national total, was the only metropolitan center over half a million population. Nine cities between 20,000 and 500,000 in size were classified as complex urban centers, and they accounted for 25.2 percent of the national population. The three largest complex urban centers were Gran Santa Cruz (319,000), Gran Cochabamba (299,000) and Gran Oruro (159,000).

RURAL TRENDS

The overwhelming majority of Bolivians in 1976 were still living in rural areas (55 percent), with many living dispersed on the landscape outside of nucleated core settlements. The percentage rural is down from 74 percent in 1950, but is up by nearly 14 percent in absolute terms to more than 2,500,000 rural inhabitants.

SETTLEMENT HIERARCHY

Bolivia could be classified as a dispersed–complex urban (0–3) settlement landscape in 1976, with approximately three-fourths of all Bolivians living either in rural places or in intermediate sized cities. The very small proportion of population living in simple urban centers between 2,500 and 20,000 population (only 5 percent) means that much of rural Bolivia is effectively cut off from meaningful urban services. Population density nationally is the lowest in Latin America with only five persons per square kilometer, thus compounding the problem of extending services to the rural inhabitants.

OTHER DEMOGRAPHIC DATA

The annual rate of population growth in Bolivia has been between 2.5 percent and 2.9 percent since the mid-1960s. Life expectancy in 1982 was 49 years, and 42 percent of the population was under fifteen years of age. Per capita GNP in 1982 of $570 was up by 185 percent from $200 in 1975, ranking Bolivia number 18 among the twenty Latin American republics in that category.

Table 6-1

POPULATION DATA AND DENSITY BY DEPARTMENT IN BOLIVIA, 1976[a]

1976 Rank	Department	Population	Percent	Percent Change 1964-1976	Percent Change 1950-1976	Population Density 1976 (km^2)
1	La Paz	1,484,151	31.9	+26.9	+73.8	11
2	Cochabamba	730,358	15.7	+38.9	+61.5	13
3	Santa Cruz	715,072	15.4	+109.2	+192.3	2
4	Potosí	658,713	14.2	+5.3	+29.4	6
5	Chuquisaca	357,244	7.7	+10.6	+37.1	6
6	Oruro	311,245	6.7	+6.6	+61.8	6
7	Tarija	188,655	4.1	+29.4	+82.4	5
8	Beni	167,969	3.6	+61.9	+134.5	1
9	Pando	34,409	.7	+39.4	+111.3	1
	Total	4,647,816	100.0	+33.2	+71.9	4

a. The U.S. Bureau of the Census (1978) estimated a 4.2 percent net underenumeration in 1976; for an adjusted total of 4,853,000 inhabitants. In addition, they estimated the population on July 1, 1979, to be 5,213,000 (1981).

SOURCE: Census of November 29, 1976; *Censo Nacional de Bolivia 1976*: Resultos Provisionales (La Paz: Instituto Nacional de Estadística, 1977), pp. 1-3.

Table 6–2

MAJOR URBAN CENTERS IN BOLIVIA, 1976

Rank	Major Urban Centers	Population	Percent
1	✪ Gran La Paz (1)	695,566	15.0
	La Paz proper	654,713	14.1
	Others in Murillo Dept.	40,853	.9
2	● Gran Santa Cruz (3)	318,804	6.9
	Santa Cruz proper	256,946	5.5
	Others in Andrés Ibáñez Dept.	61,858	1.3
3	Gran Cochabamba (2)	298,567	6.4
	Cochabamba proper	205,002	4.4
	Others in Cercado Dept.	16,854	.4
	Quillacolla	19,433	.4
	Others in Quillacolla Dept.	57,278	1.2
4	● Gran Oruro (6)	158,713	3.4
	Oruro proper	124,121	2.7
	Others in Cercado Dept.	34,592	.7
5	Gran Potosí (4)	122,677	2.6
	Potosí proper	77,253	1.7
	Others in Tomas Frías Dept.	45,424	1.0

Table 6–2 (Continued)

MAJOR URBAN CENTERS IN BOLIVIA, 1976

Rank	Major Urban Centers	Population	Percent
6	✪ Gran Sucre (5)	106,082[a]	2.3
	Sucre proper	62,207[a]	1.3
	Others in Oropeza Dept.	43,875	1.0
7	● Gran Tarija (7)	57,655	1.2
	Tarija proper	39,087	.8
	Others in Cercado Dept.	18,568	.4
8	Gran Llalloqua Mining Area (4)	54,889	1.2
	Llalloqua	23,361	.5
	Siglo XX	10,766	.2
	Catavi/Catavi Civil	8,860	.2
	Uncía	7,396	.2
	Chayanta	2,937	.1
	Cancañiri	1,569	.03
9	● Montero (3)	28,647	.6
10	Trinidad (8)	27,583	.6
			40.2
11	○ Camiri (3)	19,782	
12	Riberalta (8)	18,032	
13	Huanuni (6)	17,292	
14	Centro Minero Colquiri (1)	15,334	
15	Bermejo (7)	13,022	
16	Villazón (4)	12,536	
17	Guayaramerín (8)	12,504	
18	Yucuiba (7)	10,791	
19	Tupza (4)	10,682	
20	Punata (2)	10,216	

a. The *U.N. Demographic Yearbook 1978*, p. 215, states that the population of
Sucre proper on XI-30-1973 was 106,590. Sucre is the legal capital and seat
of the judiciary, while La Paz is the actual capital and seat of the government.

SOURCE: *Censo Nacional de Población y Vivienda* (La Paz: Instituto
Nacional de Estadística, 1977), pp. 8–22.

Map 6-2

BASE MAP OF DEPARTMENTS IN BOLIVIA AND LOCATION OF
MAJOR URBAN CENTERS

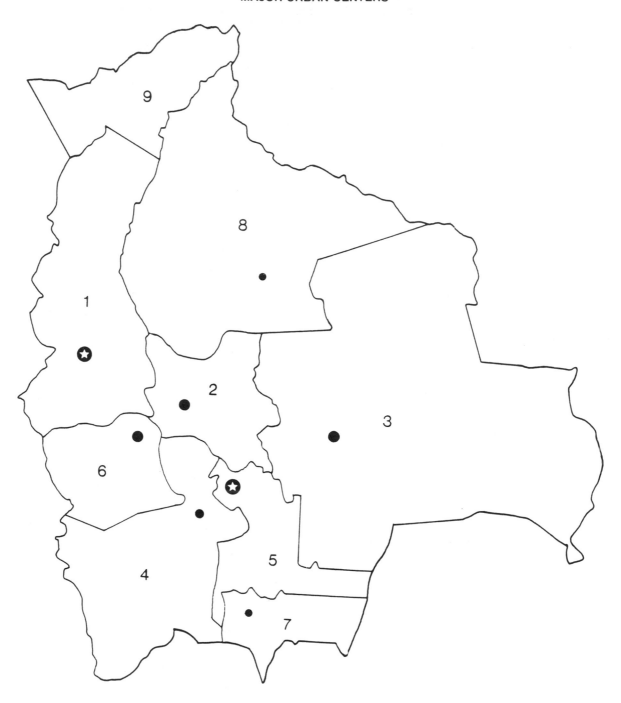

Note: Department numbers are rank ordered according to population data listed in Table 6-1.

Map 6-3

POPULATION CARTOGRAM OF BOLIVIA, 1976

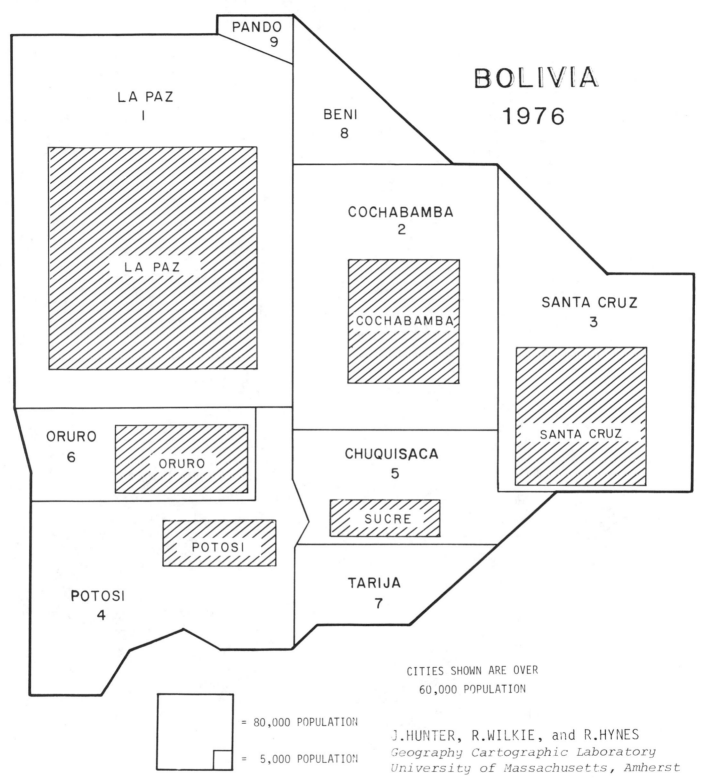

BOLIVIA
1976

PANDO
9

LA PAZ
1

LA PAZ

BENI
8

COCHABAMBA
2

COCHABAMBA

SANTA CRUZ
3

SANTA CRUZ

ORURO
6

ORURO

CHUQUISACA
5

SUCRE

POTOSI

POTOSI
4

TARIJA
7

CITIES SHOWN ARE OVER
60,000 POPULATION

= 80,000 POPULATION

= 5,000 POPULATION

J.HUNTER, R.WILKIE, and R.HYNES
Geography Cartographic Laboratory
University of Massachusetts, Amherst

Map 6-4

THREE-DIMENSIONAL CHOROPLETH MAP OF TOTAL POPULATION
BY DEPARTMENT IN BOLIVIA, 1976
(By Major Civil Division)

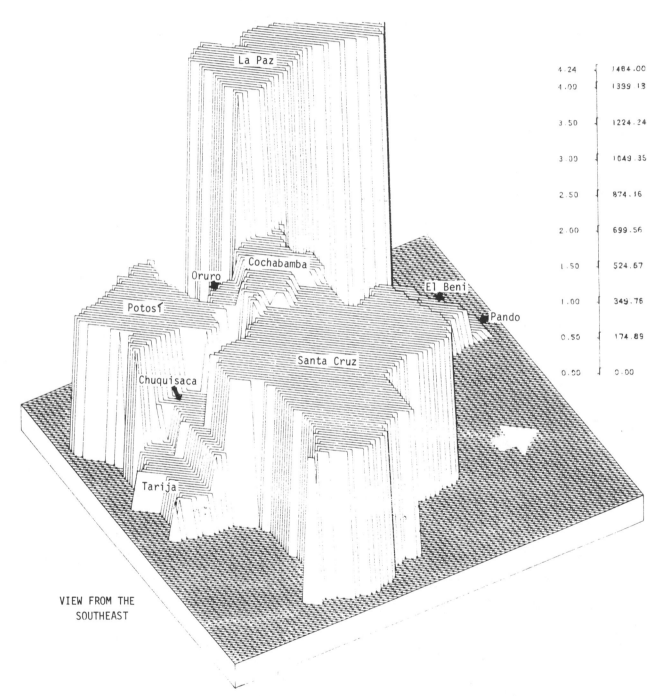

VIEW FROM THE
SOUTHEAST

S.CONNOR, T.GALLAGHER, and R.WILKIE, 1980
Geography Cartographic Laboratory, University of Massachusetts, Amherst
using the SYMVU program from the Harvard Univ. Center for Computer Graphics

Map 6-5

THREE-DIMENSIONAL CHOROPLETH MAP OF POPULATION DENSITY
IN BOLIVIA, 1976
(Persons per km²)

BOLIVIA
POPULATION DENSITY
(PERSONS PER KM²)
1976

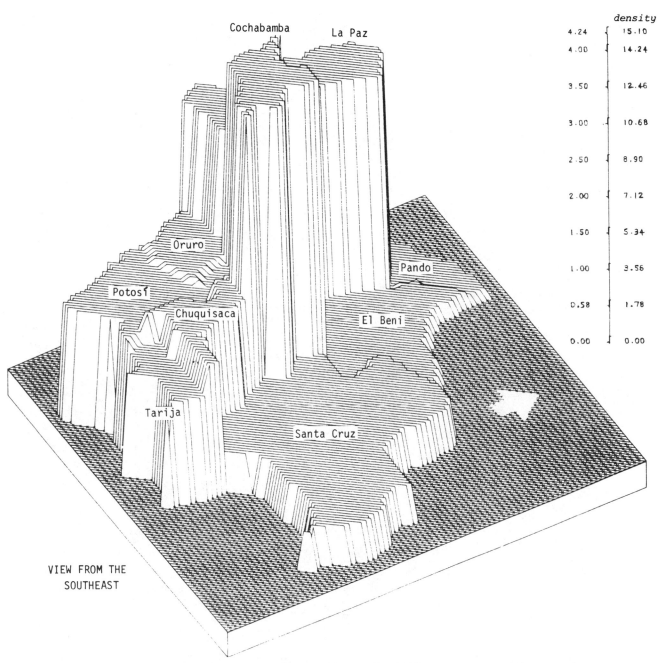

density
4.24	15.10
4.00	14.24
3.50	12.46
3.00	10.68
2.50	8.90
2.00	7.12
1.50	5.34
1.00	3.56
0.58	1.78
0.00	0.00

VIEW FROM THE
SOUTHEAST

S.CONNOR, T.GALLAGHER, and R.WILKIE, 1980
Geography Cartographic Laboratory, University of Massachusetts, Amherst
using the SYMVU program from the Harvard Univ. Center for Computer Graphics

Map 6-6

**THREE-DIMENSIONAL CHOROPLETH MAP OF POPULATION CHANGE
IN BOLIVIA, 1950−1976
(%)**

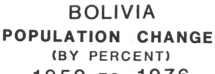

BOLIVIA
POPULATION CHANGE
(BY PERCENT)
1950 TO 1976

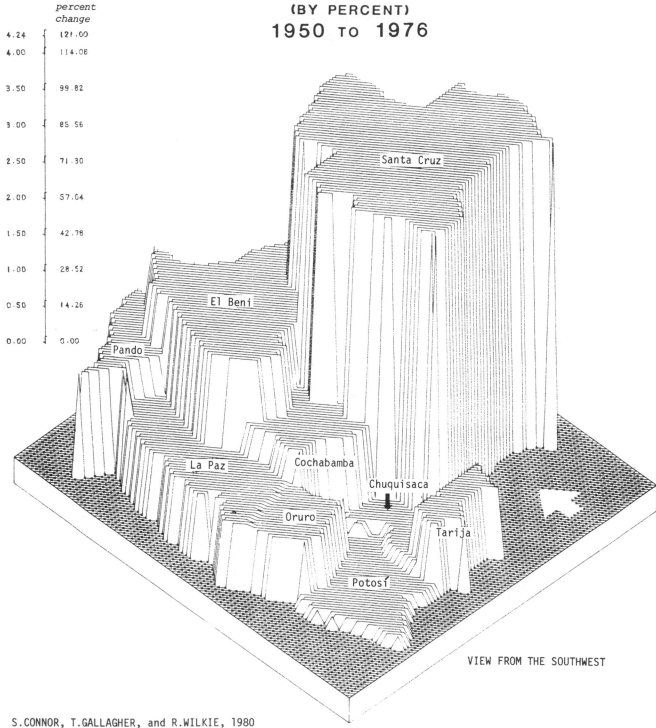

VIEW FROM THE SOUTHWEST

S.CONNOR, T.GALLAGHER, and R.WILKIE, 1980
Geography Cartographic Laboratory, University of Massachusetts, Amherst
using the SYMVU program from the Harvard Univ. Center for Computer Graphics

Photo 6-1

**DISPERSED SETTLEMENT PATTERNS, ALTIPLANO NEAR PUCARANI,
LA PAZ, BOLIVIA (1966)**

Table 6-3

POPULATION FOR EACH NATIONAL CENSUS IN BOLIVIA, 1831–1976[a]

Census Year	Population
1831	1,018,900
1835	992,700
1845	1,031,500
1854	1,544,300
1882	1,097,600
1900	1,696,400
1950	3,019,031
1960	3,782,000[b]
1976	4,647,816[c]

a. Territorial variations have been taken into account; the figures refer to the population within the present boundaries of Bolivia.
b. Estimated.
c. Recommended adjustment of population to 4,853,000 by the U.S. Bureau of the Census (1978).

Table 6-4

TOTAL AND PERCENT POPULATION IN FIVE LEVELS OF THE URBAN-RURAL SETTLEMENT HIERARCHY OF BOLIVIA SINCE 1950

CENSUS YEAR	0 DISPERSED Population 1 to 99	1 VILLAGE 100 to 2,500	2 SIMPLE URBAN 2,501– 20,000	3 COMPLEX URBAN 20,001– 500,000	4 METROPOLITAN over 500,000	SETTLEMENT HIERARCHY Classification	PERCENT in top 2 levels
TOTAL							
1950	. . . .	2,234,083	261,392	523,556	- -		
1960	. . . .	2,760,860	155,062	866,078	- -		
1976	. . . .	2,542,533	236,100	1,173,617	695,566		
PERCENT							
1950	. . . .	74.0	8.7	17.3	- -	0–1	74.0
1960	. . . .	73.0[a]	4.1	22.9	- -	0–3	74 to 84
1976	. . . .	54.7	5.0	25.3	15.0	0–3	70 to 80

a. Estimated.

Table 6-5

SELECTED INDICATORS OF POPULATION CHANGE AND PER CAPITA GNP IN BOLIVIA

Years	Per 1000 Population		Rate of Natural Increase (Annual %)	Number of Years to Double Population	Percent Population Under Age 15	Life Expectancy at Birth	Per Capita GNP (US)
	Births	Deaths					
1940–45	36	17	1.8	- -	- -	- -	- -
1945–50	40	16	1.9	- -	- -	- -	- -
1950–55	42	15	2.0	- -	40[a]	50[b]	- -
1955–60	31	9	2.2	- -	- -	- -	66[c]
1960–65	45	8	2.3	- -	- -	- -	- -
1965–70	44	8	2.9	- -	- -	- -	- -
1970–74	44	20[d]	2.4	29[d]	44[d]	- -	170[d]
1975	44	18	2.6	28	43	47	200
1976	44	18	2.6	27	43	47	250
1977	44	18	2.6	27	42	47	320
1978	47	18	2.9	24	42	48	390
1979	44	16	2.8	25	42	48	540
1980	44	19	2.5	28	42	47	510
1981	44	.19	2.5	28	42	51	550
1982	45	18	2.7	25	42	49	570

a. 1950.
b. 1949-51.
c. 1955.
d. 1970.

MAJOR SOURCES:
   Births: SALA, 19-204; SALA, 20-705 through 1975.
   Deaths: SALA, 18-703d and 706 through 1970.
   Life expectancy: SALA 19-700 through 1970.
   Per capita GNP: 1955 data from Ginsburg, *Atlas of Economic Development* (Chicago: University of Chicago Press, 1961).
   Rate of natural increase: SALA, 22-626 from CELADE-BD 10 (1972) through 1970.
   All other data: Population Reference Bureau, Washington, D.C., annual world population data sheets.

Map 6-7

**PHYSIOGRAPHIC DRAWING OF THE TITICACA LAKE SHORE
LANDSCAPE, COPACABANA, BOLIVIA**

COPACABANA, BOLIVIA

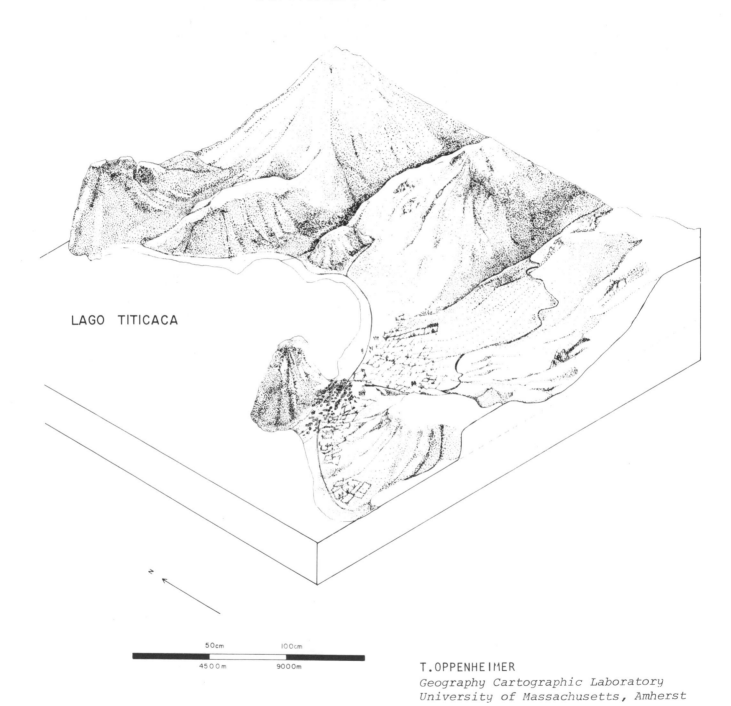

LAGO TITICACA

N

50cm	100cm
4500m	9000m

T.OPPENHEIMER
*Geography Cartographic Laboratory
University of Massachusetts, Amherst*

Photo 6-2

SIMPLE URBAN SETTLEMENT PATTERN ON LAKE TITICACA, COPACABANA, BOLIVIA (1974)

Table 6-6

BOLIVIAN DEPARTMENTS BY GEOGRAPHICAL
SIZE AND SUBDIVISION, 1967

Department	Civil Subdivisions (N)	Area km^2	%
Total	99	1,098,581	100.0
Departments			
Beni	8	213,564	19.4
Cochabamba	14	55,631	5.1
Chuquisaca	10	51,524	4.7
La Paz	18	133,985	12.2
Oruro	10	53,588	4.9
Pando	5	63,827	5.8
Potosi	15	118,218	10.8
Santa Cruz	13	370,621	33.7
Tarija	6	37,623	3.4

SOURCE: SALA, 21-301.

Photo 6-3

COLONIAL STREET AND ROOF PATTERNS, SUCRE, BOLIVIA (1977)

Map 7-1

PHYSIOGRAPHIC MAP OF BRAZIL

BRAZIL

GUY-HAROLD SMITH

7

Brazil

Brazil has had nine official censuses over a 111-year period. The first census (1872) counted 10,112,061 inhabitants. By the fourth census (1920) the population had tripled to 30,635,605, and it slightly more than tripled again by 1970 to 94,508,554. The latest census (1980) documented an increase of 28.2 percent for the decade to 121,113,084 inhabitants.

The population totals, trends, and characteristics of Brazil are presented in six tables and fifteen maps. Some of the findings concerning Brazil include those outlined below.

URBAN TRENDS

Brazil in 1980 had thirteen metropolitan centers with more than half a million population each. Greater São Paulo (12,578,045) and greater Rio de Janeiro (9,018,961) are the second and fourth largest cities in Latin America respectively, and the greater metropolitan populations of eight other cities are all over one million inhabitants each, including Belo Horizonte (2,534,576), Recife (2,346,196), and Pôrto Alegre (2,232,370) with more than two million inhabitants each. The metropolitan population of Brazil in 1980 was more than 37 million and represented 31 percent of the nation's population. The complex urban and simple urban levels are relatively underdeveloped with only 12 to 14 percent of the population in each of those city size ranges.

RURAL TRENDS

The rural dispersed population in Brazil in 1970 (41,603,810) was greater than the total population of any other country in Latin America except Mexico. Thus in spite of rapid urbanization in the metropolitan sector, nearly half the Brazilian population continues to live in rural areas. While the percent rural declined from 65 percent in 1950, to 55 percent in 1960, and to 48 percent in 1970, in absolute terms the rural population grew by 34 percent during the twenty years.

SETTLEMENT HIERARCHY

Brazil can be classified as a dispersed-metropolitan settlement landscape (0-4) since 1960, with between two-thirds and three-fourths of all Brazilians living at either of the two extreme ends of the urban-rural hierarchy. This means that rural villages, simple urban, and complex urban centers all lack the kind of development that is needed for a healthy urban system.

OTHER DEMOGRAPHIC DATA

The annual rate of population growth in Brazil has been between 2.4 and 2.9 percent since 1960. Life expectancy in 1982 was 62 years, and 41 percent of the population was under fifteen years of age. Per capita GNP in 1982 of $2050 was up by 287 percent from $530 in 1975, ranking Brazil number 6 among the twenty Latin American republics in that category.

Table 7-1

POPULATION DATA AND DENSITY BY STATE IN BRAZIL, 1970 AND 1980[a]

1980 Rank	State	1970 Population	1980 Population	1980 Percent	Percent Change 1970-1980	Population Density 1980 (km^2)
1	São Paulo	17,958,693	25,358,245	20.9	+41.2	102
2	Minas Gerais	11,645,095	13,643,886	11.3	+17.2	23
3	Rio de Janeiro[1]	9,110,324	11,490,471	9.5	+26.1	260
4	Bahía	7,583,140	9,593,687	7.9	+26.5	17
5	Rio Grande do Sul	6,755,458	7,942,047	6.6	+17.6	28
6	Paraná	6,997,682	7,749,523	6.4	+10.7	39
7	Pernambuco	5,252,590	6,240,836	5.2	+18.8	64
8	Ceará	4,491,590	5,379,927	4.4	+19.8	36
9	Maranhão	3,037,135	4,097,311	3.4	+34.9	13
10	Goiás	2,997,570	3,967,310	3.3	+32.3	6
11	Santa Catarina	2,930,411	3,687,659	3.0	+25.8	38
12	Pará	2,197,072	3,506,592	2.9	+59.6	3
13	Paraíba	2,445,419	2,810,003	2.3	+14.9	50
14	Piauí	1,734,865	2,188,148	1.8	+26.1	9
15	Espírito Santo	1,617,857	2,063,610	1.7	+27.5	45
16	Alagoas	1,606,174	2,011,956	1.7	+25.3	73
17	Rio Grande do Norte	1,611,606	1,933,131	1.6	+19.9	37
18	Amazonas	960,934	1,447,373	1.2	+50.6	1
19	Mato Grosso do Sul[2]	- -	1,399,468	1.1	(+58.2)	4
20	Distrito Federal	546,015	1,202,683	1.0	+120.3	207
21	Sergipe	911,251	1,157,176	1.0	+27.0	53
22	Mato Grosso[3]	1,623,618	1,169,287	1.0	(+58.2)	1
23	Rondônia	116,620	503,059	.4	+331.4	2
24	Acre	218,006	306,916	.2	+40.8	2
25	Amapá	116,480	180,078	.1	+54.6	1
26	Roraima	41,638	81,896	.1	+96.7	0.4
27	Fernando de Noronha	1,311	1,342	- -	+2.4	52
	Total	94,508,554	121,113,084	100.0	+28.2	14

1. Guanabara and Rio de Janeiro states were combined to create the new state of Rio de Janeiro.
2. Mato Grosso do Sul is a new state, occupying approximately the southern 30 percent of the old state of Mato Grosso.
3. Mato Grosso is a new state, occupying approximately the northern 70 percent of the old state of Mato Grosso.

a. 1980 census definitions:
"População Residente": Persons residents of the domicile present or not on the date of the census (119,061,470).
"Não Moradores Presentes": Persons not residents of the domicile present on the date of the census (2,051,614).
"População Recenseada" (121,113,084).

SOURCES: *Censo Demográfico do Brasil 1980: Resultados Preliminares* (Rio de Janeiro: Instituto Brasileiro de Geografia e Estadística, 1980), p. 1; SALA, 20-301.

Table 7–2

MAJOR URBAN CENTERS IN BRAZIL, 1970 AND 1980

Rank	Major Urban Centers	1970 Population	1980 Population	1980 Percent	Percent Change 1970–1980
1	✪ Greater São Paulo (1)	8,137,401	12,578,045	10.6	+54.6
	São Paulo proper	5,921,796	8,490,763	7.1	+43.4
	Santo André	418,578	552,751	.5	+32.1
	Guarulhos	236,865	532,948	.4	+125.0
	Osasco	283,203	472,535	.4	+66.9
	São Bernardo do Campo	201,462	425,122	.4	+111.0
	Diadema	78,957	327,946	.3	+315.3
	Mauá	101,726	205,817	.2	+102.3
	Mogi das Cruzes	138,746	198,082	.2	+42.8
	Carapicuíba	54,907	185,250	.2	+237.4
	São Caetano do Sul	150,171	162,901	.1	+8.5
	Suzano	55,622	101,067	.1	+81.7
	Other population	495,368	922,863	.8	+86.3
2	Greater Rio de Janeiro (3)	7,082,404	9,018,961	7.5	+27.3
	Rio de Janeiro proper	4,252,009	5,093,496	4.3	+19.8
	Nova Iguaçu	727,674	1,094,650	.9	+50.4
	São Gonçalo	430,349	615,059	.5	+42.9
	Duque de Caxias	431,345	575,533	.5	+33.4
	Niterói	324,367	400,140	.4	+23.4
	São João de Meriti	303,108	398,686	.3	+31.5
	Petrópolis	189,118	241,573	.2	+27.7
	Magé	113,032	116,576	.1	+3.1
	Nilópolis	128,098	151,700	.1	+18.4
	Itaboraí	65,851	114.494	.1	+73.9
	Other population	117,453	217,054	.2	+84.8
3	● Greater Belo Horizonte (2)	1,605,663	2,534,576	2.1	+57.8
	Belo Horizonte proper	1,235,001	1,774,712	1.5	+43.7
	Contagem	111,338	280,721	.2	+152.1
	Other population	259,324	479,143	.4	+84.8
4	Greater Recife (7)	1,792,688	2,346,196	2.0	+30.9
	Recife proper	1,060,752	1,204,794	1.0	+13.6
	Jaboatão	201,460	330,919	.3	+64.3
	Olinda	196,471	281,828	.2	+43.4
	Paulista	70,279	164,066	.1	+133.4
	São Lourenço da Mata	94,137	144,066	.1	+53.0
	Cabo	75,980	104,235	.1	+37.2
	Other population	93,609	116,288	.1	+24.2
5	Greater Pôrto Alegre (5)	1,531,168	2,232,370	1.9	+45.8
	Pôrto Alegre proper	885,564	1,125,901	1.0	+27.1
	Canoas	153,759	220,569	.2	+43.5
	Novo Hamburgo	85,356	136,551	.1	+60.0
	Viamão	66,367	117,756	.1	+77.4
	Gravataí	52,457	107,500	.1	+104.9
	Other population	287,665	524,093	.4	+82.2
6	Greater Salvador (4)	1,148,828	1,766,075	1.5	+53.7
	Salvador proper	1,007,744	1,501,219	1.3	+49.0
	Other population	141,084	264,856	.2	+87.7
7	Greater Fortaleza (8)	1,038,041	1,581,457	1.3	+52.4
	Fortaleza proper	859,135	1,308,859	1.1	+52.4
	Other population	178,906	272,598	.2	+52.4
8	Greater Ritiba (Curitiba) (6)	820,766	1,441,743	1.2	+75.7
	Curitiba proper	608,417	1,025,979	.9	+68.6
	Other population	212,349	415,764	.3	+95.8
9	✪ Greater Brazília (20)	538,351	1,176,748	1.0	+118.6

Table 7-2 (Continued)

MAJOR URBAN CENTERS IN BRAZIL, 1970 AND 1980

Rank	Major Urban Centers		1970 Population	1980 Population	1980 Percent	Percent Change 1970–1980
10	Greater Belém (12)		656,351	1,000,357	.8	+52.4
	Belém proper		633,749	934,330	.8	+47.4
	Other population		22,602	66,027	.05	+192.1
11	Goiânia (10)		381,055	717,948	.6	+88.4
12	Manaus (18)		312,160	634,759	.5	+103.3
13	Greater Rondônia (23)		113,659	492,744[a]	.4	+333.5
	Pôrto Velho		64,522	134,621	.1	+108.6
	Ji-Parana		8,904	122,124	.1	+1271.6
	Other population		40,233	235,999	.2	+486.6
					31.6%[b]	
14	● Campinas (1)		328,629[c]	- -	- -	- -
15	Santos (1)		314,317	- -	- -	- -
16	São Luis (9)		265,595	449,906	.4	+69.4
17	Natal (17)		264,567	416,906	.4	+57.6
18	Maceió (16)		263,583	400,041	.3	+51.8
19	João Pessoa (13)		221,484	330,176	.3	+49.1
20	Teresina (14)		220,520	378,026	.3	+71.4
21	Juiz de Fora (2)		218,832	- -	- -	- -
22	Ribeirão Prêto (1)		190,897	- -	- -	- -
23	Aracaju (21)		183,908	293,485	.2	+59.6
24	Sorocaba (1)		165,990	- -	- -	- -
25	Campina Grande (13)		163,206	- -	- -	- -
26	Londrina (6)		156,670	- -	- -	- -
27	Campos (3)		153,310	- -	- -	- -
28	Ponta Grossa (6)	1968	152,581	- -	- -	- -
29	Pelotas (5)		150,287	- -	- -	- -
30	Jundiaí (1)		145,785	- -	- -	- -
31	Colatina (15)	1968	140,729	- -	- -	- -
32	Campo Grande (19)		140,366	290,586	.2	+107.0
33	Florianópolis (11)		138,556	187,800	.2	+35.5
34	Teófilo Otonia (2)	1968	134,476	- -	- -	- -
35	Vitoria (15)		133,117	207,560	.2	+55.9
36	Feira de Santana (4)		127,105	- -	- -	- -
37	Guarapauva (6)	1968	126,080	- -	- -	- -
38	Piracicaba (1)		125,490	- -	- -	- -
39	Governador Valadares (15)		125,175	- -	- -	- -
40	Caxias (9)	1968	124,403	- -	- -	- -
41	Caratinga (2)	1968	123,344	- -	- -	- -
42	Montes Claros (2)	1968	121,428	- -	- -	- -
43	Santa María (5)		120,667	- -	- -	- -
44	Volta Redonda (3)		120,645	- -	- -	- -
45	Baurú (1)		120,178	- -	- -	- -
46	Rio Grande (5)	1968	117,500	- -	- -	- -
47	Maringá (6)	1968	111,773	- -	- -	- -
48	Bacabal (9)	1968	111,753	- -	- -	- -
49	Santarém (12)	1968	111,706	- -	- -	- -
50	Caxias do Sul (5)		107,487	- -	- -	- -
51	Marilia (1)	1968	107,305	- -	- -	- -
52	Caruaru (7)	1968	101,006	- -	- -	- -
53	Cuiabá (22)		100,865	212,929	.2	+111.1

a. Brazil considers Rondônia a metropolitan area of over 500,000 in 1980 because its population with residents not present (10,315) is 503,059.
b. Total percent (1980) in cities over 500,000.
c. Cities under 500,000 revert to 1970 rankings owing to lack of 1980 data.

SOURCES: 1980: *Censo Demográfico de 1980: Resultados Preliminares* (Rio de Janeiro: Instituto Brasileiro de Geografia e Estatística [IBGE], 1980), pp. 2–6; 1970: Ibid.; SALA, 20–629; 1968: SALA, 20–629. Percent and Percent Change 1970–1980 were calculated by the author.

Photo 7-1

**HOUSES BUILT ON THE AMAZON RIVER FLOODPLAIN,
MANAUS, AMAZONAS, BRAZIL (1974)**

Map 7-2A

BASE MAP OF STATES IN BRAZIL AND LOCATION OF
MAJOR URBAN CENTERS

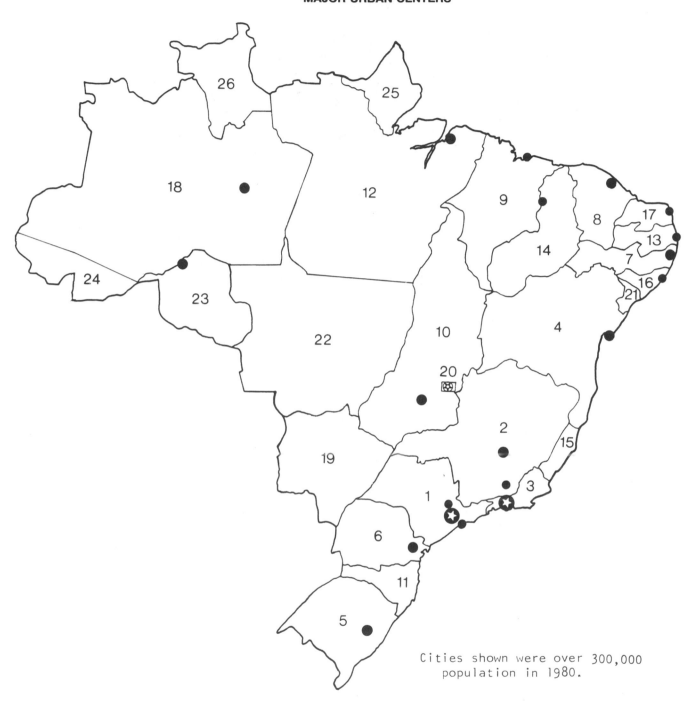

Cities shown were over 300,000
population in 1980.

Note: State numbers are rank ordered according to
1980 population data listed in Table 7-1.

Map 7-2B

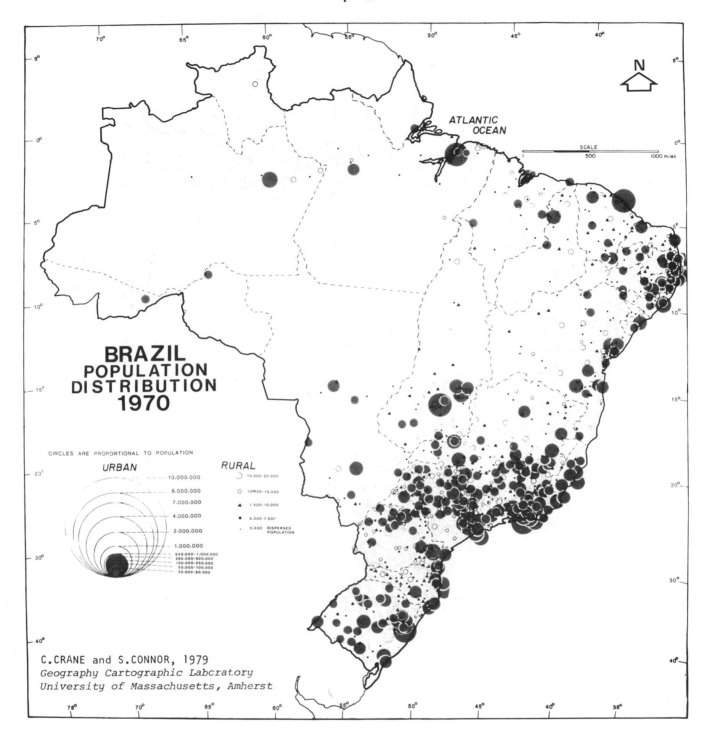

BRAZIL
POPULATION
DISTRIBUTION
1970

ATLANTIC
OCEAN

N

SCALE
500   1000 miles

CIRCLES ARE PROPORTIONAL TO POPULATION

URBAN   RURAL

10.000.000   15.000-20.000
8.000.000   10.000-15.000
7.000.000   7.500-10.000
4.000.000   5.000-7.500
2.000.000   5.000 DISPERSED
1.000.000   POPULATION
500.000-1.000.000
250.000-500.000
100.000-250.000
50.000-100.000
20.000-50.000

C.CRANE and S.CONNOR, 1979
Geography Cartographic Laboratory
University of Massachusetts, Amherst

Map 7-3A

POPULATION CARTOGRAM OF BRAZIL, 1970

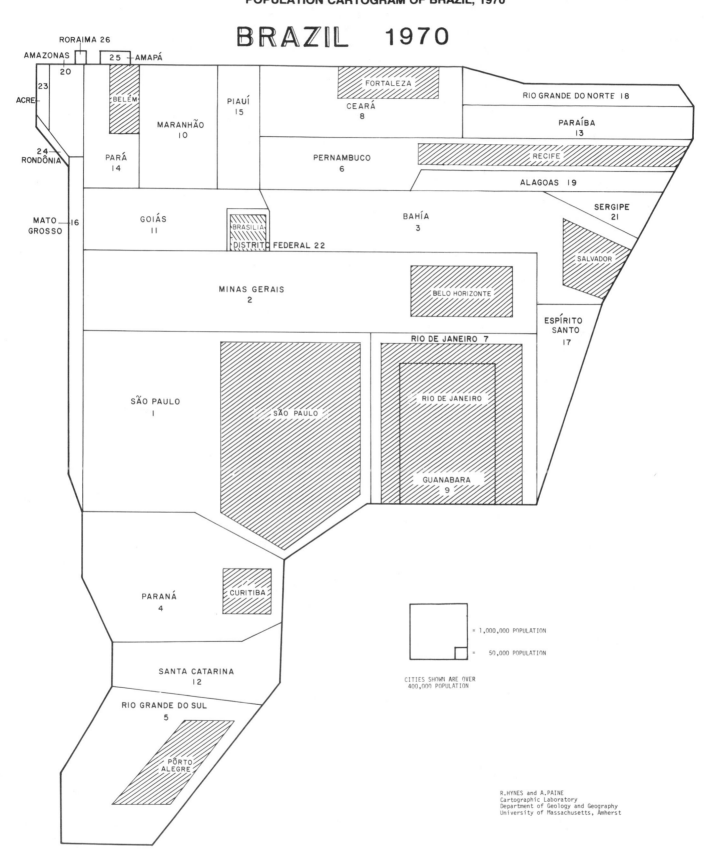

BRAZIL   1970

RORAIMA 26

AMAZONAS   25   AMAPÁ

20

23

ACRE

BELÉM

PARÁ
14

24
RONDÔNIA

MARANHÃO
10

PIAUÍ
15

FORTALEZA

CEARÁ
8

RIO GRANDE DO NORTE 18

PARAÍBA
13

PERNAMBUCO
6

RECIFE

ALAGOAS 19

MATO
GROSSO   16

GOIÁS
11

BRASILIA

DISTRITO FEDERAL 22

BAHÍA
3

SERGIPE
21

SALVADOR

MINAS GERAIS
2

BELO HORIZONTE

ESPÍRITO
SANTO
17

RIO DE JANEIRO 7

SÃO PAULO
1

SÃO PAULO

RIO DE JANEIRO

GUANABARA
9

PARANÁ
4

CURITIBA

= 1,000,000 POPULATION

= 50,000 POPULATION

CITIES SHOWN ARE OVER
400,000 POPULATION

SANTA CATARINA
12

RIO GRANDE DO SUL
5

PÔRTO
ALEGRE

R.HYNES and A.PAINE
Cartographic Laboratory
Department of Geology and Geography
University of Massachusetts, Amherst

Map 7-3B

POPULATION CARTOGRAM OF BRAZIL, 1980

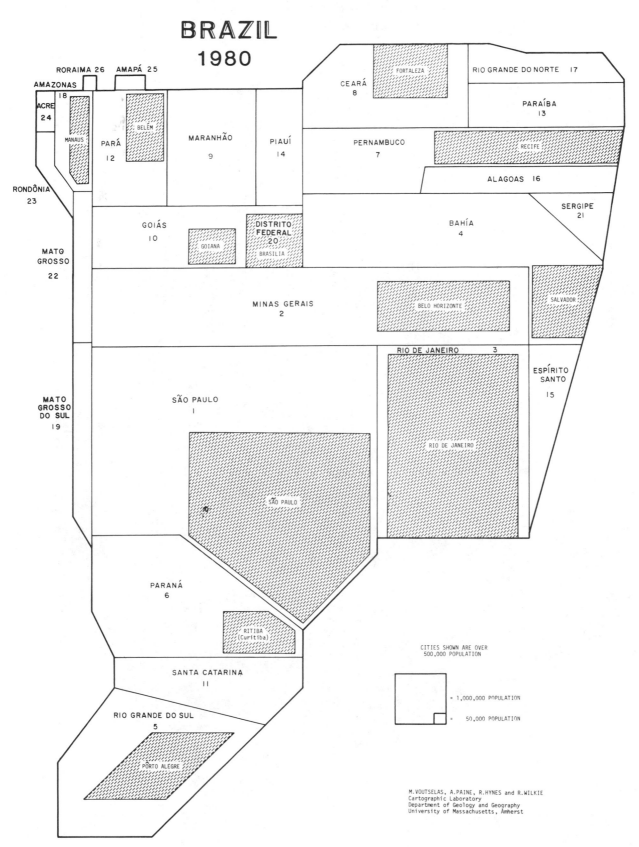

BRAZIL
1980

RORAIMA 26   AMAPÁ 25

AMAZONAS
18

ACRE
24

MANAUS

BELÉM

PARÁ
12

MARANHÃO
9

PIAUÍ
14

RONDÔNIA
23

CEARÁ
8

FORTALEZA

RIO GRANDE DO NORTE   17

PARAÍBA
13

PERNAMBUCO
7

RECIFE

ALAGOAS   16

SERGIPE
21

MATO
GROSSO
22

GOIÁS
10

GOIANA

DISTRITO
FEDERAL
20

BRASILIA

BAHÍA
4

SALVADOR

MINAS GERAIS
2

BELO HORIZONTE

RIO DE JANEIRO   3

MATO
GROSSO
DO SUL
19

SÃO PAULO
1

RIO DE JANEIRO

ESPÍRITO
SANTO
15

SÃO PAULO

PARANÁ
6

RITIBA
(Curitiba)

SANTA CATARINA
11

RIO GRANDE DO SUL
5

PÔRTO ALEGRE

CITIES SHOWN ARE OVER
500,000 POPULATION

= 1,000,000 POPULATION

= 50,000 POPULATION

M.VOUTSELAS, A.PAINE, R.HYNES and R.WILKIE
Cartographic Laboratory
Department of Geology and Geography
University of Massachusetts, Amherst

Map 7-4A

THREE-DIMENSIONAL ISOPLETH MAP OF TOTAL POPULATION BY
STATE IN BRAZIL, 1980
(By Major Civil Division)

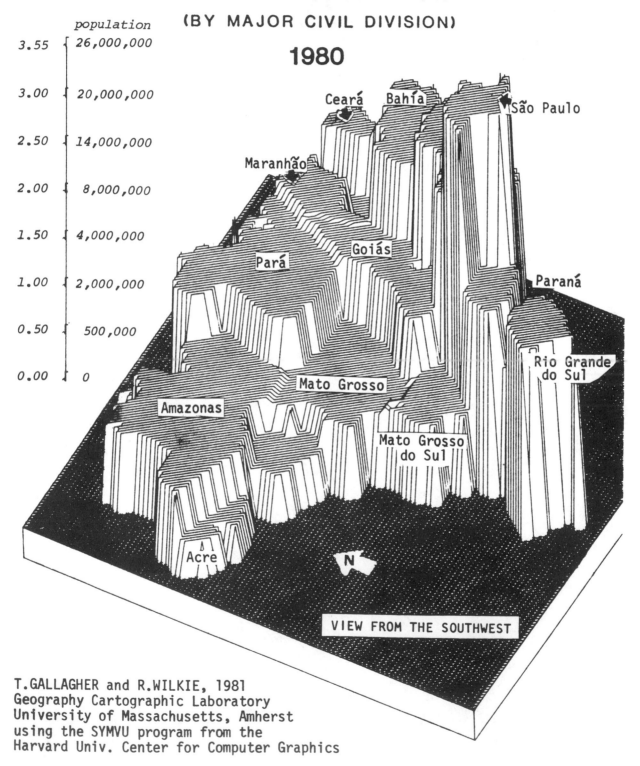

BRAZIL
TOTAL POPULATION
(BY MAJOR CIVIL DIVISION)
1980

population	
3.55	26,000,000
3.00	20,000,000
2.50	14,000,000
2.00	8,000,000
1.50	4,000,000
1.00	2,000,000
0.50	500,000
0.00	0

Ceará   Bahía   São Paulo

Maranhão

Goiás

Pará

Paraná

Mato Grosso

Amazonas

Rio Grande do Sul

Mato Grosso do Sul

Acre

N

VIEW FROM THE SOUTHWEST

T.GALLAGHER and R.WILKIE, 1981
Geography Cartographic Laboratory
University of Massachusetts, Amherst
using the SYMVU program from the
Harvard Univ. Center for Computer Graphics

Map 7-4B

THREE-DIMENSIONAL CHOROPLETH MAP OF THE TOTAL POPULATION BY
STATE IN BRAZIL, 1980
(By Major Civil Division)

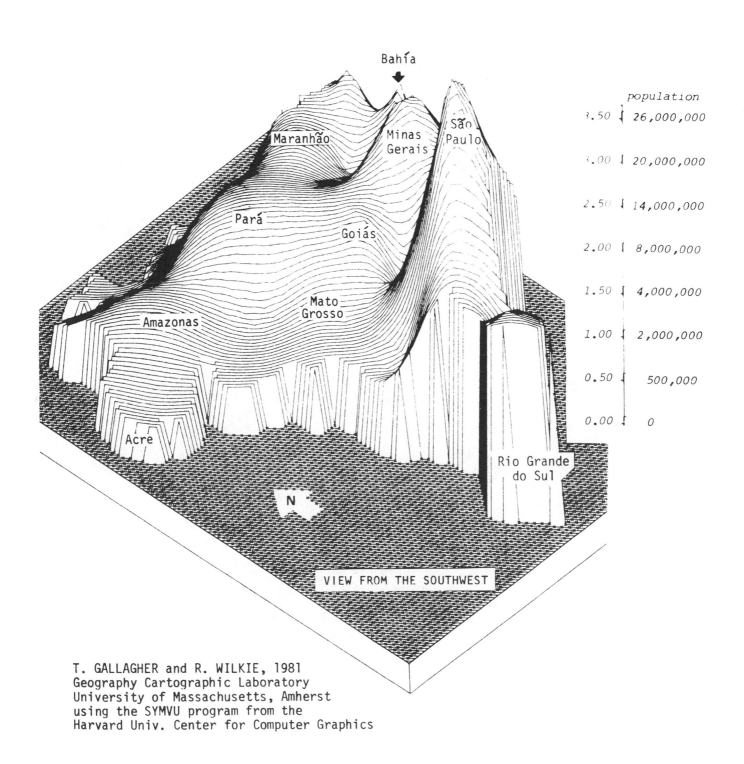

T. GALLAGHER and R. WILKIE, 1981
Geography Cartographic Laboratory
University of Massachusetts, Amherst
using the SYMVU program from the
Harvard Univ. Center for Computer Graphics

Map 7-5A

**THREE-DIMENSIONAL CHOROPLETH MAP OF POPULATION DENSITY
IN BRAZIL, 1970**
(Persons per km²)

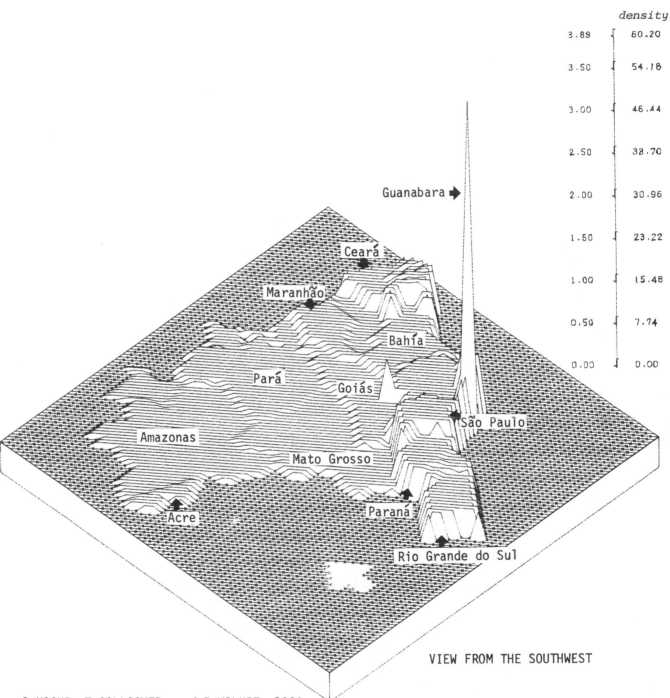

VIEW FROM THE SOUTHWEST

S.KOCUR, T.GALLAGHER, and R.WILKIE, 1980
Geography Cartographic Laboratory, University of Massachusetts, Amherst
using the SYMVU program from the Harvard Univ. Center for Computer Graphics

Map 7-5B

THREE-DIMENSIONAL CHOROPLETH MAP OF POPULATION DENSITY
IN BRAZIL, 1980
(Persons per km²)

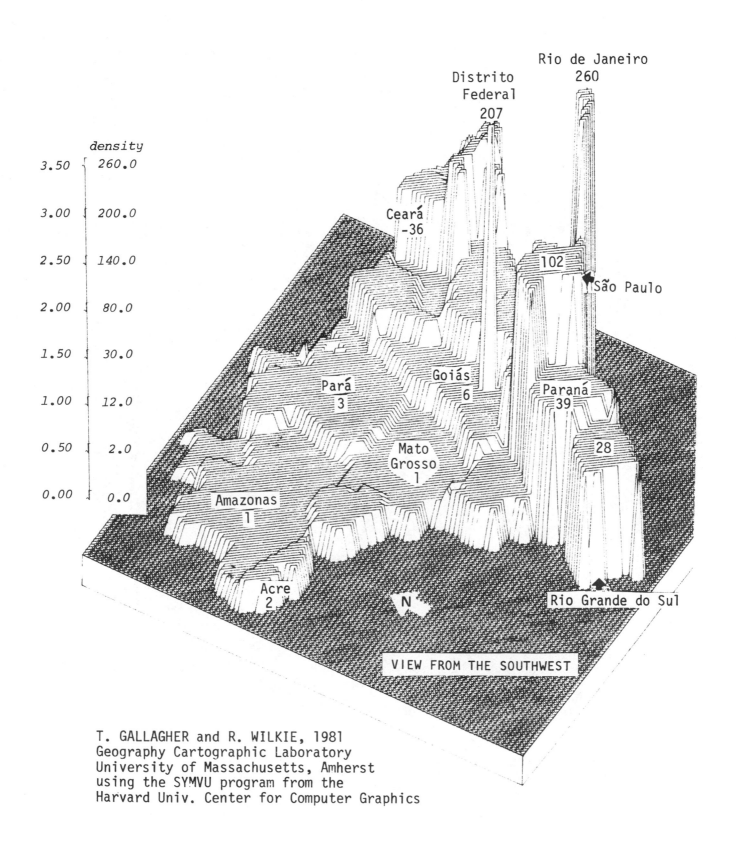

T. GALLAGHER and R. WILKIE, 1981
Geography Cartographic Laboratory
University of Massachusetts, Amherst
using the SYMVU program from the
Harvard Univ. Center for Computer Graphics

Map 7-5C

**THREE-DIMENSIONAL ISOPLETH MAP OF POPULATION DENSITY
IN BRAZIL, 1980**
(Persons per km²)

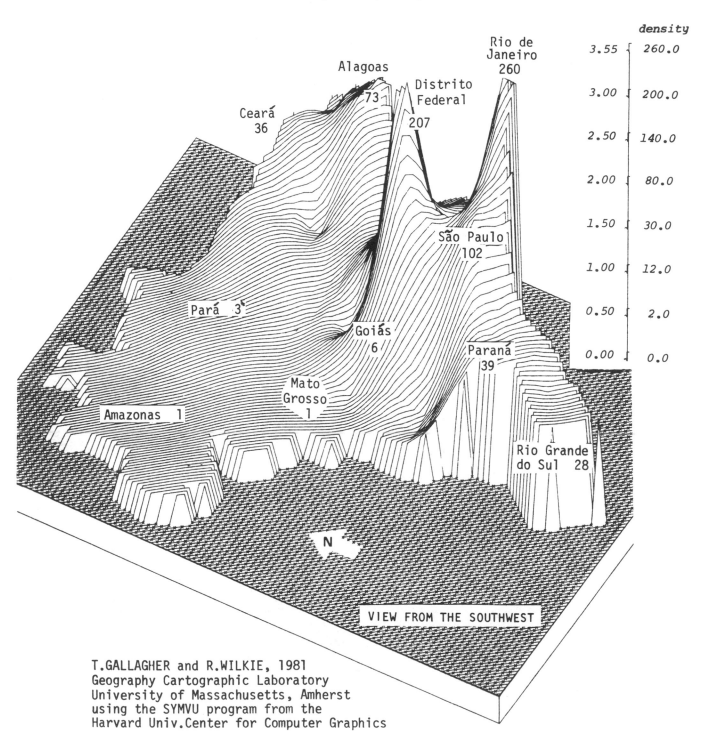

VIEW FROM THE SOUTHWEST

T.GALLAGHER and R.WILKIE, 1981
Geography Cartographic Laboratory
University of Massachusetts, Amherst
using the SYMVU program from the
Harvard Univ.Center for Computer Graphics

Map 7-6A

THREE-DIMENSIONAL CHOROPLETH MAP OF POPULATION
CHANGE IN BRAZIL, 1960–1970
(%)

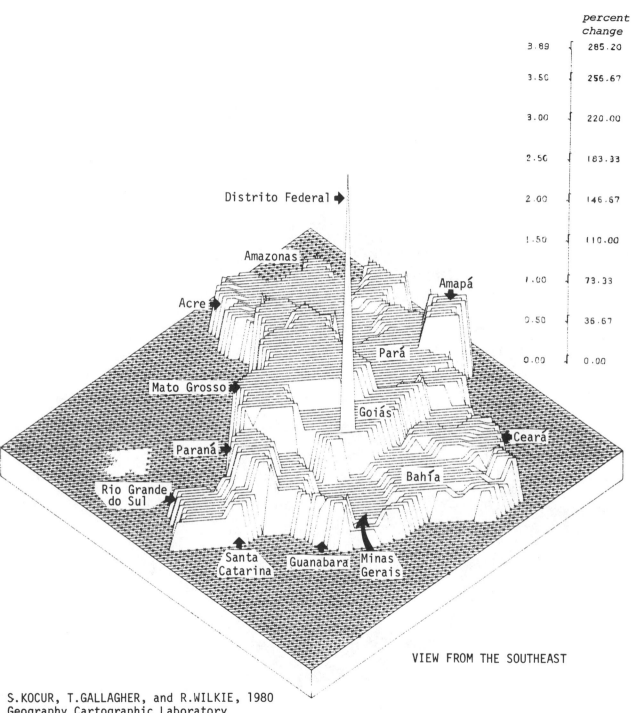

	percent change
3.89	285.20
3.50	256.67
3.00	220.00
2.50	183.33
2.00	146.67
1.50	110.00
1.00	73.33
0.50	36.67
0.00	0.00

VIEW FROM THE SOUTHEAST

S.KOCUR, T.GALLAGHER, and R.WILKIE, 1980
Geography Cartographic Laboratory
University of Massachusetts, Amherst
using the SYMVU program from the
Harvard Univ. Center for Computer Graphics

Map 7-6B

THREE-DIMENSIONAL CHOROPLETH MAP OF POPULATION
CHANGE IN BRAZIL, 1970–1980
(%)

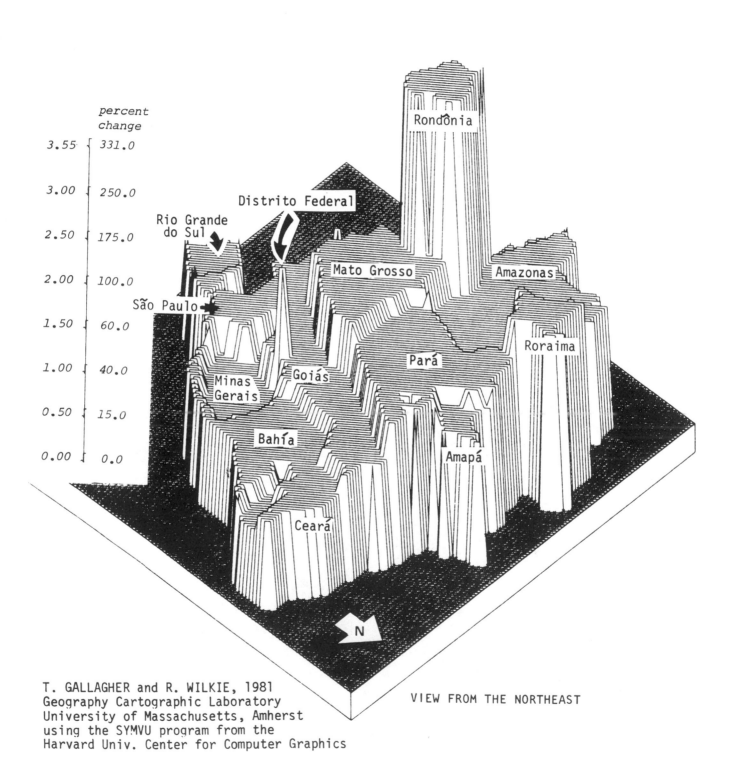

percent
change

3.55	331.0
3.00	250.0
2.50	175.0
2.00	100.0
1.50	60.0
1.00	40.0
0.50	15.0
0.00	0.0

Rondônia

Distrito Federal

Rio Grande
do Sul

Mato Grosso

Amazonas

São Paulo

Roraima

Minas
Gerais

Goiás

Pará

Bahía

Amapá

Ceará

N

T. GALLAGHER and R. WILKIE, 1981
Geography Cartographic Laboratory
University of Massachusetts, Amherst
using the SYMVU program from the
Harvard Univ. Center for Computer Graphics

VIEW FROM THE NORTHEAST

Map 7-6C

THREE-DIMENSIONAL ISOPLETH MAP OF POPULATION CHANGE
IN BRAZIL, 1970–1980
(%)

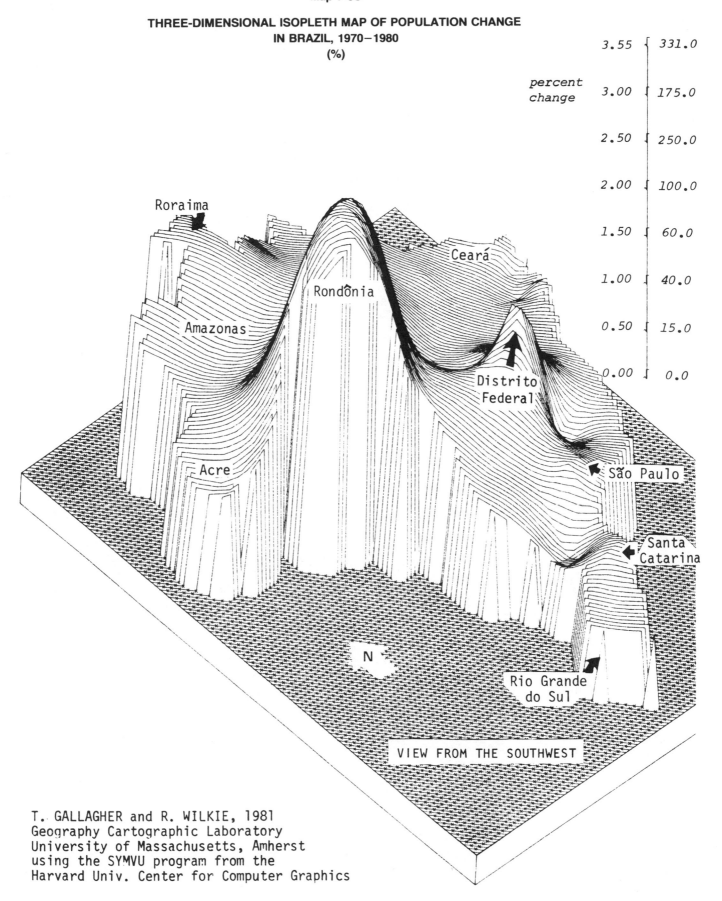

percent change	
3.55	331.0
3.00	175.0
2.50	250.0
2.00	100.0
1.50	60.0
1.00	40.0
0.50	15.0
0.00	0.0

VIEW FROM THE SOUTHWEST

T. GALLAGHER and R. WILKIE, 1981
Geography Cartographic Laboratory
University of Massachusetts, Amherst
using the SYMVU program from the
Harvard Univ. Center for Computer Graphics

Table 7-3

POPULATION FOR EACH NATIONAL CENSUS IN
BRAZIL, 1872–1980

Census Year	Population
1872	10,112,061
1890	14,333,915
1900	17,318,556
1920	30,635,605
1940	41,236,315
1950	51,944,397
1960	70,992,343
1970	94,508,544[a]
1980	121,113,084[b]

a. Recommended adjustment of population to 96,137,000 by
   the U.S. Bureau of the Census (1978).
b. Consisting of 119,061,470 resident population (whether in
   house or not) and 2,051,614 nonresidents in domicile at the
   time of the census.

Table 7-4

TOTAL AND PERCENT POPULATION IN FIVE LEVELS OF THE URBAN-RURAL
SETTLEMENT HIERARCHY OF BRAZIL SINCE 1950

	0	1	2	3	4	SETTLEMENT HIERARCHY	
CENSUS YEAR	DISPERSED Population 1 to 99	VILLAGE 100 to 2,500	SIMPLE URBAN 2,501– 20,000	COMPLEX URBAN 20,001– 500,000	METROPOLITAN over 500,000	Classification	PERCENT in top 2 levels
TOTAL							
1950	30,930,373	2,781,534	5,518,286	6,620,756	6,193,448		
1960	35,693,970	3,293,556	8,775,192	10,093,242	13,136,383		
1970	41,603,810	3,591,325	11,938,792	13,022,966	24,351,661		
1980	- -	- -	- -	- -	37,029,235		
PERCENT							
1950	59.5	5.3	10.6	12.6	11.9	0–3	72.1
1960	50.3	4.6	12.4	14.2	18.5	0–4	68.8
1970	44.0	3.8	12.6	13.8	25.8	0–4	69.8
1980	- -	- -	- -	- -	31.1	- -	- -

SOURCE: Dispersed and village populations for 1950 from Donald Dyer, "Growth of Brazil's Population," *Journal of Geography* 65:9.
All other data are calculated from various Brazilian national censuses since 1950, and from SALA, 20-631, 632, 634, 635, 636, 637, and 638.

Table 7-5

SELECTED INDICATORS OF POPULATION CHANGE AND PER CAPITA GNP IN BRAZIL

Years	Per 1000 Population		Rate of Natural Increase (Annual %)	Number of Years to Double Population	Percent Population Under Age 15	Life Expectancy at Birth	Per Capita GNP (US)
	Births	Deaths					
1940–45	43	- -	2.3	- -	- -	- -	- -
1945–50	43	16	2.6	- -	- -	- -	- -
1950–55	43	14	3.0	- -	- -	- -	- -
1955–60	40	13	3.0	- -	- -	- -	262[a]
1960–65	39	- -	2.9	- -	- -	59	- -
1965–70	38	- -	2.9	- -	- -	59	- -
1970–74	37	11[b]	2.8[b]	25[b]	43[b]	61[b]	250[b]
1975	37	9	2.8	25	42	61	530
1976	37	9	2.8	25	42	61	900
1977	37	9	2.8	25	42	61	1,010
1978	36	8	2.8	25	42	61	1,140
1979	36	8	2.8	25	41	61	1,390
1980	36	8	2.8	25	41	64	1,570
1981	32	8	2.4	29	41	64	1,690
1982	32	9	2.4	29	41	62	2,050

a. 1955.
b. 1970.

MAJOR SOURCES:
   Births: SALA, 19-204; SALA, 20-705 through 1975.
   Deaths: SALA, 18-703d and 706 through 1970.
   Life expectancy: SALA, 19-700 through 1970.
   Per capita GNP: 1955 data from Ginsburg, *Atlas of Economic Development* (Chicago: University of Chicago Press, 1961).
   Rate of natural increase: SALA, 22-626 from CELADE-BD 10 (1972) through 1970.
   All other date: Population Reference Bureau, Washington, D.C., annual world population data sheets.

Table 7-6

BRAZILIAN STATES BY GEOGRAPHICAL SIZE AND SUBDIVISION, 1970

State	Civil Subdivisions (N)	Area km^2	%
Total	3,952[a]	8,456,508[b]	100.0
Federal District	1	5,771	.1
States and Territories			
Acre	7	152,589	1.8
Alagoas	94	27,652	.3
Amapá (territory)	5	139,068	1.6
Amazonas	44	1,558,987	18.4
Bahía	336	559,951	6.6
Ceará	142	146,817	1.7
Espírito Santo	53	45,597	.5
Fernando de Noronha (territory)	1	25	.0
Gioás	221	642,036	7.5
Guanabara	1	1,171	#
Maranháo	130	324,616	3.8
Mato Grosso	84	1,231,549	14.5
Minas Gerais	722	582,586	6.9
Pará	83	1,227,530	14.5
Paraíba	171	56,372	.7
Paraná	288	199,060	2.4
Pernambuco	164	98,281	1.2
Piauí	114	250,934	3.0
Rio de Janeiro	63	42,134	.5
Rio Grande do Norte	150	53,015	.6
Rio Grande do Sul	232	267,528	3.2
Rondònia (territory)	2	243,044	2.9
Roraima	2	230,104	2.7
Santa Catarina	197	95,483	1.1
São Paulo	571	247,320	2.9
Sergipe	74	21,994	.3
Zones in Litigation			
Amazonas-Pará	* *	2,680	#
Piauí-Ceará	* *	2,614	#

a. Municipios.
b. Including zones of litigation, total is 8,511,965.

SOURCE: SALA, 21-301.

Photo 7-2

**EARLY MORNING SUN ACROSS GUANABARA BAY, SUGARLOAF,
AND BOTAFOGO, RIO DE JANEIRO, BRAZIL (1974)**

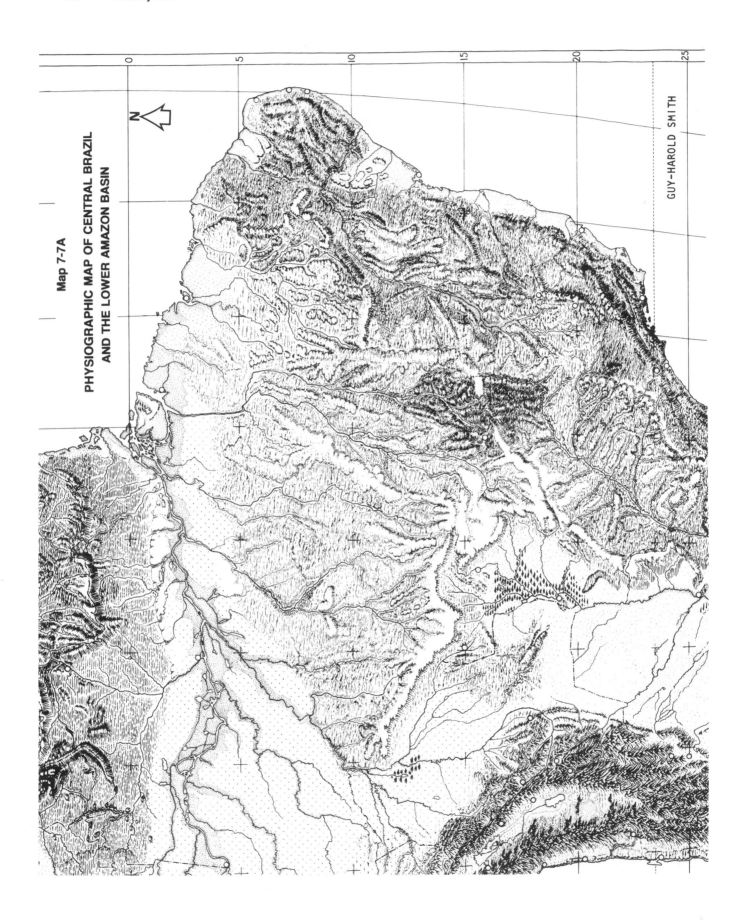

Map 7-7A

PHYSIOGRAPHIC MAP OF CENTRAL BRAZIL
AND THE LOWER AMAZON BASIN

GUY-HAROLD SMITH

Photo 7-3

AMAZON RIVERBOAT TRANSPORTATION, BELEM, BRAZIL

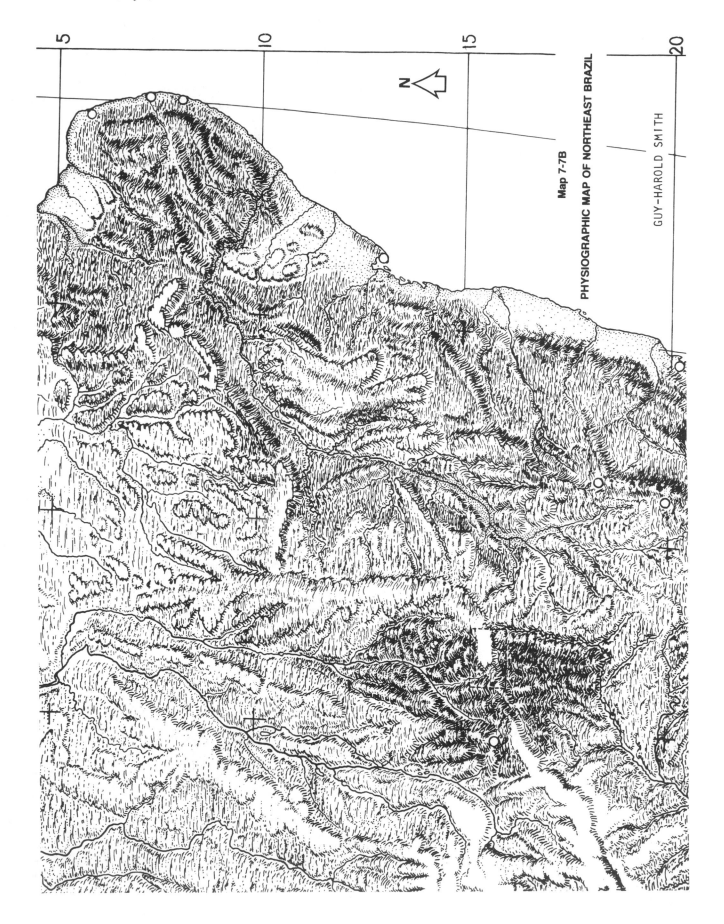

Map 7-7B

PHYSIOGRAPHIC MAP OF NORTHEAST BRAZIL

GUY-HAROLD SMITH

Map 7-7C

PHYSIOGRAPHIC MAP OF SOUTHERN BRAZIL

N

GUY-HAROLD SMITH

Map 8-1

PHYSIOGRAPHIC MAP OF CHILE

CHILE

GUY-HAROLD SMITH

8

Chile

Chile has had fourteen official population censuses over a 148-year period. The first census (1835) counted 1,010,336 inhabitants. The number of Chileans doubled to 2,075,971 by the fifth census (1875) and more than doubled again to 4,287,445 in the tenth census (1930). The latest census, taken on April 22, 1982, counted 11,275,440 inhabitants.

The population totals, trends, and characteristics of Chile are presented in six tables and six maps. Some of the findings concerning Chile include those outlined below.

URBAN TRENDS

Chile in 1970 had three greater metropolitan centers of more than half a million population each. Gran Santiago with 3,351,000 represented 38 percent of the nation's population, while Gran Valparaíso (841,000) and Gran Concepción (697,000) jointly accounted for another 18 percent. In the census of 1982, the population of Gran Santiago had grown 28 percent to 4,295,000 inhabitants. Beyond these three metropolitan centers which accounted for nearly three-fifths of the population of Chile in 1970, there were thirteen regional centers in the urban hierarchy between 50,000 and 155,000 in population.

RURAL TRENDS

Rural population has dropped significantly from nearly 40 percent in 1952 to just under 17 percent in 1970. In absolute terms this is a decline from just over 2.3 million rural inhabitants in 1952 to 1.5 million in 1970.

SETTLEMENT HIERARCHY

In 1970 Chile could be classified as a metropolitan—complex urban (4−3) settlement landscape, with nearly three-quarters of all Chileans living in cities of more than 20,000 population.

OTHER DEMOGRAPHIC DATA

The annual rate of population growth in Chile reached a peak of 2.5 percent during the early 1960s and by 1980 had declined to 1.4 percent. Life expectancy in 1980 was 66 years and 35 percent of the national population was under fifteen years of age. Per capita GNP in 1982 of $2160 was up by 170 percent from $800 in 1975, ranking Chile number 5 among the twenty Latin American republics in that category.

Table 8-1A

POPULATION DATA AND DENSITY BY PROVINCE IN CHILE, 1970[a]

1970 Rank	Province	Population	Percent	Percent Change 1960–1970	Population Density 1970 (km^2)
1	Santiago	3,218,155	36.4	+32.1	182
2	Valparaíso	721,156	8.2	+17.6	142
3	Concepción	638,118	7.2	+18.3	112
4	Cautín	420,682	4.8	+ 6.6	23
5	Coquimbo	336,821	3.8	+ 8.9	9
6	Ñuble	314,738	3.6	+10.2	23
7	O'Higgins	306,863	3.5	+18.1	43
8	Valdivia	274,642	3.1	+ 6.0	15
9	Antofagasta	250,665	2.8	+16.4	2
10	Talca	231,008	2.6	+12.0	23
11	Llanquihue	197,986	2.2	+18.2	11
12	Bío-Bío	193,027	2.2	+14.3	17
13	Linares	189,030	2.1	+10.3	20
14	Malleco	176,060	2.0	+ 1.1	13
15	Tarapacá	174,730	2.0	+42.0	3
16	Aconcagua	169,821	1.9	+14.4	16
17	Colchagua	167,899	1.9	+ 5.9	20
18	Osorno	158,673	1.8	+10.1	17
19	Atacama	152,326	1.7	+31.0	2
20	Curicó	113,710	1.3	+ 7.4	22
21	Chiloé	110,720	1.3	+11.6	4
22	Arauco	97,720	1.1	+10.4	19
23	Magallanes	88,244	1.0	+20.8	1
24	Maule	82,339	.9	+ 3.2	15
25	Aysén	51,082	.6	+35.0	1
	Total	8,836,223	100.0	+19.8	12

a. The U.S. Bureau of the Census (1978) noted an official midyear adjustment which implied a 4.8 percent net underenumeration, for a new figure of 9,336,000 inhabitants. In addition, they estimated (1981) the population on July 1, 1979, to be 10,848,000.

SOURCES: Census of April 22, 1970; SALA, 18-602a.

Table 8–2

MAJOR URBAN CENTERS IN CHILE, 1970, 1978, AND 1982

Rank	Major Urban Centers	April 22, 1970	Percent	June 30, 1978	April 21, 1982	Percent
1	✪ Gran Santiago[1] (1)	3,350,680	37.9	3,691,548	4,294,938	36.1
	Santiago proper	- -	- -	3,448,700	- -	- -
2	● Gran Valparaíso (2)	841,020	9.5	882,280	- -	- -
	Valparaíso	601,360	- -	620,180	- -	- -
	Viña del Mar	239,660	- -	262,100	- -	- -
3	Gran Concepción (3)	696,969	7.9	723,050	- -	- -
	Concepción	506,530	- -	518,950	- -	- -
	Talcahuano	190,439	- -	204,100	- -	- -
4	● Antafagasta (9)	154,800	1.8	- -	- -	- -
5	Temuco (4)	144,400	1.6	- -	- -	- -
6	Talca (10)	119,620	1.4	- -	- -	- -
7	Arica (15)	117,020	1.3	- -	- -	- -
8	Rancagua (7)	112,710	1.3	- -	- -	- -
9	Chillán (6)	105,310	1.2	- -	- -	- -
10	Valdivia (8)	100,470	1.1	- -	- -	- -
			65.0			
11	● Osorno (18)	78,000[a]	- -	- -	- -	- -
12	Iquique (15)	68,000	- -	- -	- -	- -
13	Punta Arenas (23)	64,000	- -	- -	- -	- -
14	Lota (3)	63,000	- -	- -	- -	- -
15	Puerto Montt (11)	55,000	- -	- -	- -	- -
16	La Serena (5)	52,000	- -	- -	- -	- -

1. Gran Santiago includes the *comunas* of Barrancas, Conchali, La Cisterna, La Florida, La Granja, Las Condes, Maipú, Nuñoa, Providencia, Quilicura, Quinta Normal, Renca, San Bernardo, and San Miguel.

a. Lines 11–16 are 1970 estimates.

SOURCES: Census of April 22, 1970: SALA, 20–629; *América en Cifras*; Census of June 30, 1978: *U.N. Demographic Yearbook, 1978*; Census of April 21, 1982.

Table 8-1B

POPULATION OF CHILE IN 1970 AND 1982 USING NEW REGIONAL BOUNDARIES

1982 Rank	Region	1970 Population	1982 Population	1982 Percent	Percent Change 1970-1982
1	Región Metropolitana de Santiago	3,151,765	4,294,938	38.1	+36.1
	Santiago Province	2,671,761	3,672,374	33.6	+37.5
	Other Metropolitan Santiago	480,004	622,564	4.5	+30.0
2	Bío-Bío	1,255,393	1,516,552	13.5	+20.8
3	Valparaíso	966,609	1,204,693	10.7	+24.6
4	Los Lagos	744,610	843,430	7.5	+13.3
5	Maule	617,543	723,224	6.4	+17.1
6	La Aramcanía	600,499	692,924	6.1	+15.4
7	Libertador General Bernardo O'Higgins	485,987	584,989	5.2	+20.4
8	Coquimbo	338,203	419,178	3.7	+23.9
9	Antofagasta	252,119	341,203	3.0	+35.5
10	Tarapacá	175,209	273,427	2.4	+56.1
11	Atacama	154,187	183,071	1.6	+18.7
12	Magallanes y la Antártica Chilena	89,443	132,333	1.2	+48.0
13	Aysén del General Carlos Ibañez del Campo	50,201	65,478	.6	+30.4
	Total	8,884,768	11,275,440	100.0	+27.0

SOURCE: Chilean Statistical Office (May 1982), report on the Census of April 21, 1982.

Photo 8-1

**WORKING-CLASS SUBURB ON THE NORTHERN EDGE OF
SANTIAGO, GREATER SANTIAGO, CHILE (1977)**

Map 8-2

BASE MAP OF OLD PROVINCIAL AND NEW REGIONAL BOUNDARIES
IN CHILE AND LOCATION OF MAJOR URBAN CENTERS

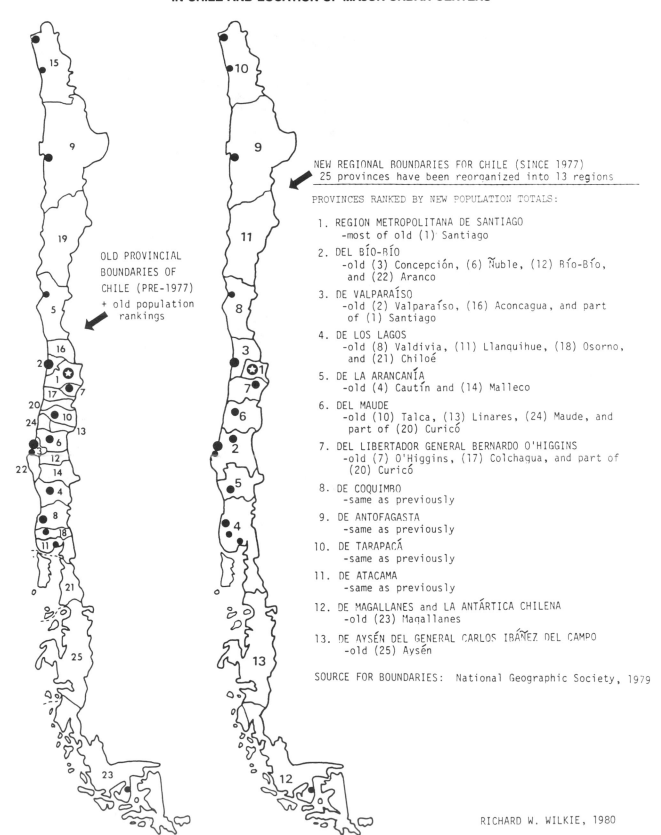

OLD PROVINCIAL
BOUNDARIES OF
CHILE (PRE-1977)
+ old population
rankings

NEW REGIONAL BOUNDARIES FOR CHILE (SINCE 1977)
25 provinces have been reorganized into 13 regions

PROVINCES RANKED BY NEW POPULATION TOTALS:

1. REGION METROPOLITANA DE SANTIAGO
   -most of old (1) Santiago

2. DEL BÍO-BÍO
   -old (3) Concepción, (6) Ñuble, (12) Bío-Bío,
   and (22) Aranco

3. DE VALPARAÍSO
   -old (2) Valparaíso, (16) Aconcagua, and part
   of (1) Santiago

4. DE LOS LAGOS
   -old (8) Valdivia, (11) Llanquihue, (18) Osorno,
   and (21) Chiloé

5. DE LA ARANCANÍA
   -old (4) Cautín and (14) Malleco

6. DEL MAUDE
   -old (10) Talca, (13) Linares, (24) Maude, and
   part of (20) Curicó

7. DEL LIBERTADOR GENERAL BERNARDO O'HIGGINS
   -old (7) O'Higgins, (17) Colchagua, and part of
   (20) Curicó

8. DE COQUIMBO
   -same as previously

9. DE ANTOFAGASTA
   -same as previously

10. DE TARAPACÁ
    -same as previously

11. DE ATACAMA
    -same as previously

12. DE MAGALLANES and LA ANTÁRTICA CHILENA
    -old (23) Magallanes

13. DE AYSÉN DEL GENERAL CARLOS IBÁÑEZ DEL CAMPO
    -old (25) Aysén

SOURCE FOR BOUNDARIES: National Geographic Society, 1979

RICHARD W. WILKIE, 1980

Map 8-3

POPULATION CARTOGRAM OF CHILE, 1970

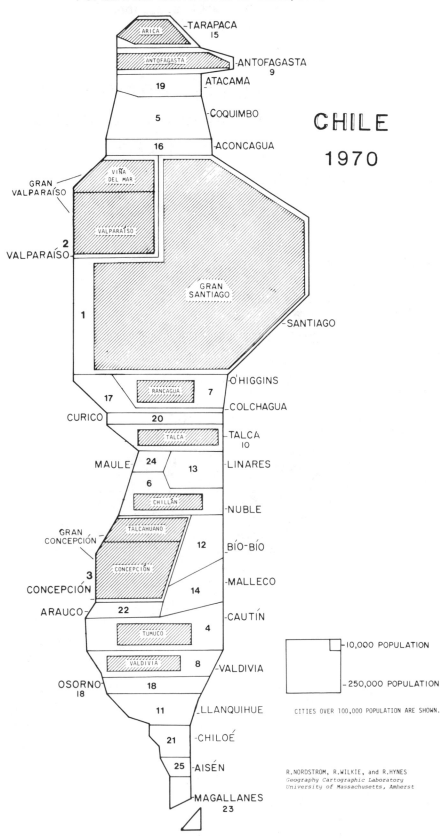

CHILE
1970

CITIES OVER 100,000 POPULATION ARE SHOWN.

R.NORDSTROM, R.WILKIE, and R.HYNES
Geography Cartographic Laboratory
University of Massachusetts, Amherst

Map 8-4

**THREE-DIMENSIONAL CHOROPLETH MAP OF TOTAL POPULATION
BY PROVINCE IN CHILE, 1970
(By Major Civil Division)**

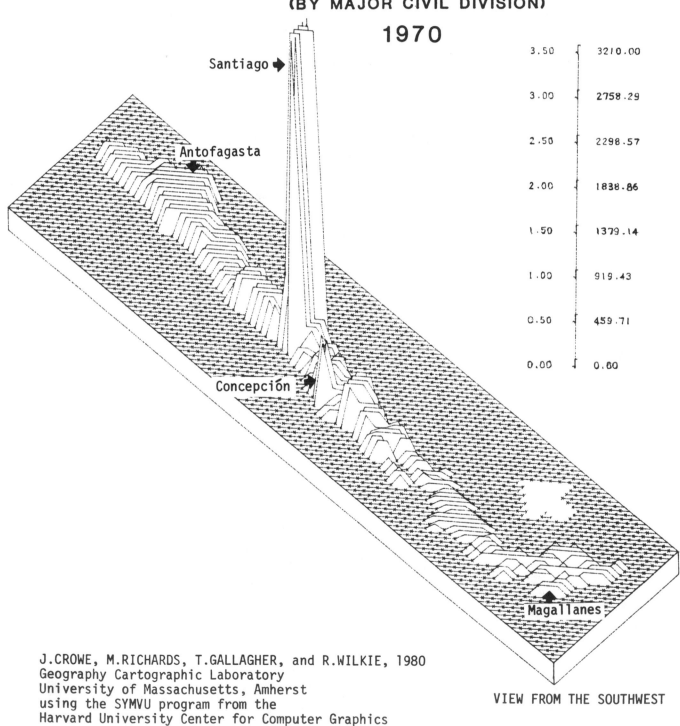

CHILE
TOTAL POPULATION
(BY MAJOR CIVIL DIVISION)
1970

3.50	3210.00
3.00	2758.29
2.50	2298.57
2.00	1838.86
1.50	1379.14
1.00	919.43
0.50	459.71
0.00	0.00

Santiago ➤

Antofagasta

Concepción ➤

Magallanes

J.CROWE, M.RICHARDS, T.GALLAGHER, and R.WILKIE, 1980
Geography Cartographic Laboratory
University of Massachusetts, Amherst
using the SYMVU program from the
Harvard University Center for Computer Graphics

VIEW FROM THE SOUTHWEST

Map 8-5

**THREE-DIMENSIONAL CHOROPLETH MAP OF POPULATION DENSITY
IN CHILE, 1970
(Persons per km²)**

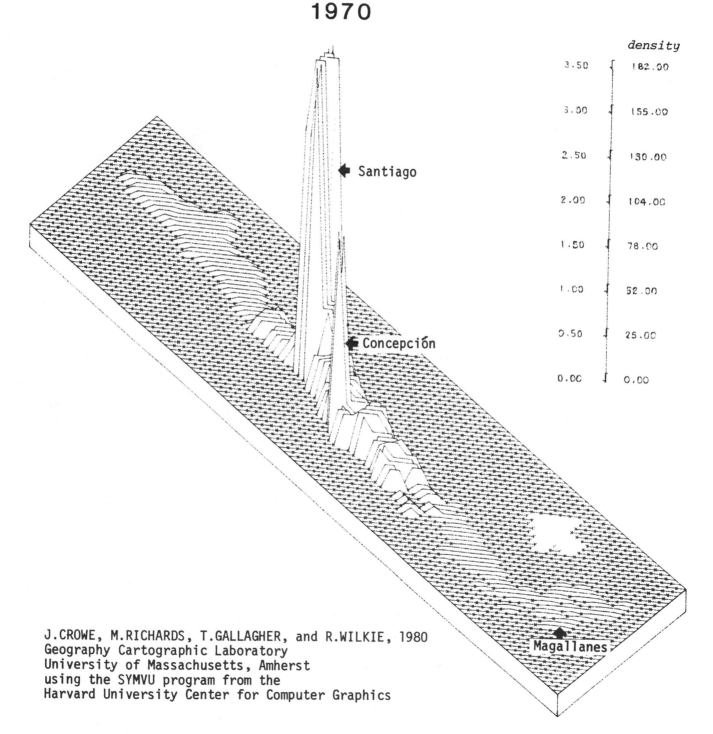

CHILE
POPULATION DENSITY
(PERSONS PER KM²)
1970

density

3.50	182.00
3.00	155.00
2.50	130.00
2.00	104.00
1.50	78.00
1.00	52.00
0.50	25.00
0.00	0.00

Santiago

Concepción

Magallanes

J.CROWE, M.RICHARDS, T.GALLAGHER, and R.WILKIE, 1980
Geography Cartographic Laboratory
University of Massachusetts, Amherst
using the SYMVU program from the
Harvard University Center for Computer Graphics

Map 8-6

**THREE-DIMENSIONAL CHOROPLETH MAP OF POPULATION
CHANGE IN CHILE, 1960–1970
(%)**

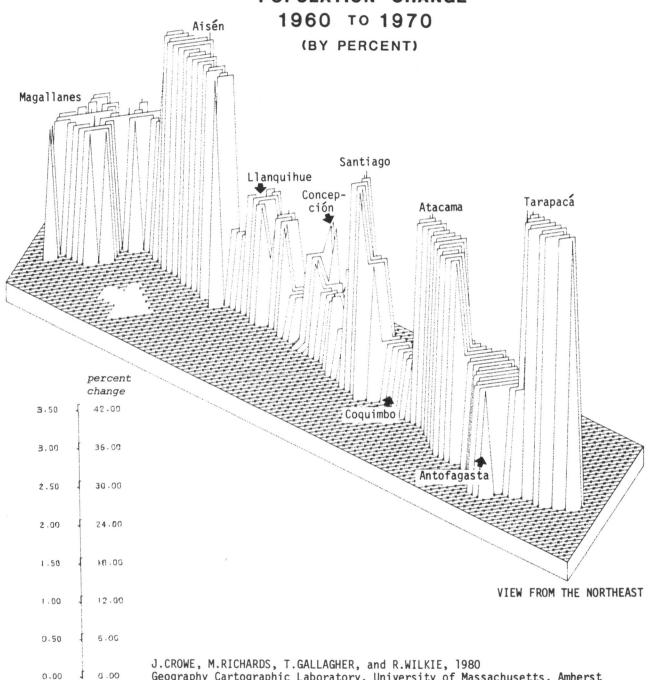

CHILE
POPULATION CHANGE
1960 TO 1970
(BY PERCENT)

Magallanes

Aisén

Llanquihue

Concep-
ción

Santiago

Atacama

Tarapacá

Coquimbo

Antofagasta

percent change	
3.50	42.00
3.00	36.00
2.50	30.00
2.00	24.00
1.50	18.00
1.00	12.00
0.50	6.00
0.00	0.00

VIEW FROM THE NORTHEAST

J.CROWE, M.RICHARDS, T.GALLAGHER, and R.WILKIE, 1980
Geography Cartographic Laboratory, University of Massachusetts, Amherst
using the SYMVU program from the Harvard Univ. Center for Computer Graphics

Photo 8-2

**TYPICAL INTERIOR COURTYARD OF A SPANISH COLONIAL
ADMINISTRATIVE BUILDING, CHILE (1977)**

Table 8-3

POPULATION FOR EACH NATIONAL CENSUS IN
CHILE, 1835–1982

Census Year	Population	Census Year	Population
1835	1,010,336	1907	3,231,022
1843	1,083,801	1920	3,730,235
1854	1,439,120	1930	4,287,445
1865	1,819,223	1952	5,932,995
1875	2,075,971	1960	7,374,712
1885	2,507,005	1970	8,836,223[a]
1895	2,695,625	1982	11,275,440

a. Recommended adjustment of population to 9,336,000 by
the U.S. Bureau of the Census (1978).

Table 8-4

TOTAL AND PERCENT POPULATION IN FIVE LEVELS OF THE URBAN-RURAL
SETTLEMENT HIERARCHY OF CHILE SINCE 1952

	0	1	2	3	4	SETTLEMENT HIERARCHY	
CENSUS YEAR	DISPERSED Population 1 to 99	VILLAGE 100 to 2,500	SIMPLE URBAN 2,501– 20,000	COMPLEX URBAN 20,001– 500,000	METROPOLITAN over 500,000	Classification	PERCENT in top 2 levels
TOTAL							
1952	.... 2,360,000		922,751	1,226,621	1,423,623		
1960	.... 2,485,000		967,804	1,937,963	1,983,945		
1970	.... 1,496,580		941,534	1,509,440	4,888,669		
PERCENT							
1952	.... 39.8		15.5	20.7	24.0	4-0	50 to 55
1960	.... 33.7		13.1	26.3	26.9	4-3	53.2
1970	.... 16.9		10.7	17.1	55.3	4-3	72.4

SOURCE: Calculated from various Chilean national censuses since 1950, and from SALA, 20–631, 632, 634, 635, 636, 637, and 638.

Table 8-5

SELECTED INDICATORS OF POPULATION CHANGE AND PER CAPITA GNP IN CHILE

Years	Per 1000 Population		Rate of Natural Increase (Annual %)	Number of Years to Double Population	Percent Population Under Age 15	Life Expectancy at Birth	Per Capita GNP (US)
	Births	Deaths					
1940–45	36	17	1.5	- -	- -	- -	- -
1945–50	36	14	1.7	- -	- -	- -	- -
1950–55	34	13	2.4	- -	- -	- -	- -
1955–60	36	12	2.4	- -	- -	- -	180[a]
1960–65	37	12	2.5	- -	- -	- -	- -
1965–70	32	10	2.3	- -	- -	- -	- -
1970–74	27	8	1.8	31[b]	40[b]	63[b]	470[b]
1975	25	9	1.8	38	36	63	800
1976	24	8	1.7	41	39	63	820
1977	24	8	1.6	43	36	63	760
1978	25	7	1.8	38	35	63	1,050
1979	24	8	1.6	43	35	63	1,170
1980	21	7	1.4	48	35	66	1,410
1981	22	7	1.5	47	34	67	1,690
1982	22	7	1.5	47	34	66	2,160

a. 1955.
b. 1970.

MAJOR SOURCES:
   Births: SALA, 19-204; SALA, 20-705 through 1976.
   Deaths: SALA, 18-703d and 706 through 1970.
   Life expectancy: SALA, 19-700 through 1970.
   Per capita GNP: 1955 data from Ginsburg, *Atlas of Economic Development* (Chicago: University of Chicago Press, 1961).
   Rate of natural increase: SALA, 22-626 from CELADE-BD 10 (1972) through 1970.
   All other data: Population Reference Bureau, Washington, D.C., annual world population data sheets.

Table 8-6

CHILEAN PROVINCES BY GEOGRAPHICAL
SIZE AND SUBDIVISION, 1970

Province	Civil Subdivisions (N)	Area km^2	%
Total	93[a]	756,629[b]	100.0
Provinces			
Aconcagua	3	9,874	1.3
Antofagasta	4	125,306	16.6
Arauco	3	5,240	.7
Atacama	4	78,268	10.3
Aysen	3	103,584	13.7
Bío-Bío	3	11,135	1.5
Cautín	5	18,377	2.4
Colchagua	2	8,327	1.1
Concepción	5	5,681	.8
Coquimbo	6	39,647	5.2
Curicó	2	5,266	.7
Chiloé	4	26,695	3.5
Linares	3	9,414	1.2
Llanquihue	4	18,205	2.4
Magallanes	3	132,034[b]	17.5
Malleco	5	14,095	1.9
Maule	3	5,697	.8
Ñuble	5	13,951	1.8
O'Higgins	4	7,106	.9
Osorno	2	9,236	1.2
Santiago	8	17,686	2.3
Talca	3	10,141	1.3
Tarapacá	3	58,073	7.7
Valdivia	3	18,473	2.4
Valparaíso	3	5,118	.7

a. Departamentos.
b. Excludes 1,150,000 km^2 of the Territorio Antártico.

SOURCE: SALA, 21-301.

Photo 8-3

PUSHING AGRICULTURE TO THE LIMIT IN THE ANDES (1977)

Map 9-1

PHYSIOGRAPHIC MAP OF COLOMBIA

COLOMBIA

GUY-HAROLD SMITH

9

Colombia

Colombia has had fourteen official censuses over a 158-year period. The first census (1825) counted 1,223,598 inhabitants. By 1905 the population had passed 4 million, and that total more than doubled to 8,701,816 by 1938. The latest census (1973) enumerated 21,070,115 inhabitants, but the U.S. Bureau of the Census (1978) estimated an 8.4 percent underenumeration for a real total of 23,228,000. In 1980 the population was estimated by the Latin American Economic Commission to be 25,614,000 inhabitants.

The population totals, trends, and characteristics of Brazil are presented in six tables and six maps. Some of the findings concerning Brazil include those outlined below.

URBAN TRENDS

Colombia in 1973 had four metropolitan centers of more than half a million population. Greater Bogotá, with a population of 2,870,594, was the largest center in the country with 13.6 percent of the nation's population. Medellín (1,410,154), Cali (926,264), and Barranquilla (728,533) are all major regional centers. In addition, twelve complex urban centers between 100,000 and 400,000 population also served as important regional centers.

RURAL TRENDS

The percentage of the Colombian population living in rural areas fell from nearly two-thirds in 1951 (64 percent) to just over one-third in 1973 (36 percent), but in real terms the rural population actually increased by one-quarter of a million to 7,670,000.

SETTLEMENT HIERARCHY

Colombia in 1973 could be classified as a dispersed−metropolitan settlement landscape (0−4), with nearly three-fifths of the population living either in isolated rural dwellings or in one of four major metropolitan centers. Colombia has a more highly developed level of complex urban centers than most countries in Latin America, and nearly one-quarter of the nation's population (24 percent) lives in cities between 20,000 and 500,000 in size.

OTHER DEMOGRAPHIC DATA

The annual rate of population growth in Colombia has dropped rapidly to 2 percent after remaining higher than 3 percent between 1950 and 1976. Life expectancy in 1982 was 62 years, and 40 percent of the population was under fifteen years of age. Per capita GNP in 1982 of $1180 was up by 195 percent from $400 in 1975, ranking Colombia number 12 among the twenty Latin American republics in that category.

Table 9-1

POPULATION DATA AND DENSITY BY DEPARTMENT IN COLOMBIA, 1973[a]

Rank	Department	Population	Percent	Percent Change 1964-1973	Population Density 1973 (km²)
1	Cundinamarca region	3,961,691	18.9	+39.2	165
	◐ Bogotá, D.E.	2,855,065	13.6	+59.4	1799
	Cundinamarca	1,106,626	5.3	-1.4	50
2	Antioquia	2,976,153	14.1	+20.1	47
3	Valle del Cauca	2,204,722	10.5	+27.2	104
4	Santander	1,130,977	5.3	+13.0	37
5	Boyacá	1,084,766	5.1	+2.5	16
6	Atlántico	958,560	4.5	+33.6	293
7	Tolima	903,520	4.3	+7.4	39
8	Nariño	807,112	3.8	+14.0	26
9	Bolívar	802,402	3.8	+15.7	27
10	Caldas	700,954	3.3	-1.7	96
11	Norte de Santander	693,298	3.3	+29.7	33
12	Córdoba	645,478	3.1	+10.2	26
13	Cauca	603,894	2.9	-0.5	20
14	Magdalena	536,112	2.5	+1.4	23
15	Huila	469,834	2.2	+12.9	24
16	Risaralda	452,626	2.1	+3.5	114
17	Sucre	354,412	1.7	+13.4	34
18	Cesar	339,843	1.6	+30.2	14
19	Quindío	321,677	1.5	+5.2	176
21	Meta	245,176	1.2	+48.1	3
22	Chocó	201,915	1.0	+11.0	4
23	La Guajira	180,520	.9	+22.7	9
	National territories total	494,458	2.3	+105.2	0.5
	Intendencia				
20	Caquetá[1]	250,028	1.2	+141.1	3
24	Putumayo[1]	110,336	.5	+96.0	4
25	Arauca[1]	46,391	.2	+92.1	2
27	S. Andrés y Providencia	22,719	.1	+35.8	516
	Comisaria				
26	Vaupés[1,2]	24,783	.1	+84.9	0.3
28	Amazonas[1]	22,405	.1	+72.9	0.2
29	Vichada[1]	10,780	.1	+6.4	0.1
30	Guainía[1]	7,016	.1	+94.8	0.1
	Total	21,070,115	100.0	+20.5	18.5

1. Four *intendencias* and four *comisarias* have been estimated from the known total for all national territories and the estimated rates of growth between 1964 and 1968 published in the *Diccionario Geográfico de Colombia* (1970), p. 334.
2. In 1982 a new political unit named Guaviare was created by dividing Vaupés. The capital is San José del Guaviare.

a. The U.S. Bureau of the Census (1978) estimated an 8.4 percent net underenumeration in 1973, for a suggested adjusted total of 23,115,000 inhabitants. In addition, they estimated the population on July 1, 1979, to be 26,205,000 (1981).

SOURCES: Censuses of July 15, 1964, and October 24, 1973; SALA, 20-626; *Diccionario Geográfico de Colombia* (Instituto Augustin Codazzi, 1970).

Table 9-2

MAJOR URBAN CENTERS IN COLOMBIA, 1973

| Rank | Major Urban Centers | Population | Percent | United Nations Figures for | |
				City Proper	Urban Agglomeration
1	✪ Gran Bogotá (1)	2,870,594	13.6	2,836,361	2,855,065
2	● Medellín (2)	1,410,154	6.7	1,112,390	1,281,974[a]
3	Cali (3)	926,264	4.4	967,908	990,304
4	Barranquilla (6)	728,533	3.5	690,471	691,728
5	● Bucaramanga (4)	377,149	1.8	315,565	322,883
6	Cartagena (9)	356,424	1.7	309,428	354,735
7	● Pereira (16)	245,214	1.2	186,615	226,888
8	Cúcuta (11)	216,509	1.0	223,868	278,933
9	Manizales (10)	204,024	1.0	205,780	231,888
10	Ibagúe (7)	180,734	.9	193,879	223,112
11	Armenia (19)	158,388	.8	147,635	160,345
12	Palmira (3)	140,481	.7	140,338	184,970
13	Santa Marta (14)	126,719	.6	108,007	150,987
14	Pasto (8)	119,339	.6	127,811	158,533
15	Buenaventura (3)	115,770	.5	108,710	136,308
16	Neiva (15)	105,595	.5	112,479	128,784
17	● Valledupar (18)	92,187	.4	97,066	160,654
18	Villavicencio (21)	90,211	.4	- -	- -
19	Montería (12)	89,552	.4	98,897	172,407
20	Tuluá (3)	86,736	.4	86,104	110,509
21	Barrancabermeja (4)	82,171	.4	- -	- -
22	Popayán (13)	77,669	.4	- -	- -
23	Sincelejo (17)	73,465	.3	- -	- -
24	Girardot (1)	71,964	.3	- -	- -
25	Buga (3)	71,016	.3	- -	- -
26	Cartago (3)	69,154	.3	- -	- -
27	Sogamoso (5)	51,474	.2	- -	- -
28	Tunja (5)	51,301	.2	- -	- -
29	● Ciénaga (14)	43,048	.2	- -	- -
30	Magangué (9)	40,613	.2	- -	- -
31	Tumaco (8)	38,742	.2	- -	- -
32	Ocaña (11)	37,935	.2	- -	- -
33	Chiquinquirá (5)	37,504	.2	- -	- -
34	Duitama (5)	36,551	.2	- -	- -
35	Aguachica (18)	33,237	.2	- -	- -
36	Espinal (7)	31,838	.2	- -	- -
37	Zipaquirá (1)	31,267	.1	- -	- -
38	Sevilla (3)	31,143	.1	- -	- -
39	La Dorada (10)	30,995	.1	- -	- -
40	Ipiales (8)	30,871	.1	- -	- -
41	Pamplona (11)	28,911	.1	- -	- -
42	Quibdó (22)	27,318	.1	- -	- -
43	Facatativá (1)	27,238	.1	- -	- -
44	Sabanalarga (6)	27,110	.1	- -	- -
45	Plato (14)	26,985	.1	- -	- -
46	Maicao (23)	26,887	.1	- -	- -
47	Fusasusagá (1)	25,026	.1	- -	- -
			46.2		

a. Includes Bello (122, 780).

SOURCES: D.A.N.E., *Censo Nacional de Población, X-24-73*; A. Gilbert, "Urban and Regional Development Programs in Colombia since 1951," in Cornelius and Trueblood, eds., *Urbanization and Inequality* (Beverly Hills: Sage Publications (1975), p. 48; United Nations, *Demographic Yearbook 1978* (New York: United Nations, 1979), p. 126.

Map 9-2

BASE MAP OF MAJOR CIVIL DIVISIONS IN COLOMBIA
AND LOCATION OF MAJOR URBAN CENTERS

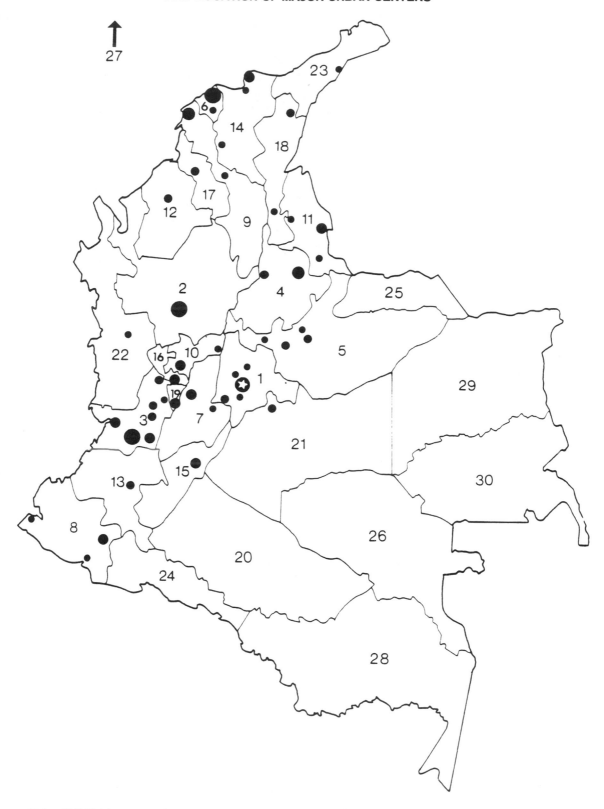

Note: Civil Divisions are rank ordered according to population data listed in Table 9-1.

Map 9-3

POPULATION CARTOGRAM OF COLOMBIA, 1973

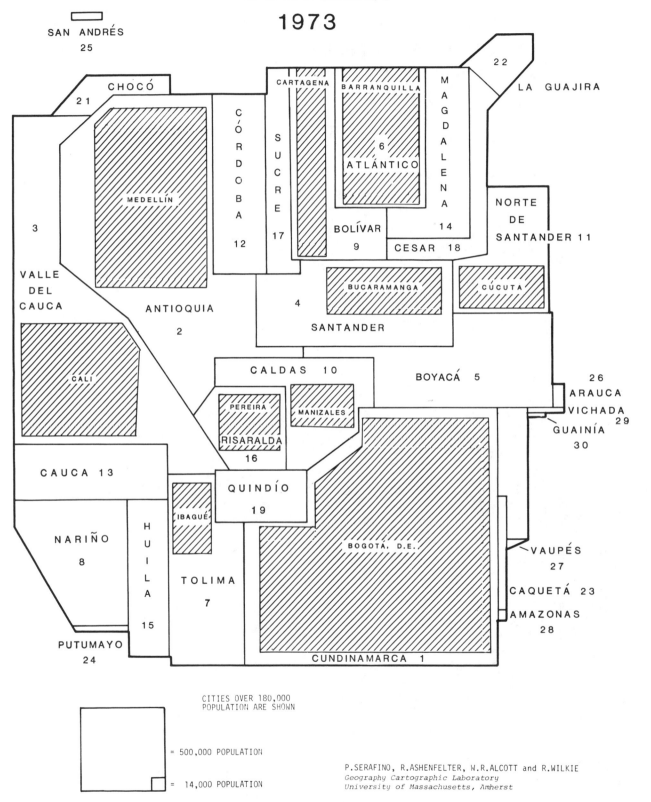

COLOMBIA
1973

SAN ANDRÉS
25

CHOCÓ 21

CARTAGENA

BARRANQUILLA

LA GUAJIRA

22

CÓRDOBA 12

SUCRE 17

MAGDALENA 14

MEDELLÍN

ATLÁNTICO 6

NORTE DE SANTANDER 11

VALLE DEL CAUCA 3

BOLÍVAR 9

CESAR 18

ANTIOQUIA 2

4

BUCARAMANGA

CÚCUTA

CALI

SANTANDER

CALDAS 10

BOYACÁ 5

26
ARAUCA

VICHADA 29

PEREIRA

MANIZALES

GUAINÍA 30

CAUCA 13

RISARALDA 16

QUINDÍO 19

NARIÑO 8

HUILA 15

IBAGUÉ

BOGOTÁ, D.E.

VAUPÉS 27

CAQUETÁ 23

TOLIMA 7

AMAZONAS 28

PUTUMAYO 24

CUNDINAMARCA 1

CITIES OVER 180,000
POPULATION ARE SHOWN

= 500,000 POPULATION

= 14,000 POPULATION

P.SERAFINO, R.ASHENFELTER, W.R.ALCOTT and R.WILKIE
Geography Cartographic Laboratory
University of Massachusetts, Amherst

Map 9-4

**THREE-DIMENSIONAL CHOROPLETH MAP OF TOTAL POPULATION
BY DEPARTMENT IN COLOMBIA, 1973
(By Major Civil Division)**

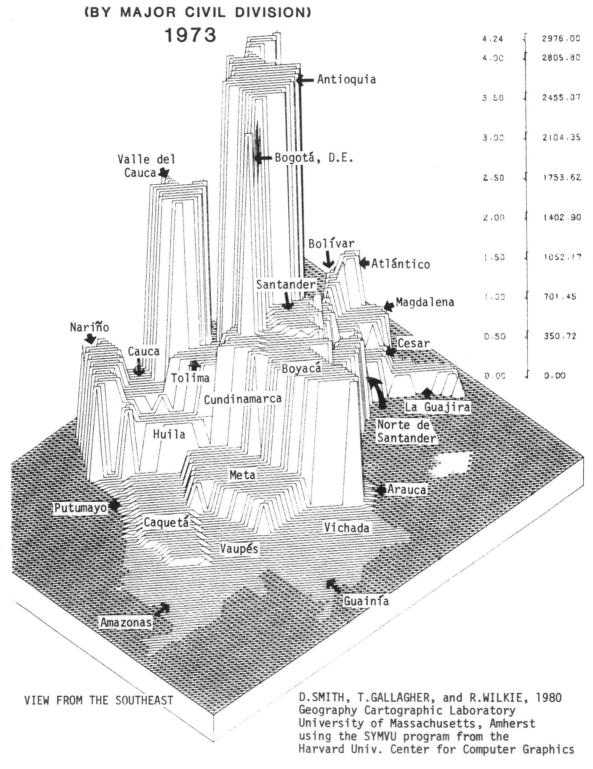

COLOMBIA
TOTAL POPULATION
(BY MAJOR CIVIL DIVISION)
1973

4.24	2976.00
4.00	2805.80
3.50	2455.07
3.00	2104.35
2.50	1753.62
2.00	1402.90
1.50	1052.17
1.00	701.45
0.50	350.72
0.00	0.00

Antioquia

Bogotá, D.E.

Valle del Cauca

Bolívar

Atlántico

Santander

Magdalena

Nariño

Cesar

Cauca

Boyacá

Tolima

Cundinamarca

La Guajira

Huila

Norte de Santander

Meta

Arauca

Putumayo

Caquetá

Vichada

Vaupés

Guainía

Amazonas

VIEW FROM THE SOUTHEAST

D.SMITH, T.GALLAGHER, and R.WILKIE, 1980
Geography Cartographic Laboratory
University of Massachusetts, Amherst
using the SYMVU program from the
Harvard Univ. Center for Computer Graphics

Map 9-5

THREE-DIMENSIONAL CHOROPLETH MAP OF POPULATION DENSITY
IN COLOMBIA, 1973
(Persons per km²)

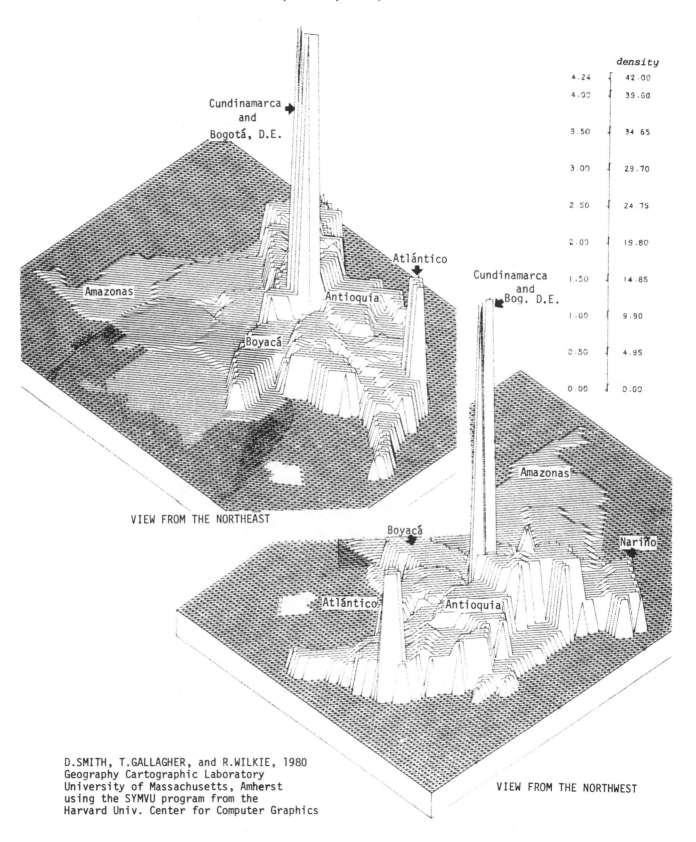

VIEW FROM THE NORTHEAST

VIEW FROM THE NORTHWEST

D.SMITH, T.GALLAGHER, and R.WILKIE, 1980
Geography Cartographic Laboratory
University of Massachusetts, Amherst
using the SYMVU program from the
Harvard Univ. Center for Computer Graphics

Map 9-6A

THREE-DIMENSIONAL CHOROPLETH MAP OF POPULATION CHANGE
IN COLOMBIA, NORTHEAST VIEW, 1964–1975
(%)

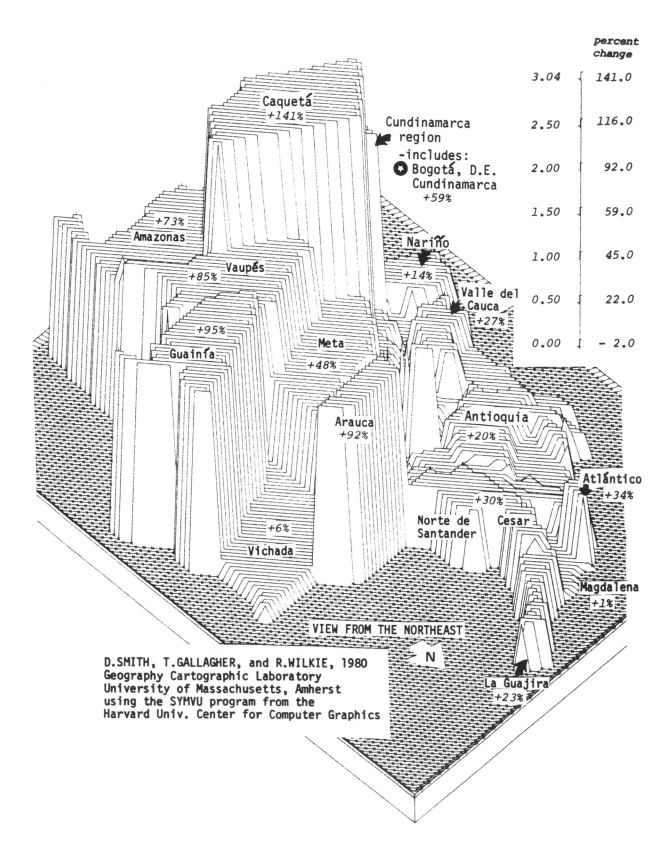

Caquetá
+141%

Cundinamarca
region
-includes:
⊕ Bogotá, D.E.
Cundinamarca
+59%

+73%
Amazonas

Nariño
+14%

Vaupés
+85%

Valle del
Cauca
+27%

+95%

Meta

Guainía
+48%

Arauca
+92%

Antioquia
+20%

Atlántico
+34%

+30%

+6%

Norte de
Santander   Cesar

Vichada

Magdalena
+1%

VIEW FROM THE NORTHEAST

N

La Guajira
+23%

	percent change
3.04	141.0
2.50	116.0
2.00	92.0
1.50	59.0
1.00	45.0
0.50	22.0
0.00	– 2.0

D.SMITH, T.GALLAGHER, and R.WILKIE, 1980
Geography Cartographic Laboratory
University of Massachusetts, Amherst
using the SYMVU program from the
Harvard Univ. Center for Computer Graphics

Map 9-6B

THREE-DIMENSIONAL CHOROPLETH MAP OF POPULATION
CHANGE IN COLOMBIA, NORTHWEST VIEW, 1964–1975
(%)

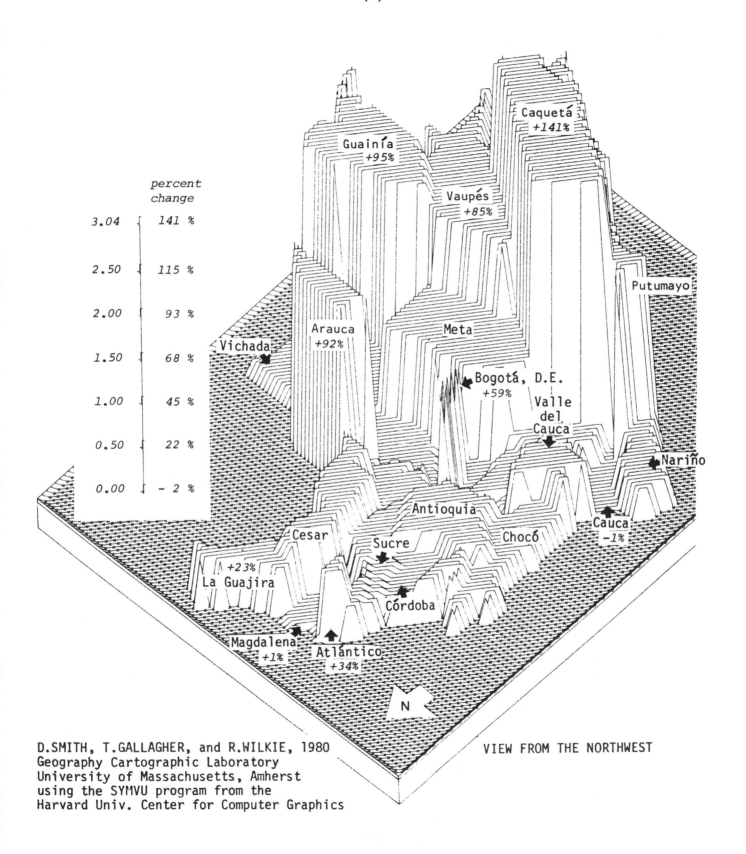

percent change

3.04	141 %
2.50	115 %
2.00	93 %
1.50	68 %
1.00	45 %
0.50	22 %
0.00	- 2 %

Caquetá +141%

Guainía +95%

Vaupés +85%

Putumayo

Arauca +92%

Meta

Vichada

Bogotá, D.E. +59%

Valle del Cauca

Nariño

Antioquia

Cauca -1%

Cesar

Sucre

Chocó

+23%

La Guajira

Córdoba

Magdalena +1%

Atlántico +34%

N

D.SMITH, T.GALLAGHER, and R.WILKIE, 1980
Geography Cartographic Laboratory
University of Massachusetts, Amherst
using the SYMVU program from the
Harvard Univ. Center for Computer Graphics

VIEW FROM THE NORTHWEST

Table 9-3

POPULATION FOR EACH NATIONAL CENSUS IN COLOMBIA, 1825–1973

Census Year	Population	Census Year	Population
1825	1,223,598	1912	5,072,604
1835	1,686,038	1918	5,855,077
1843	1,955,264	1928	7,851,000[a]
1851	2,243,730	1938	8,701,816
1864	2,694,487	1951	11,548,172
1870	2,391,984	1964	17,484,508
1905	4,143,632	1973	21,070,115[b]

a. The 1928 census was not accepted by the National Congress because it was believed that the figures for certain civil divisions were inflated.
b. Recommended adjustment of population to 23,228,000 by the U.S. Bureau of the Census (1978).

Table 9-4

TOTAL AND PERCENT POPULATION IN FIVE LEVELS OF THE URBAN-RURAL SETTLEMENT HIERARCHY OF COLOMBIA SINCE 1950

	0	1	2	3	4	SETTLEMENT HIERARCHY	
CENSUS YEAR	DISPERSED Population 1 to 99	VILLAGE 100 to 1,500	SIMPLE URBAN 1,501– 20,000	COMPLEX URBAN 20,001– 500,000	METROPOLITAN over 500,000	Classification	PERCENT in top 2 levels
TOTAL							
1951	.... 7,390,830		1,501,223	1,940,869	715,250		
1964	7,083,593	1,383,912	2,623,371	3,360,241	3,033,391		
1973	.... 7,669,522		2,495,289	5,086,233	5,819,071		
PERCENT							
1951	.... 64.0		13.0	16.8	6.2	0–3	65 to 70
1964	40.5	7.9	15.0	19.2	17.3	0–3	59.7
1973	.... 36.4		11.8	24.2	27.6	0–4	56 to 58

SOURCE: Calculated from various Colombian national censuses since 1950, and from SALA, 20-631, 632, 634, 635, 636, 637, and 638.

Table 9-5

SELECTED INDICATORS OF POPULATION CHANGE AND PER CAPITA GNP IN COLOMBIA

Years	Per 1000 Population		Rate of Natural Increase (Annual %)	Number of Years to Double Population	Percent Population Under Age 15	Life Expectancy at Birth	Per Capita GNP (US)
	Births	Deaths					
1940–45	33	16	2.4	- -	- -	- -	- -
1945–50	34	15	2.7	- -	- -	- -	- -
1950–55	37	13	3.1	- -	- -	- -	330[a]
1955–60	40	12	3.3	- -	- -	- -	- -
1960–65	45	11	3.3	- -	- -	57[b]	- -
1965–70	44	9	3.5	- -	- -	- -	- -
1970–74	41	10	3.1	21[c]	47[c]	- -	300[c]
1975	41	9	3.2	22	46	61	400
1976	41	9	3.2	22	46	61	510
1977	33	9	2.5	28	43	61	550
1978	33	9	2.4	29	44	61	630
1979	31	9	2.2	32	43	59	710
1980	29	8	2.1	33	45	62	870
1981	29	8	2.1	33	41	62	1,010
1982	28	8	2.0	35	40	62	1,180

a. 1955.
b. 1964.
c. 1970.

MAJOR SOURCES:

Births: SALA, 19-204; SALA, 20-705 through 1975.

Deaths: SALA, 18-703d and 706 through 1970.

Life expectancy: SALA, 19-700 through 1970.

Per capita GNP: 1955 data from Ginsburg, *Atlas of Economic Development* (Chicago: University of Chicago Press, 1961).

Rate of natural increase: SALA, 22-626 from CELADE-BD 10 (1972) through 1970.

All other data: Population Reference Bureau, Washington, D.C., annual world population data sheets.

Table 9-6

COLOMBIAN DEPARTMENTS BY GEOGRAPHICAL
SIZE AND SUBDIVISION, 1968

Department	Civil Subdivisions (N)	Area km^2	%
Total	915^a	1,138,914	100.0
Departments			
Antioquia	109	62,870	5.5
Atlántico	23	3,270	.3
Bogotá, D.E.	7	1,587	.1
Bolívar	29	29,392	2.3
Boyacá	133	67,750	5.9
Caldas	24	7,283	.6
Cauca	36	30,495	2.7
César	13	23,792	2.1
Córdoba	22	25,175	2.2
Cundinamarca	111	22,373	2.0
Chocó	18	47,205	4.1
Huila	36	19,990	1.8
La Guarjira	7	20,180	1.8
Magdalena	20	22,903	2.0
Meta	16	85,770	7.5
Narino	51	31,045	2.7
Norte de Santander	35	20,815	1.8
Quindío	12	1,825	.2
Risaralda	13	3,962	.3
Santander	77	30,950	2.7
Sucre	23	10,523	.9
Tolima	44	23,325	2.0
Valle del Cauca	42	21,245	1.9
Intendencias			
Arauca	2	23,490	2.1
Caquetá	7	90,185	7.9
Putumayo	2	25,570	2.2
San Andrés y Providencia	2	44	#
Comisarías			
Amazonas	1	121,240	10.6
Guainía	* *	78,065	6.9
Vaupés	* *	90,625	8.0
Vichada	* *	98,970	8.7

a. Municipios.

SOURCE: SALA, 21-301.

Map 9-7

SETTLEMENT LANDSCAPE AROUND MEDELLÍN, COLOMBIA, 1955

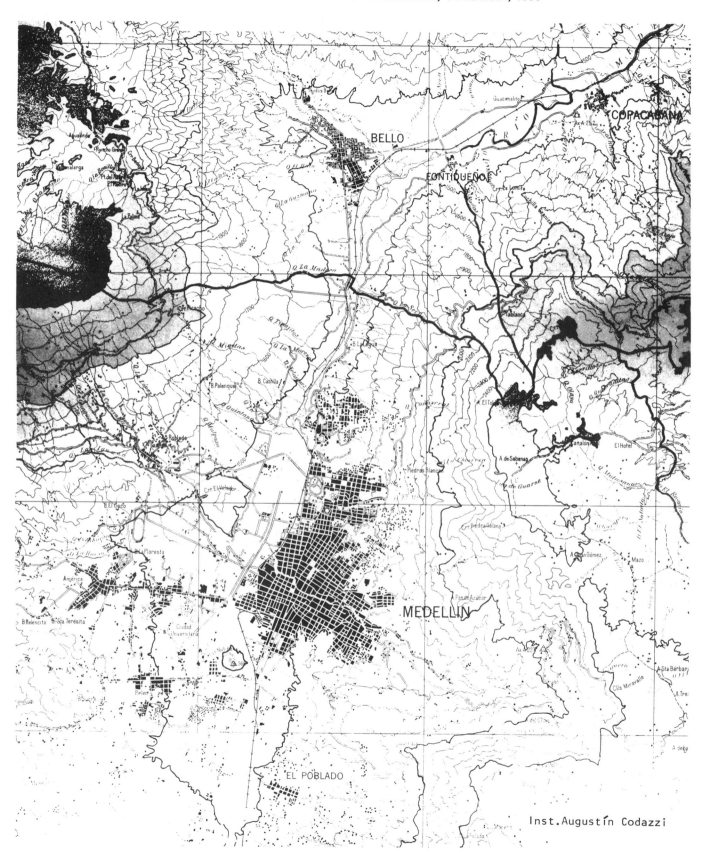

Inst. Augustín Codazzi

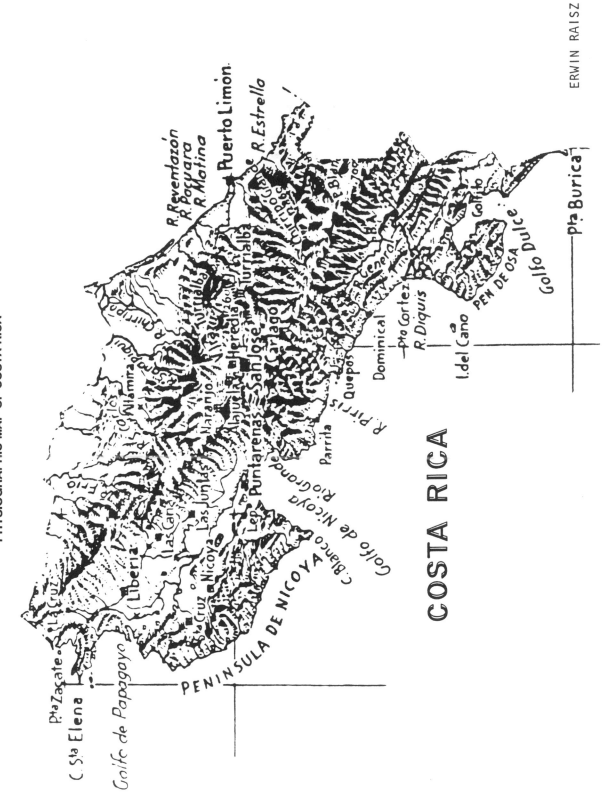

Map 10-1

PHYSIOGRAPHIC MAP OF COSTA RICA

COSTA RICA

ERWIN RAISZ

10

Costa Rica

Costa Rica has had seven official censuses over a 119-year period. The first census (1864) counted only 120,499 inhabitants. By the fourth census in 1927 the total population had risen to 471,524, and that total nearly doubled in 1950 to 800,875. The latest census (1973) documented an increase of 134 percent to 1,871,780 inhabitants. In 1980 the population was estimated by the Latin American Economic Commission to be 2,111,000.

The population totals, trends, and characteristics of Costa Rica are presented in six tables and six maps. Some of the findings concerning Costa Rica are outlined below.

URBAN TRENDS

Understanding the complexity of the urban hierarchy of Costa Rica is complicated by dense clustering of most of the major urban centers in the central highland valleys. No urban center alone is large enough to be classified as a metropolitan city of more than half a million population, although the urbanized area of Greater San José is close with 481,000 inhabitants (26 percent of the nation's population). If the nonurban population in the region is included in the greater metropolitan region, the population of Greater San José totals 806,000 (43 percent of the nation's population). At a second level of urban centers, no other city had more than 35,000 (inhabitants) in 1973.

RURAL TRENDS

Three-fifths of the population of Costa Rica lived in rural areas in 1973. While this percentage was down slightly from two-thirds in 1950, the actual population in rural areas nearly doubled to 1,110,680.

SETTLEMENT HIERARCHY

Costa Rica could be classified in 1973 as a dispersed−complex urban settlement landscape (0−3). Since the population of Greater San José has continued to grow rapidly, by the early 1980s Costa Rica will most likely be dispersed—metropolitan (0−4).

OTHER DEMOGRAPHIC DATA

The annual rate of population growth in Costa Rica remains high—between 2.5 and 2.8 since 1970—but well below the more than 4 percent growth rate of the late 1950s. Life expectancy in 1982 was 70 years, and 38 percent of the population was under fifteen years of age. Per capita GNP in 1982 of $1730 was down from $1810 in 1981 but up overall by 175 percent from $630 in 1975, ranking Costa Rica number 7 (with Panama) among the twenty Latin American republics in that category.

Table 10-1

POPULATION DATA AND DENSITY BY PROVINCE IN COSTA RICA, 1973[a]

Rank	Province	Population	Percent	Percent Change 1963-1973	Population Density 1974 (km^2)
1	San José	695,163	37.1	+42.6	134
2	Alajuela	326,032	17.4	+35.4	34
3	Puntarenas	218,208	11.7	+39.4	20
4	Cartago	204,699	10.9	+31.7	79
5	Guanacaste	178,691	9.5	+25.4	17
6	Heredia	133,844	7.2	+57.4	46
7	Limón	115,143	6.2	+68.3	12
	Total	1,871,780	100.0	+40.1	37

a. The U.S. Bureau of the Census (1978) estimated a net underenumeration of .4 percent, for an adjusted population of 1,879,000 inhabitants. In addition, they estimated the population on July 1, 1979, to be 2,184,000.

SOURCES: Census of May 14, 1973; SALA, 20-626.

Table 10-2

MAJOR URBAN CENTERS IN COSTA RICA, 1973

Rank	Major Urban Centers	Urbanized Area		Metropolitan Region	
		Population	Percent	Population	Percent
1	Gran San José	480,938	25.7	806,100	43.1
	✪ San José Province　(1)	401,038	21.4	532,300	28.4
	Canton Central	215,441	11.5	215,441	11.5
	Canton Goicoechea	43,418		61,600	
	Canton Tibás	35,602		35,602	
	Canton Desamparados	35,469		68,100	
	Canton Montes de Oca	27,636		33,700	
	Canton Moravia	14,381		18,800	
	Canton Escazú	13,903		25,000	
	Canton Curribat	8,615		15,600	
	Canton Alajuelita	6,673		23,000	
	Canton Santa Ana	- -		14,500	
	Canton Aserri	- -		11,700	
	Canton Coronado	- -		9,800	
5	Heredia Province　(6)			101,200	5.4
	● Canton Central	23,600	1.3	36,500	2.0
	Canton Santo Domingo			16,400	
	Canton San Rafael			11,700	
	Canton Belén			8,500	
	Canton San Pablo			6,700	
	Canton Flores			6,500	
	Canton Barba			5,600	
	Canton Santa Barbara			5,600	
	Canton San Isidro			3,700	
6	Cartago Province　(4)			95,100	5.1
	● Canton Central	22,000	1.2	54,900	2.9
	Canton La Union			23,400	
	Canton Oreamuno			10,400	
	Canton el Guarco			6,400	
2	● Alajuela Province　(3)			78,200	4.2
	Canton Central	34,300	1.8	78,200	4.2
	Complex Urban Centers outside Metropolitan San José				
3	● Puerto Limón　(7)	29,600	1.6		
4	Puntarenas　(3)	26,300	1.4		
	Total over 20,000	536,838	28.7		
7	○ Turrialba　(4)	12,200	.7		
8	Liberia　(5)	10,800	.6		

Other cities over 10,000 population
○ Nicoya　(5)
Golfito　(3)
Ciudad Quesada　(2)

SOURCES: Robert Fox and Jerrold Huguet, *Population and Urban Trends in Central America and Panama* (Washington, D.C.: Inter-American Development Bank, 1977), pp. 69, 78, 82; *América en Cifras 1974*.

Map 10-2

BASE MAP OF PROVINCES IN COSTA RICA AND
LOCATION OF MAJOR URBAN CENTERS

Note: Province numbers are rank ordered according
to 1973 population data listed in Table 10-1.

Map 10-3

POPULATION CARTOGRAM OF COSTA RICA, 1973

COSTA RICA
1973

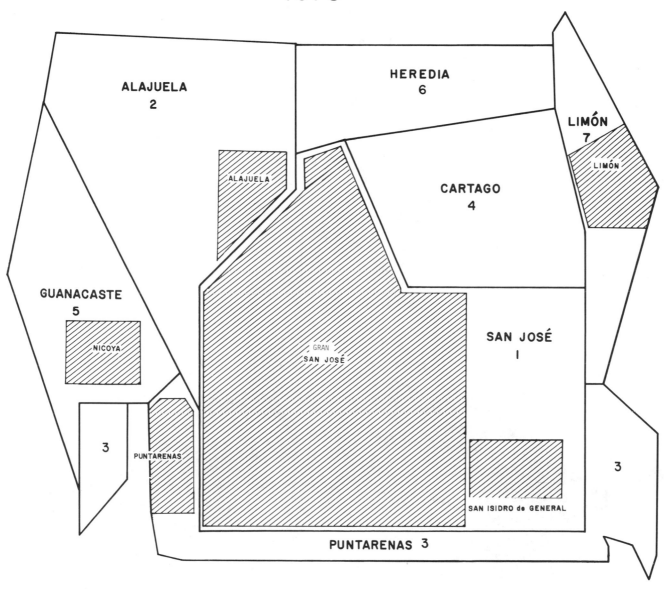

ALAJUELA
2

HEREDIA
6

LIMÓN
7

ALAJUELA

CARTAGO
4

LIMÓN

GUANACASTE
5

NICOYA

GRAN
SAN JOSÉ

SAN JOSÉ
I

3

PUNTARENAS

3

SAN ISIDRO de GENERAL

PUNTARENAS 3

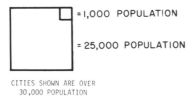

= 1,000 POPULATION

= 25,000 POPULATION

CITIES SHOWN ARE OVER
30,000 POPULATION

D.COTTON, J.F.HUNTER and P.CUTTS
Geography Cartographic Laboratory
University of Massachusetts, Amherst

Map 10-4

**THREE-DIMENSIONAL CHOROPLETH MAP OF TOTAL POPULATION
BY PROVINCE IN COSTA RICA, 1973
(By Major Civil Division)**

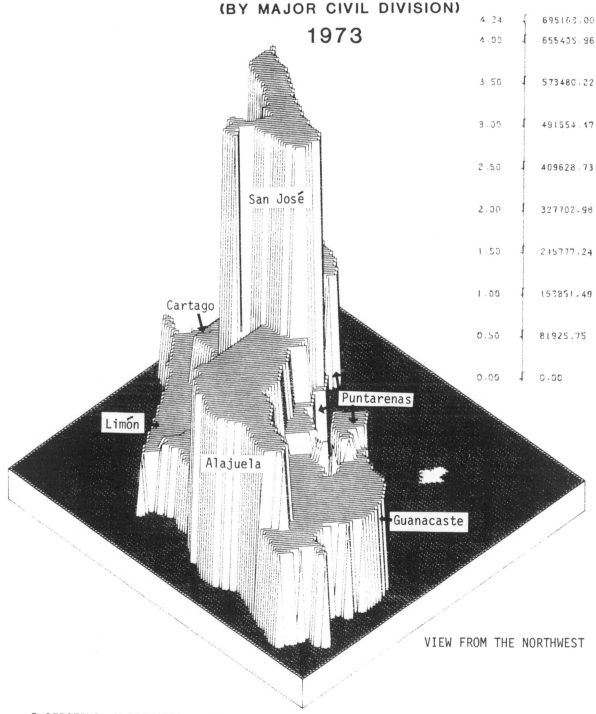

COSTA RICA
TOTAL POPULATION
(BY MAJOR CIVIL DIVISION)
1973

4.24	695163.00
4.00	655405.96
3.50	573480.22
3.00	491554.47
2.50	409628.73
2.00	327702.98
1.50	245777.24
1.00	163851.49
0.50	81925.75
0.00	0.00

San José

Cartago

Limón

Puntarenas

Alajuela

Guanacaste

VIEW FROM THE NORTHWEST

P.SERAFINO, M.RICHARDS, and R.WILKIE, 1980
Geography Cartographic Laboratory, University of Massachusetts, Amherst,
using the SYMVU program from Harvard Laboratory for Computer Graphics

Map 10-5

THREE-DIMENSIONAL CHOROPLETH MAP OF POPULATION DENSITY
IN COSTA RICA, 1973
(Persons per km²)

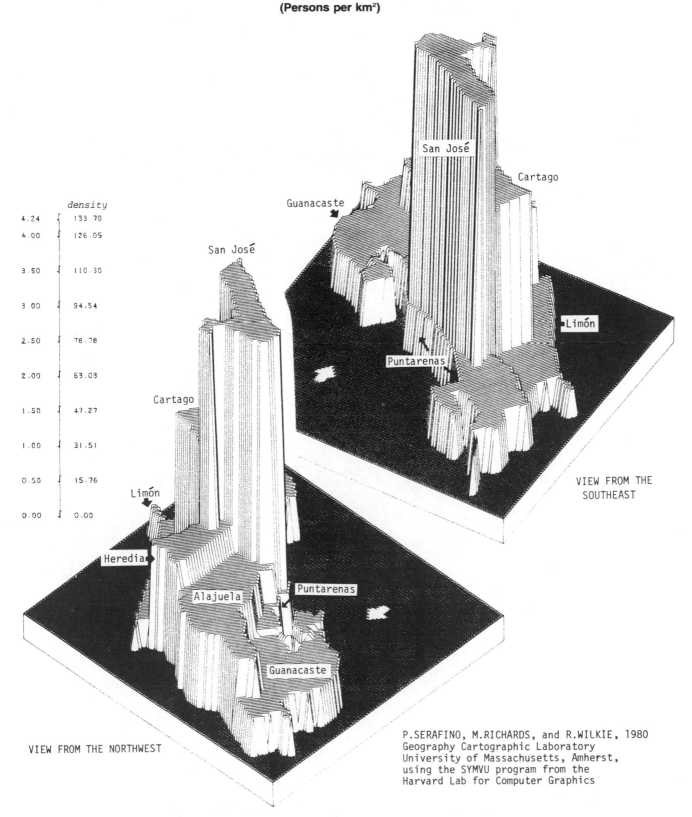

density

4.24	133.70
4.00	126.05
3.50	110.30
3.00	94.54
2.50	78.78
2.00	63.03
1.50	47.27
1.00	31.51
0.50	15.76
0.00	0.00

San José

Cartago

Guanacaste

Limón

Puntarenas

VIEW FROM THE SOUTHEAST

San José

Cartago

Limón

Heredia

Alajuela

Puntarenas

Guanacaste

VIEW FROM THE NORTHWEST

P.SERAFINO, M.RICHARDS, and R.WILKIE, 1980
Geography Cartographic Laboratory
University of Massachusetts, Amherst,
using the SYMVU program from the
Harvard Lab for Computer Graphics

Map 10-6

THREE-DIMENSIONAL CHOROPLETH MAP OF
POPULATION CHANGE IN COSTA RICA, 1963−1975

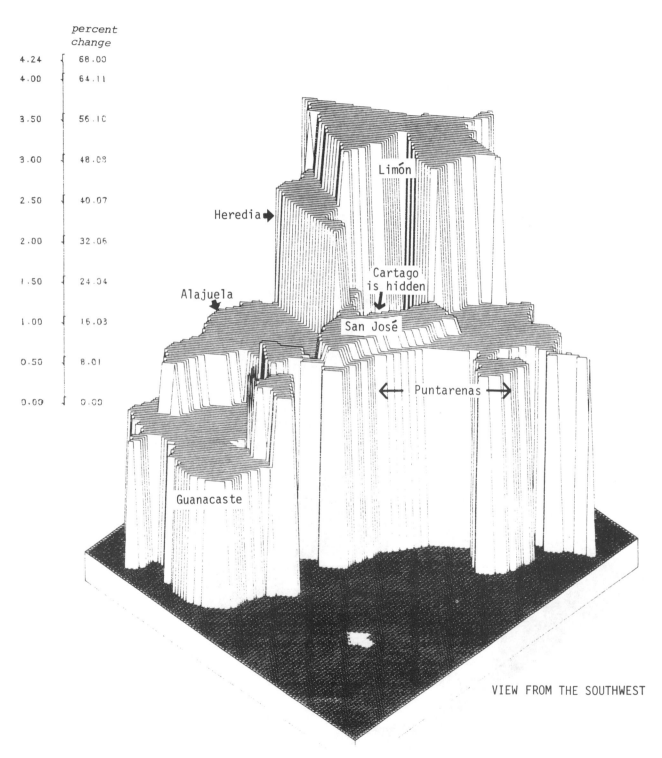

P.SERAFINO, M.RICHARDS, and R.WILKIE, 1980
Geography Cartographic Laboratory, University of Massachusetts, Amherst,
using the SYMVU program from the Harvard Laboratory for Computer Graphics

Photo 10-1

BUILDING CONSTRUCTION IN LATIN AMERICA (1977)

Table 10-3

POPULATION FOR EACH NATIONAL CENSUS IN
COSTA RICA, 1864–1973

Census Year	Population
1864	120,499
1883	182,073
1892	243,205
1927	471,524
1950	800,875
1963	1,336,274
1973	1,871,780[a]

a. Recommended adjustment of population to 1,879,000 by
   the U.S. Bureau of the Census (1978).

Table 10-4

TOTAL AND PERCENT POPULATION IN FIVE LEVELS OF THE URBAN-RURAL
SETTLEMENT HIERARCHY OF COSTA RICA SINCE 1950

	0	1	2	3	4	SETTLEMENT HIERARCHY	
CENSUS YEAR	DISPERSED Population 1 to 99	VILLAGE 100 to 2,500	SIMPLE URBAN 2,501– 20,000	COMPLEX URBAN 20,001– 500,000	METROPOLITAN over 500,000	Classification	PERCENT in top 2 levels
TOTAL							
1950	.... 536,586		122,432	141,857	- -		
1963	.... 875,774		107,724	352,776	- -		
1973	.... 1,110,680		207,925	552,175	- -		
PERCENT							
1950	.... 66.5		15.8	17.7	- -	0–3	67 to 72
1963	.... 65.5		8.1	26.4	- -	0–3	67 to 72
1973	.... 59.4		11.1	29.5	- -	0–3	68 to 75

SOURCE: Calculated from the various Costa Rican national censuses since 1950, and from SALA, 20-631, 632, 634, 635, 636, 637, and 638. The complex urban and simple urban level populations for 1963 and 1973 were calculated in Robert Fox and Jerrold Huguet, *Population and Urban Trends in Central America and Panama* (Washington, D.C.: Inter-American Development Bank, 1977), p. 70.

Table 10-5

SELECTED INDICATORS OF POPULATION CHANGE AND PER CAPITA GNP IN COSTA RICA

Years	Per 1000 Population Births	Per 1000 Population Deaths	Rate of Natural Increase (Annual %)	Number of Years to Double Population	Percent Population Under Age 15	Life Expectancy at Birth	Per Capita GNP (US)
1940–45	45	18	3.0	- -	- -	- -	- -
1945–50	46	14	3.4	- -	- -	- -	- -
1950–55	46	12	3.7	- -	- -	- -	307[a]
1955–60	48	10	4.1	- -	- -	- -	- -
1960–65	45	8	3.7	- -	- -	63	- -
1965–70	37	7	3.1	- -	- -	- -	- -
1970–74	31	6	2.7	19[b]	48	- -	410
1975	29	6	2.8	25	42	68	630
1976	30	5	2.3	30	42	69	790
1977	31	5	2.4	29	44	68	910
1978	29	5	2.4	29	44	68	1,040
1979	30	5	2.5	28	44	68	1,240
1980	31	4	2.7	26	44	70	1,540
1981	32	4	2.8	25	39	70	1,810
1982	29	4	2.5	28	38	70	1,730

a. 1955.
b. 1970.

MAJOR SOURCES:
   Births: SALA, 19-204; SALA, 20-705 through 1977.
   Deaths: SALA, 18-703d and 706 through 1970.
   Life expectancy: SALA, 19-700 through 1970.
   Per capita GNP: 1955 data from Ginsburg, *Atlas of Economic Development* (Chicago: University of Chicago Press, 1961).
   Rate of natural increase: SALA, 22-626 from CELADE-BD 10 (1972) through 1970.
   All other data: Population Reference Bureau, Washington, D.C., annual world population data sheets.

Table 10-6

COSTA RICAN PROVINCES BY GEOGRAPHICAL SIZE AND SUBDIVISION, 1969

Province	Civil Subdivisions (N)	Area km^2	Area %
Total	72[a]	50,900	100.0
Provinces			
Alajuela	12	9,500	18.7
Cartago	8	2,600	5.1
Guanacaste	10	10,400	20.4
Heredia	9	2,900	5.7
Limón	5	9,300	18.3
Puntarenas	8	11,000	21.6
San José	20	5,200	10.2

a. Cantones.

SOURCE: SALA, 21-301.

Map 11-1

PHYSIOGRAPHIC MAP OF CUBA

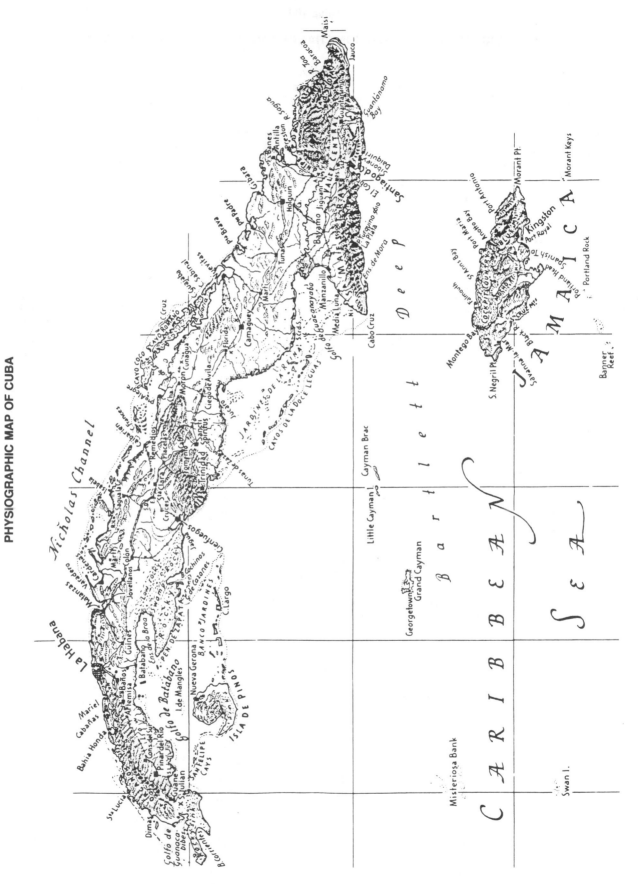

11

Cuba

Cuba has had seventeen official censuses over a 209-year period. The first census (1774) counted 171,620 inhabitants. By the fifth census (1841), Cuba had surpassed one million population, and 66 years later, in 1907, it counted 2,049,000 inhabitants. That population again nearly doubled to just under 4 million by 1931, and by 1953 there were just under 6 million persons in the nation. The latest census (1976) documented a 64 percent increase over twenty-six years to 9,537,036 inhabitants. In 1980 the population was estimated by the Latin American Economic Commission to be 9,718,000, although the U.S. Bureau of the Census estimated its population on July 1, 1979, to be 9,824,000 inhabitants.

The population totals, trends, and characteristics of Cuba are presented in six tables and six maps. Some of the findings concerning Cuba are outlined below.

URBAN TRENDS

In spite of a policy in Cuba to limit the size of Greater Habana, the percentage of the nation's population living in its capital city has remained at about 20 percent since the early 1940s. In 1978 Greater Habana counted 1,986,000 inhabitants (20.4 percent), and it was the only metropolitan center in the country. Six regional centers had between 100,000 and 350,000, including Santiago de Cuba (333,000), Camagüey (236,000), Holguín (164,000), Guantánamo (159,000), Santa Clara (154,000), and Matanzas (100,000). Cuba's policy of urban dispersement has benefited the complex urban level of cities between 20,000 and 500,000 population,

and 22.6 percent of the Cubans live in cities in that range. The simple urban level is also moderately well developed with 16.4 percent of the population living in urban towns between 2,000 and 20,000 in size.

RURAL TRENDS

Two out of every five Cubans (40.5 percent) lived in rural areas in 1970. While the percent rural gradually declined, the absolute number of rural inhabitants has remained relatively constant at about 3.5 million since the early 1960s.

SETTLEMENT HIERARCHY

The growth of population in the complex urban centers means that in 1970 Cuba could be classified as having a dispersed–complex urban (0–3) settlement landscape after being classified dispersed–metropolitan (0–4) for the 1950s and 1960s. Overall, Cuba has a reasonably well balanced hierarchy of settlement sizes, with the greatest imbalance in rural areas between an underdeveloped village level and a moderately high percentage of population living dispersed.

OTHER DEMOGRAPHIC DATA

The annual rate of population growth in Cuba dropped markedly to .8 percent from a high of more than 2 percent, which lasted from 1945 through 1975. Life expectancy in 1982 was seventy-three years, and 35 percent of the population was under fifteen years of age. Per capita GNP in 1981 of $1410 was up by 176 percent from $510 in 1975, ranking Cuba number 9 among the twenty Latin American republics in that category.

Table 11-1A

POPULATION DATA AND DENSITY BY PROVINCE IN CUBA,[1] 1976

Rank	Province	1976 Population	1976 Percent	Population Density 1976 (km^2)
1	Ciudad de Habana	1,961,674	20.5	2647
2	Santiago de Cuba	891,168	9.2	140
3	Holguín	887,654	9.2	100
4	Villa Clara	762,838	8.9	94
5	Granma	715,016	7.5	85
6	Camagüey	626,205	6.4	44
7	Pinar del Río	617,087	6.4	57
8	Habana	570,945	5.9	101
	Isla de la Juventud (Pines)	46,148	.5	21
9	Matanzas	551,685	5.8	47
10	Guantánamo	458,641	4.7	72
11	Las Tunas	428,100	4.5	67
12	Sancti Spiritus	398,257	4.1	59
13	Cienfuegos	317,039	3.2	76
14	Ciego de Avila	304,579	3.2	47
	Total	9,537,036	100.0	86

1. In 1976 Cuba divided the six existing provinces into fourteen new provinces and one municipio (Isla de la Juventud) which is administered by Havana province.

SOURCES: Census of December 31, 1976; *Cuba Handbook of Historical Statistics* (Boston, Mass.: G. K. Hall, 1982), p. 43.

Table 11-1B

POPULATION DATA AND DENSITY BY PROVINCE IN CUBA,[1] 1970

Rank	Province	1970 Population	1970 Percent	Percent Change 1961-1970	Population Density 1970 (km^2)
1	Oriente	2,998,972	35.1	+66.8	82
2	Habana	2,335,344	27.3	+51.8	284
3	Las Villas	1,362,179	15.9	+32.2	64
4	Camagüey	813,204	9.5	+31.5	31
5	Pinar del Río	542,423	6.3	+21.0	40
6	Matanzas	501,273	5.9	+26.7	59
	Total	8,553,395	100.0	+46.7	75

1. The U.S. Bureau of the Census (1978) did not evaluate the 1970 census for possible coverage errors. They did estimate the population on July 1, 1977 to be 9,604,000, and on July 1, 1979 to be 9,824,000 (1981).

SOURCES: Census of September 6, 1970, and SALA, 20-626.

Table 11-2

MAJOR URBAN CENTERS IN CUBA, 1970, 1976, AND 1978

Rank	Major Urban Centers	1970 Population	1970 Percent	1976 Population	1976 Percent	1978 Population
1	✪ Gran Habana (2)	1,751,216	20.5	1,949,000	20.4	1,986,000
	Habana proper	1,008,500	11.8	- -	- -	- -
2	● Santiago de Cuba (1)	277,600	3.2	322,000	3.4	333,000
3	● Camagüey (4)	197,720	2.3	228,000	2.4	236,000
4	Holguín (1)	131,000	1.5	158,000	1.7	164,000
5	Guantánamo (1)	130,000	1.5	153,000	1.6	159,000
6	Santa Clara (3)	130,000	1.5	150,000	1.6	154,000
7	Matanzas (6)	89,000	1.0	98,000	1.0	100,000
8	Cienfuegos (3)	80,000	.9	91,000	1.0	93,000
9	Pinar del Río (5)	72,000	.8	89,000	.9	91,000
10	Bayamo (1)	70,000	.8	87,000	.9	90,000
11	Sancti Spíritus (3)	57,000	.7	67,000	.7	68,000
12	Ciego de Avila (4)	56,000	.7	66,000	.7	69,000
13	Victoria de las Tunas (1)	53,000	.6	64,000	.7	68,000
			36.0		37.0	

SOURCE: *Cuba Handbook of Historical Statistics* (Boston, Mass.: G. K. Hall, 1982), p. 49.

Map 11-2A

BASE MAP OF PROVINCES IN CUBA AND LOCATION OF
MAJOR URBAN CENTERS, 1976

Map 11-2B

BASE MAP OF PROVINCES IN CUBA AND LOCATION OF MAJOR
URBAN CENTERS, 1970

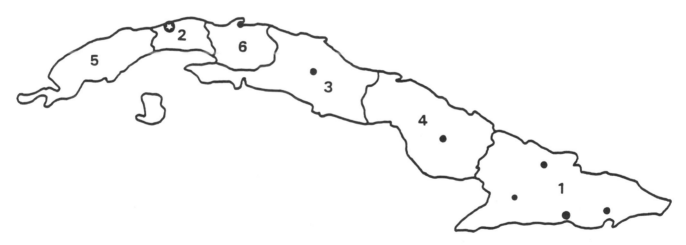

Note: Provincial numbers are rank ordered according to population data listed in Tables 11-1A and 11-1B.

Map 11-3

POPULATION CARTOGRAMS OF CUBA, 1970 AND 1976

CUBA

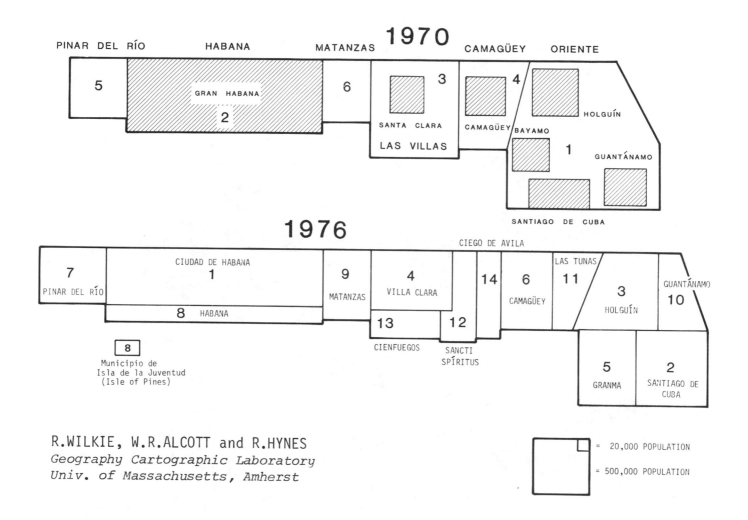

R.WILKIE, W.R.ALCOTT and R.HYNES
Geography Cartographic Laboratory
Univ. of Massachusetts, Amherst

Map 11-4

THREE-DIMENSIONAL CHOROPLETH MAP OF TOTAL POPULATION
BY PROVINCE IN CUBA, 1970
(By Major Civil Division)

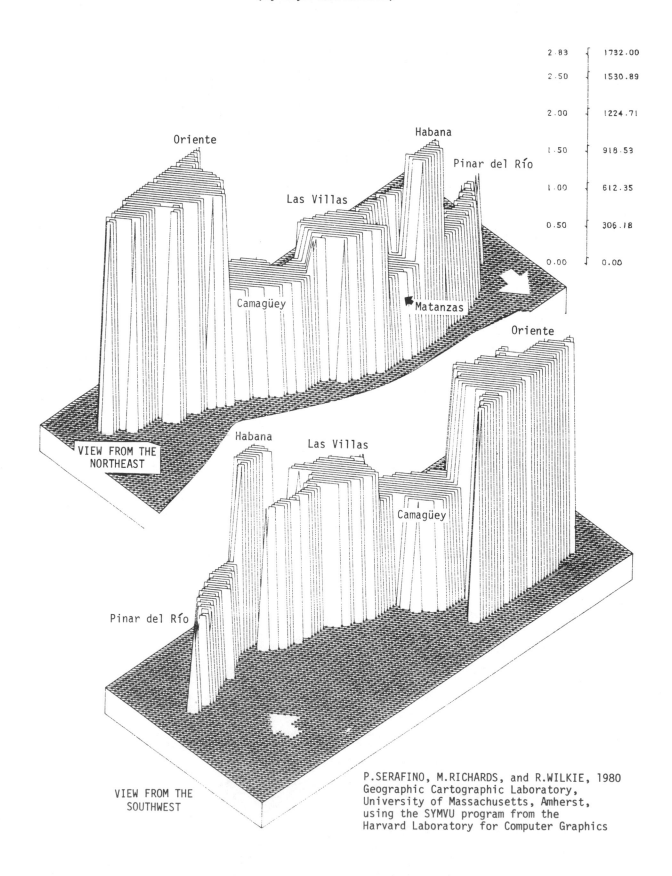

2.83	1732.00
2.50	1530.89
2.00	1224.71
1.50	918.53
1.00	612.35
0.50	306.18
0.00	0.00

VIEW FROM THE NORTHEAST

VIEW FROM THE SOUTHWEST

P.SERAFINO, M.RICHARDS, and R.WILKIE, 1980
Geographic Cartographic Laboratory,
University of Massachusetts, Amherst,
using the SYMVU program from the
Harvard Laboratory for Computer Graphics

Map 11-5

THREE-DIMENSIONAL CHOROPLETH MAP OF POPULATION DENSITY
IN CUBA, 1970
(Persons per km²)

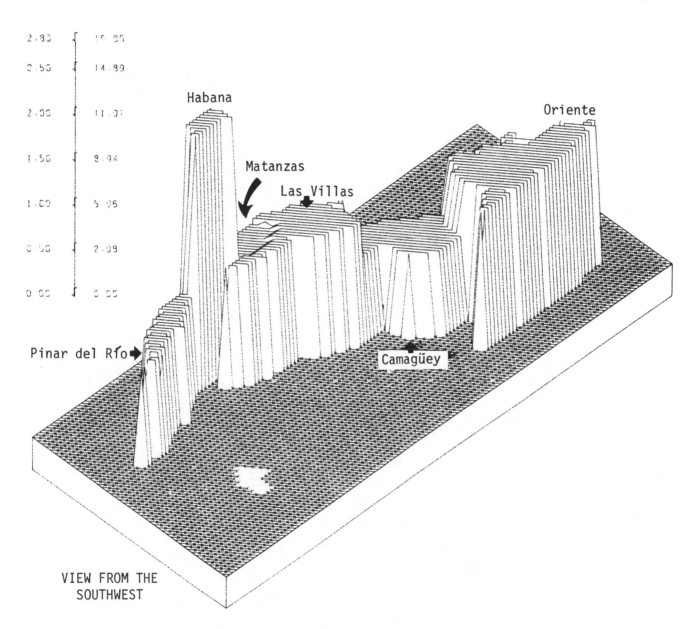

VIEW FROM THE
SOUTHWEST

P.SERAFINO, M.RICHARDS, and R.WILKIE, 1980
Geography Cartographic Laboratory, University of Massachusetts, Amherst
using the SYMVU program from Harvard Laboratory for Computer Graphics

Map 11-6

THREE-DIMENSIONAL CHOROPLETH MAP OF POPULATION CHANGE
IN CUBA, 1953–1970

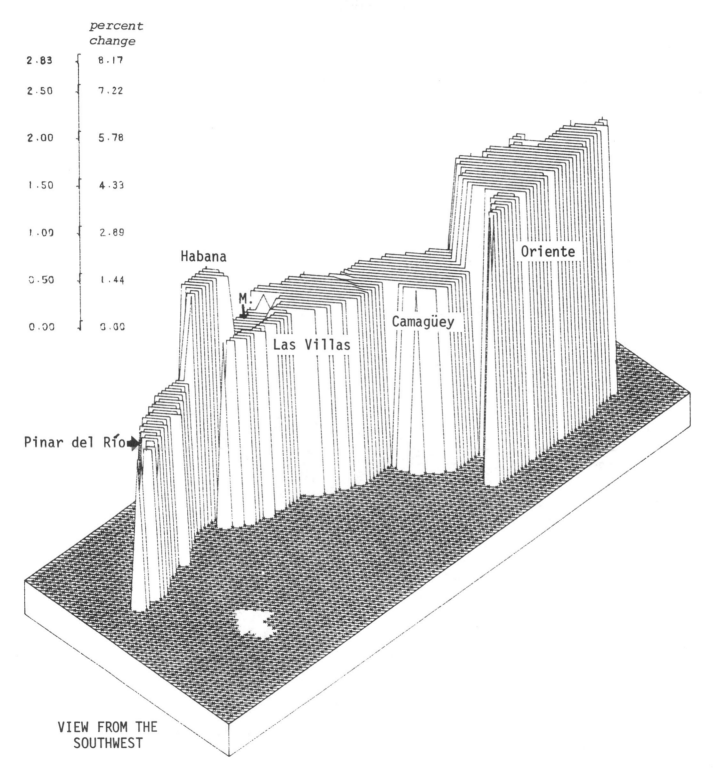

P.SERAFINO, M.RICHARDS, and R.WILKIE, 1980
Geography Cartographic Laboratory, University of Massachusetts, Amherst
using the SYMVU program from Harvard Laboratory for Computer Graphics

Photo 11-1

CARIBBEAN FISHING BOAT (1978)

Table 11-3

POPULATION FOR EACH NATIONAL CENSUS IN CUBA, 1774–1970

Census Year	Population	Census Year	Population
1774	171,620	1899	1,572,797
1792	272,300	1907	2,048,980
1817	572,363	1919	2,889,004
1827	704,487	1931	3,962,344
1841	1,007,624	1943	4,778,583
1861	1,396,530	1953	5,829,029
1877	1,509,291	1964	7,434,200[a]
1887	1,631,687	1970	8,553,395

a. Estimated.

Table 11-4

TOTAL AND PERCENT POPULATION IN FIVE LEVELS OF THE URBAN-RURAL SETTLEMENT HIERARCHY OF CUBA SINCE 1950

	0	1	2	3	4	SETTLEMENT HIERARCHY	
CENSUS YEAR	DISPERSED Population 1 to 99	VILLAGE 100 to 2,500	SIMPLE URBAN 2,501– 20,000	COMPLEX URBAN 20,001– 500,000	METROPOLITAN over 500,000	Classification	PERCENT in top 2 levels
TOTAL							
1953	2,541,440	347,000	838,280	1,003,722	1,098,587		
1964	.... 3,568,416		1,051,784	1,220,000	1,594,000		
1970	.... 3,461,307		1,407,381	1,933,491	1,751,216		
PERCENT							
1953	43.6	6.0	14.4	17.2	18.8	0–4	62.4
1964	.... 48.0		14.1	16.4	21.4	0–4	62 to 64
1970	.... 40.5		16.4	22.6	20.5	0–3	60 to 65

SOURCE: Calculated from the various Cuban national censuses since 1950, and from SALA, 20–631, 632, 634, 635, 636, 637, and 638, and from *Cuba Handbook of Historical Statistics* (Boston, Mass.: G.K. Hall, 1982), table 11.10.

Table 11-5

SELECTED INDICATORS OF POPULATION CHANGE AND PER CAPITA GNP IN CUBA

Years	Per 1000 Population		Rate of Natural Increase (Annual %)	Number of Years to Double Population	Percent Population Under Age 15	Life Expectancy at Birth	Per Capita GNP (US)
	Births	Deaths					
1940–45	22	10	1.6	- -	- -	- -	- -
1945–50	31	12	2.3	- -	- -	- -	- -
1950–55	31	12	2.1	- -	- -	- -	- -
1955–60	30	7	2.1	- -	- -	- -	361[a] in 1955
1960–65	34	6	2.1	- -	- -	- -	- -
1965–70	31	6	2.0	- -	- -	67	- -
1970–74	26	6	2.3	37[b]	37[b]	- -	330[b]
1975	21	5	2.0	35	38	70	510
1976	20	6	1.8	38	37	70	640
1977	18	6	1.6	43	37	70	800
1978	21	5	1.5	46	37	70	860
1979	20	6	1.4	50	37	71	900
1980	18	6	1.2	59	37	72	810
1981	15	6	.9	77	32	72	1,410
1982	14	6	.8	85	35	73	- -

a. 1955.
b. 1970.

MAJOR SOURCES:

Births: SALA, 19-204; SALA, 20-705 through 1977.
Deaths: SALA, 18-703d and 706 through 1970; Cuba Handbook of Historical Statistics (Boston, Mass.: G. K. Hall, 1982) for 1970–1976.
Life expectancy: SALA 19-700 through 1970.
Per capita GNP: 1955 data from Ginsburg, Atlas of Economic Development (Chicago: University of Chicago Press, 1961).
Rate of natural increase: SALA, 22-626 from CELADE-BD 10 (1972) through 1970.
All other data: Population Reference Bureau, Washington, D.C., annual world population data sheets.

Table 11-6

CUBAN PROVINCES BY GEOGRAPHICAL SIZE AND SUBDIVISION, 1966

Province	Civil Subdivisions (N)	Area	
		km^2	%
Total	131[a]	114,524	100.0
Provinces			
Camagüey	10	26,346	23.0
La Habana	27	8,221	7.2
Las Villas	32	21,411	18.7
Matanzas	22	8,444	7.4
Oriente	25	36,602	32.0
Pinar del Río	15	13,500	11.8

a. Municipios.

SOURCE: SALA, 21-301.

Map 12-1

PHYSIOGRAPHIC MAP OF THE DOMINICAN REPUBLIC

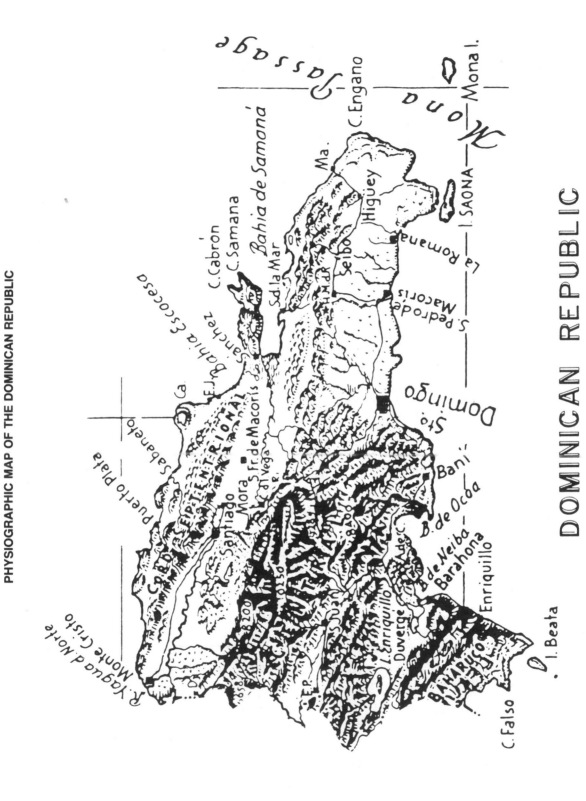

DOMINICAN REPUBLIC

ERWIN RAISZ

12

Dominican Republic

The Dominican Republic has had six official censuses over only a 63-year period. The first census (1920) counted 894,665 inhabitants. By the third census (1950) the population grew 145 percent to 2,135,872, and the last census (1981) showed an addition gain of 163 percent to 5,621,985 inhabitants.

The population totals, trends, and characteristics of the Dominican Republic are presented in six tables and six maps. Some of the findings concerning the Dominican Republic are those outlined below.

URBAN TRENDS

Greater Santo Domingo has continued to grow at a much faster rate than the rest of the country as a whole. Between 1970 and 1981 Santo Domingo increased by 96 percent from 700,000 to 1,318,172, and it had nearly one-fourth of the nation's population (23.4 percent). The second city of the country is Greater Santiago de los Caballeros (278,654). Twelve other complex urban cities had more than 20,000 population in 1970, and together with Santiago de los Caballeros had 15.6 percent of the nation's inhabitants.

RURAL TRENDS

The majority of Dominicans continued to live in rural areas of the country in 1970, even though there had been a gradual decline from 76 percent in 1950, to 70 percent in 1960, and ultimately to 58 percent in 1970. In absolute terms, however, the rural population has increased from 1.6 million in 1950 to 2.3 million in 1970.

SETTLEMENT HIERARCHY

The Dominican Republic could be classified in 1970 as a dispersed—metropolitan settlement landscape (0−4), with approximately two-thirds of the population living in dispersed rural clusters of under 100 individuals or in the capital city.

OTHER DEMOGRAPHIC DATA

The annual rate of population growth in the Dominican Republic has only dropped below 3 percent since 1979, after reaching a high of 3.7 percent in the early 1970s. Life expectancy in 1982 was sixty years, and 45 percent of the population was under fifteen years of age. Per capita GNP in 1982 of $1140 was up by 143 percent from $470 in 1975, ranking the Dominican Republic number 13 among the twenty Latin American republics in that category.

Table 12-1

POPULATION DATA AND DENSITY BY PROVINCE IN THE DOMINICAN REPUBLIC, 1970 AND 1981[a]

1970 Rank	Province	1970 Population	1970 Percent	Percent Change 1960-1970	Population Density 1970 (km²)	1981 Population	Percent Change 1970-1981	Population Density 1981 (km²)
1	Distrito Nacional	817,467	20.4	+75.1	554	1,555,739	+90.3	1,053
2	Santiago	386,269	9.6	+32.4	124	548,644	+42.0	176
3	San Cristóbal	324,395	8.1	+28.6	87	444,983	+37.2	119
4	La Vega	293,694	7.3	+18.8	87	383,455	+30.6	111
5	Duarte	200,813	5.0	+23.7	155	235,570	+17.3	182
6	San Juan	191,065	4.8	+25.4	54	239,967	+25.6	67
7	Puerto Plata	185,800	4.6	+13.3	99	202,735	+9.1	108
8	Espaillat	139,579	3.5	+15.5	140	164,645	+18.0	169
9	El Seibo	132,795	3.3	+9.1	44	160,775	+21.1	54
10	Peravia	127,587	3.2	+18.1	79	166,356	+30.4	103
11	Barahona	112,914	2.8	+41.1	45	137,160	+21.5	54
12	Sánchez Ramírez	106,177	2.6	+17.6	90	126,356	+19.0	108
13	San Pedro de Macorís	105,490	2.6	+55.5	91	131,310	+24.5	113
14	María Trinidad Sánchez	97,043	2.4	+8.4	74	111,199	+14.6	85
15	Azúa	91,511	2.3	+23.0	38	143,628	+57.0	59
16	Salcedo	89,773	2.2	+26.1	168	99,013	+10.3	201
17	La Altagracia	87,180	2.2	+34.4[b]	28	100,112	+14.8	32
18	Valverde	76,608	1.9	+26.3	75	100,274	+30.9	173
19	Monte Cristi	69,276	1.7	+15.4	35	83,407	+20.4	42
20	Bahoruco	66,572	1.7	+26.1	48	78,508	+17.9	57
21	La Romana	56,955	1.4	-[b]	105	109,769	+92.7	190
22	Samaná	53,893	1.3	+25.2	55	64,886	+20.4	66
23	La Estrelleta (Elias Piña)	53,228	1.3	+22.1	30	65,813	+23.6	64
24	Dajabón	50,780	1.3	+21.2	57	57,709	+13.6	65
25	Santiago Rodríguez	49,598	1.2	+21.8	49	55,411	+11.7	54
26	Independencia	32,580	.8	+17.1	18	38,052	+16.8	20
27	Perdernales	12,547	.3	+41.6	13	16,509	+31.6	16
	Total	4,011,589	100.0	+31.7	83	5,621,985	+40.1	116

a. The U.S. Bureau of the Census (1978) recommended adjusting the 1970 census figure based on an implied 6.4 percent net underenumeration to 4,284,000 inhabitants. In addition, they estimated the population on July 1, 1979, to be 5,551,000 (1981).

b. On July 9, 1962, La Altagracia province was divided into La Altagracia and La Romana provinces.

SOURCE: *Santo Domingo News,* Jan. 1-7, 1982.

Table 12-2

MAJOR URBAN CENTERS IN THE DOMINICAN REPUBLIC, 1970 AND 1981

Rank	Major Urban Centers 1970	1970 Population	1970 Percent	1981 Population	1981 Percent	Percent Change 1970–1981
1	✪ Gran Santo Domingo (1)	699,000[a]	17.4	- -	- -	- -
	Santo Domingo proper	673,000	16.8	1,318,172	23,4	+95.9
	Bajos de Haina	11,000	.2	- -	- -	- -
	Vicente Noble	8,000	.2	- -	- -	- -
	Sabana Grande de Boya	7,000	.2	- -	- -	- -
2	● Gran Santiago de los Caballeros (2)	245,000	6.1	- -	- -	- -
	Santiago proper	155,000	3.9	278,654	5.0	+79.8
3	● S. Francisco de Macorís (5)	45,000	1.1	64,906	1.2	+44.2
4	San Pedro de Macorís (13)	43,000	1.1	77,498	1.4	+80.2
5	Barahona (11)	37,000	.9	- -	- -	- -
6	La Romana (21)	37,000	.9	- -	- -	- -
7	S.Juan de la Maguana (6)	32,000	.9	- -	- -	- -
8	Puerto Plata (7)	32,000	.9	45,348	.8	+41.7
9	La Vega (4)	31,000	.9	51,928	.8	+67.5
10	San Cristóbal (3)	26,332	.7	58,520	1.0	+122.2
11	Mao (18)	26,000	.6	- -	- -	- -
12	Moca (8)	24,000	.6	- -	- -	- -
13	Baní (10)	24,000	.6	- -	- -	- -
14	Monseñor Nouel (4)	22,000	.5	- -	- -	- -
			33.0[b]			
15	○ Higüey (17)	18,000				
16	Azúa (15)	14,000				
17	Nagua (14)	14,000				
18	Villa Altagracia (3)	12,000				
19	Bajos de Haina (3)	11,000				
20	Esperanza (18)	11,000				
21	Hato Mayor (9)	10,000				

a. The United Nations (1978) listed the population of Gran Santo Domingo in 1970 as 817,645 (20.4%).

b. The United Nations figure with 118,645 more population for Gran Santo Domingo increases the percentage of population in urban centers over 20,000 population to 36.0 percent.

SOURCES: Censuses of January 9-10, 1970, and December 12-13, 1981; *América en Cifras 1974; U.N. Demographic Yearbook 1978;* SALA, 20-626.

Map 12-2

BASE MAP OF PROVINCES IN THE DOMINICAN REPUBLIC AND
LOCATION OF MAJOR URBAN CENTERS

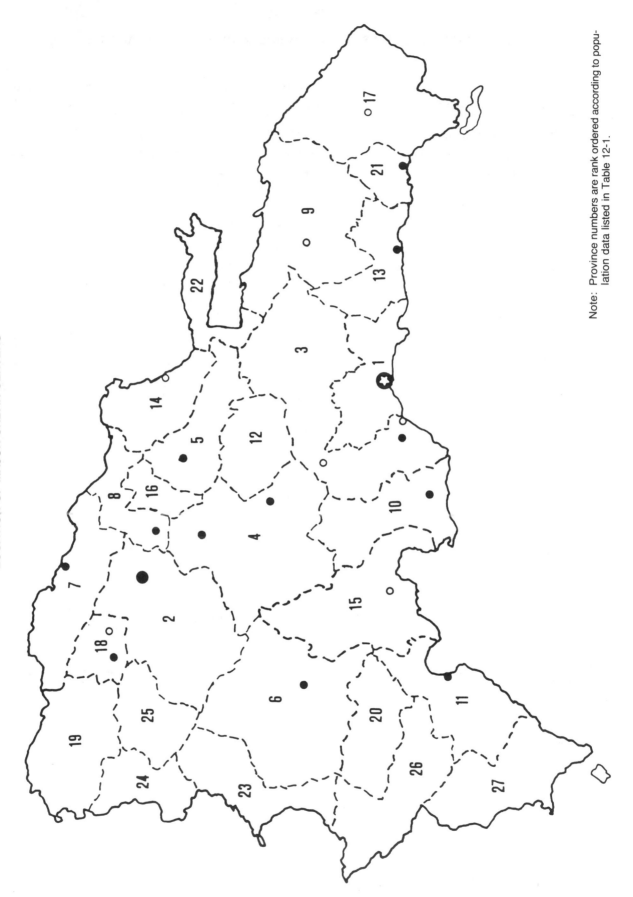

Note: Province numbers are rank ordered according to population data listed in Table 12-1.

Map 12-3

POPULATION CARTOGRAM OF THE DOMINICAN REPUBLIC, 1970

DOMINICAN REPUBLIC
1970

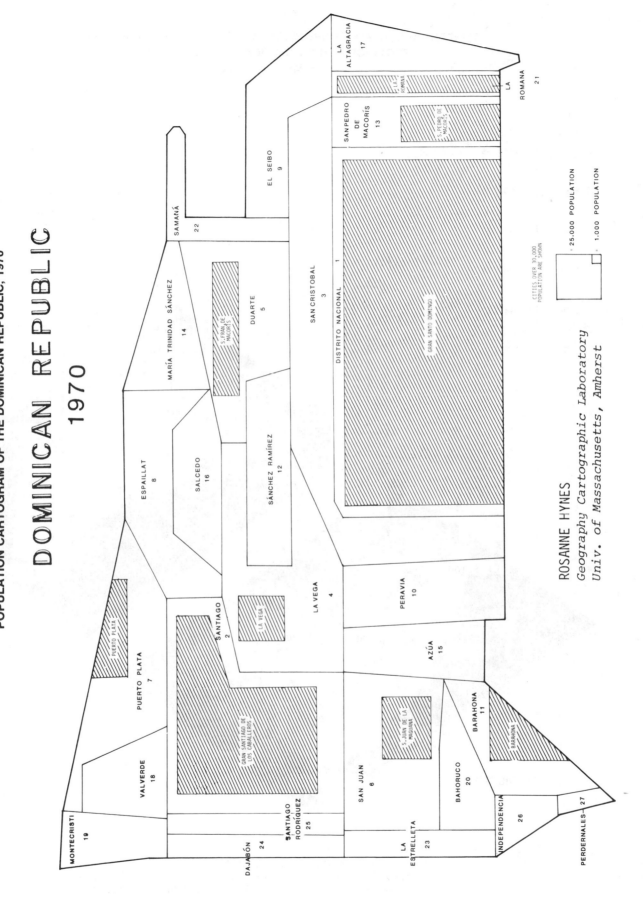

ROSANNE HYNES
Geography Cartographic Laboratory
Univ. of Massachusetts, Amherst

CITIES OVER 30,000
POPULATION ARE SHOWN

☐ = 25,000 POPULATION

□ = 1,000 POPULATION

Map 12-4

THREE-DIMENSIONAL CHOROPLETH MAP OF TOTAL POPULATION BY
PROVINCE IN THE DOMINICAN REPUBLIC, 1970
(By Major Civil Division)

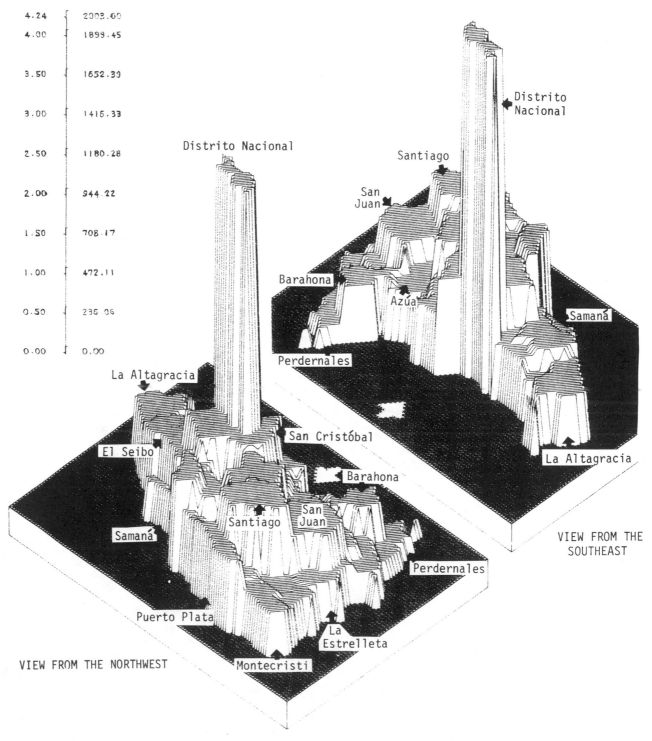

S.MORGAN, M.RICHARDS, and R.WILKIE, 1980
Geography Cartographic Laboratory, University of Massachusetts, Amherst
using the SYMVU program from the Harvard Univ. Computer Graphics Center

Map 12-5

THREE-DIMENSIONAL CHOROPLETH MAP OF POPULATION DENSITY
IN THE DOMINICAN REPUBLIC, 1970
(Persons per km³)

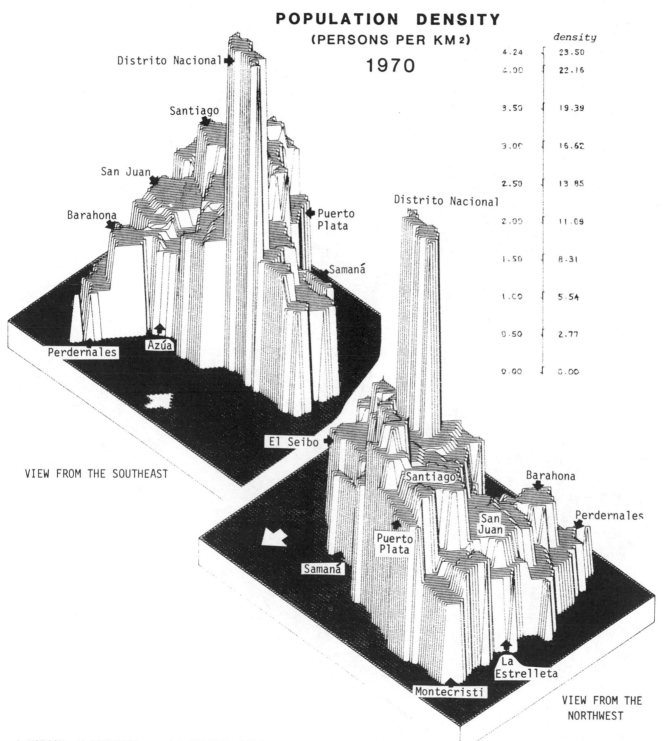

DOMINICAN REPUBLIC
POPULATION DENSITY
(PERSONS PER KM²)
1970

	density
4.24	23.50
4.00	22.16
3.50	19.39
3.00	16.62
2.50	13.85
2.00	11.09
1.50	8.31
1.00	5.54
0.50	2.77
0.00	0.00

Distrito Nacional

Santiago

San Juan

Barahona

Puerto Plata

Samaná

Perdernales

Azúa

El Seibo

VIEW FROM THE SOUTHEAST

Distrito Nacional

Santiago

Barahona

Perdernales

San Juan

Puerto Plata

Samaná

La Estrelleta

Montecristi

VIEW FROM THE NORTHWEST

S.MORGAN, M.RICHARDS, and R.WILKIE, 1980
Geography Cartographic Laboratory, University of Massachusetts, Amherst
using the SYMVU program from the Harvard Univ. Computer Graphics Center

Map 12-6

THREE-DIMENSIONAL CHOROPLETH MAP OF POPULATION
CHANGE IN THE DOMINICAN REPUBLIC, 1960–1970
(%)

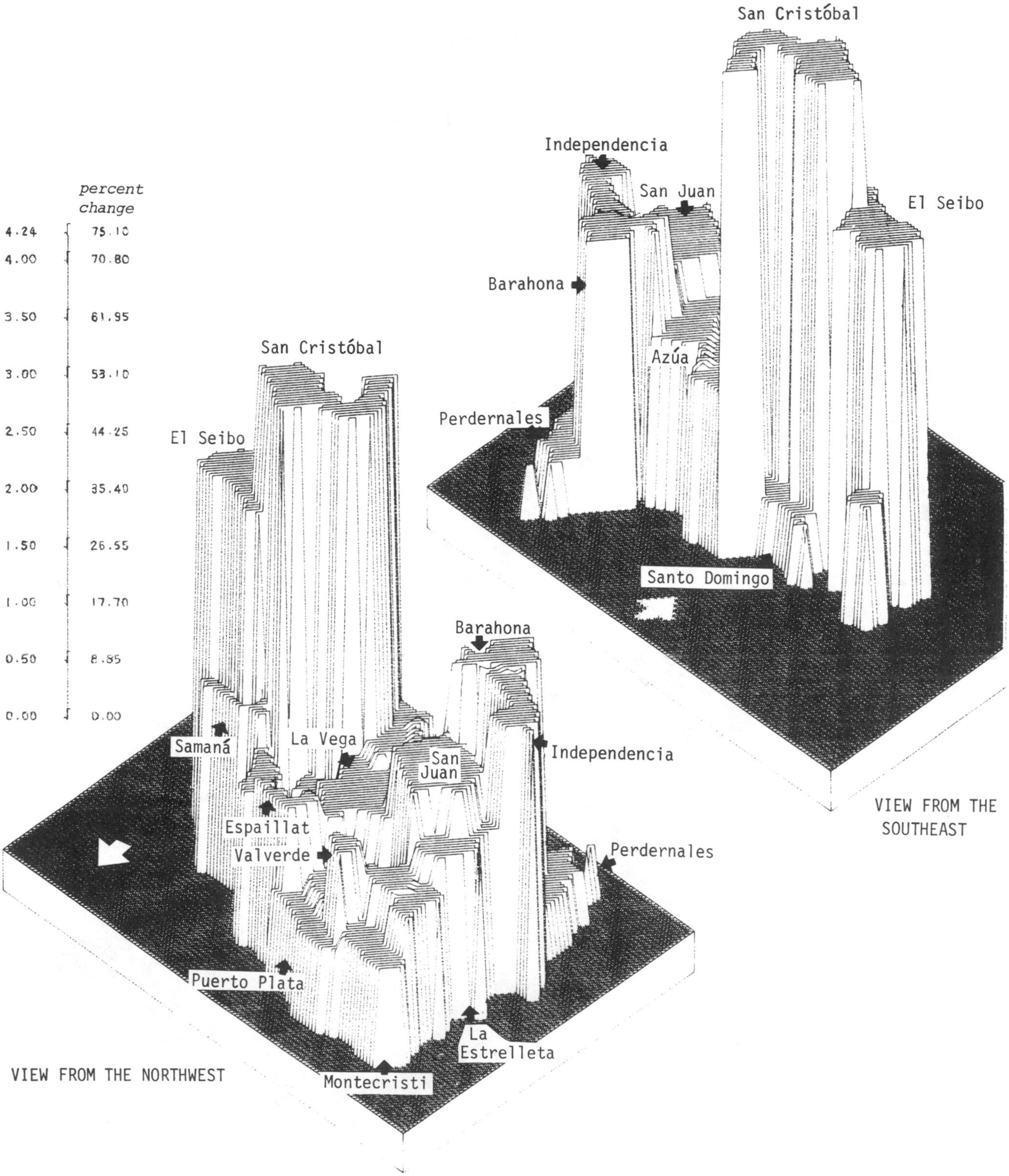

percent change	
4.24	75.10
4.00	70.80
3.50	61.95
3.00	53.10
2.50	44.25
2.00	35.40
1.50	26.55
1.00	17.70
0.50	8.85
0.00	0.00

San Cristóbal

Independencia

San Juan

Barahona

El Seibo

Azúa

Perdernales

Santo Domingo

VIEW FROM THE SOUTHEAST

San Cristóbal

El Seibo

Samaná   La Vega   San Juan   Independencia

Espaillat
Valverde   Perdernales

Puerto Plata

La Estrelleta

Barahona

VIEW FROM THE NORTHWEST

Montecristi

S.MORGAN, M.RICHARDS, and R.WILKIE, 1980
Geography Cartographic Laboratory, University of Massachusetts, Amherst
using the SYMVU program from the Harvard Univ. Computer Graphics Center

Photo 12-1

TWO-STORY WOODEN HOUSE CONSTRUCTION IN THE
CARIBBEAN REGION (1978)

Table 12-3

POPULATION FOR EACH NATIONAL CENSUS IN
THE DOMINICAN REPUBLIC, 1920–1981

Census Year	Population
1920	894,665
1935	1,479,417
1950	2,135,872
1960	3,047,070
1970	4,011,589[a]
1981	5,621,985

a. Recommended adjustment of population to 4,284,000 by
the U.S. Bureau of the Census (1978).

Table 12-4

TOTAL AND PERCENT POPULATION IN FIVE LEVELS OF THE URBAN-RURAL
SETTLEMENT HIERARCHY OF THE DOMINICAN REPUBLIC SINCE 1950

CENSUS YEAR	0 DISPERSED Population 1 to 99	1 VILLAGE 100 to 2,500	2 SIMPLE URBAN 2,501– 20,000	3 COMPLEX URBAN 20,001– 500,000	4 METROPOLITAN over 500,000	SETTLEMENT HIERARCHY Classification	PERCENT in top 2 levels
TOTAL							
1950	....	1,623,263	216,587	296,022	- -		
1960	....	2,132,949	238,401	675,720	- -		
1970	....	2,312,383	375,206	625,000	699,000		
1981	- -	- -	- -	- -	1,318,000		
PERCENT							
1950	....	76.0	10.1	13.9	- -	0–1	76.0
1960	....	70.0	7.8	22.2	- -	0–3	72 to 80
1970	....	57.6	9.4	15.6	17.4	0–4	60 to 70
1981	- -	- -	- -	- -	23.4	- -	- -

SOURCES: Calculated from the various Dominican Republic national censuses since 1950, and from SALA, 20–631, 632, 634, 635, 636, 637, and 638.

Table 12-5

SELECTED INDICATORS OF POPULATION CHANGE AND PER CAPITA GNP
IN THE DOMINICAN REPUBLIC

Years	Per 1000 Population		Rate of Natural Increase (Annual %)	Number of Years to Double Population	Percent Population Under Age 15	Life Expectancy at Birth	Per Capita GNP (US)
	Births	Deaths					
1940–45	35	11	2.6	- -	- -	- -	- -
1945–50	38	11	2.8	- -	- -	- -	- -
1950–55	44	9	3.0	- -	- -	- -	- -
1955–60	40	9	3.2	- -	- -	- -	205[a]
1960–65	47	9	3.3	- -	- -	58[b]	- -
1965–70	47	7	3.4	- -	- -	55	- -
1970–74	36	9	3.7	21[c]	47[c]	- -	260[c]
1975	36	11	3.3	21	48	58	470
1976	37	11	3.0	23	48	58	590
1977	37	11	3.5	20	48	58	720
1978	39	9	3.0	23	48	58	780
1979	37	9	2.8	25	48	58	840
1980	37	9	2.8	25	48	60	910
1981	37	9	2.8	25	45	60	990
1982	37	9	2.8	25	45	60	1,140

a. 1955.
b. 1960-1961.
c. 1970.

MAJOR SOURCES:

Births: SALA, 19-204; SALA, 20-705 through 1977.

Deaths: SALA, 18-703d and 706 through 1970.

Life expectancy: SALA, 19-700 through 1970.

Per capita GNP: 1955 data from Ginsburg, *Atlas of Economic Development* (Chicago: University of Chicago Press, 1961).

Rate of natural increase: SALA, 22-626 from CELADE-BD 10 (1972) through 1970.

All other data: Population Reference Bureau, Washington, D.C., annual world population data sheet.

Table 12-6

DOMINICAN REPUBLIC PROVINCES BY GEOGRAPHICAL
SIZE AND SUBDIVISION, 1970

Province	Civil Subdivisions (N)	Area km^2	%
Total	98[a]	48,442	100.0
Distrito Nacional	1	1,477	3.1
Provinces			
Azúa	2	2,430	5.0
Bahoruco	3	1,377	2.8
Barahona	5	2,528	5.2
Dajabón[1]	3	890	1.8
Duarte	5	1,292	2.7
El Seibo	5	2,989	6.2
Espaillat	4	974	2.0
Independencia	4	1,861	3.9
La Altagracia	2	3,166	6.5
La Estrelleta[2]	4	1,788	3.7
La Romana[3]	2	577	1.2
La Vega	4	3,442	7.1
María Trinidad Sánchez[4]	3	1,310	2.7
Montecristi	5	1,989	4.1
Perdernales	2	1,011	2.1
Peravia[5]	3	1,622	3.4
Puerto Plata	6	1,881	3.9
Salcedo	3	493	1.0
Samaná	2	989	2.0
San Cristóbal[6]	9	3,743	7.7
San Juan[7]	3	3,561	7.4
San Pedro de Macorís	3	1,166	2.4
Sánchez Ramírez	3	1,174	2.4
Santiago	7	3,112	6.4
Santiago Rodríguez	2	1,020	2.1
Valverde	3	580	1.2

1. Ex-provincia Libertador.
2. Ex-provincia San Rafael.
3. Ex-provincia Altagracia.
4. Ex-provincia Julia Molina.
5. Ex-provincia Trujillo Valdez.
6. Ex-provincia Trujillo.
7. Ex-provincia Benefactor.

a. Municipios.

SOURCE: SALA, 21-301.

Photo 12-2

COASTAL FISHERMEN (1967)

Map 13-1

PHYSIOGRAPHIC MAP OF ECUADOR

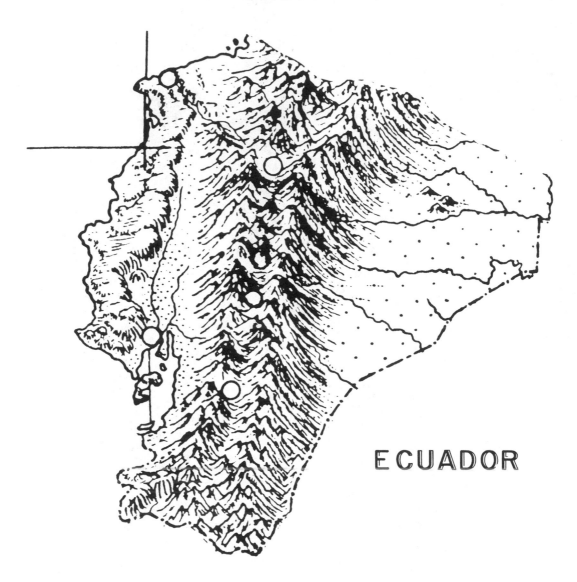

ECUADOR

GUY-HAROLD SMITH

13

Ecuador

Ecuador has had only three official censuses, and all three have been taken within the last thirty-three years. The first census (1950) counted 3,202,757 inhabitants. The number of Ecuadorians grew by 40 percent to 4,476,000 in 1962, and by 1974 the total had increased another 66 percent to 6,829,967. In 1982 the population of Ecuador was 8,072,702.

The population totals, trends, and characteristics of Ecuador are presented in six tables and six maps. Some of the findings concerning Ecuador are outlined below.

URBAN TRENDS

Ecuador has two metropolitan centers of over half a million inhabitants which dominate the urban hierarchy of the country. Guayaquil, the coastal port, is the largest city, with over a million people in 1978. Quito, the highland capital, has a quarter of a million less than Guayaquil, and dominates the north-south settlement hierarchy of the Andes. In 1974 thirteen complex-urban cities between 20,000 and 110,000 were either regional centers (10) or satellite cities (3), and they accounted for 11.3 percent of the nation's population. Even less developed is the simple urban level of small cities between 2,500 and 20,000 population, and fewer than one person in twenty (4.8 percent) live in communities of this size. Without further development in the smaller to intermediate-sized cities, the large rural population of the country will have little, if any, access to economic, social, and political services.

RURAL TRENDS

The percentage of rural population in Ecuador has gradually declined from 72 percent in 1950 to 62 percent in 1974, but in absolute terms the rural population has increased 75 percent from 2.3 million to more than 4 million inhabitants. Much of this rural population is dispersed on the settlement landscape and is relatively isolated from the larger urban centers of the nation.

SETTLEMENT HIERARCHY

In 1974 Ecuador could be classified as a dispersed-metropolitan (0–4) settlement landscape, with between two-thirds and three-fourths of all Ecuadorians living either dispersed in small clusters of population or in one of the two metropolitan centers of over half a million. The middle-sized communities in the urban-rural settlement hierarchy of cities were grossly underdeveloped.

OTHER DEMOGRAPHIC DATA

The annual rate of population growth in Ecuador rose to more than 3 percent a year in the late 1950s and has remained above that rate since then, reaching a peak of 3.4 percent during the 1960s. Life expectancy since 1970 has remained at sixty years, while 45 percent of the population of Ecuador has been under fifteen years of age since 1977. Per capita GNP in 1982 of $1,220 was up by 229 percent from $360 in 1975, ranking Ecuador number 11 among the twenty Latin American republics in that category.

Table 13-1

POPULATION DATA AND DENSITY BY PROVINCE IN ECUADOR, 1974 AND 1982

1974 Rank	Province	1974 Population	Population Density 1974 (km^2)	1982 Population	1982 Percent	Percent Change 1972-82	Population Density 1982 (km^2)
1	Guayas	1,594,345	85	2,016,819	25.0	+26.5	108
2	Pichincha	1,033,909	60	1,369,059	17.0	+32.4	80
3	Manabí	852,181	41	874,803	10.9	+2.7	42
4	Los Ríos	404,808	61	451,064	5.6	+11.4	68
5	Azuay	385,357	41	440,571	5.5	+14.3	47
6	Loja	361,641	30	358,558	4.4	-0.9	29
7	Chimborazo	332,632	52	329,922	4.1	-0.8	51
8	Tungurahua	290,990	83	328,070	4.1	+12.7	94
9	El Oro	274,238	42	335,630	4.2	+22.4	51
10	Cotopaxi	248,309	43	279,622	3.5	+12.6	48
11	Imbabura	229,548	40	244,421	3.0	+6.5	43
12	Esmeraldas	214,365	12	247,870	3.1	+15.6	14
13	Cañar	155,408	34	180,285	2.2	+16.0	40
14	Bolívar	154,313	39	148,161	1.8	-3.9	37
15	Carchi	126,742	29	128,113	1.6	+1.1	29
16	Napo	63,417	1	113,042	1.4	+78.3	2
17	Morona Santiago	54,381	2	67,094	.8	+23.4	3
18	Zamora Chinchipe	35,176	2	44,841	.6	+27.5	2
19	Pastaza	23,930	1	32,536	.4	+36.0	1
20	Archipielago de Colón	4,277	1	6,201	.1	+45.0	1
	Zones not delimited	- -	- -	- -	- -	- -	- -
	Total	6,829,967	24	8,053,280	100.0	+17.9	29

SOURCES: 1974 census: CONADE y Naciones Unidas, *Estructura Urbana-Regional del Ecuador (Último Informe)*, (Quito: Gobierno del Ecuador, June 1981), p. 11. 1982 Census (Nov. 28, 1982): Instituto Nacional de Estadística y Censos, *IV Censo de Población, 1982 (Resultados Provisionales)*, (Quito: INEC, Feb. 1983), pp. 1-4. Percent, percent change 1974-82, and population density figures were calculated by the author.

Table 13-2

MAJOR URBAN CENTERS IN ECUADOR, 1974 AND 1982

1982 Rank	Major Urban Centers	1982 Population	1982 Percent	1974 Population	Percent Change 1974–1982
1	Gran Guayaquil (1)	1,242,055	15.4	851,758	+46
	Guayaquil proper	1,175,276	14.6	814,064	+44
	Remainder of Guayaquil parroquias	5,087		2,360	+115
	Other parroquias				
	15. Eloy Alfaro (44,269)[a]	47,768		25,418	+88
	Pascuales	13,924		9,916	+40
2	Gran Quito (2)	1,049,165	13.0	724,893	+45
	Quito proper	858,736	10.7	597,133	+44
	Remainder of Quito parroquia	22,678		24,978	−9
	Other parroquias				
	Alangasí	7,507		4,798	+56
	Amaguaña	16,262		12,147	+34
	Calderón	18,037		12,998	+39
	Conocoto	19,614		11,763	+67
	Cumbayá	10,236		4,276	+134
	Guangopolo	1,627		1,263	+29
	La Merced	3,538		2,477	+43
	Llano Chico	3,377		2,672	+26
	Lloa	1,411		1,434	−2
	Nayón	4,627		3,190	+45
	P.V. Maldonado	15,306		- -	- -
	Pomasqui	7,748		5,664	+37
	San Antonio	8,196		5,234	+57
	Tumbaco	17,034		10,820	+57
	Zámbiza	2,668		1,753	+52
	Parroquias in Canton Sangolquí				
	33. Sangolquí (14,523)	22,034		15,927	+38
	S. Pedro de'Taboada	4,030		2,703	+49
	San Rafael	4,499		2,563	+76
	Total Metropolitan	2,291,220	28.4	1,576,651	+45
3	Cuenca (5)	150,902	1.9	104,667	+44
4	Machala (9)	105,283	1.3	69,235	+52
5	Portoviejo (3)	101,771[b]	1.3	59,404	+71
6	Ambato (8)	100,605	1.2	77,052	+31
7	Manta (3)	98,827	1.2	63,514	+56
8	Esmeraldas (12)	90,078	1.1	60,132	+50
9	Milagro (1)	76,237	.9	53,058	+44
10	Riobamba (7)	72,217	.9	58,029	+24
11	Loja (7)	71,130	.9	47,268	+50
12	Santo Domingo de Los Colorados (2)	66,661	.8	30,487	+119
13	Quevedo (4)	66,311	.8	43,123	+54
14	Ibarra (11)	52,808	.7	53,965	−2
15	Eloy Alfaro (1)	- -	- -	- -	- -
16	Babahoyo (4)	42,958	.5	28,345	+52
17	La Libertad (1)	40,331[c]	.5	25,069	+61

Table 13-2 (Continued)

MAJOR URBAN CENTERS IN ECUADOR, 1974 AND 1982

1982 Rank	Major Urban Centers	1982 Population	1982 Percent	1974 Population	Percent Change 1974–1982
18	Chone (3)	33,640	.4	23,618	+42
19	Tulcán (15)	31,143	.4	24,443	+27
20	Latacunga (10)	28,857	.4	22,106	+31
21	Santa Rosa (9)	27,239	.3	18,848	+45
22	Jipijapa (3)	26,872	.3	19,644	+37
23	Pasaje (9)	26,773	.3	20,822	+29
24	Huaquillas (9)	20,036	.2	9,164	+119
	Total population between 20,000 and 500,000	1,297,039	16.1	864,335(12.75%)	+50
25	Daule (1)	18,895		13,014	+45
26	Otavalo (11)	17,479		13,544	+29
27	Balzar (1)	17,438		11,144	+56
28	Salinas (Sta.Rosa) (1)	17,150		12,243	+40
29	Velasco Ibarra (1)	16,505		11,818	+40
30	Ventanas (3)	15,835		8,890	+78
31	Vinces (4)	14,851		9,717	+53
32	Azoguez (13)	14,542		10,939	+33
33	Sangolquí (2)[d]	- -		- -	- -
34	Cayambe (2)	14,168		11,042	+28
35	Guaranda (14)	13,610		11,387	+20
36	Atuntaqui (A.Ante) (11)	13,273		9,862	+35
37	Santa Elena (1)	12,607		7,762	+62
38	Bahía de Caráquez (Sucre) (3)	12,335		11,327	+9
39	El Carmen (3)	11,928		7,200	+66
40	Pedro Carbo (1)	11,848		5,728	+107
41	S. Gabriel (Montúfar) (15)	11,203		10,578	+6
42	Rosa Zárate (12)	10,697		4,835	+121
43	Cañar (13)	10,541		6,728	+56
44	Naranjito (1)	10,541		6,246	+69
45	Nacará (6)	10,115		8,060	+25
46	Calceta (3)	10,046		7,299	+38
	Total population between 10,000 and 20,000	285,606(3.5%)		164,690(2.4%)	+73

a. City population of Eloy Alfaro (Alfaro Durán) is estimated by the author to be 44,269, based on the 1974 figure of 92.7% of the population of the parroquia.
b. Includes Picoaza (4,006 in 1974) and Colón (811 in 1974).
c. City population of La Libertad is estimated by the author to be 40,331, based on the 1974 figure of 96.1% of the population of the parroquia.
d. See Gran Quito.

Photo 13-1

RESIDENTIAL AREA OF QUITO, ECUADOR

Map 13-2

BASE MAP OF PROVINCES IN ECUADOR AND LOCATION OF MAJOR URBAN CENTERS

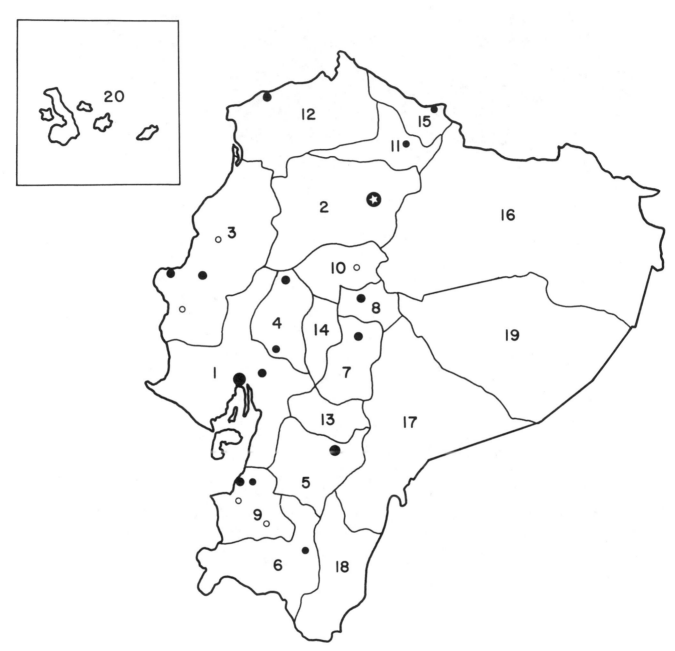

Note: Province numbers are rank ordered according to population data listed in Table 13-1.

Map 13-3

POPULATION CARTOGRAM OF ECUADOR, 1974

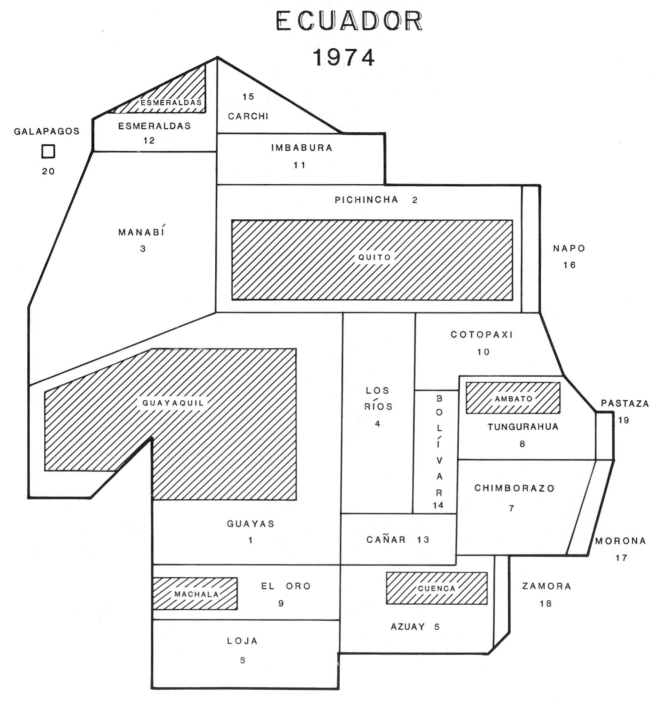

ECUADOR
1974

CITIES SHOWN ARE OVER
60,000 POPULATION

= 100,000 POPULATION

= 5,000 POPULATION

P.SERAFINO and W.R.ALCOTT
Geography Cartographic Laboratory
Univ. of Massachusetts, Amherst

Map 13-4

**THREE-DIMENSIONAL CHOROPLETH MAP OF TOTAL POPULATION
BY PROVINCE IN ECUADOR, 1975
(By Major Civil Division)**

ECUADOR
TOTAL POPULATION
(BY MAJOR CIVIL DIVISION)
1974

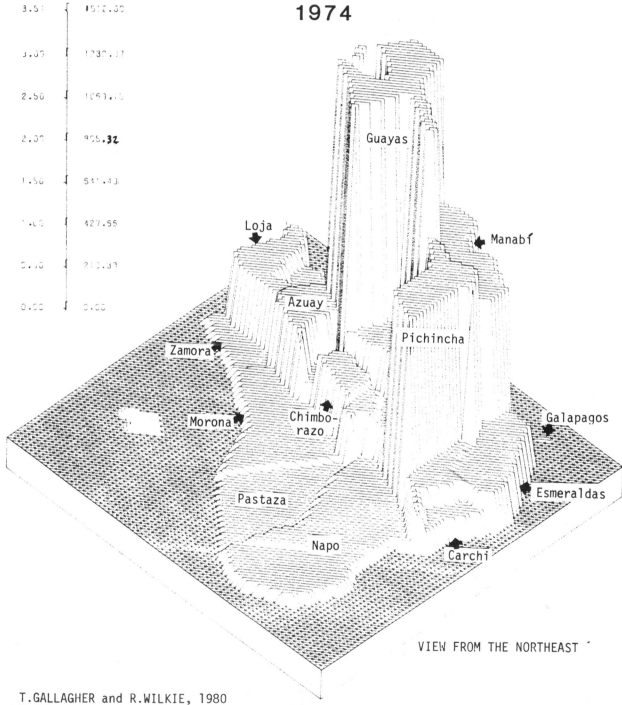

T.GALLAGHER and R.WILKIE, 1980
Geography Cartographic Laboratory, University of Massachusetts, Amherst
using the SYMVU program from the Harvard Univ. Center for Computer Graphics

Map 13-5

**THREE-DIMENSIONAL CHOROPLETH MAP OF POPULATION DENSITY
IN ECUADOR, 1974
(Persons per km²)**

ECUADOR
POPULATION DENSITY
(PERSONS PER KM²)
1974

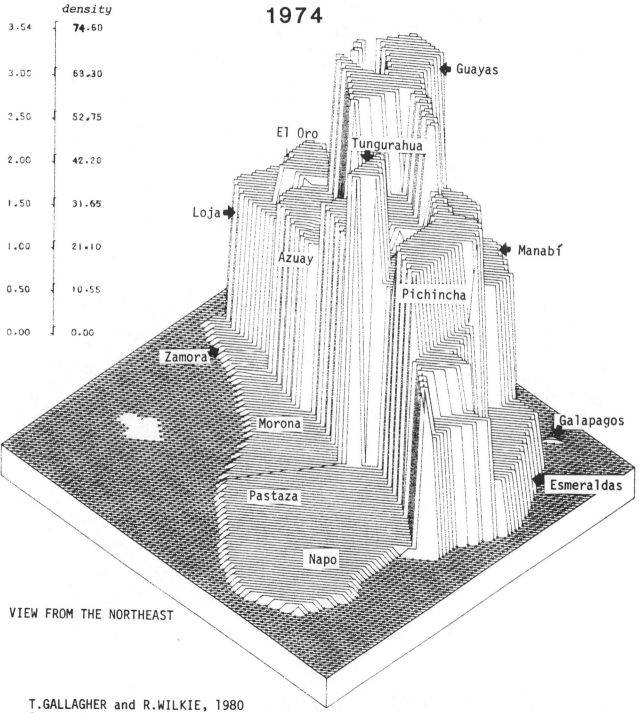

VIEW FROM THE NORTHEAST

T.GALLAGHER and R.WILKIE, 1980
Geography Cartographic Laboratory, University of Massachusetts, Amherst
using the SYMVU program from the Harvard Univ. Center for Computer Graphics

Map 13-6

**THREE-DIMENSIONAL CHOROPLETH MAP OF POPULATION CHANGE
IN ECUADOR, 1962–1974
(%)**

ECUADOR
POPULATION CHANGE
(BY PERCENT)
1962 TO 1974

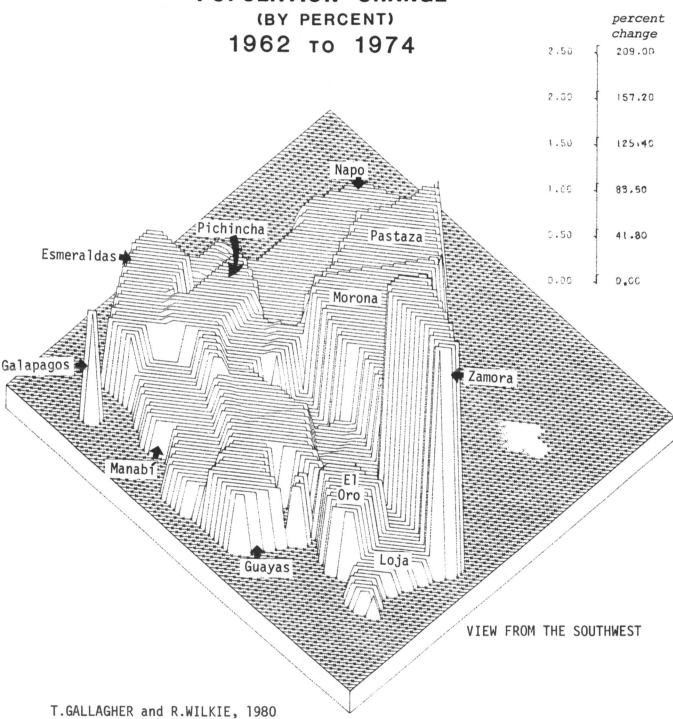

percent
change

2.50	209.00
2.00	157.20
1.50	125.40
1.00	83.50
0.50	41.80
0.00	0.00

VIEW FROM THE SOUTHWEST

T.GALLAGHER and R.WILKIE, 1980
Geography Cartographic Laboratory, University of Massachusett, Amherst
using the SYMVU program from the Harvard Univ. Center for Computer Graphics

Photo 13-2

ATTENDING A FIREWORKS FESTIVAL

Table 13-3

POPULATION FOR EACH NATIONAL CENSUS IN ECUADOR, 1950–1974

Census Year	Population
1950	3,202,757
1962	4,476,000
1974	6,500,845[a]
1982	8,072,702

a. Recommended adjustment of population to 6,686,000 by the U.S. Bureau of the Census (1978)

Table 13-4

TOTAL AND PERCENT POPULATION IN FIVE LEVELS OF THE URBAN-RURAL SETTLEMENT HIERARCHY OF ECUADOR SINCE 1950

CENSUS YEAR	0 DISPERSED Population 1 to 99	1 VILLAGE 100 to 2,500	2 SIMPLE URBAN 2,501– 20,000	3 COMPLEX URBAN 20,001– 500,000	4 METROPOLITAN over 500,000	SETTLEMENT HIERARCHY Classification	PERCENT in top 2 levels
TOTAL							
1950	. . . . 2,305,985		326,749	570,023	- -		
1962	. . . . 2,932,145		397,518	741,028	510,785		
1974	. . . . 3,782,174		562,601	919,755	1,565,437		
1982	. . . . 3,676,606		770,950	1,348,136	2,277,010		
PERCENT							
1950	. . . . 72.0		10.2	17.8	- -	0–3	73 to 80
1962	. . . . 64.0		8.7	16.2	11.1	0–3	65 to 75
1974	. . . . 55.4		8.2	13.5	22.9	0–4	68 to 74
1982	. . . . 45.5		9.6	16.7	28.2	0–4	65 to 73

SOURCE: Calculated from the various Ecuadorian national censuses since 1950, and from SALA, 20–631, 632, 634, 635, 636, 637, and 638.

Table 13-5

SELECTED INDICATORS OF POPULATION CHANGE AND PER CAPITA GNP IN ECUADOR

Years	Per 1000 Population		Rate of Natural Increase (Annual %)	Number of Years to Double Population)	Percent Population Under Age 15	Life Expectancy at Birth	Per Capita GNP (US)
	Births	Deaths					
1940–45	46	21	2.1	- -	- -	- -	- -
1945–50	46	19	2.4	- -	- -	- -	- -
1950–55	45	16	2.8	- -	- -	- -	204[a]
1955–60	46	15	3.1	- -	- -	- -	- -
1960–65	45	14	3.4	- -	- -	52[b]	- -
1965–70	45	11	3.4	- -	- -	- -	- -
1970–74	42	11	3.1	21[c]	48[c]	- -	210[c]
1975	42	10	3.2	22	46	60	360
1976	42	10	3.2	22	47	60	460
1977	42	10	3.2	22	45	60	550
1978	40	9	3.2	22	45	60	640
1979	42	10	3.1	22	44	60	770
1980	42	10	3.1	22	44	60	910
1981	42	10	3.1	22	45	60	1,050
1982	42	10	3.1	22	45	60	1,220

a. 1955.
b. 1961–1963.
c. 1970

MAJOR SOURCES:
   Births: SALA, 19-204; SALA, 20-705 through 1975.
   Deaths: SALA, 18-703d and 706 through 1970.
   Life expectancy: SALA, 19-700 through 1970.
   Per capita GNP: 1955 data from Ginsburg, *Atlas of Economic Development* (Chicago: University of Chicago Press, 1961).
   Rate of natural increase: SALA, 22-626 from CELADE-BD 10 (1972) through 1970.
   All other data: Population Reference Bureau, Washington, D.C., annual world population data sheets.

Table 13-6

ECUADORIAN PROVINCES BY GEOGRAPHICAL
SIZE AND SUBDIVISION, 1981

Province	Civil Subdivisions (N)	Area km^2	Area %
Total	126[a]	281,334	100.0
Provinces			
Archipiélago de Colón	3	8,006	2.9
Azuay	6	9,323	3.3
Bolívar	4	3,983	1.4
Cañar	3	4,514	1.6
Carchi	4	4,411	1.6
Cotopaxi	5	5,834	2.1
Chimborazo	6	6,414	2.3
El Oro	9	6,522	2.3
Esmeraldas	5	17,807	6.3
Guayas	12	18,711	6.7
Imbabura	5	5,669	2.0
Loja	12	12,192	4.3
Los Ríos	7	6,668	2.4
Manabí	13	20,669	7.3
Morona-Santiago	6	25,423	9.0
Napo	8	51,798	18.4
Pastaza	2	32,008	11.4
Pichincha	6	17,090	6.1
Tungurahua	6	3,493	1.2
Zamora Chinchipe	4	20,799	7.4

a. Cantones.

SOURCE: Civil Subdivisions: Instituto Nacional de Estadística y Censos, División Político-Administrativa de la República del Ecuador, 1981, p. 3.

Area: United Nations, *Estructuración Urbana Regional del Ecuador* (New York: United Nations, 1981), p. 11.

Photo 13-3
CENTRAL RESIDENTIAL BLOCK, QUITO, ECUADOR (1983)

Photo 13-4
CENTRAL COMMERCIAL BLOCK, QUITO, ECUADOR (1983)

Map 14-1

PHYSIOGRAPHIC MAP OF EL SALVADOR

ERWIN RAISZ

14

El Salvador

El Salvador has had only four official censuses in the fifty-three years since 1930. Between the first census and the fourth census (1971) the population rose one and a half times from 1,434,000 to approximately 3,600,000. In 1980 the population was estimated by the Latin American Economic Commission to be 4,524,000, 1.3 percent of the population of Latin America.

The population totals, trends, and characteristics of El Salvador are presented in six tables and six maps. Some of the findings concerning El Salvador are outlined below.

URBAN TRENDS

The only metropolitan center with over half a million population in 1971 was Greater San Salvador with 565,000 inhabitants (16 percent of the national total). There were only five complex urban centers with more than 20,000 population at that time, including Santa Ana (98,400), San Miguel (61,900), and Sonsonate (33,300). These five cities together only had 234,000 population, making the complex urban level with only 6.6 percent on the nation's population the least developed in the urban-rural hierarchy of places. Simple urban centers between 2,500 and 20,000 population had 586,000 for 16.5 percent of the national population.

RURAL TRENDS

More than three out of every five Salvadorans lived in rural areas in 1971. The percentage of the rural popula-

tion dropped from 72 percent in 1950 to 59 percent in 1961, before rising to 61 percent in 1971. In real terms, however, the rural population has grown 61 percent from 1,342,000 in 1950 to 2,165,000 in 1971.

SETTLEMENT HIERARCHY

El Salvador could be classified as a dispersed−simple urban (0−2) settlement landscape in both 1961 and 1971, with nearly two-thirds of the inhabitants living either dispersed on the landscape in units under 100 population or in simple urban centers between 2,000 and 20,000 in size. Population density of 170 persons per square kilometer in 1971 was the highest in Latin America.

OTHER DEMOGRAPHIC DATA

The annual rate of population growth in El Salvador has been extremely high since the early 1950s. Between 1960 and 1981 the rate exceeded 3 percent, peaking at 3.4 percent twice (during the late 1960s and 1979). In 1982 the rate had declined slightly to 2.7 percent. Life expectancy was sixty-two years, and 46 percent of the population was under fifteen years of age in 1982. Per capita GNP was up by only 74 percent from $340 in 1975 to $590 in 1982, ranking El Salvador number 17 among the twenty Latin American republics in that category.

Table 14-1

POPULATION DATA AND DENSITY BY DEPARTMENT IN EL SALVADOR, 1971[a]

Rank	Department	Population	Percent	Percent Change 1961-1971	Population Density 1971 (km^2)
1	San Salvador	731,679	20.6	+58.0	843
2	Santa Ana	332,958	9.4	+28.5	163
3	San Miguel	323,039	9.1	+39.3	151
4	Usulután	293,292	8.3	+41.6	138
5	La Libertad	282,762	8.0	+39.0	172
6	Sonsonate	233,604	6.6	+39.9	168
7	La Unión	220,014	6.2	+48.5	89
8	La Paz	184,420	5.2	+41.1	153
9	Ahuachapán	179,820	5.1	+37.6	153
10	Chalatenango	172,075	4.8	+32.5	114
11	Morazán	157,971	4.5	+32.3	114
12	San Vicente	156,224	4.4	+38.3	130
13	Cuscatlán	152,203	4.3	+34.6	206
14	Cabañas	129,199	3.6	+36.6	126
	Total	3,549,260	100.0	+41.3	170

a. The U.S. Bureau of the Census (1978) estimated a 3.6 net underenumeration, for a recommended adjustment to 3,687,000 inhabitants. In addition, they estimated the population on July 1, 1979, to be 4,662,000 (1981).

SOURCES: Census of June 28, 1971; SALA 20-626.

Table 14-2

MAJOR URBAN CENTERS IN EL SALVADOR, 1971

Rank	Major Urban Centers	Population	Percent
1	✪ Gran San Salvador (1)	565,000	15.9
	San Salvador proper	335,930	9.5
	● Mejicanos	55,000	
	● Villa Delgado	44,000	
	● Nueva San Salvador/Antiguo Cuscatlán (5)	41,400	
	San Marcos	23,000	
	Soyapango	22,000	
	Ilopango	19,000	
	Cuscatancingo	19,000	
	Ayutuxtepeque	6,000	
2	● Santa Ana (2)	98,400	2.8
3	San Miguel (3)	61,900	1.7
4	● Sonsonate (6)	33,300	.9
5	Cojutepeque (13)	20,000	.6
6	Usulután (4)	20,000	.6
			22.5
7	○ Chalchuapa (2)	18,900	
8	San Vicente (12)	18,500	
9	La Unión (7)	17,200	
10	Zacatecoluca (8)	16,800	
11	Ahuachapán (9)	16,300	
12	Quezaltepeque (5)	12,600	
13	Ajautla (6)	10,300	

SOURCE: Census of June 28, 1971; Robert Fox and Jerrold Huguet, *Population and Urban Trends in Central America and Panama* (Washington, D.C.: Inter-American Development Bank, 1977), p. 100.

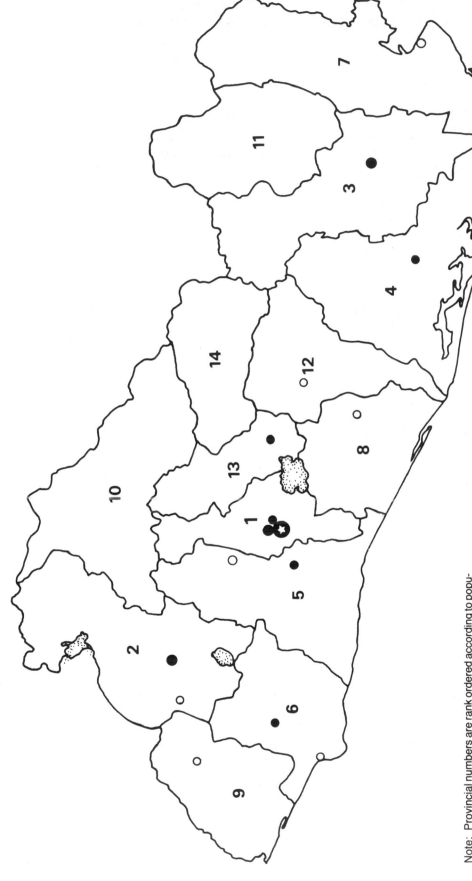

Map 14-2

BASE MAP OF DEPARTMENTS IN EL SALVADOR AND
LOCATION OF MAJOR URBAN CENTERS

Note: Provincial numbers are rank ordered according to population data listed in Table 14-1.

Map 14-3

POPULATION CARTOGRAM OF EL SALVADOR, 1971

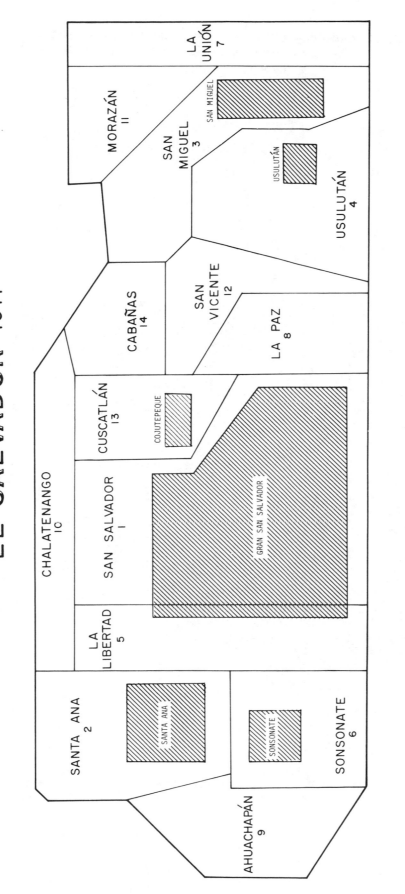

EL SALVADOR 1971

L.R.WARREN and R.WILKIE
Geography Cartographic Laboratory
University of Massachusetts, Amherst

Map 14-4

**THREE-DIMENSIONAL CHOROPLETH MAP OF TOTAL POPULATION
BY DEPARTMENT IN EL SALVADOR, 1971
(By Major Civil Division)**

EL SALVADOR
TOTAL POPULATION
(BY MAJOR CIVIL DIVISION)
1971

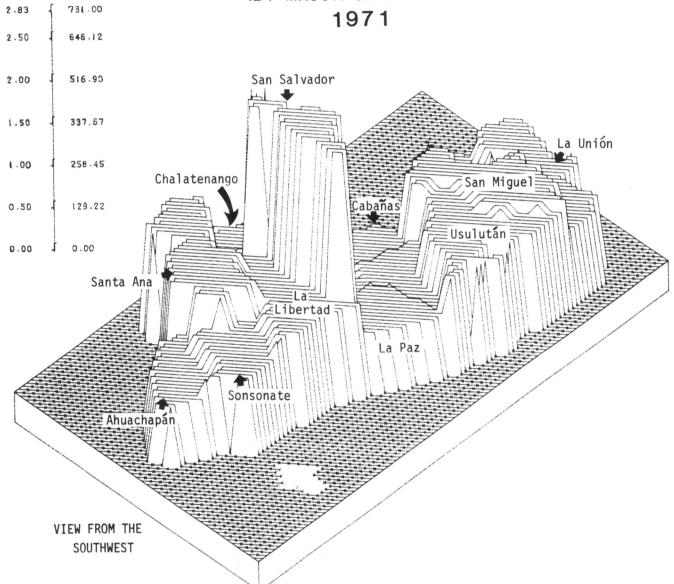

2.83	731.00
2.50	646.12
2.00	516.90
1.50	337.67
1.00	258.45
0.50	129.22
0.00	0.00

San Salvador

La Unión

Chalatenango

San Miguel

Cabañas

Usulután

Santa Ana

La Libertad

La Paz

Sonsonate

Ahuachapán

VIEW FROM THE
SOUTHWEST

T.GALLAGHER and R.WILKIE, 1980
Geography Cartographic Laboratory, University of Massachusetts, Amherst
using the SYMVU program from the Harvard Univ. Center for Computer Graphics

Map 14-5

**THREE-DIMENSIONAL CHOROPLETH MAP OF POPULATION DENSITY
IN EL SALVADOR, 1971
(Persons per km²)**

EL SALVADOR
POPULATION DENSITY
(PERSONS PER KM²)
1971

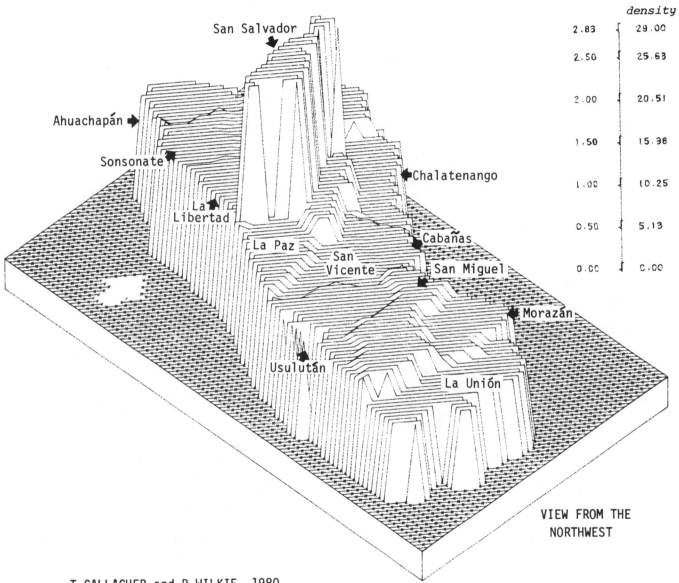

	density
2.83	29.00
2.50	25.63
2.00	20.51
1.50	15.38
1.00	10.25
0.50	5.13
0.00	0.00

VIEW FROM THE
NORTHWEST

T.GALLAGHER and R.WILKIE, 1980
Geography Cartographic Laboratory, University of Massachusetts, Amherst
using the SYMVU program from the Harvard Univ. Center for Computer Graphics

Map 14-6

**THREE-DIMENSIONAL CHOROPLETH MAP OF POPULATION CHANGE
IN EL SALVADOR, 1961−1971
(%)**

EL SALVADOR
POPULATION CHANGE
(BY PERCENT)
1961 TO 1971

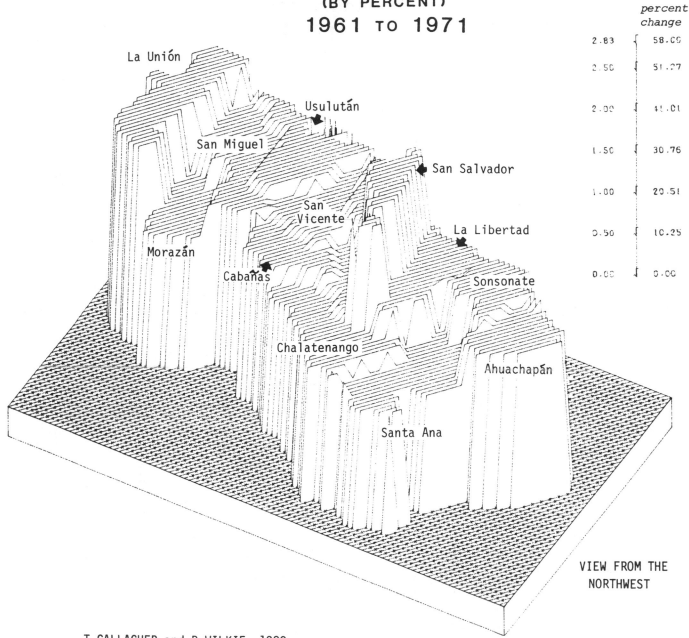

*percent
change*

2.83	58.09
2.50	51.27
2.00	41.01
1.50	30.76
1.00	20.51
0.50	10.25
0.00	0.00

La Unión
Usulután
San Miguel
San Salvador
San Vicente
La Libertad
Morazán
Cabañas
Sonsonate
Chalatenango
Ahuachapán
Santa Ana

VIEW FROM THE
NORTHWEST

T.GALLAGHER and R.WILKIE, 1980
Geography Cartographic Laboratory, University of Massachusetts, Amherst
using the SYMVU program from the Harvard Univ. Computer Graphics Center

Table 14-3

POPULATION FOR EACH NATIONAL CENSUS IN EL SALVADOR, 1930–1971

Census Year	Population
1930	1,434,361
1950	1,855,917
1961	2,510,984
1971	3,549,260[a]

a. Recommended adjustment of population to 3,687,000 by the U.S. Bureau of the Census (1978).

Table 14-4

TOTAL AND PERCENT POPULATION IN FIVE LEVELS OF THE URBAN-RURAL SETTLEMENT HIERARCHY OF EL SALVADOR SINCE 1950

	0	1	2	3	4	SETTLEMENT HIERARCHY	
CENSUS YEAR	DISPERSED Population 1 to 99	VILLAGE 100 to 2,500	SIMPLE URBAN 2,501– 20,000	COMPLEX URBAN 20,001– 500,000	METROPOLITAN over 500,000	Classification	PERCENT in top 2 levels
TOTALS							
1950	.... 1,341,562		274,000	240,355	- -		
1961	.... 1,491,418		535,887	483,679	- -		
1971	.... 2,165,049		585,611	233,600	565,000		
PERCENT							
1950	.... 72.2		14.8	13.0	- -	0–1	72.2
1961	.... 59.4		21.3	19.3	- -	0–2	61 to 65
1971	.... 61.0		16.5	6.6	15.9	0–2	61 to 65

SOURCE: The data were reorganized and calculated from the various El Salvadoran national censuses since 1950, and from SALA, 20-631, 632, 634, 635, 636, 637, and 638.

Table 14-5

SELECTED INDICATORS OF POPULATION CHANGE AND PER CAPITA GNP IN EL SALVADOR

Years	Per 1000 Population		Rate of Natural Increase (Annual %)	Number of Years to Double Population	Percent Population Under Age 15	Life Expectancy at Birth	Per Capita GNP (US)
	Births	Deaths					
1940–45	43	21	1.2	- -	- -	- -	- -
1945–50	44	17	2.1	- -	- -	- -	- -
1950–55	49	15	2.5	- -	- -	- -	244[a]
1955–60	49	14	2.9	- -	- -	- -	- -
1960–65	48	11	3.0	- -	- -	58[b]	- -
1965–70	44	·10	3.4	- -	- -	- -	- -
1970–74	40	9	3.3	21[c]	45[c]	- -	270[c]
1975	40	11	3.1	22	46	58	340
1976	40	8	3.2	22	46	58	390
1977	42	8	3.2	22	46	58	450
1978	40	8	3.3	21	46	58	490
1979	42	8	3.4	20	46	59	570
1980	40	7	3.3	21	46	62	600
1981	39	7	3.2	22	45	63	670
1982	35	8	2.7	26	46	62	590

a. 1955.
b. 1960–1961.
c. 1970.

MAJOR SOURCES:
   Births: SALA, 19-204; SALA, 20-705 through 1977.
   Deaths: SALA, 18-703d and 706 through 1970.
   Life expectancy: SALA, 19-700 through 1970.
   Per capita GNP: 1955 data from Ginsburg, *Atlas of Economic Development* (Chicago: University of Chicago Press, 1961).
   Rate of natural increase: SALA, 22-626 from CELADE-BD 10 (1972) through 1970.
   All other data: Population Reference Bureau, Washington, D.C., annual world population data sheets.

Table 14-6

EL SALVADOR DEPARTMENTS BY GEOGRAPHICAL
SIZE AND SUBDIVISION, 1969

Department	Civil Subdivisions (N)	Area km^2	%
Total	261[a]	20,935	100.0
Departments			
Ahuachapán	12	1,181	5.6
Cabañas	9	1,028	4.9
Cuscatlán	16	740	3.5
Chalatenango	33	1,511	7.2
La Libertad	22	1,643	7.8
La Paz	21	1,207	5.8
La Unión	18	2,478	11.8
Morazán	26	1,388	6.6
San Miguel	20	2,133	10.2
San Salvador	19	868	4.1
San Vicente	13	1,204	5.8
Santa Ana	13	2,043	9.8
Sonsonate	16	1,388	6.6
Usulután	23	2,123	10.1

a. Municipios.

SOURCE: SALA, 21-301.

Map 15-1

PHYSIOGRAPHIC MAP OF GUATEMALA

ERWIN RAISZ

15

Guatemala

Guatemala has had nine official censuses over a 103-year period. The first census (1880) counted 1,224,602 inhabitants. It took until the 1940s for the population to double, and by the fifth census (1950) the population of Guatemala was 2,790,686. The last census (1973) documented a rise of 87 percent to 5,212,000. Problems of underenumeration exist in Guatemala, however, and the Dirección General de Estadística adjusted that total to 5,879,000 (up 111 percent). In 1980 the population was estimated by the Latin American Economic Commission to be 6,839,000 inhabitants.

   The population totals, trends, and characteristics of Guatemala are presented in six tables and six maps. Some of the findings concerning Guatemala are outlined below.

URBAN TRENDS

Greater Guatemala City in 1973, with just under 1 million population representing 17 percent of the nation's total, was the only metropolitan center with over half a million population. Only five other cities in Guatemala were over 20,000 population in the complex urban classification, and together they only had 3.1 percent of Guatemala's inhabitants. Quezaltenango (55,200) and Escuintla (43,400) rank as the second and third largest cities in the nation.

RURAL TRENDS

The percentage of the population living in rural areas was still an overwhelming 60 percent in 1973, after gradually declining from 75 percent in 1950. In real terms, the number of rural inhabitants increased by 1.5 million in those twenty-three years to 3,528,000 individuals.

SETTLEMENT HIERARCHY

Guatemala could be classified as a dispersed–simple urban (0–2) settlement landscape in both 1964 and 1973, with more than two-thirds of all Guatemalans living in those two levels in the urban-rural hierarchy. The greatest weakness in the hierarchy of cities in Guatemala is the almost total lack of complex urban centers.

OTHER DEMOGRAPHIC DATA

The annual rate of population growth in Guatemala has remained over 3 percent for all but brief periods since the 1940s. Life expectancy in 1982 was fifty-eight years, and 45 percent of the population was under fifteen years of age. Per capita GNP in 1982 of $1,110 was up 164 percent from $420 in 1975, ranking Guatemala number 14 among the twenty Latin American republics in that category.

Table 15-1

POPULATION DATA AND DENSITY BY DEPARTMENT IN GUATEMALA, 1973 AND 1981[a]

1973 Rank	Department	1981 Population	Percent	1973 Population	Percent Change 1973-81	Percent Change 1964-73	Population Density 1981 (km^2)
1.	Guatemala	1,307,340	21.6	1,127,845	+15.9	+38.6	615
2.	San Marcos	470,985	7.8	388,100	+21.4	+16.8	124
3.	Huehuetenango	429,460	7.1	368,807	+16.4	+28.5	58
4.	Quezaltenango	364,641	6.1	311,613	+17.0	+15.9	187
5.	Quiché	326,188	5.4	300,641	+8.5	+21.3	39
6.	Escuintla	332,551	5.5	300,140	+10.8	+11.2	76
7.	Alta Verapaz	322,132	5.3	276,370	+16.6	+6.3	37
8.	Jutiapa	251,642	4.2	231,005	+8.9	+16.1	78
9.	Suchitepéquez	237,472	3.9	212,017	+12.0	+13.8	95
10.	Chimaltenango	230,724	3.8	193,557	+19.2	+18.2	117
11.	Santa Rosa	200,845	3.3	176,198	+14.0	+13.8	68
12.	Izabal	193,972	3.2	170,864	+13.5	+49.4	21
13.	Totonicapán	203,545	3.4	166,622	+22.2	+19.3	192
14.	Chiquimula	169,428	2.8	158,146	+7.1	+4.6	71
15.	Retalhuleu	150,105	2.5	133,993	+12.0	+9.1	81
16.	Sololá	153,874	2.6	126,884	+21.3	+16.6	145
17.	Jalapa	135,366	2.2	118,103	+14.6	+20.5	66
18.	Baja Verapaz	115,206	1.9	106,909	+7.8	+11.8	37
19.	Zacapa	115,818	1.9	106,726	+8.5	+11.2	43
20.	Sacatepéquez	120,060	2.0	99,710	+20.4	+23.9	258
21.	El Progreso	81,121	1.3	73,176	+10.9	+9.7	42
22.	Petén	131,084	2.2	64,503	+103.2	+141.4	4
	Total	6,043,559	100.0	5,211,929	+16.0	+21.6	56

a. The Dirección General de Estadística in Guatemala estimated for 1973 an underenumeration of 2.8 percent in urban areas and 4.1 percent in rural areas, for an adjusted total of 5,879,700. The U.S. Bureau of the Census (1978) estimated the net underenumeration at 9.5 percent, for a total in 1973 of 5,699,000. In addition, they estimated the population on July 1, 1979, to be 6,849,000.

SOURCES: Censuses of 1973 and 1981; SALA 20-626.

Table 15-2

MAJOR URBAN CENTERS IN GUATEMALA, 1973

Rank	Major Urban Centers	Census of March 26, 1973			
		Enumerated Population	Percent	Adjusted Population[1]	Percent
1	✪ Gran Guatemala City (1)	979,430	18.8	989,100	16.8
	● Guatemala City proper	717,322	13.8		
	● Mixco	129,627	2.5		
	Villa Nueva	42,045	.8		
	Amatitlán	26,436	.5		
	Chinautla	24,682	.5		
	Sta. Catarina Pinula	12,968	.2		
	Villa Canales	9,557	.2		
	Petapa	8,067	.2		
	San Pedro Sacatepéquez	4,920	.1		
	San José Pinula	3,806	.1		
2	● Quezaltenango (4)	46,000	.9	55,200	.9
3	● Escuintla (6)	37,200	.7	43,400	.7
4	Mazatenango (9)	24,200	.5	29,100	.5
5	Retalhuleu (15)	20,200	.4	23,400	.4
6	Puerto Barrios (12)	20,000	.4	29,400	.5
			21.6		19.9
7	○ Antigua Guatemala (20)	17,994		19,600	
8	San Pedro Sacatepequez/San Marcos (2)	16,700		19,800	
9	Chiquimula (14)	16,126		19,600	
10	Coatepéque (4)	15,900		19,100	
11	Sta. Lucía Cotzumalguapa (6)	13,900		16,300	
12	Jalapa (17)	13,800		15,900	
13	Chimaltenango (10)	13,100		14,900	
14	Zacapa (19)	12,700		16,800	
15	Huehuetenango (3)	12,570		14,100	
16	Cobán (7)	11,900		14,700	
17	Santiago Atitlán (16)	11,416		14,800	
18	Tiquisate (6)	10,800		12,600	
19	Jutiapa (8)	10,100		13,400	
20	San José (6)	10,100		11,800	
	National Total	5,211,929		5,879,700[a]	

1. Adjusted for underenumeration by the Dirección General de Estadística. Underenumeration was estimated to be 2.8 percent in urban areas and 4.1 percent in rural areas.

a. See note 1.

SOURCE: Robert Fox and Jerrold Huguet, *Population and Urban Trends in Central America and Panama* (Washington, D.C.: Inter-American Development Bank, 1977), pp. 118–121.

Map 15-2

BASE MAP OF DEPARTMENTS IN GUATEMALA AND LOCATION
OF MAJOR URBAN CENTERS

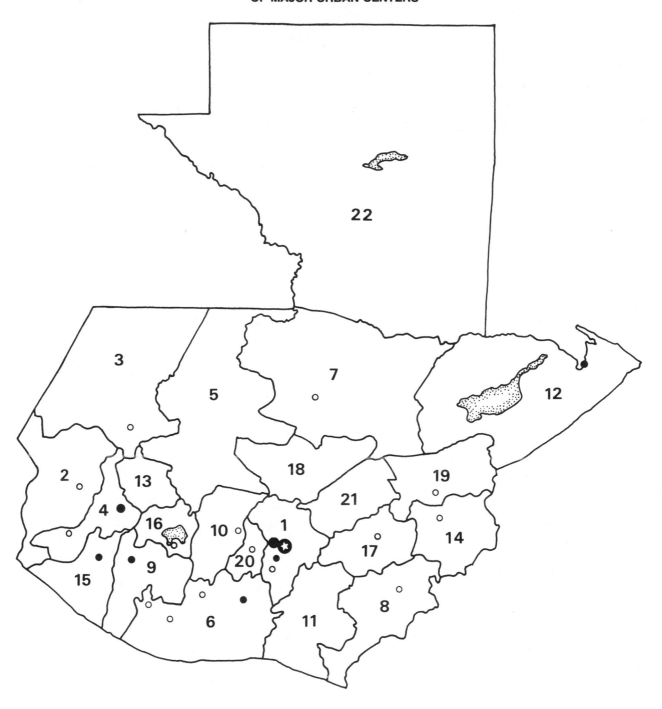

Note: Department numbers are rank ordered according to
population data listed in Table 15-1.

Map 15-3

POPULATION CARTOGRAM OF GUATEMALA, 1973

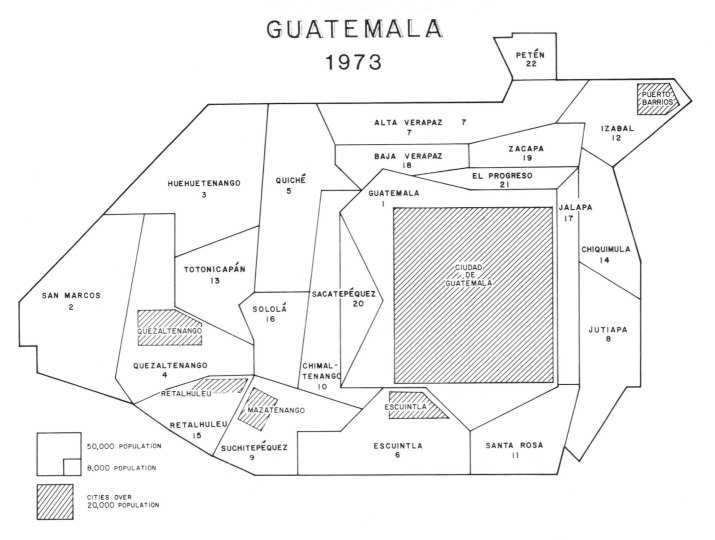

GUATEMALA
1973

PETÉN 22

PUERTO BARRIOS

ALTA VERAPAZ 7
7

IZABAL 12

BAJA VERAPAZ 18

ZACAPA 19

HUEHUETENANGO 3

QUICHÉ 5

EL PROGRESO 21

GUATEMALA 1

JALAPA 17

CHIQUIMULA 14

TOTONICAPÁN 13

CIUDAD DE GUATEMALA

SAN MARCOS 2

SACATEPÉQUEZ 20

SOLOLÁ 16

QUEZALTENANGO

JUTIAPA 8

QUEZALTENANGO 4

CHIMAL-TENANGO 10

RETALHULEU

MAZATENANGO

ESCUINTLA

RETALHULEU 15

ESCUINTLA 6

SANTA ROSA 11

SUCHITEPÉQUEZ 9

50,000 POPULATION
8,000 POPULATION

CITIES OVER 20,000 POPULATION

PATRICIA CUTTS
Geography Cartographic Laboratory
Univ. of Massachusetts, Amherst

Map 15-4

THREE-DIMENSIONAL CHOROPLETH MAP OF TOTAL
POPULATION BY DEPARTMENT IN GUATEMALA, 1973
(By Major Civil Division)

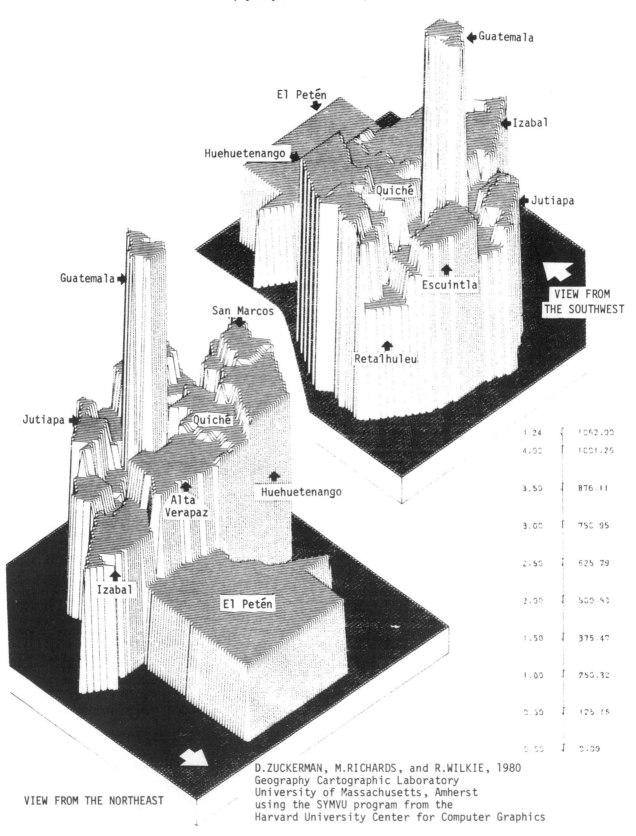

1.24	1062.00
4.00	1001.26
3.50	876.11
3.00	750.95
2.50	625.79
2.00	500.63
1.50	375.47
1.00	250.32
0.50	125.16
0.00	0.00

VIEW FROM THE SOUTHWEST

VIEW FROM THE NORTHEAST

D.ZUCKERMAN, M.RICHARDS, and R.WILKIE, 1980
Geography Cartographic Laboratory
University of Massachusetts, Amherst
using the SYMVU program from the
Harvard University Center for Computer Graphics

Map 15-5

THREE-DIMENSIONAL CHOROPLETH MAP OF POPULATION DENSITY
IN GUATEMALA, 1973
(Persons per km²)

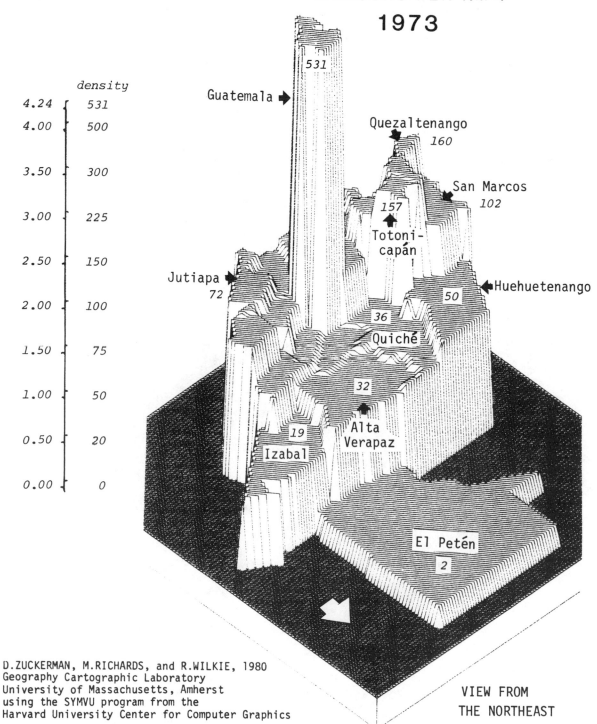

GUATEMALA
POPULATION DENSITY
(PERSONS PER KM²)
1973

density

4.24	531
4.00	500
3.50	300
3.00	225
2.50	150
2.00	100
1.50	75
1.00	50
0.50	20
0.00	0

531

Guatemala ►

Quezaltenango
160

San Marcos
102

157
Totoni-
capán

Jutiapa ►
72

◄ Huehuetenango
50

36

Quiché

32

19
Alta
Verapaz

Izabal

El Petén
2

D.ZUCKERMAN, M.RICHARDS, and R.WILKIE, 1980
Geography Cartographic Laboratory
University of Massachusetts, Amherst
using the SYMVU program from the
Harvard University Center for Computer Graphics

VIEW FROM
THE NORTHEAST

Map 15-6

**THREE-DIMENSIONAL CHOROPLETH MAP OF POPULATION CHANGE
IN GUATEMALA, 1964–1973
(%)**

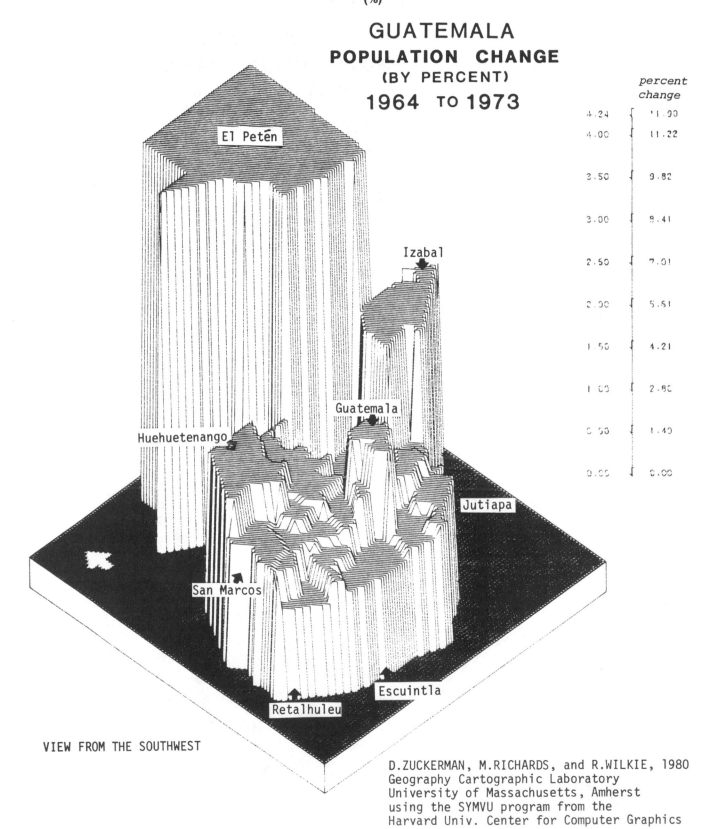

GUATEMALA
POPULATION CHANGE
(BY PERCENT)
1964 TO 1973

percent change

4.24	11.90
4.00	11.22
3.50	9.82
3.00	8.41
2.50	7.01
2.00	5.61
1.50	4.21
1.00	2.80
0.50	1.40
0.00	0.00

El Petén

Izabal

Guatemala

Huehuetenango

Jutiapa

San Marcos

Escuintla

Retalhuleu

VIEW FROM THE SOUTHWEST

D.ZUCKERMAN, M.RICHARDS, and R.WILKIE, 1980
Geography Cartographic Laboratory
University of Massachusetts, Amherst
using the SYMVU program from the
Harvard Univ. Center for Computer Graphics

Photo 15-1

SETTLEMENT LANDSCAPE AROUND LAKE ATITLÁN, GUATEMALA (1979)

Table 15-3

**POPULATION FOR EACH NATIONAL CENSUS IN
GUATEMALA, 1880-1973**

Census Year	Population
1880	1,224,602
1893	1,364,678
1921	2,004,900
1930	1,771,000
1935	1,996,000
1940	2,222,000
1950	2,790,686
1964	4,282,473
1973	5,879,700[a]

a. Figure adjusted from 5,211,929 by the Guatemalan Dirección General de Estadística.

Table 15-4

**TOTAL AND PERCENT POPULATION IN FIVE LEVELS OF THE URBAN-RURAL
SETTLEMENT HIERARCHY OF GUATEMALA SINCE 1950**

	0	1	2	3	4	SETTLEMENT HIERARCHY	
CENSUS YEAR	DISPERSED Population 1 to 99	VILLAGE 100 to 2,500	SIMPLE URBAN 2,501– 20,000	COMPLEX URBAN 20,001– 500,000	METROPOLITAN over 500,000	Classification	PERCENT in top 2 levels
TOTAL							
1950	....	2,082,947	....	385,723	322,016	- -	
1964	....	2,827,752	....	791,781	92,269	572,937	
1973	....	3,527,820	....	1,182,280	180,500	989,100	
PERCENT							
1950	....	74.6	....	13.8	11.5	- -	0–1	74.6
1964	....	66.0	....	18.4	2.2	13.4	0–2	66 to 70
1973	....	60.0	....	20.1	3.1	16.8	0–2	66 to 70

SOURCE: Calculated from the various Guatemalan national censuses since 1950, and from SALA, 20–631, 632, 634, 635, 636, 637, and 638.

Table 15-5

SELECTED INDICATORS OF POPULATION CHANGE AND PER CAPITA GNP IN GUATEMALA

Years	Per 1000 Population		Rate of Natural Increase (Annual %)	Number of Years to Double Population	Percent Population Under Age 15	Life Expectancy at Birth	Per Capita GNP (US)
	Births	Deaths					
1940–45	47	28	3.4	- -	- -	- -	- -
1945–50	51	24	3.1	- -	- -	- -	- -
1950–55	51	22	2.7	- -	- -	- -	- -
1955–60	49	20	2.8	- -	- -	- -	- -
1960–65	46	17	3.0	- -	- -	- -	- -
1965–70	45	16	2.9	- -	- -	49	- -
1970–74	43	13	3.0	24[a]	46[a]	52[b]	310[a]
1975	41	14	2.9	24	44	53	420
1976	43	15	2.8	25	44	53	570
1977	43	12	3.1	22	45	53	650
1978	43	12	3.1	22	45	53	630
1979	43	10	3.3	21	45	58	790
1980	43	12	3.1	23	45	58	910
1981	43	12	3.1	22	45	58	1,020
1982	42	10	3.2	22	45	58	1,110

a. 1970.
b. 1971.

MAJOR SOURCES:
  Births: SALA, 19-204; SALA, 20-705 through 1976.
  Deaths: SALA, 18-703d and 706 through 1970.
  Life expectancy: SALA, 19-700 through 1970.
  Per capita GNP: 1955 data from Ginsburg, *Atlas of Economic Development* (Chicago: University of Chicago Press, 1961).
  Rate of natural increase: SALA, 22-626 from CELADE-BD 10 (1972) through 1970.
  All other data: Population Reference Bureau, Washington, D.C., annual world population data sheets.

Table 15-6

GUATEMALAN DEPARTMENTS BY GEOGRAPHICAL
SIZE AND SUBDIVISION, 1968

Department	Civil Subdivisions (N)	Area	
		km^2	%
Total	325[a]	108,889	100.0
Departments			
Alta Verapaz	14	8,686	8.0
Baja Verapaz	8	3,124	2.9
Chimaltenango	16	1,979	1.8
Chiquimula	11	2,376	2.2
El Progreso	8	1,922	1.8
Escuintla	13	4,384	4.0
Guatemala	17	2,126	2.0
Huehuetenango	31	7,400	6.8
Izabal	5	9,038	8.3
Jalapa	7	2,063	1.9
Jutiapa	17	3,219	3.0
Petén	11	35,854	32.9
Quezaltenango	24	1,951	1.8
Quiché	18	8,378	7.7
Retalhuleu	9	1,856	1.7
Sacatepéquez	16	465	.4
San Marcos	29	3,791	3.5
Santa Rosa	14	2,955	2.7
Sololá	19	1,061	1.0
Suchitepéquez	20	2,510	2.3
Totonicapán	8	1,061	1.0
Zacapa	10	2,690	2.5

a. Municipios.

SOURCE: SALA, 21-301.

Map 15-7

SOUTHWESTERN GUATEMALA

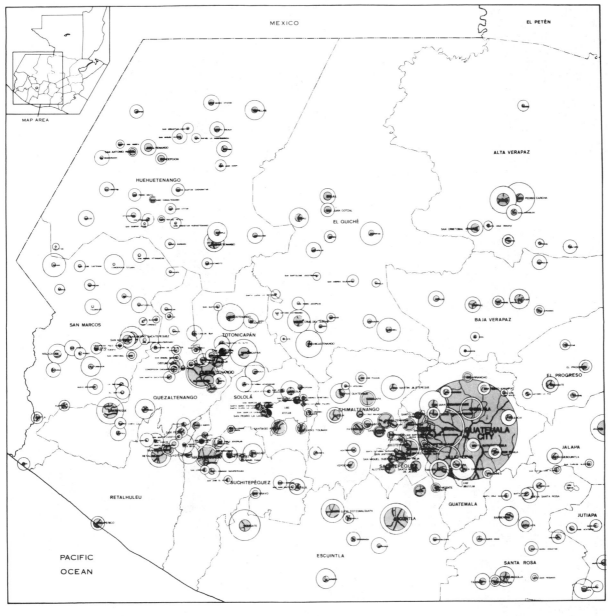

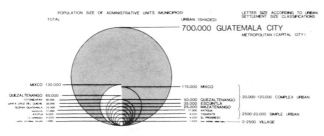

POPULATION SIZE OF ADMINISTRATIVE UNITS (MUNICIPIOS)

LETTER SIZE ACCORDING TO URBAN
SETTLEMENT SIZE CLASSIFICATIONS

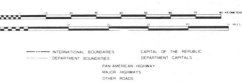

Source: Guatemalan Census
of Population, 1973

Photo 15-2

TURKEY VENDOR ARRIVING AT SUNDAY MARKET, MOMOSTENANGO, TOTONICAPÁN,
GUATEMALA (1967)

Map 15-8

**STYLIZED MAP OF MARKET SIZES AND TRANSPORTATION
LINKAGES, GUATEMALA, 1979**

PERIODIC MARKET SYSTEMS OF GUATEMALA, 1979

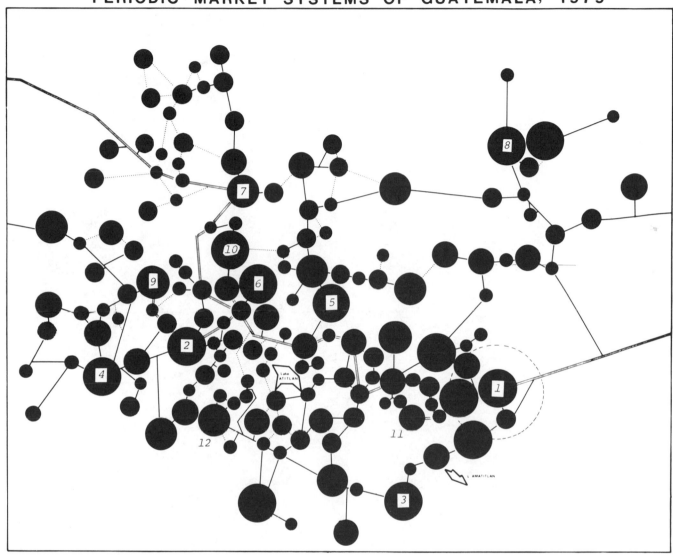

**TOTAL POPULATION of TOWNS
having MARKETS**

- 0 - 10.000 PERSONS
- 10.000 - 20.000 PERSONS
- 20.000 - 30.000 PERSONS
- 30.000 - 40.000 PERSONS
- ABOVE 40.000 PERSONS

Selected Market Centers:
1. Guatemala City   7. Huehuetenango
2. Quezaltenango   8. Cobán
3. Escuintla   9. San Marcos/ S.P.Sac.
4. Coatepéque   10. Momostenango
5. Chichicastenango   11. Antigua
6. Totonicapán   12. Mazatenango

LINKAGES

===== MAJOR ALL WEATHER HIGHWAY
───── IMPROVED SECONDARY ROADS
········· UNIMPROVED ROADS & PATHS

**STUDY AREA
(shaded)**

D.Zuckerman and R.Wilkie, 1981
Geography Cartographic Laboratory
University of Massachusetts, Amherst

Map 15-9A

SUNDAY MARKETS, SOUTHWESTERN GUATEMALA

SUNDAY MARKETS
SOUTHWESTERN GUATEMALA

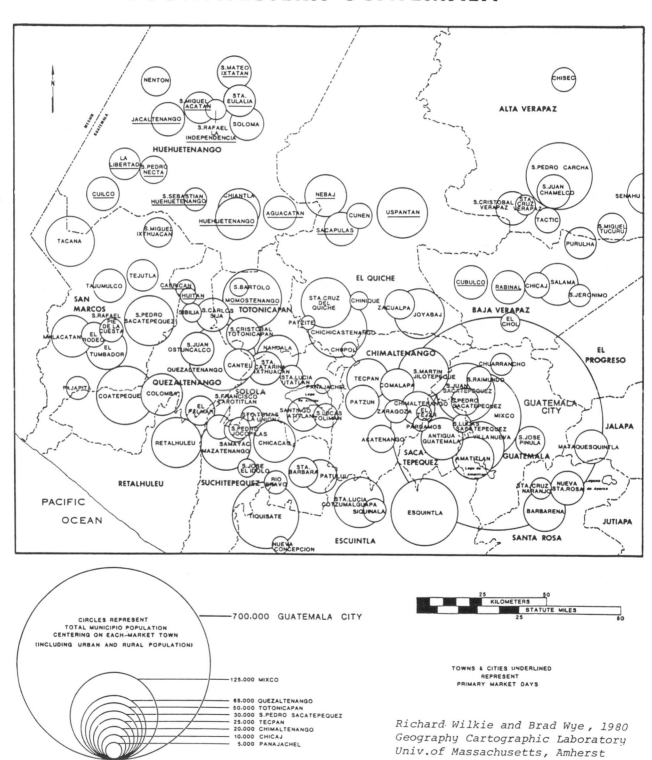

CIRCLES REPRESENT
TOTAL MUNICIPIO POPULATION
CENTERING ON EACH—MARKET TOWN
(INCLUDING URBAN AND RURAL POPULATION)

——— 700,000 GUATEMALA CITY

——— 125,000 MIXCO

——— 65,000 QUEZALTENANGO
——— 50,000 TOTONICAPAN
——— 30,000 S.PEDRO SACATEPEQUEZ
——— 25,000 TECPAN
——— 20,000 CHIMALTENANGO
——— 10,000 CHICAJ
——— 5,000 PANAJACHEL

TOWNS & CITIES UNDERLINED
REPRESENT
PRIMARY MARKET DAYS

Richard Wilkie and Brad Wye, 1980
Geography Cartographic Laboratory
Univ.of Massachusetts, Amherst

Map 15-9B

MONDAY MARKETS, SOUTHWESTERN GUATEMALA

MONDAY MARKETS
SOUTHWESTERN GUATEMALA

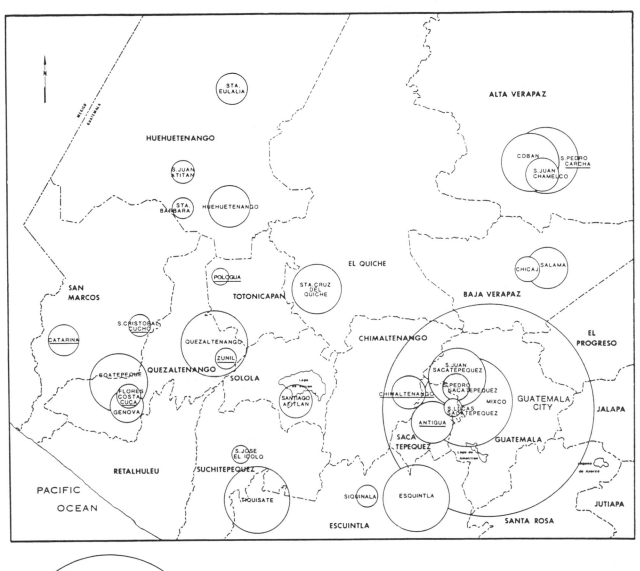

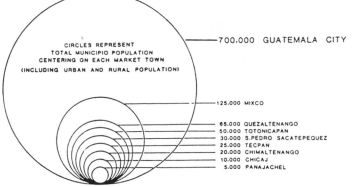

CIRCLES REPRESENT
TOTAL MUNICIPIO POPULATION
CENTERING ON EACH MARKET TOWN
(INCLUDING URBAN AND RURAL POPULATION)

——— 700,000 GUATEMALA CITY

——— 125,000 MIXCO

——— 65,000 QUEZALTENANGO
——— 50,000 TOTONICAPAN
——— 30,000 S.PEDRO SACATEPEQUEZ
——— 25,000 TECPAN
——— 20,000 CHIMALTENANGO
——— 10,000 CHICAJ
——— 5,000 PANAJACHEL

KILOMETERS
STATUTE MILES

TOWNS & CITIES UNDERLINED
REPRESENT
PRIMARY MARKET DAYS

Richard Wilkie and Brad Wye, 1980
Geography Cartographic Laboratory
Univ. of Massachusetts, Amherst

Map 15-9C

TUESDAY MARKETS, SOUTHWESTERN GUATEMALA

TUESDAY MARKETS
SOUTHWESTERN GUATEMALA

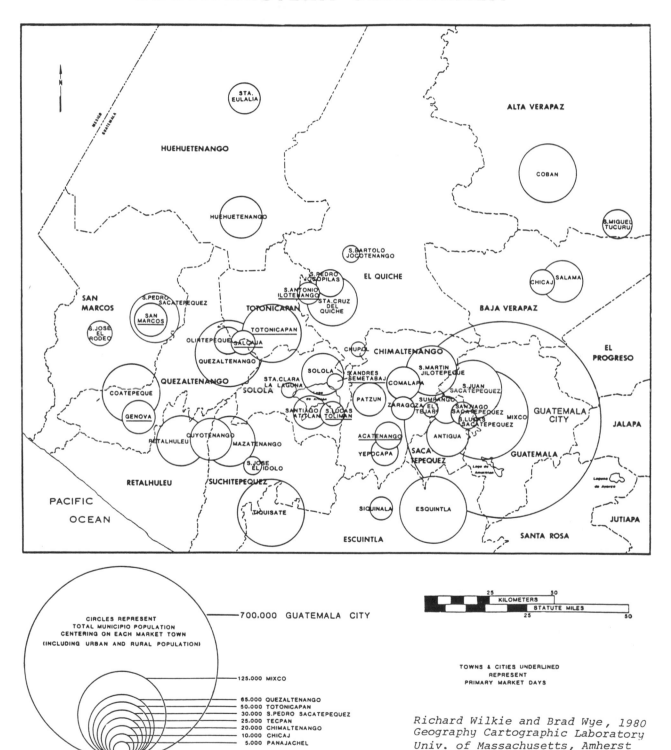

CIRCLES REPRESENT
TOTAL MUNICIPIO POPULATION
CENTERING ON EACH MARKET TOWN
(INCLUDING URBAN AND RURAL POPULATION)

—— 700,000 GUATEMALA CITY

—— 125,000 MIXCO

—— 65,000 QUEZALTENANGO
—— 50,000 TOTONICAPAN
—— 30,000 S.PEDRO SACATEPEQUEZ
—— 25,000 TECPAN
—— 20,000 CHIMALTENANGO
—— 10,000 CHICAJ
—— 5,000 PANAJACHEL

KILOMETERS
STATUTE MILES

TOWNS & CITIES UNDERLINED
REPRESENT
PRIMARY MARKET DAYS

*Richard Wilkie and Brad Wye, 1980
Geography Cartographic Laboratory
Univ. of Massachusetts, Amherst*

Map 15-9D

WEDNESDAY MARKETS, SOUTHWESTERN GUATEMALA

WEDNESDAY MARKETS
SOUTHWESTERN GUATEMALA

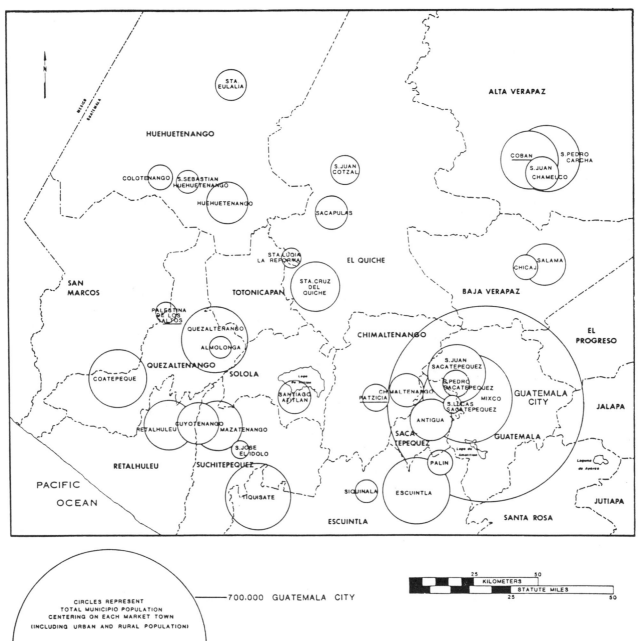

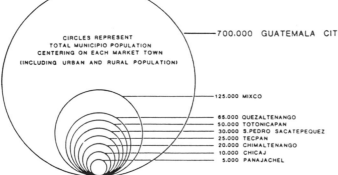

CIRCLES REPRESENT
TOTAL MUNICIPIO POPULATION
CENTERING ON EACH MARKET TOWN
(INCLUDING URBAN AND RURAL POPULATION)

——— 700,000 GUATEMALA CITY

——— 125,000 MIXCO

——— 65,000 QUEZALTENANGO
——— 50,000 TOTONICAPAN
——— 30,000 S.PEDRO SACATEPEQUEZ
——— 25,000 TECPAN
——— 20,000 CHIMALTENANGO
——— 10,000 CHICAJ
——— 5,000 PANAJACHEL

TOWNS & CITIES UNDERLINED
REPRESENT
PRIMARY MARKET DAYS

*Richard Wilkie and Brad Wye, 1980
Geography Cartographic Laboratory
Univ. of Massachusetts, Amherst*

Map 15-9E

THURSDAY MARKETS, SOUTHWESTERN GUATEMALA

THURSDAY MARKETS
SOUTHWESTERN GUATEMALA

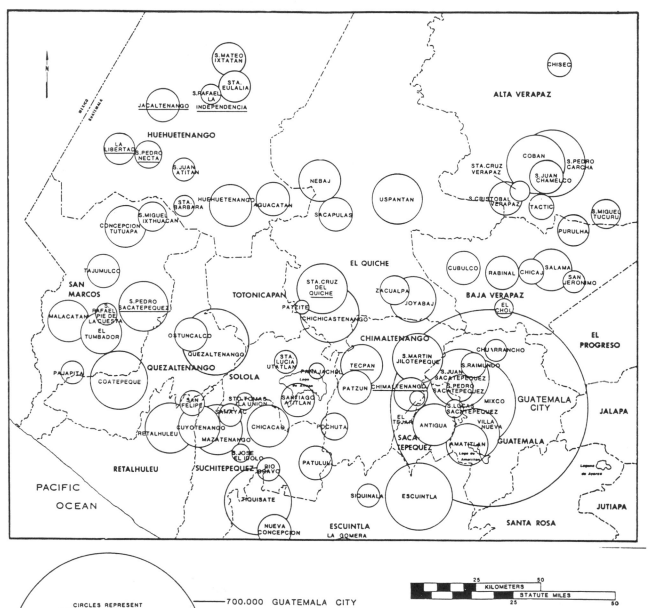

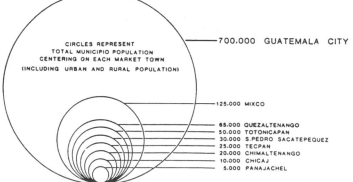

CIRCLES REPRESENT
TOTAL MUNICIPIO POPULATION
CENTERING ON EACH MARKET TOWN
(INCLUDING URBAN AND RURAL POPULATION)

—— 700,000 GUATEMALA CITY

—— 125,000 MIXCO

—— 65,000 QUEZALTENANGO
—— 50,000 TOTONICAPAN
—— 30,000 S.PEDRO SACATEPEQUEZ
—— 25,000 TECPAN
—— 20,000 CHIMALTENANGO
—— 10,000 CHICAJ
—— 5,000 PANAJACHEL

TOWNS & CITIES UNDERLINED
REPRESENT
PRIMARY MARKET DAYS

Richard Wilkie and Brad Wye, 1980
Geography Cartographic Laboratory
Univ.of Massachusetts, Amherst

Map 15-9F

FRIDAY MARKETS, SOUTHWESTERN GUATEMALA

FRIDAY MARKETS
SOUTHWESTERN GUATEMALA

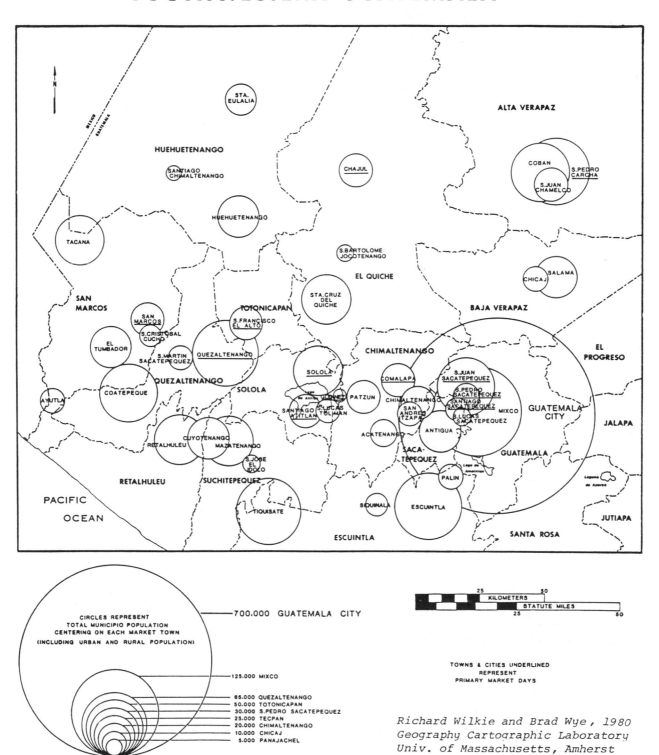

CIRCLES REPRESENT
TOTAL MUNICIPIO POPULATION
CENTERING ON EACH MARKET TOWN
(INCLUDING URBAN AND RURAL POPULATION)

——— 700,000 GUATEMALA CITY

——— 125,000 MIXCO

——— 65,000 QUEZALTENANGO
——— 50,000 TOTONICAPAN
——— 30,000 S.PEDRO SACATEPEQUEZ
——— 25,000 TECPAN
——— 20,000 CHIMALTENANGO
——— 10,000 CHICAJ
——— 5,000 PANAJACHEL

25   50
KILOMETERS
STATUTE MILES
25   50

TOWNS & CITIES UNDERLINED
REPRESENT
PRIMARY MARKET DAYS

*Richard Wilkie and Brad Wye, 1980
Geography Cartographic Laboratory
Univ. of Massachusetts, Amherst*

Map 15-9G

SATURDAY MARKETS, SOUTHWESTERN GUATEMALA

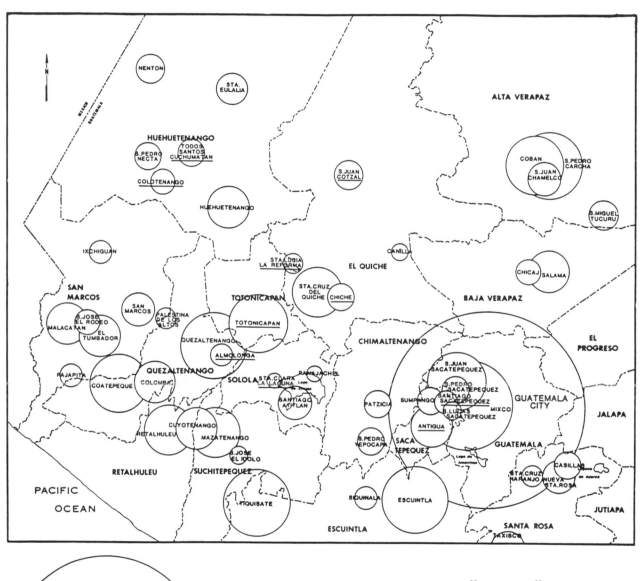

SATURDAY MARKETS
SOUTHWESTERN GUATEMALA

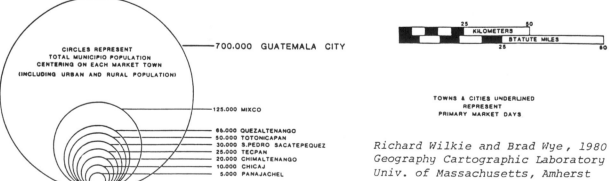

CIRCLES REPRESENT
TOTAL MUNICIPIO POPULATION
CENTERING ON EACH MARKET TOWN
(INCLUDING URBAN AND RURAL POPULATION)

——— 700,000 GUATEMALA CITY

——— 125,000 MIXCO

——— 65,000 QUEZALTENANGO
——— 50,000 TOTONICAPAN
——— 30,000 S.PEDRO SACATEPEQUEZ
——— 25,000 TECPAN
——— 20,000 CHIMALTENANGO
——— 10,000 CHICAJ
——— 5,000 PANAJACHEL

TOWNS & CITIES UNDERLINED
REPRESENT
PRIMARY MARKET DAYS

Richard Wilkie and Brad Wye, 1980
Geography Cartographic Laboratory
Univ. of Massachusetts, Amherst

Photo 15-3

RURAL INHABITANTS LEAVING A WEEKLY MARKET, SAN FRANCISCO EL ALTO, TOTONICAPÁN, GUATEMALA (1979)

Figure 15-1

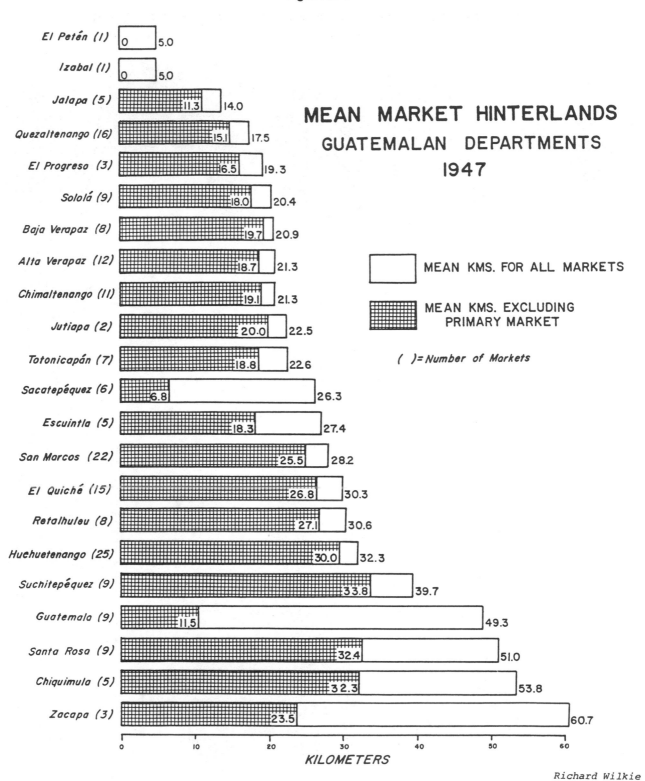

MEAN MARKET HINTERLANDS
GUATEMALAN DEPARTMENTS
1947

El Petén (1)   0   5.0
Izabal (1)   0   5.0
Jalapa (5)   11.3   14.0
Quezaltenango (16)   15.1   17.5
El Progreso (3)   16.5   19.3
Sololá (9)   18.0   20.4
Baja Verapaz (8)   19.7   20.9
Alta Verapaz (12)   18.7   21.3
Chimaltenango (11)   19.1   21.3
Jutiapa (2)   20.0   22.5
Totonicapán (7)   18.8   22.6
Sacatepéquez (6)   6.8   26.3
Escuintla (5)   18.3   27.4
San Marcos (22)   25.5   28.2
El Quiché (15)   26.8   30.3
Retalhuleu (8)   27.1   30.6
Huehuetenango (25)   30.0   32.3
Suchitepéquez (9)   33.8   39.7
Guatemala (9)   11.5   49.3
Santa Rosa (9)   32.4   51.0
Chiquimula (5)   32.3   53.8
Zacapa (3)   23.5   60.7

MEAN KMS. FOR ALL MARKETS

MEAN KMS. EXCLUDING
PRIMARY MARKET

( )=Number of Markets

0   10   20   30   40   50   60
KILOMETERS

Richard Wilkie

Photo 15-4

DISPERSED SETTLERS WALKING TO SUNDAY MARKET, TOTONICAPÁN, GUATEMALA
(1979)

Map 16-1

PHYSIOGRAPHIC MAP OF HAITI

ERWIN RAISZ

16

Haiti

Haiti has had only four official censuses in sixty-five years. The first census (1918) counted 1,631,260 inhabitants, and the second census thirty-two years later (1950) counted 3,097,220. In 1960 population totals were estimated to be 3,676,938, up 19 percent in ten years. The last census (1971) documented a further rise of 17 percent in eleven years to 4,314,628 inhabitants. In 1980 the population was estimated by the Latin American Economic Commission to be 5,534,000.

The population totals, trends, and characteristics of Haiti are presented in six tables and six maps. Some of the findings concerning Haiti are outlined below.

URBAN TRENDS

With a total population of 494,000 in 1971, greater Port-au-Prince was just below the metropolitan classification. This means that the capital city was one of only four cities in the complex urban category of more than 20,000 population. Cap-Haïtien (46,000), Gonaives (29,000), and Les Cayes (22,000) were all much smaller than Port-au-Prince. With only 13.7 percent of the population in complex urban cities and only 5.3 percent in simple urban centers, the urban hierarchy of Haiti is completely inadequate for the population as a whole.

RURAL TRENDS

Haiti is one of the most rural countries in the world. In 1971 more than four out of every five Haitians (81 per-

cent) lived in rural areas. That figure was down from nearly nine out of every ten (88 percent) in 1950, but overall the actual number of rural inhabitants was up from 2,726,000 in 1950 to 3,495,000 in 1971. It is very likely as well that a large number of rural inhabitants were never tabulated in either of the censuses, making the actual figures for rural population even higher.

SETTLEMENT HIERARCHY

Haiti in 1971 still had the most rural dominated settlement landscape in Latin America, and could be classified as dispersed-village (0−1). In addition, population density of 156 persons per square kilometer, of those actually counted, places Haiti just behind El Salvador as the most densely settled area in Latin America.

OTHER DEMOGRAPHIC DATA

The annual rate of population growth in Haiti has, for the greater part of thirty years, remained between 2 and 2.6 percent. That figure would be higher except for the fact that Haiti still has a relatively high death rate compared to the birth rate. Life expectancy in 1982 was fifty-one years, and 41 percent of the population was under fifteen years of age. Per capita GNP was up by 108 percent from $130 a year in 1975 to $270 a year in 1982, ranking Haiti lowest among the twenty Latin American republics in that category.

Table 16-1

POPULATION DATA AND DENSITY BY DEPARTMENT IN HAITI, 1971[a]

Rank	Department	Population	Percent	Percent Change 1950-1971	Population Density 1971 (km^2)
1	Ouest	1,670,140	38.6	+54.2	198
2	Sud	976,409	22.5	+31.9	147
3	Artibonite	765,228	17.7	+35.0	124
4	Nord	700,725	16.2	+30.0	166
5	Nord-Ouest	217,489	5.0	+29.5	92
	Total	4,329,991	100.0	+39.8	156

a. According to the U.S. Bureau of the Census (1977), the 1971 census of Haiti has not been evaluated for possible coverage error. However, based on a United Nations projection and other midyear estimates, a net underenumeration of 8.4 percent is implied, for a population of 4,694,000. In addition, they estimated (1981) the population on July 1, 1979, to be 5,670,000.

SOURCE: Census of September 1, 1971; SALA 20-626.

Table 16-2

MAJOR URBAN CENTERS IN HAITI, 1971

Rank	Major Urban Centers	1971 Population	1971 Percent	July 1, 1978[a]
1	✪ Gran Port-au-Prince (1)	493,932	11.4	
	Port-au-Prince proper	306,000		745,700
	Carrefour et Martissant	153,000		
	Petion-Ville	35,000		
2	● Cap-Haïtien (4)	46,000	1.1	
3	Gonaives (3)	29,000	.7	
4	Les Cayes (2)	22,000	.5	
			13.7	
5	○ Jérémie (2)	18,000		
6	St. Marc (3)	17,000		
7	Port-de-Paix (5)	14,000		
8	Jacmel (1)	11,000		

a. United Nations, *Demographic Yearbook 1978*, p. 211.

SOURCES: *América en Cifras 1974*; Census of September 1, 1971; SALA, 20–629.

Photo 16-1

STREET SCENE IN CAP-HAITIEN, HAITI (1981)

Map 16-2

BASE MAP OF DEPARTMENTS IN HAITI AND LOCATION OF
MAJOR URBAN CENTERS

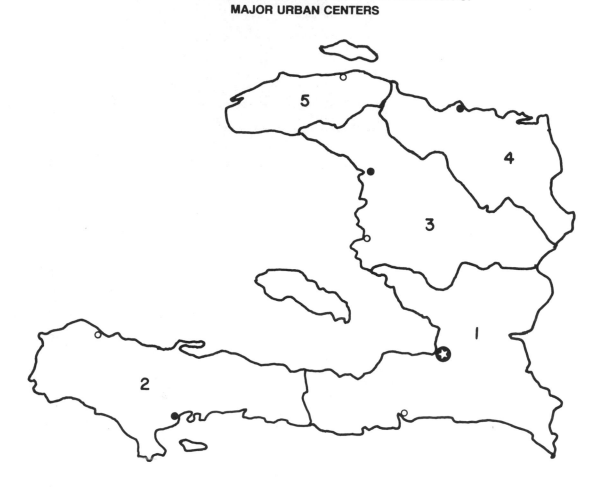

Note: Provincial numbers are rank ordered according to popu-
       lation data listed in Table 16-1.

Map 16-3

POPULATION CARTOGRAM OF HAITI, 1971

HAITI   1971

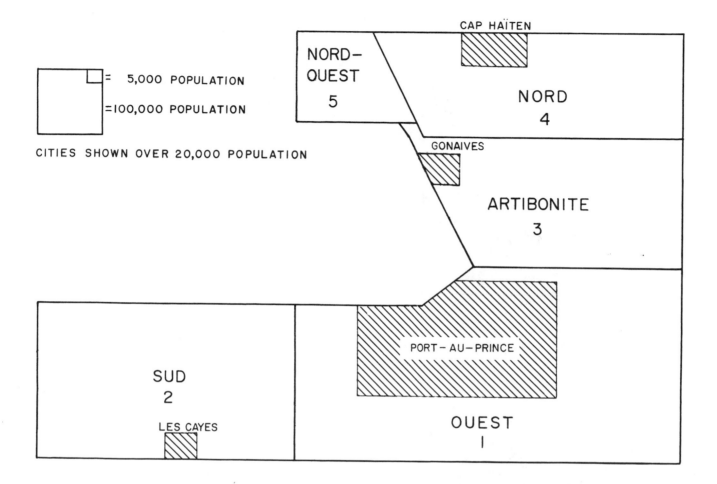

J.F. HUNTER and R.HYNES
Geography Cartographic Laboratory
Univ. of Massachusetts, Amherst

Map 16-4

**THREE-DIMENSIONAL CHOROPLETH MAP OF TOTAL POPULATION BY
DEPARTMENT IN HAITI, 1971
(By Major Civil Division)**

HAITI
TOTAL POPULATION
(BY MAJOR CIVIL DIVISION)
1971

4.07	1292.08
3.50	1112.19
3.00	953.30
2.50	794.42
2.00	635.54
1.50	476.65
1.00	317.77
0.50	158.89
0.00	0.00

VIEW FROM THE NORTHWEST

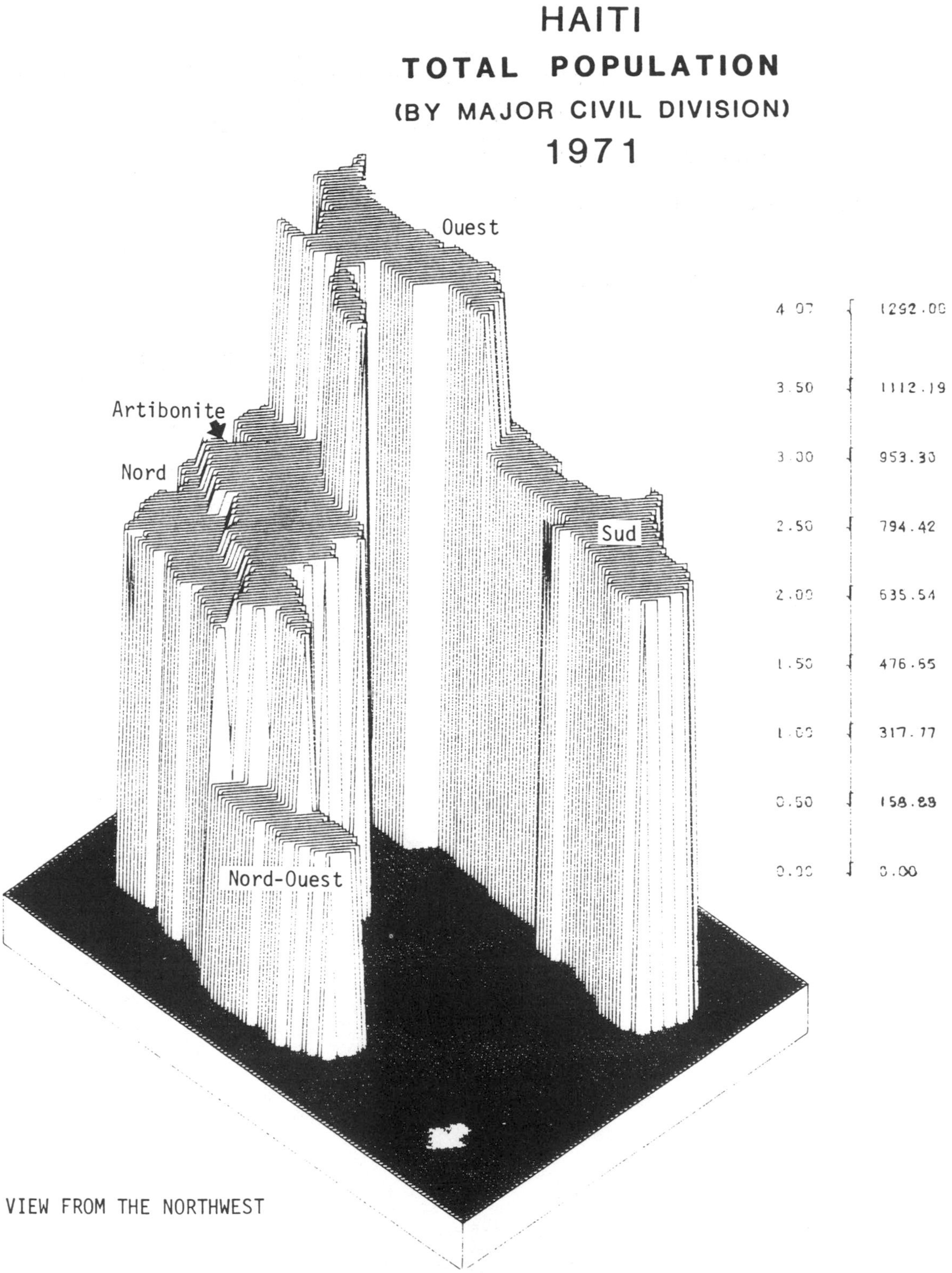

R.HYNES, M.RICHARDS, and R.WILKIE, 1980
Geography Cartographic Laboratory, University of Massachusetts, Amherst
using the SYMVU program from the Harvard Univ. Center for Computer Graphics

Map 16-5

**THREE-DIMENSIONAL CHOROPLETH MAP OF POPULATION DENSITY
IN HAITI, 1971
(Persons per km²)**

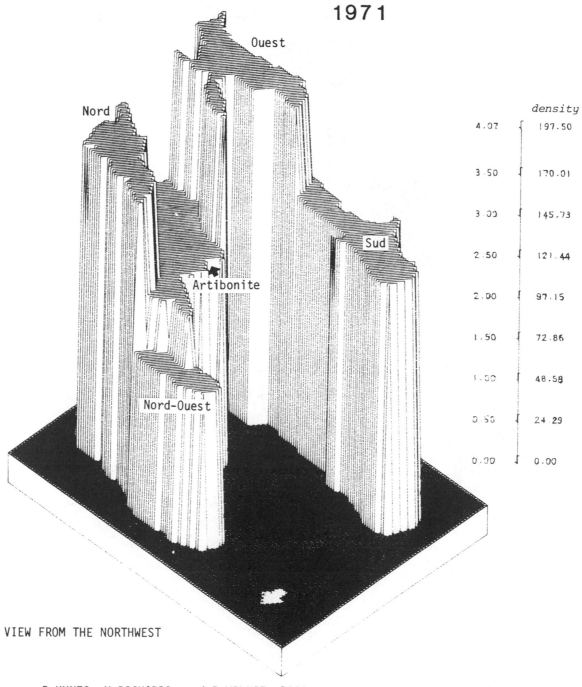

HAITI
POPULATION DENSITY
(PERSONS PER KM²)
1971

Ouest

Nord

Sud

Artibonite

Nord-Ouest

density

4.07	197.50
3.50	170.01
3.00	145.73
2.50	121.44
2.00	97.15
1.50	72.86
1.00	48.58
0.50	24.29
0.00	0.00

VIEW FROM THE NORTHWEST

R.HYNES, M.RICHARDS, and R.WILKIE, 1980
Geography Cartographic Laboratory, University of Massachusetts, Amherst
using the SYMVU program from the Harvard Univ. Center for Computer Graphics

Map 16-6

THREE-DIMENSIONAL CHOROPLETH MAP OF POPULATION CHANGE IN HAITI,
1950–1971
(%)

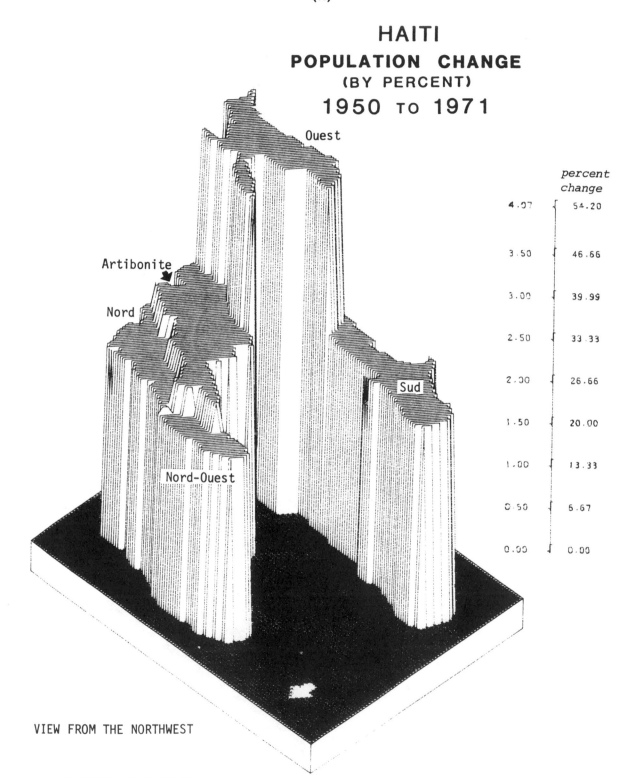

HAITI
POPULATION CHANGE
(BY PERCENT)
1950 TO 1971

Ouest

Artibonite

Nord

Sud

Nord-Ouest

VIEW FROM THE NORTHWEST

	percent change
4.07	54.20
3.50	46.66
3.00	39.99
2.50	33.33
2.00	26.66
1.50	20.00
1.00	13.33
0.50	6.67
0.00	0.00

R.HYNES, M.RICHARDS, and R.WILKIE, 1980
Geography Cartographic Laboratory, University of Massachusetts, Amherst
using the SYMVU program from the Harvard Univ. Center for Computer Graphics

Photo 16-2

FRENCH COLONIAL ARCHITECTURE, PORT-AU-PRINCE, HAITI (1980)

Table 16-3

POPULATION FOR EACH NATIONAL CENSUS IN
HAITI, 1918–1971

Census Year	Population
1918	1,631,260
1950	3,097,220
1960	3,676,938[a]
1971	4,314,628

a. Estimated.

Table 16-4

TOTAL AND PERCENT POPULATION IN FIVE LEVELS OF THE URBAN-RURAL
SETTLEMENT HIERARCHY OF HAITI SINCE 1950

| | 0 | 1 | 2 | 3 | 4 | SETTLEMENT HIERARCHY | |
| | DISPERSED | VILLAGE | SIMPLE URBAN | COMPLEX URBAN | | | PERCENT in top 2 levels |
CENSUS YEAR	Population 1 to 99	100 to 2,500	2,501– 20,000	20,001– 500,000	METROPOLITAN over 500,000	Classification	
TOTAL							
1950	. . . .	2,725,554	131,073	240,593	- -		
1960	. . . .	3,125,397[a]	280,485	271,056	- -		
1971	. . . .	3,494,849	228,847	590,932	- -		
PERCENT							
1950	. . . .	88.0	4.2	7.8	- -	0–1	88.0
1960	. . . .	85.0[a]	7.6	7.4	- -	0–1	85.0
1971	. . . .	81.0	5.3	13.7	- -	0–1	81.0

a. Estimated.

SOURCES: Calculated from the various Haitian national censuses since 1950, and from SALA, 20–631, 632, 634, 635, 636, 637, and 638.

Table 16-5

SELECTED INDICATORS OF POPULATION CHANGE AND PER CAPITA GNP IN HAITI

Years	Per 1000 Population Births	Per 1000 Population Deaths	Rate of Natural Increase (Annual %)	Number of Years to Double Population	Percent Population Under Age 15	Life Expectancy at Birth	Per Capita GNP (US)
1940–45	- -	- -	1.8	- -	- -	- -	- -
1945–50	- -	- -	1.8	- -	- -	- -	- -
1950–55	- -	- -	2.0	- -	- -	33[a] in 1950	75[b]
1955–60	- -	- -	2.2	- -	- -	- -	- -
1960–65	45	- -	2.3	- -	- -	- -	- -
1965–70	45	16	2.5	- -	- -	- -	- -
1970–74	36	20[c]	2.5[c]	28[c]	42[c]	- -	- -
1975	36	17	1.4	50	40	50	130
1976	36	16	1.6	43	41	50	140
1977	36	16	2.0	35	42	50	180
1978	39	17	2.2	32	42	50	200
1979	42	16	2.6	27	41	49	230
1980	42	16	2.6	26	41	51	260
1981	42	16	2.6	26	41	51	260
1982	42	16	2.6	27	41	51	270

a. 1950.
b. 1955.
c. 1970.

MAJOR SOURCES:
  Births: SALA, 19-204; SALA, 20-705 through 1975.
  Deaths: SALA, 18-703d and 706 through 1970.
  Life expectancy: SALA, 19-700 through 1970.
  Per capita GNP: 1955 data from Ginsburg, *Atlas of Economic Development* (Chicago: University of Chicago Press, 1961).
  Rate of natural increase: SALA, 22-626 from CELADE-BD 10 (1972) through 1970.
  All other data: Population Reference Bureau, Washington, D.C., annual world population data sheets.

Table 16-6

HAITIAN DEPARTMENTS BY GEOGRAPHICAL
SIZE AND SUBDIVISION, 1950

Department	Civil Subdivisions (N)	Area km^2	Area %
Total	108[a]	27,844	100.0
Departments			
Artibonite	16	6,192	22.2
Nord	28	4,223	15.2
Nord-ouest	9	2,355	8.5
Ouest	26	8,452	30.3
Sud	29	6,622	23.8

a. Municipios.

SOURCE: SALA, 21-301.

Map 17-1

PHYSIOGRAPHIC MAP OF HONDURAS

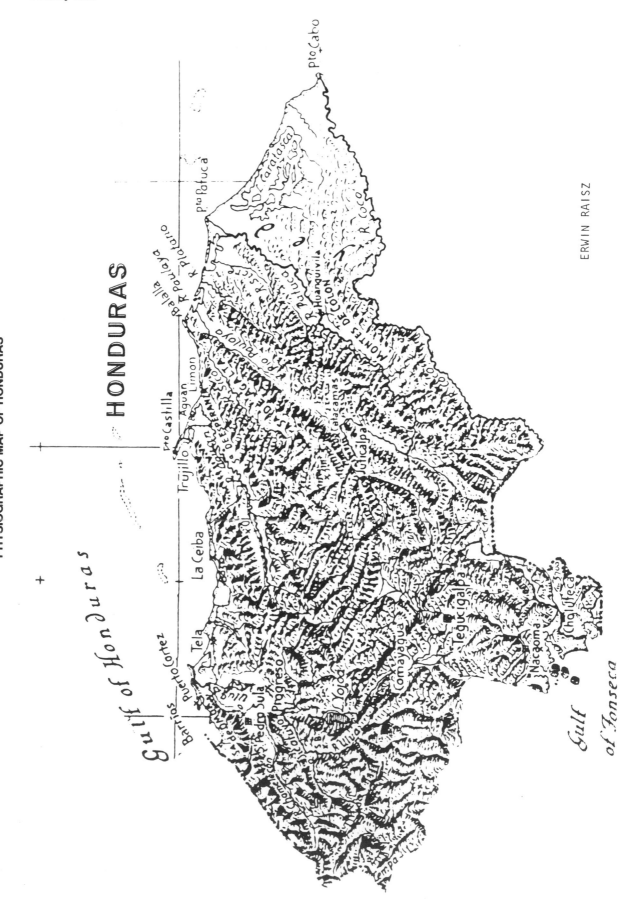

HONDURAS

Gulf of Honduras

Gulf of Fonseca

ERWIN RAISZ

17

Honduras

Honduras has had sixteen official censuses over 192 years. The first census (1791) counted 93,505 inhabitants. By the fifth census 114 years later in 1905, the number of Hondurans had risen to 500,136. From that date the population more than doubled to 1,107,859 in 1940 and more than doubled again to 2,495,000 in 1967. The latest census (1974) had a tabulated population of 2,653,857, but the U.S. Bureau of the Census suggested a 12.5 percent underenumeration and recommended a figure of 3,032,000. In 1980 the population was estimated by the Latin American Economic Commission to be 3,439,000 inhabitants.

The population totals, trends, and characteristics of Honduras are presented in six tables and six maps. Some of the findings concerning Honduras are outlined below.

URBAN TRENDS

There were no metropolitan centers with more than half a million population in 1974, but there were seven complex urban centers. Greater Tegucigalpa with 302,483 is the largest city in the country and it had 11.4 percent of the nation's inhabitants in 1974. Other large cities include San Pedro Sula (161,700), La Ceiba (42,100), and El Progreso (30,600). Overall, complex urban centers over 20,000 population account for 22.4 percent of the national total. The least developed level in the urban-rural hierarchy is the simple urban level of cities between 2,000 and 20,000, and it accounts for less than 4 percent of the population.

RURAL TRENDS

Honduras is one of the most rural countries in Latin America. In 1974 three-fourths of the inhabitants lived in rural areas (down from 81 percent in 1950), and ten out of eleven of those individuals lived dispersed rather than in villages.

SETTLEMENT HIERARCHY

Honduras could be classified as a dispersed−complex urban (0−3) settlement landscape since 1961, with close to 90 percent of the nation's population living in those two levels in the urban-rural hierarchy. Clearly most rural peasants in Honduras are essentially cut off from any meaningful economic and social services that would normally radiate down from larger urban centers through a developed hierarchy of regional centers. Without those centers in the hierarchy, people must travel much greater distances to the largest cities in order to have the selection of services they need.

OTHER DEMOGRAPHIC DATA

The annual rate of population growth in Honduras has been higher than 3 percent since 1950 and higher than 3.5 percent since 1970. Life expectancy in 1982 was fifty-seven years, and 48 percent of the population was under fifteen years of age. Per capita GNP in 1982 of $560 was up by only 75 percent from $320 in 1975, ranking Honduras number 19 among the twenty Latin American republics in that category.

Table 17-1

POPULATION DATA AND DENSITY BY DEPARTMENT IN HONDURAS, 1974[a]

Rank	Department	Population	Percent	Percent Change 1961-1974	Population Density 1974 (km^2)
1	Francisco Morazán	451,778	17.0	+62.9	57
2	Cortés	373,629	14.1	+86.7	95
3	Yoro	194,953	7.3	+49.3	25
4	Choluteca	192,145	7.2	+28.8	46
5	Santa Bárbara	185,163	7.0	+26.1	36
6	Olancho	151,923	5.7	+37.2	6
7	Copán	151,331	5.7	+19.9	47
8	Atlántida	148,440	5.6	+59.8	35
9	El Paraíso	140,340	5.3	+31.4	20
10	Comayagua	135,455	5.1	+40.6	26
11	Lempira	127,465	4.8	+14.3	30
12	Valle	90,954	3.4	+12.4	59
13	Intibucá	81,685	3.1	+11.7	27
14	Colón	77,239	2.9	+84.3	9
15	La Paz	65,390	2.5	+7.9	28
16	Ocotepeque	51,161	1.9	-2.6	31
17	Gracias a Dios	21,079	.8	+93.2	1
18	Islas de la Bahía	13,227	.5	+46.7	51
	Total	2,653,857	100.0	+41.6	24

a. CELADE (Centro Latinoamericano de Demografía) estimated a 9.2 percent underenumeration, for a figure of 2,897,500. The U.S. Bureau of the Census (1978) estimated a net underenumeration of 12.5 percent for a population in 1974 of 3,032,000. In addition, they estimated the population on July 1, 1979, to be 3,645,000 (1981).

SOURCES: Census of March 6, 1974; SALA, 20-626.

Table 17-2

MAJOR URBAN CENTERS IN HONDURAS, 1974

| Rank | Major Urban Centers | Census of March 6, 1974 | | | |
		Enumerated Population	Percent	Adjusted Population[1]	Percent
1	✪ Gran Tegucigalpa, D.C. (1)	302,483	11.4	- -	- -
	Tegucigalpa proper	273,894	10.3	295,500	10.2
2	● San Pedro Sula (2)	153,307	5.8	161,700	5.6
3	● La Ceiba (8)	38,600	1.5	42,100	1.5
4	El Progreso (3)	28,000	1.1	30,600	1.1
5	Puerto Cortés (2)	25,700	1.0	28,000	1.0
6	Choluteca (4)	25,100	.9	27,400	.9
7	Tela (8)	20,000	.8	21,000	.8
			22.4		
8	○ La Lima (2)	14,300		15,600	
9	Comayagua (10)	13,400		14,600	
10	Santa Rosa de Copán (7)	12,100		13,200	
11	Siguatepeque (10)	12,000		13,100	
12	Danlí (9)	11,400		12,400	
13	Juticalpa (6)	10,100		11,000	

1. Adjusted for underenumeration by CELADE (Centro Latinoamericano de Demografía).

SOURCES: Census of March 6, 1974; SALA, 20–629; CELADE, *Boletín Demográfico* 7:13 (Jan. 1974); Robert Fox and Jerrold Huguet, *Population and Urban Trends in Central America and Panama* (Washington, D.C.: Inter-American Development Bank, 1977), pp. 147-148.

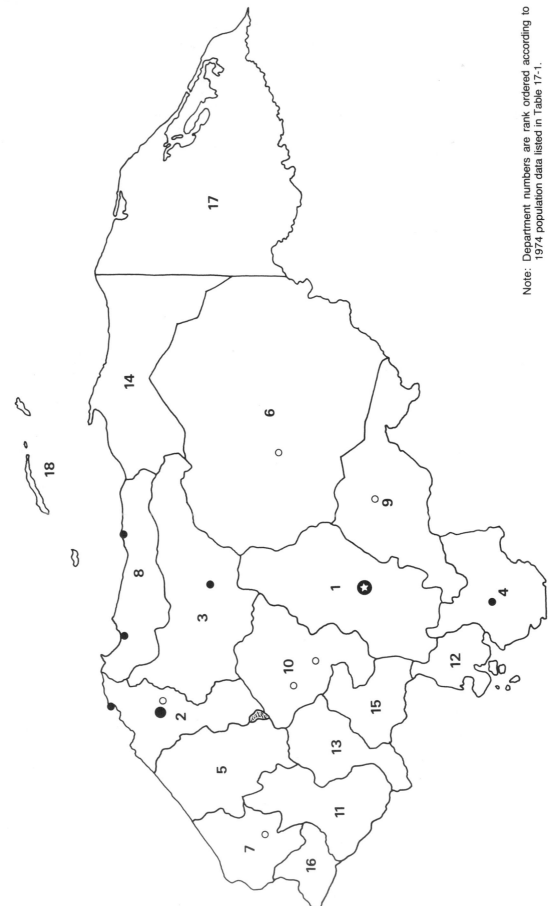

Map 17-2

BASE MAP OF DEPARTMENTS IN HONDURAS AND LOCATION
OF MAJOR URBAN CENTERS

Note: Department numbers are rank ordered according to
1974 population data listed in Table 17-1.

Map 17-3

POPULATION CARTOGRAM OF HONDURAS, 1974

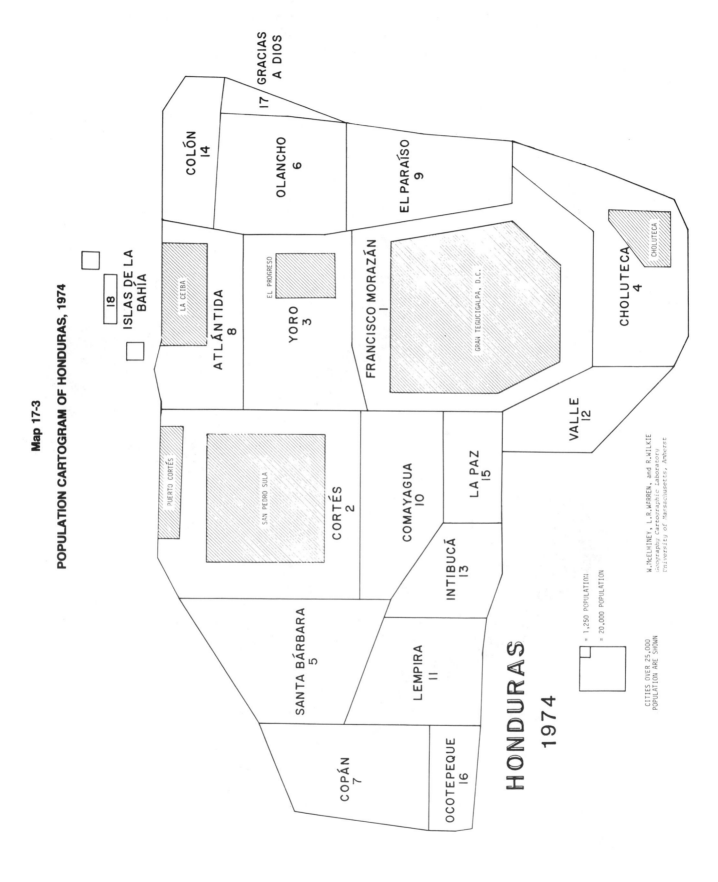

CITIES OVER 25,000
POPULATION ARE SHOWN

□ = 1,250 POPULATION

□ = 20,000 POPULATION

W.McELHINEY, L.R.WARREN, and R.WILKIE
Geography Cartographic Laboratory
University of Massachusetts, Amherst

HONDURAS 1974

Map 17-4

THREE-DIMENSIONAL CHOROPLETH MAP OF TOTAL POPULATION BY
DEPARTMENT IN HONDURAS, 1974
(By Major Civil Division)

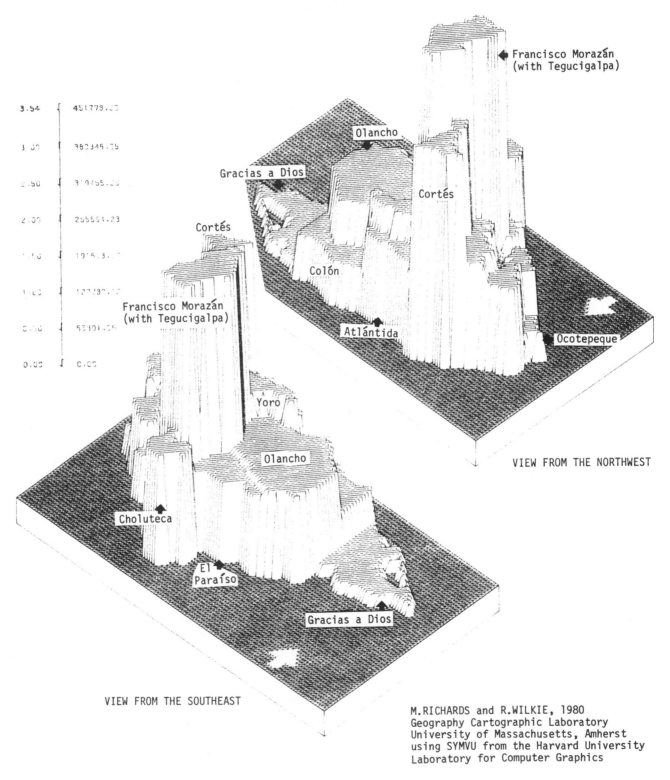

VIEW FROM THE NORTHWEST

VIEW FROM THE SOUTHEAST

M.RICHARDS and R.WILKIE, 1980
Geography Cartographic Laboratory
University of Massachusetts, Amherst
using SYMVU from the Harvard University
Laboratory for Computer Graphics

Map 17-5

THREE-DIMENSIONAL CHOROPLETH MAP OF POPULATION DENSITY
IN HONDURAS, 1974
(Persons per km²)

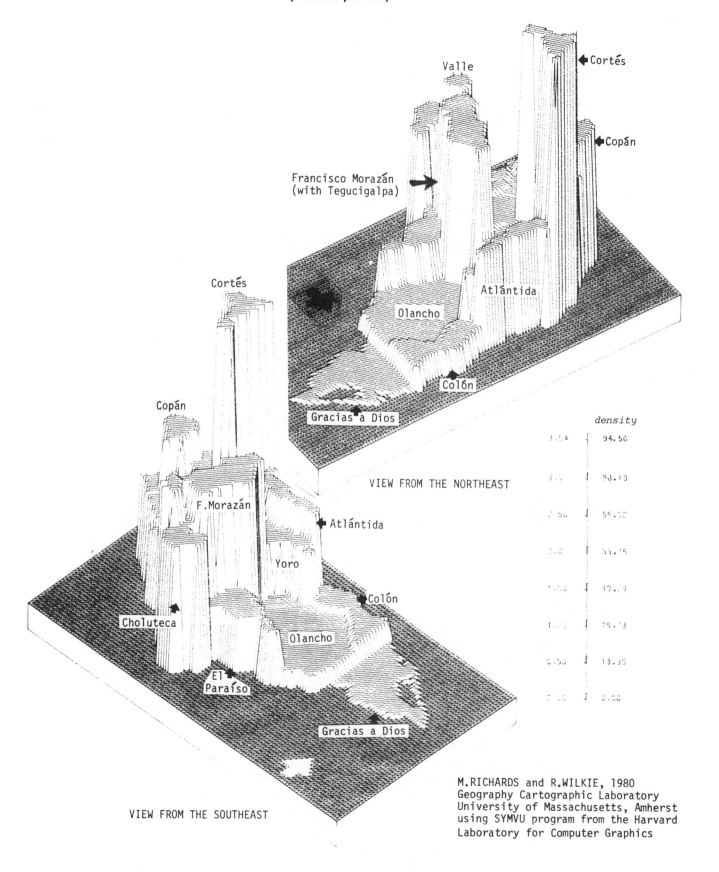

VIEW FROM THE NORTHEAST

VIEW FROM THE SOUTHEAST

M. RICHARDS and R. WILKIE, 1980
Geography Cartographic Laboratory
University of Massachusetts, Amherst
using SYMVU program from the Harvard
Laboratory for Computer Graphics

Map 17-6

THREE-DIMENSIONAL CHOROPLETH MAP OF POPULATION CHANGE
IN HONDURAS, 1961–1974
(%)

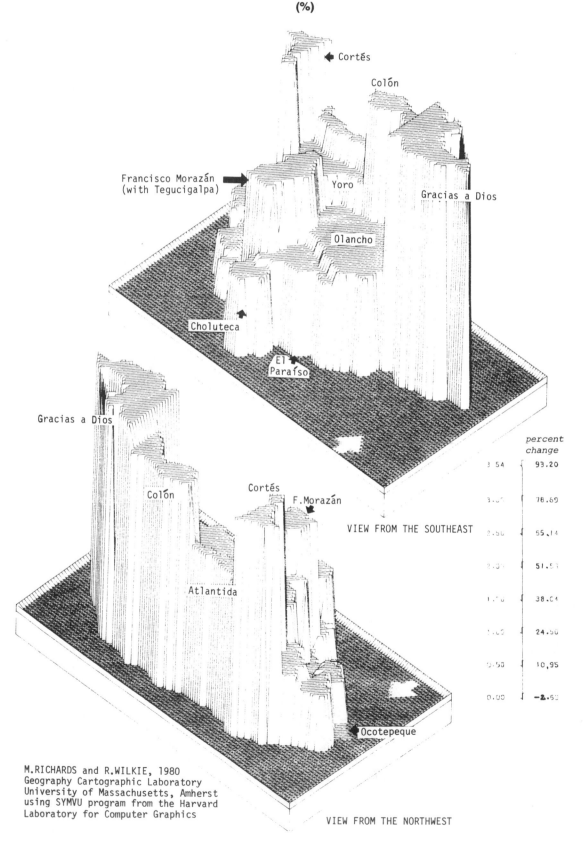

percent change

3.54	93.20
3.00	78.69
2.50	55.14
2.00	51.53
1.70	38.04
1.00	24.50
0.50	10.95
0.00	−2.50

VIEW FROM THE SOUTHEAST

M.RICHARDS and R.WILKIE, 1980
Geography Cartographic Laboratory
University of Massachusetts, Amherst
using SYMVU program from the Harvard
Laboratory for Computer Graphics

VIEW FROM THE NORTHWEST

Photo 17-1

RAISED WOODEN HOUSE TYPICAL OF THE CARIBBEAN
COAST OF CENTRAL AMERICA (1979)

Table 17-3

POPULATION FOR EACH NATIONAL CENSUS IN HONDURAS, 1791–1974

Census Year	Population	Census Year	Population	Census Year	Population
1791	93,505	1910	553,446	1940	1,107,859
1801	130,000	1916	605,997	1945	1,200,542
1881	307,289	1926	700,811	1950	1,368,605
1887	331,917	1930	854,184	1961	1,884,765
1905	500,136	1935	962,000	1967	2,495,000
				1974	2,653,857[a]

a. Recommended adjustment of population to 3,032,000 by the U.S. Bureau of the Census (1978).

Table 17-4

**TOTAL AND PERCENT POPULATION IN FIVE LEVELS OF THE URBAN-RURAL
SETTLEMENT HIERARCHY OF HONDURAS SINCE 1950**

	0	1	2	3	4	SETTLEMENT HIERARCHY	
CENSUS YEAR	DISPERSED Population 1 to 99	VILLAGE 100 to 2,500	SIMPLE URBAN 2,501– 20,000	COMPLEX URBAN 20,001– 500,000	METROPOLITAN over 500,000	Classification	PERCENT in top 2 levels
TOTAL							
1950	. . . .	1,109,939	165,142	93,524	- -		
1961	. . . .	1,449,760	197,078	237,927	- -		
1967	1,703,278	163,997	281,693	346,032	- -		
1974	. . . .	1,963,854	96,813	593,190	- -		
PERCENT							
1950	. . . .	81.1	11.2	6.8	- -	0–2	80 to 86
1961	. . . .	76.9	10.5	12.6	- -	0–3	82.7
1967	68.2	6.6	11.3	13.9	- -	0–3	82.1
1974	. . . .	74.0	3.6	22.4	- -	0–3	84 to 90

SOURCES: Calculated from the various Honduran national censuses since 1950, and from SALA, 20–631, 632, 634, 635, 636, 637, and 638.

Table 17-5

SELECTED INDICATORS OF POPULATION CHANGE AND PER CAPITA GNP IN HONDURAS

Years	Per 1000 Population Births	Per 1000 Population Deaths	Rate of Natural Increase (Annual %)	Number of Years to Double Population	Percent Population Under Age 15	Life Expectancy at Birth	Per Capita GNP (US)
1940-45	37	17	2.0	- -	- -	- -	- -
1945-50	41	14	2.4	- -	- -	- -	- -
1950-55	41	12	2.6	- -	- -	- -	- -
1955-60	43	11	3.2	- -	- -	- -	137[a]
1960-65	52	10	3.4	- -	- -	- -	- -
1965-70	51	9	3.4	- -	- -	- -	- -
1970-74	49	11	3.8	21[b]	51[b]	53[c]	240[b]
1975	49	15	3.5	20	47	54	320
1976	49	14	3.5	20	47	54	340
1977	49	15	3.5	20	47	54	350
1978	47	13	3.5	20	47	55	390
1979	47	12	3.5	20	48	55	450
1980	47	12	3.5	20	48	57	480
1981	47	12	3.5	20	48	57	530
1982	47	12	3.5	20	48	57	560

a. 1955.
b. 1970.
c. 1971.

MAJOR SOURCES:
Births: SALA, 19-204; SALA, 20-705 through 1975.
Deaths: SALA, 18-703d and 706 through 1970.
Life expectancy: SALA, 19-700 through 1970.
Per capita GNP: 1955 data from Ginsburg, *Atlas of Economic Development* (Chicago: University of Chicago Press, 1961).
Rate of natural increase: SALA, 22-626 from CELADE-BD 10 (1972) through 1970.
All other data: Population Reference Bureau, Washington, D.C., annual world population data sheets.

Table 17-6

HONDURAN DEPARTMENTS BY GEOGRAPHICAL SIZE AND SUBDIVISION, 1970

Department	Civil Subdivisions (N)	Area km^2	Area %
Total	281[a]	112,088	100.0
Departments			
Atlántida	7	4,251	3.8
Colón	9	8,875	7.9
Comayagua	18	5,196	4.6
Copán	23	3,203	2.9
Cortés	11	3,954	3.5
Choluteca	16	4,211	3.8
El Paraíso	18	7,218	6.4
Francisco Morazán	27	7,946	7.1
Gracias a Dios	2	16,630	14.8
Intibucá	16	3,072	2.7
Islas de la Bahía	4	261	.2
La Paz	19	2,331	2.1
Lempira	27	4,290	3.8
Ocotepeque	16	1,680	1.5
Olancho	22	24,351	21.7
Santa Bárbara	26	5,115	4.6
Valle	9	1,565	1.4
Yoro	11	7,939	7.1

a. Municipios.
SOURCE: SALA, 21-301.

Map 18-1

PHYSIOGRAPHIC MAP OF MEXICO

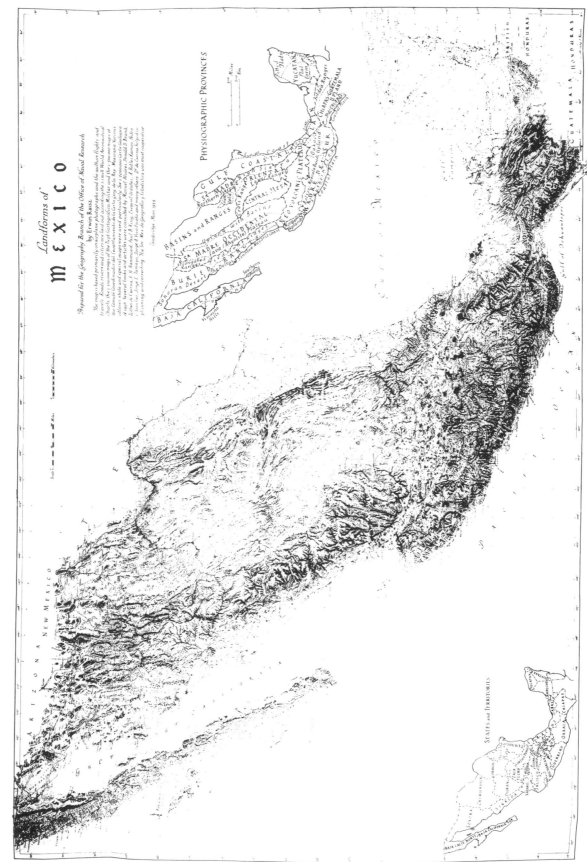

ERWIN RAISZ

18

Mexico

Mexico has had ten official censuses over an 88-year period. The first census (1895) counted 12,632,427 inhabitants. Beginning in 1900, Mexico conducted a census every ten years, with the exception of 1921 rather than 1920. It took until 1950 for the population to slightly more than double to 25,791,017, but by 1970 it had nearly doubled again to 48,225,238. The latest census in 1980 had a tabulated population of 67,405,700, for a rise of 40 percent in the decade. The growth of population alone between 1970 and 1980 equalled the total population living in Mexico in 1940.

The population totals, trends, and characteristics of Mexico are presented in this chapter in eight tables, twelve maps, and three figures. Some of the findings concerning Mexico are outlined below.

URBAN TRENDS

Mexico had three metropolitan centers with more than half a million population in 1970. Greater Mexico City with 10,223,000 had 21.2 percent of the nation's population, and Greater Guadalajara (1,445,000) and Greater Monterrey (1,213,000) were both very dominant regional centers. Together these three centers accounted for 26.7 percent of Mexico's population in 1970, while complex urban cities between 20,000 and 500,000 in size had another 16.2 percent of the population.

RURAL TRENDS

Mexico has been a predominantly rural country throughout most of this century, declining from 71 percent in 1910, to 58 percent in 1950, to 41 percent in 1970. The majority of the inhabitants of rural areas live in villages between 100 and 2,500 in population. In 1970 rural villages still had 38.4 percent of the population of Mexico.

SETTLEMENT HIERARCHY

By 1970 Mexico had moved from the village–simple urban settlement classification (1–2) which dominated the national settlement hierarchy for almost the entire century into a village–metropolitan settlement landscape (1–4), with two-thirds of the population (65 percent) living in those two levels. Compared to other Latin American countries, however, Mexico has gradually evolved a more balanced hierarchy of places.

OTHER DEMOGRAPHIC DATA

The annual rate of population growth in Mexico has been well over 3 percent for most of the time since the 1940s, with peaks of 3.5 percent during the 1960s and again in 1976–77. In 1981–82 the figure came down to 2.5 percent growth a year, a rather dramatic reduction in a short time. Life expectancy in 1982 was sixty-five years, and 42 percent of the population was under fifteen years of age. Per capita GNP in 1982 of $2130 was up by 188 percent from $740 in 1975, ranking Mexico number 5 among the twenty Latin American republics in that category. Because of drastic devaluation of the peso in 1982, however, much of the gains over the last several years might be lost.

Table 18-1

POPULATION DATA AND DENSITY BY STATE IN MEXICO, 1970 AND 1980

1980 Rank	State	1970 Population	1980 Population	1980 Percent	Percent Change 1970-1980	Population Density 1980 (km^2)
1	Distrito Federal	6,874,165	9,373,958	13.9	+36.4	6337
2	México	3,833,185	7,545,692	11.2	+96.9	353
3	Veracruz	3,815,422	5,264,611	7.8	+38.0	73
4	Jalisco	3,296,586	4,293,549	6.4	+30.2	53
5	Puebla	2,508,226	3,279,960	4.9	+30.8	97
6	Michoacán	2,324,226	3,048,704	4.5	+31.2	51
7	Guanajuato	2,270,370	3,044,402	4.5	+34.1	100
8	Oaxaca	2,015,424	2,518,157	3.7	+24.9	27
9	Nuevo León	1,694,689	2,463,298	3.7	+45.3	38
10	Guerrero	1,597,360	2,174,162	3.2	+36.1	34
11	Chiapas	1,569,053	2,096,812	3.1	+33.6	28
12	Chihuahua	1,612,525	1,933,856	2.9	+19.9	8
13	Tamaulipas	1,456,858	1,924,934	2.9	+32.1	24
14	Sinaloa	1,266,528	1,880,098	2.8	+48.4	32
15	San Luis Potosí	1,281,996	1,670,637	2.5	+30.3	26
16	Coahuila	1,114,956	1,558,401	2.3	+39.8	10
17	Hidalgo	1,193,845	1,516,511	2.3	+27.0	73
18	Sonora	1,098,720	1,498,931	2.2	+36.0	8
19	Baja California	870,421	1,225,436	1.8	+40.8	18
20	Durango	939,208	1,160,196	1.7	+23.5	9
21	Tabasco	768,327	1,149,756	1.7	+49.7	46
22	Zacatecas	951,462	1,145,327	1.7	+20.4	16
23	Yucatán	758,355	1,034,648	1.5	+36.4	27
24	Morelos	616,119	931,675	1.4	+51.2	188
25	Querétaro	485,523	726,054	1.1	+49.6	63
26	Nayarit	544,031	730,024	1.1	+34.2	27
27	Tlaxcala	420,638	547,261	.8	+30.1	136
28	Aguascalientes	338,142	503,410	.7	+48.9	92
29	Campeche	251,556	372,227	.6	+48.0	7
30	Colima	241,153	339,202	.5	+40.7	65
31	Baja California Sur	128,019	221,389	.3	+72.9	3
32	Quintana Roo	88,150	209,858	.3	+138.1	4
	Total	48,225,238	67,383,000	100.0	+39.7	34

SOURCES: *X Censo General de Población y Vivienda, Cifras Preliminares* (México, D.F.: Dirección General de Estadística, 1980); SALA, 20-301 and 626.

Table 18–2
MAJOR URBAN CENTERS IN MEXICO, 1970 AND 1978

1978 Rank	Major Urban Centers	1970 Population	1970 Percent	1978 Population
1	◉ Gran Mexico City (1/2)	10,223,102	21.2	13,993,866
	Mexico City proper	8,590,000	17.8	8,988,230
	Netzahualcóyotl	580,000	1.2	2,067,992
	other population	1,053,102	2.2	2,937,644
2	● Gran Guadalajara (4)	1,445,000	3.0	2,343,034
	Guadalajara proper	1,194,000	2.5	1,813,131
	Zapopan	- -	- -	97,000
	Tláquepaque	- -	- -	71,000
	other population	- -	- -	361,903
3	Gran Monterrey (9)	1,213,000	2.5	1,923,402
	Monterrey proper	858,000	1.8	1,054,029
4	● Puebla (5)	402,000	.8	677,959
5	Ciudad Juárez (12)	407,000	.8	597,096
6	León (7)	365,000	.8	589,950
7	Tijuana (19)	277,000	.6	534,993
8	Tampico/Ciudad Madero (13)	260,000	.6	510,088
9	● Acapulco (10)	172,000	.4	421,088
10	Torreón/Gómez Palacio (16/20)	336,695	.7	397,159
11	Chihuahua (12)	257,000	.6	369,545
12	Mexicali (19)	263,000	.6	338,423
13	San Luis Potosí (15)	230,000	.5	315,228
14	Culiacán (14)	168,000	.3	302,229
15	Hermosillo (18)	180,000	.4	299,687
16	Veracruz (3)	214,000	.4	295,297
17	Mérida (23)	212,000	.4	263,186
	Total Population	15,448,102	32.0	24,172,230(+64%)
	Other Major Cities			
18	● Aguascalientes (28)	181,000		247,764
19	Saltillo (16)	161,000		245,738
20	Morelia (6)	161,000		239,377
21	Orizaba/Córdoba (3)	141,000		234,502
22	Coatzacoalcos/Minatitlan (3)	136,000		232,636
23	Cuernavaca (24)	134,117		226,649
24	Toluca (2)	114,000		222,885
25	Reynosa (13)	137,000		218,683
26	Durango (20)	151,000		218,629
27	Nueva Laredo (13)	150,922		214,161
28	○ Jalapa (3)	122,000		191,096
29	Poza Rica (de Hidalgo) (3)	121,341		188,928
30	Matamoros (13)	138,000		186,480
31	Mazatlán (14)	120,000		177,673
32	Querétaro (25)	112,993		176,200
33	Ciudad Obregón (18)	114,000		172,974
34	Villahermosa (21)	99,565		165,468
35	Irapuato (7)	117,000		155,601
36	Uruapan (6)	83,000		138,264
37	Tepic (26)	111,300		133,353
38	Oaxaca (8)	116,800		131,193
39	Monclova (16)	99,000		130,918
40	Ciudad Victoria (13)	83,000		121,379
41	Celaya (7)	81,500		114,365
42	Los Mochis (14)	74,000		111,779
43	Pachuca (17)	83,892		105,225
44	Campeche (29)	69,506		103,613
45	Tuxtla Gutiérrez (11)	53,000		101,613
46	Ciudad Delicias (12)	86,000		- -
47	Ensenada (19)	84,000		- -
48	Piedras Negras (17)	77,000		- -
49	Colima (30)	58,450		- -

SOURCES: Census of Mexico (1970); *United Nations Demographic Yearbook 1978*, p. 212; *Atlas of Mexico* (Austin: University of Texas, 1970), p. 40; *América en Cifras 1974*, p. 40.

Map 18-2

BASE MAP OF STATES IN MEXICO AND LOCATION OF MAJOR
URBAN CENTERS

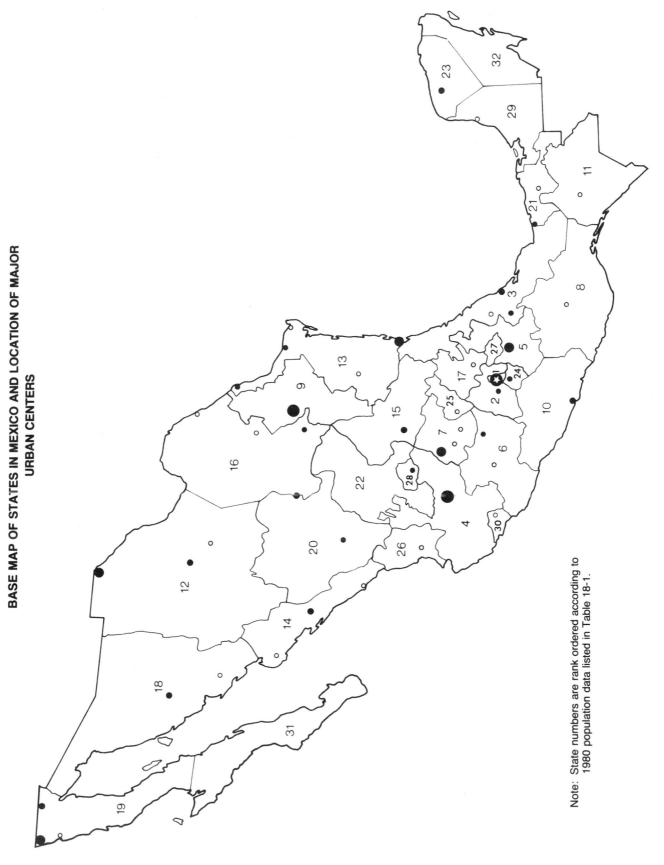

Note: State numbers are rank ordered according to
        1980 population data listed in Table 18-1.

Map 18-3A

POPULATION CARTOGRAM OF MEXICO, 1980

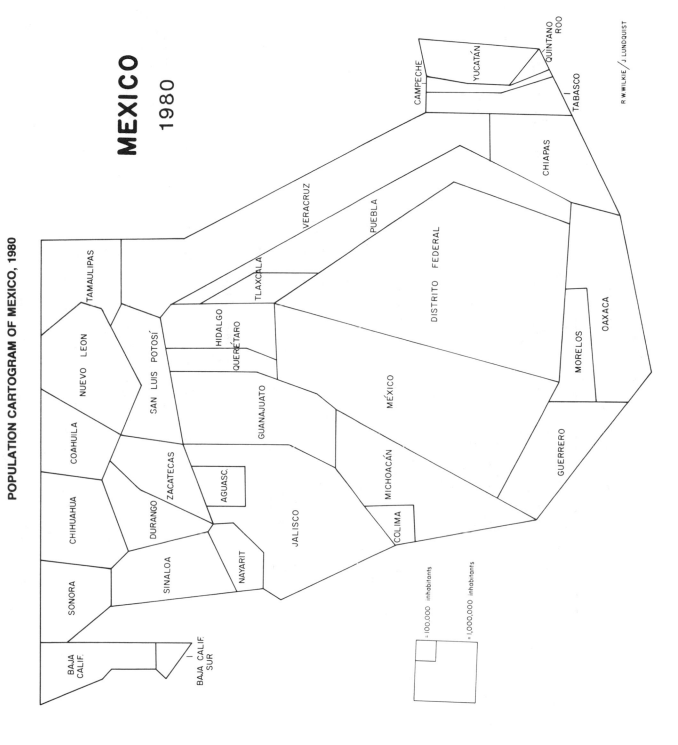

MEXICO
1980

R.W.WILKIE / J.LUNDQUIST

Map 18-3B

POPULATION CARTOGRAM OF MEXICO, 1970

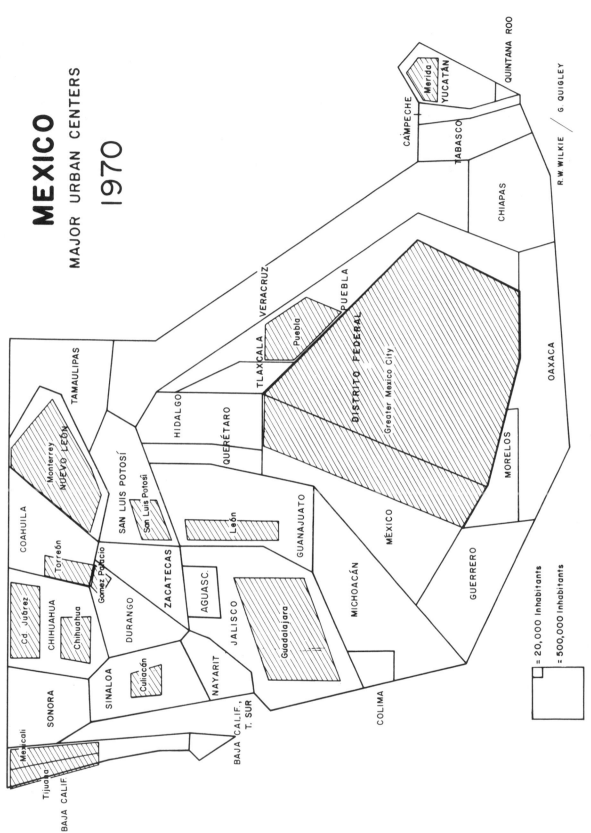

MEXICO

MAJOR URBAN CENTERS

1970

R.W. WILKIE / G. QUIGLEY

= 20,000 Inhabitants

= 500,000 Inhabitants

CITIES SHOWN OVER 250,000 POPULATION

Map 18-3C

POPULATION CARTOGRAM OF MEXICO, 1960

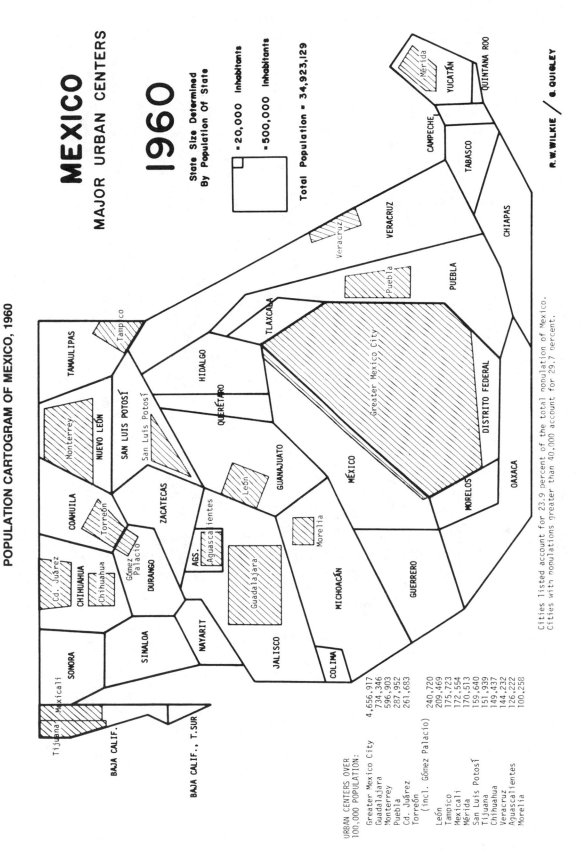

MEXICO
MAJOR URBAN CENTERS
1960

State Size Determined
By Population Of State

= 20,000 Inhabitants

= 500,000 Inhabitants

Total Population = 34,923,129

R.W. WILKIE / G. QUIGLEY

Cities listed account for 23.9 percent of the total population of Mexico.
Cities with populations greater than 40,000 account for 29.7 percent.

URBAN CENTERS OVER
100,000 POPULATION:

Greater Mexico City	4,656,917
Guadalajara	734,346
Monterrey	596,903
Puebla	287,952
Cd. Juárez	261,683
Torreón	
(incl. Gómez Palacio)	240,720
León	209,469
Tampico	175,723
Mexicali	172,554
Mérida	170,513
San Luis Potosí	159,640
Tijuana	151,939
Chihuahua	149,437
Veracruz	144,232
Aguascalientes	126,222
Morelia	100,258

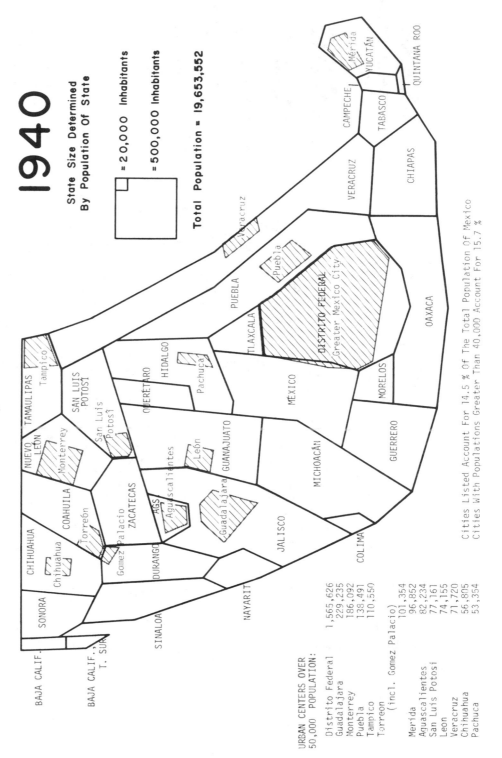

Map 18-3D

POPULATION CARTOGRAM OF MEXICO, 1940

MEXICO

MAJOR URBAN CENTERS

1940

State Size Determined
By Population Of State

= 20,000 Inhabitants

= 500,000 Inhabitants

Total Population = 19,653,552

Cities Listed Account For 14.5 % Of The Total Population Of Mexico
Cities With Populations Greater Than 40,000 Account For 15.7 %

R.W. WILKIE / **G. QUIGLEY**

URBAN CENTERS OVER
50,000 POPULATION:

Distrito Federal	1,565,626
Guadalajara	229,235
Monterrey	186,092
Puebla	138,491
Tampico	110,550
Torreon	
(incl. Gomez Palacio)	101,354
Merida	96,852
Aguascalientes	82,234
San Luis Potosí	77,161
Leon	74,155
Veracruz	71,720
Chihuahua	56,805
Pachuca	53,354

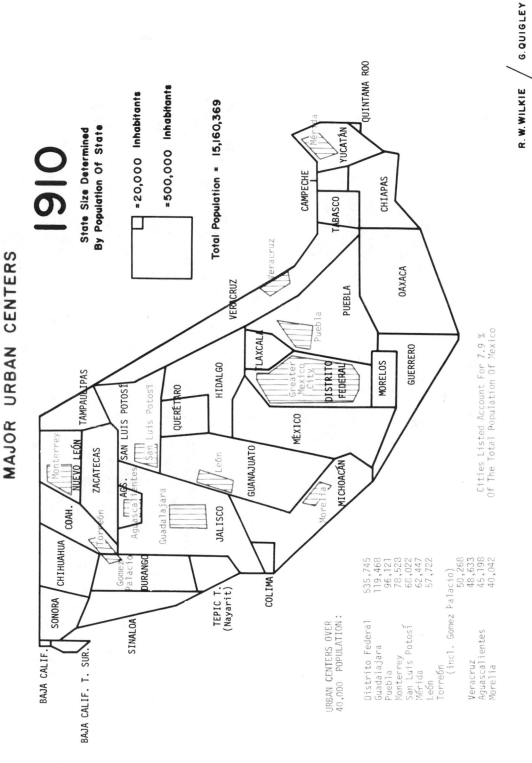

Map 18-3E

POPULATION CARTOGRAM OF MEXICO, 1910

MEXICO

MAJOR URBAN CENTERS

1910

State Size Determined By Population Of State

☐ =20,000 Inhabitants

☐ =500,000 Inhabitants

Total Population = 15,160,369

Cities Listed Account For 7.9 %
Of The Total Population Of Mexico

URBAN CENTERS OVER
40,000 POPULATION:

Distrito Federal	535,745
Guadalajara	119,468
Puebla	96,121
Monterrey	78,528
San Luis Potosí	68,022
Mérida	62,447
León	57,722
Torreón	
(incl. Gomez Palacio)	50,268
Veracruz	48,633
Aguascalientes	45,198
Morelia	40,042

R.W.WILKIE / G.QUIGLEY

Map 18-4

THREE-DIMENSIONAL CHOROPLETH MAP OF TOTAL POPULATION BY STATE IN MEXICO, 1980

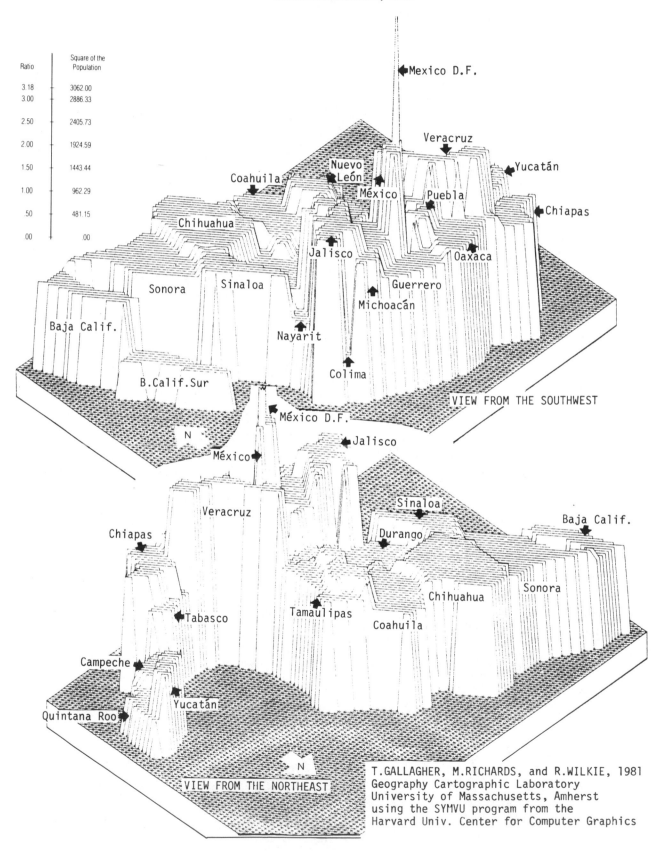

Ratio	Square of the Population
3.18	3062.00
3.00	2886.33
2.50	2405.73
2.00	1924.59
1.50	1443.44
1.00	962.29
.50	481.15
.00	.00

VIEW FROM THE SOUTHWEST

VIEW FROM THE NORTHEAST

T.GALLAGHER, M.RICHARDS, and R.WILKIE, 1981
Geography Cartographic Laboratory
University of Massachusetts, Amherst
using the SYMVU program from the
Harvard Univ. Center for Computer Graphics

Map 18-5

THREE-DIMENSIONAL CHOROPLETH MAP OF POPULATION DENSITY
IN MEXICO, 1980
(Persons per km²)

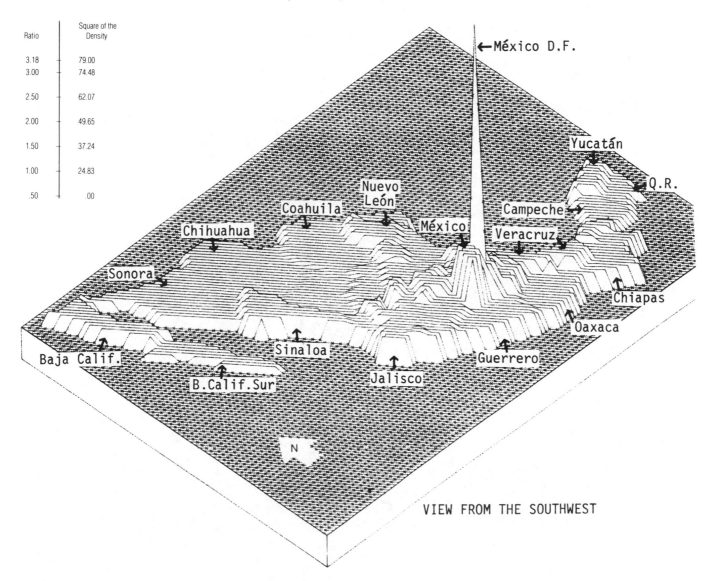

Ratio	Square of the Density
3.18	79.00
3.00	74.48
2.50	62.07
2.00	49.65
1.50	37.24
1.00	24.83
.50	.00

VIEW FROM THE SOUTHWEST

T.GALLAGHER, M.RICHARDS, and R.WILKIE, 1981
Geography Cartographic Laboratory
University of Massachusetts, Amherst
using the SYMVU program from the
Harvard Univ. Center for Computer Graphics

Map 18-6

THREE-DIMENSIONAL CHOROPLETH AND ISOPLETH MAPS OF POPULATION
CHANGE IN MEXICO, 1970–1980
(%)

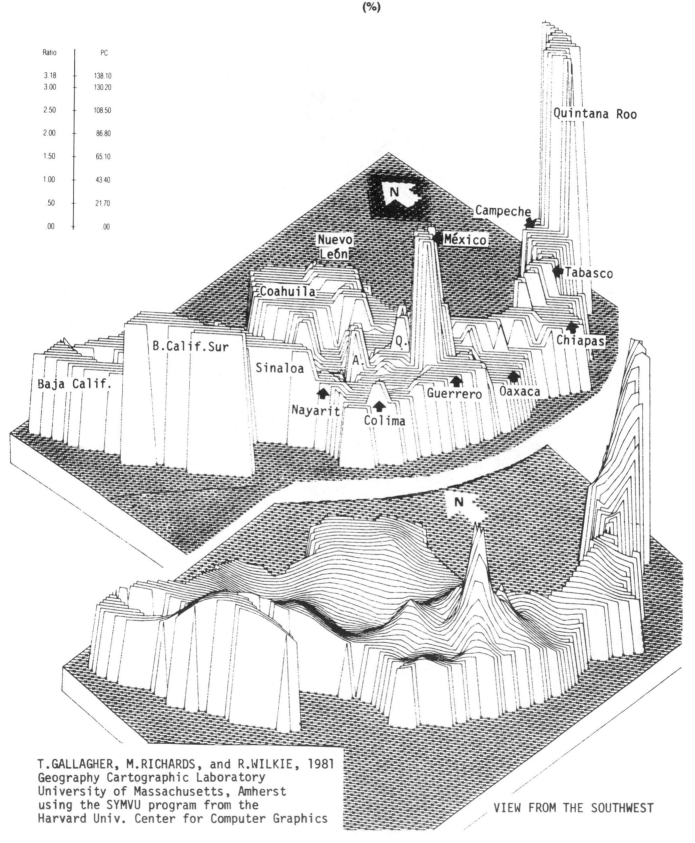

T.GALLAGHER, M.RICHARDS, and R.WILKIE, 1981
Geography Cartographic Laboratory
University of Massachusetts, Amherst
using the SYMVU program from the
Harvard Univ. Center for Computer Graphics

VIEW FROM THE SOUTHWEST

Table 18-3

POPULATION FOR EACH NATIONAL CENSUS IN
MEXICO, 1895–1980

Census Year	Population	Census Year	Population
1895	12,632,427	1940	19,653,552
1900	13,607,259	1950	25,791,017
1910	15,160,369	1960	34,923,129
1921	14,334,780	1970	48,225,238[a]
1930	16,552,722	1980	67,405,700

a. Recommended adjustment of population to 49,417,000 by the U.S.
Bureau of the Census (1978).

Table 18-4

TOTAL AND PERCENT POPULATION IN FIVE LEVELS OF THE URBAN-RURAL
SETTLEMENT HIERARCHY OF MEXICO SINCE 1950

	0	1	2	3	4	SETTLEMENT HIERARCHY	
CENSUS YEAR	DISPERSED Population 1 to 99	VILLAGE 100 to 2,500	SIMPLE URBAN 2,501– 20,000	COMPLEX URBAN 20,001– 500,000	METROPOLITAN over 500,000	Classification	PERCENT in top 2 levels
TOTAL							
1950	1,772,256	13,018,043	4,795,348	3,609,477	2,604,893		
1960	1,571,541	15,645,561	6,181,394	5,517,855	6,006,778		
1970	1,446,757	18,518,491	7,548,675	7,830,211	12,881,102		
PERCENT							
1950	6.9	50.5	18.6	13.9	10.1	1–2	69.1
1960	4.5	44.8	17.7	15.8	17.2	1–2	62.5
1970	3.0	38.4	15.7	16.2	26.7	1–4	65.1

SOURCES: Calculated from the various Mexican national censuses since 1950, and from SALA, 20–631, 632, 634, 635, 636, 637, and 638.

Map 18-7

THREE-DIMENSIONAL CHOROPLETH MAP OF POPULATION CHANGE IN MEXICO, 1960–1970

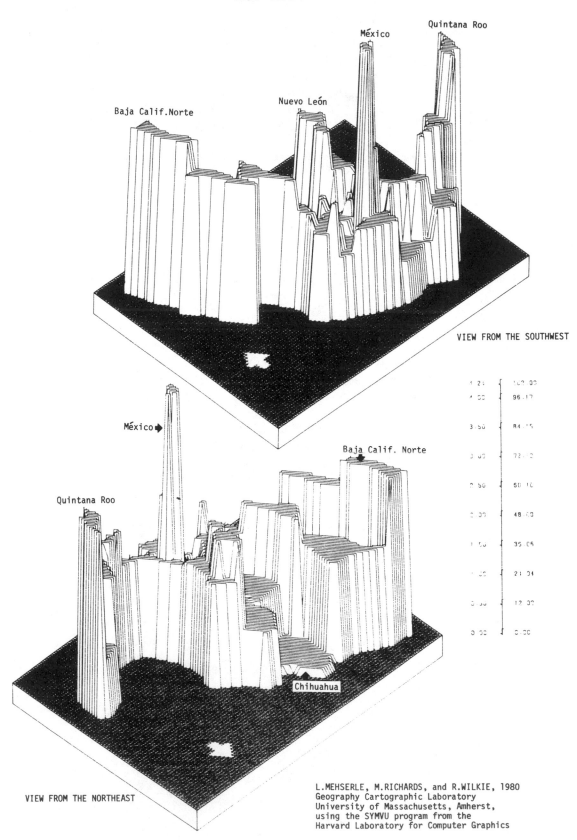

VIEW FROM THE SOUTHWEST

VIEW FROM THE NORTHEAST

L.MEHSERLE, M.RICHARDS, and R.WILKIE, 1980
Geography Cartographic Laboratory
University of Massachusetts, Amherst,
using the SYMVU program from the
Harvard Laboratory for Computer Graphics

Table 18-5

SELECTED INDICATORS OF POPULATION CHANGE AND PER CAPITA GNP IN MEXICO

Years	Per 1000 Population		Rate of Natural Increase (Annual %)	Number of Years to Double Population	Percent Population Under Age 15	Life Expectancy at Birth	Per Capita GNP (US)
	Births	Deaths					
1940–45	44	22	2.9	- -	- -	- -	- -
1945–50	44	18	3.1	- -	- -	- -	- -
1950–55	44	15	3.0	- -	- -	- -	187[a] in 1955
1955–60	45	12	3.2	- -	- -	- -	- -
1960–65	45	12	3.5	- -	- -	- -	- -
1965–70	43	10	3.5	- -	- -	- -	- -
1970–74	42	9	3.3	21[b]	46[b]	- -	490[b]
1975	42	9	3.2	22	46	63	740
1976	46	8	3.5	20	46	63	1,000
1977	42	7	3.5	20	46	63	1,190
1978	42	8	3.4	20	46	65	1,090
1979	41	7	3.4	20	46	65	1,110
1980	37	6	3.1	22	46	65	1,290
1981	33	8	2.5	28	42	65	1,590
1982	32	6	2.5	27	42	65	2,130

a. 1955.
b. 1970.

MAJOR SOURCES:

Births: SALA, 19-204; SALA, 20-705 through 1975.

Deaths: SALA, 18-703*d* and 706 through 1970.

Life expectancy: SALA, 19-700 through 1970.

Per capita GNP: 1955 data from Ginsburg, *Atlas of Economic Development* (Chicago: University of Chicago Press, 1961).

Rate of natural increase: SALA, 22-626 from CELADE-BD 10 (1972) through 1970.

All other data: Population Reference Bureau, Washington, D.C., annual world population data sheets.

Table 18-6

MEXICAN STATES BY GEOGRAPHICAL
SIZE AND SUBDIVISION, 1970

State	Civil Subdivisions (N)	Area km²	Area %
Total	2,385[a]	1,958,201	100.0
Federal District	13	1,479	.1
States			
Aguascalientes	9	5,471	.3
Baja California	4	69,921	3.6
Baja California Sur	7	73,475	3.7
Campeche	8	50,812	2.6
Coahuila	38	149,982	7.6
Colima	10	5,191	.3
Chiapas	111	74,211	3.8
Chihuahua	67	244,938	12.5
Durango	38	123,181	6.3
Guanajuato	46	30,491	1.5
Guerrero	75	64,281	3.3
Hidalgo	82	20,813	1.1
Jalisco	124	80,836	4.1
México	120	21,355	1.1
Michoacán	112	59,928	3.0
Morelos	32	4,950	.3
Nayarit	19	26,979	1.4
Nuevo León	52	64,924	3.3
Oaxaca	570	93,952	4.8
Puebla	217	33,902	1.7
Querétaro	18	11,449	.6
Quintana Roo (terr.)	4	50,212	2.6
San Luis Potosí	55	63,068	3.2
Sinaloa	17	58,328	3.0
Sonora	69	182,052	9.3
Tabasco	17	25,267	1.3
Tamaulipas	42	79,384	4.0
Tlaxcala	44	4,016	.2
Veracruz	203	71,699	3.7
Yucatán	106	38,402	2.0
Zacatecas	56	73,252	3.7

a. Municipios.
b. Excludes 5,363 km² of islands.
SOURCE: SALA, 21-301.

Figure 18-1

MEXICO PERCENT OF POPULATION IN EACH URBAN-RURAL LEVEL, 1910–1970

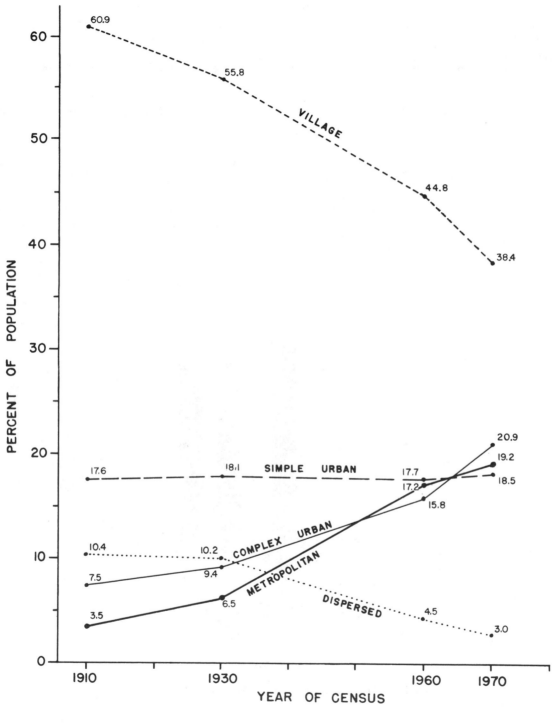

Richard Wilkie

Table 18–7

POPULATION CHANGE BY REGION IN MEXICO, 1970–1980

Region	1970 Total Population	Percent	Change, 1970 to 1980 Total Growth	Percent Increase	Percent of All Growth	1980 Total Population	Percent
CORE REGION 10 states and Federal District	24,161,025	50.1	10,718,675	44.4	55.9	34,879,700	51.7
CORE FRINGE 11 states	15,652,609	32.5	5,246,141	33.5	27.3	20,898,750	31.0
PERIPHERY (Frontier) 10 states	8,411,604	17.4	3,215,646	38.2	16.8	11,627,250	17.3
Total	48,225,238	100.0	19,180,462	39.8	100.0	67,405,700	100.0

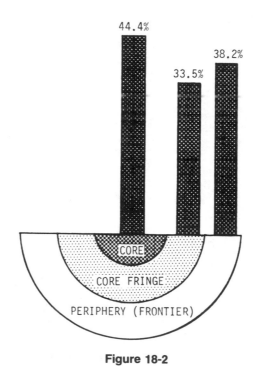

Figure 18-2

MEXICO POPULATION INCREASE BY REGION, 1970–1980

Figure 18-3

MEXICO PERCENT OF TOTAL POPULATION BY REGION, 1980

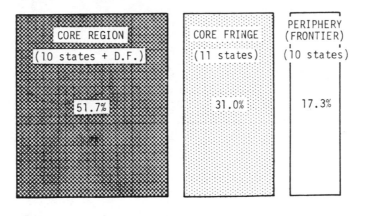

CORE REGION
(10 states + D.F.)

51.7%

CORE FRINGE
(11 states)

31.0%

PERIPHERY
(FRONTIER)
(10 states)

17.3%

CORE REGION: Distrito Federal, México, Morelos, Tlaxcala, Puebla, Hidalgo, Querétaro, Guanajuato, Aguascalientes, Michoaćan, and Jalisco.

CORE FRINGE: Colima, Guerrero, Oaxaca, Veracruz, San Luis Potosí, Nuevo León, Coahuila, Zacatecas, Durango, and Nayarit.

PERIPHERY (Frontier): Baja California, Baja California Sur, Sonora, Sinaloa, Chihuahua, Chiapas, Tabasco, Campeche, Yucatán , and Quintana Roo.

Map 18-8

LOCATION OF MEXICO POPULATION REGIONS

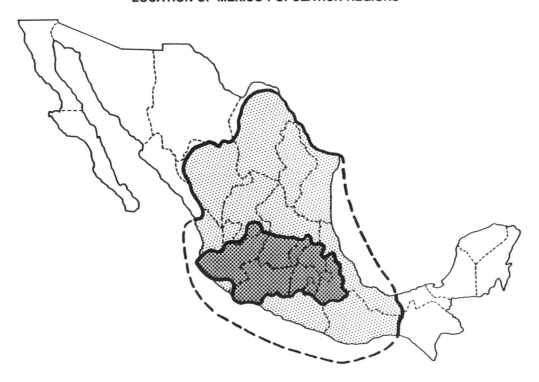

Table 18-8A

MEXICO 1910: PERCENT OF POPULATION IN EACH URBAN-RURAL LEVEL

Region	0 DISPERSED POPULATION 1-99	1 VILLAGE 100-2,500	2 SIMPLE URBAN 2,501-20,000	3 COMPLEX URBAN 20,001-500,000	4 METROPOLITAN OVER 500,000	Landscape Settlement Classification	Percent in top 2 Levels
NORTH							
Baja California / Baja California Territorio Sur	32.3	45.9	21.9	—	—	1-0	78.2
Chihuahua	19.0	55.2	33.9	—	—	1-2	89.1
Coahuila	9.7	47.6	23.5	19.2	—	1-2	71.1
Nuevo León	17.7	48.5	12.3	21.5	—	1-3	70.0
Sonora	21.4	56.0	22.5	—	—	1-2	78.5
Tamaulipas	30.5	45.9	23.7	—	—	1-0	76.4
WEST							
Durango	14.4	65.7	13.3	6.6	—	1-0	80.1
Jalisco / Colima	19.8	51.3	17.7	11.2	—	1-0	61.1
Nayarit (Tepic Terr.)	23.4	52.7	23.9	—	—	1-2	76.6
Sinaloa	23.6	60.7	9.1	6.6	—	1-0	84.3
WEST CENTRAL							
Distrito Federal	.3	—	—	—	99.7	4-0	100.0
México	2.5	70.7	21.6	5.3	—	1-2	92.3
Morelos	2.1	62.1	36.0	—	—	1-2	98.1
Guanajuato	9.9	59.3	18.2	12.6	—	1-2	98.1
Michoacán	13.0	61.7	21.3	4.0	—	1-2	83.0
EAST CENTRAL							
Aguascalientes / Zacatecas	8.8	62.6	16.7	11.9	—	1-2	79.3
Hidalgo	14.5	74.8	4.7	6.0	—	1-0	89.3
Puebla	3.0	69.9	18.8	8.7	—	1-2	88.4
Querétaro	5.2	73.7	7.6	13.5	—	1-3	87.2
San Luis Potosí	5.3	66.2	17.8	10.8	—	1-2	84.0
Tlaxcala	2.4	76.6	20.9	—	—	1-2	97.5
GULF							
Campeche	10.4	55.7	33.9	—	—	1-2	89.6
Quintana Roo, Terr.	9.6	90.4	—	—	—	1-0	100.0
Tabasco	21.7	64.4	14.0	—	—	1-0	86.1
Veracruz	5.2	66.4	18.8	9.5	—	1-2	85.2
Yucatán	12.3	56.3	13.0	18.4	—	1-2	69.3
SOUTH							
Chiapas	20.7	60.7	18.5	—	—	1-0	81.4
Guerrero	6.7	77.9	15.4	—	—	1-2	93.3
Oaxaca	2.4	77.9	16.0	3.7	—	1-2	93.9

SOURCE: *Censo General de la Población*, 1910; regions are after J.W. Wilkie, 1970a, except that Baja California Territorio Sur is here included in the North Zone not in the West Zone.

Table 18-8B

MEXICO 1930: PERCENT OF POPULATION IN EACH URBAN-RURAL LEVEL

Region	0 DISPERSED POPULATION 1-99	1 VILLAGE 100-2,500	2 SIMPLE URBAN 2,501-20,000	3 COMPLEX URBAN 20,001-500,000	4 METROPOLITAN OVER 500,000	Landscape Settlement Classification	Percent in top 2 Levels
NORTH							
Baja California	9.3	36.4	54.3	--	--	2-1	90.7
Baja California Territorio Sur	28.4	35.5	36.1	--	--	1-0	71.6
Chihuahua	18.2	48.8	15.7	17.3	--	0-1	67.0
Coahuila	10.3	47.9	16.8	25.5	--	1-3	73.4
Nuevo León	18.8	40.1	9.3	3.18	--	1-2	71.9
Sonora	15.9	47.4	36.7	--	--	1-2	84.1
Tamaulipas	21.9	35.3	10.4	32.4	--	1-3	67.7
WEST							
Durango	15.7	61.1	8.3	14.9	--	0-1	76.8
Jalisco } Colima	16.8	40.1	27.9	15.2	--	1-2	68.0
Nayarit	14.6	50.4	35.0	--	--	1-2	85.4
Sinaloa	17.2	59.9	15.5	7.4	--	0-1	77.1
WEST CENTRAL							
Distrito Federal	--	--	--	--	100.0	4-1	100.0
Guanajuato	12.4	53.5	21.6	12.5	--	1-2	75.1
México	3.8	75.7	16.3	4.2	--	1-2	92.0
Michoacán	12.7	61.0	22.5	3.8	--	1-2	83.5
Morelos	2.1	72.7	25.2	--	--	1-2	97.9
(Mexico City Metropolitan region: D.F., México, Morelos)	1.7	35.9	8.3	1.8	52.3	4-1	88.2
EAST CENTRAL							
Aguascalientes } Zacatecas	11.9	57.2	20.4	10.5	--	1-2	77.6
Hidalgo	9.5	73.5	10.6	6.4	--	1-2	84.1
Puebla	2.6	69.9	17.5	10.0	--	1-2	87.4
Querétaro	9.1	71.2	5.8	13.9	--	1-3	85.1
San Luis Potosí	12.5	60.2	14.5	12.8	--	1-2	74.7
Tlaxcala	3.3	69.2	27.5	--	--	1-2	96.7
GULF							
Campeche	9.2	45.8	21.2	23.8	--	1-3	69.6
Quintana Roo, Terr.	32.4	37.6	30.0	--	--	0-1	70.0
Tabasco	.3	82.8	16.9	--	--	1-2	99.7
Veracruz	8.5	62.7	18.1	10.7	--	1-2	80.8
Yucatán	7.1	44.7	23.6	24.6	--	1-3	69.3
SOUTH							
Chiapas	27.0	55.5	17.5	--	--	0-1	82.5
Guerrero	7.6	77.2	15.2	--	--	1-2	92.4
Oaxaca	3.6	78.4	14.9	3.1	--	1-2	93.3

SOURCE: *Censo General de la Población,* 1930.

Table 18-8C

MEXICO 1960: PERCENT OF POPULATION IN EACH URBAN-RURAL LEVEL

Region	0 DISPERSED POPULATION 1-99	1 VILLAGE 100-2,500	2 SIMPLE URBAN 2,501-20,000	3 COMPLEX URBAN 20,001-500,000	4 METROPOLITAN OVER 500,000	Landscape Settlement Classification	Landscape Settlement Percent in top 2 Levels
NORTH							
Baja California	1.2	21.2	6.6	71.0	--	3-1	92.2
Baja California Territorio Sur	22.9	40.8	6.6	29.7	--	1-3	70.5
Chihuahua	6.6	36.2	16.9	40.3	--	3-1	76.5
Coahuila	4.3	38.9	17.5	49.3	--	3-1	78.2
Nuevo León	4.6	25.0	12.5	2.5	55.3	4-1	80.3
Sonora	9.5	33.0	19.8	37.7	--	3-1	70.7
Tamaulipas	8.1	32.1	10.1	49.7	--	3-1	81.8
WEST							
Durango	6.0	58.5	14.7	20.8	--	1-3	79.3
Jalisco ⎰ Colima	7.9	33.0	24.3	6.2	28.3	1-4	61.3
Nayarit	6.0	51.4	28.8	13.9	--	1-2	80.2
Sinaloa	6.7	55.2	14.5	23.7	--	1-3	78.9
WEST CENTRAL							
Distrito Federal	--	--	--	--	100.0	4-2	100.0
Guanajuato	6.1	47.5	17.2	29.2	--	1-3	76.7
México	1.1	60.3	33.2	5.4	--	1-2	93.5
Michoacán	6.2	53.2	25.6	15.0	--	1-2	78.8
Morelos	.4	46.4	43.6	9.6	--	1-2	90.0
(Mexico City Metropolitan region: D.F., Morelos, México, Tlaxcala)	.4	22.9	28.5	10.5	37.8	4-2	66.3
EAST CENTRAL							
Aguascalientes ⎰ Zacatecas	6.8	58.5	16.4	18.3	--	1-3	76.8
Hidalgo	3.5	74.1	13.2	9.2	--	1-2	83.3
Puebla	1.3	59.5	21.4	17.8	--	1-2	80.9
Querétaro	5.3	66.6	9.1	19.0	--	1-3	85.6
San Luis Potosí	5.9	60.5	16.1	17.5	--	1-3	78.0
Tlaxcala	2.2	54.0	43.9	--	--	1-2	97.9
GULF							
Campeche	4.5	32.3	24.5	38.7	--	3-1	71.0
Quintana Roo, Terr.	15.2	53.3	31.4	--	--	1-2	84.7
Tabasco	3.4	70.0	16.1	10.5	--	1-2	86.1
Veracruz	4.7	55.7	23.3	16.3	--	1-2	78.0
Yucatán	5.2	35.0	32.0	27.8	--	1-2	67.0
SOUTH							
Chiapas	10.6	65.0	15.7	8.8	--	1-2	80.7
Guerrero	4.0	70.2	19.3	6.4	--	1-2	89.5
Oaxaca	2.0	83.5	10.4	4.2	--	1-2	93.9

SOURCE: *Censo General de Población*, 1960.

Table 18-8D

MEXICO 1980: PERCENT OF POPULATION IN EACH URBAN-RURAL LEVEL

Region	0 DISPERSED POPULATION 1-99	1 VILLAGE 100-2,500	2 SIMPLE URBAN 2,501-20,000	3 COMPLEX URBAN 20,001-500,000	4 METROPOLITAN OVER 500,000	Landscape Settlement Classification	Percent in top 2 Levels
NORTH							
Baja California	.8	13.6	8.3	77.3	--	3-1	90.9
Baja California Territorio Sur	16.0	30.1	18.0	35.9	--	3-1	66.0
Chihuahua	5.4	29.2	13.0	52.4	--	3-1	81.6
Coahuila	2.5	24.7	15.2	57.5	--	3-1	82.2
Nuevo León	4.0	19.5	18.4	7.4	50.6	4-1	70.1
Sonora	7.0	27.2	14.7	51.1	--	3-1	78.3
Tamaulipas	5.4	25.6	9.3	59.6	--	3-1	85.2
WEST							
Durango	5.4	53.1	17.0	24.5	--	1-3	77.6
Jalisco } Colima	6.1	25.3	22.7	12.1	33.8	4-2	59.1
Nayarit	4.1	45.9	30.2	19.8	--	1-2	76.1
Sinaloa	5.3	46.6	17.9	30.1	--	1-3	76.7
WEST CENTRAL							
Distrito Federal	--	--	--	--	100.0	4-2	100.0
Guanajuato	3.9	44.0	15.7	36.4	--	1-3	80.4
México	.8	38.0	40.5	5.6	15.1	2-1	78.5
Michoacán	4.8	49.0	23.4	22.8	--	1-2	72.4
Morelos	.4	29.6	48.2	21.8	--	2-1	77.8
(Mexico City Metropolitan region: D.F., Morelos, México, Tlaxcala)	.3	15.8	17.3	3.1	63.5	4-2	80.8
EAST CENTRAL							
Aguascalientes } Zacatecas	5.9	54.3	16.8	23.0	--	1-3	77.3
Hidalgo	1.9	69.9	18.2	10.3	--	1-2	88.1
Puebla	1.1	52.4	24.3	22.3	--	1-2	74.7
Querétaro	3.5	60.9	12.3	23.3	--	1-3	84.2
San Luis Potosí	4.7	56.3	15.1	23.9	--	1-3	70.2
Tlaxcala	1.7	51.0	42.3	5.0	--	1-2	93.3
GULF							
Campeche	3.1	33.0	22.4	41.4	--	3-1	74.4
Quintana Roo, Terr.	9.1	54.3	9.7	26.9	--	1-2	81.2
Tabasco	.8	65.7	20.5	13.0	--	1-3	86.2
Veracruz	1.6	51.2	21.5	25.6	--	2-1	76.8
Yucatán	3.1	33.0	35.8	28.1	--	2-1	68.8
SOUTH							
Chiapas	8.2	64.1	15.1	12.6	--	1-2	79.2
Guerrero	3.0	61.3	17.9	17.7	--	1-2	87.3
Oaxaca	1.5	70.2	20.2	8.1	--	1-2	90.4

SOURCE: *Censo General de Población*, 1970.

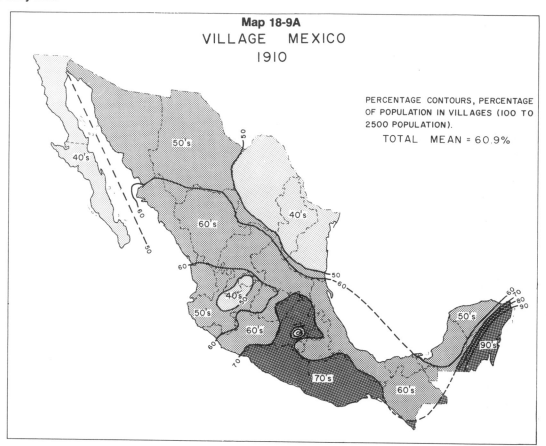

Map 18-9A
VILLAGE MEXICO
1910

PERCENTAGE CONTOURS, PERCENTAGE
OF POPULATION IN VILLAGES (100 TO
2500 POPULATION).

TOTAL MEAN = 60.9%

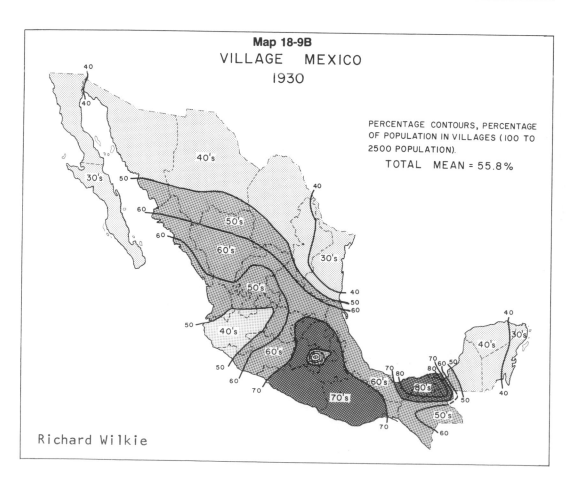

Map 18-9B
VILLAGE MEXICO
1930

PERCENTAGE CONTOURS, PERCENTAGE
OF POPULATION IN VILLAGES (100 TO
2500 POPULATION).

TOTAL MEAN = 55.8%

Richard Wilkie

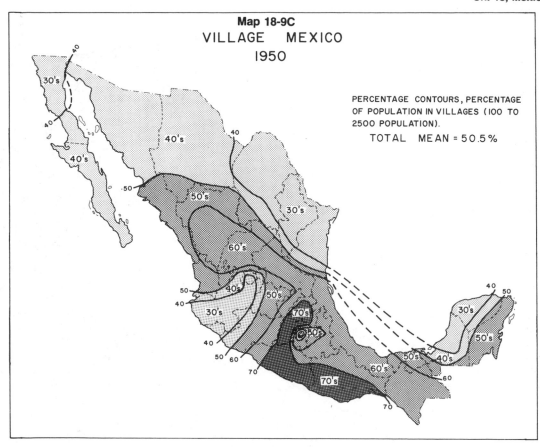

Map 18-9C
VILLAGE MEXICO
1950

PERCENTAGE CONTOURS, PERCENTAGE
OF POPULATION IN VILLAGES (100 TO
2500 POPULATION).

TOTAL   MEAN = 50.5%

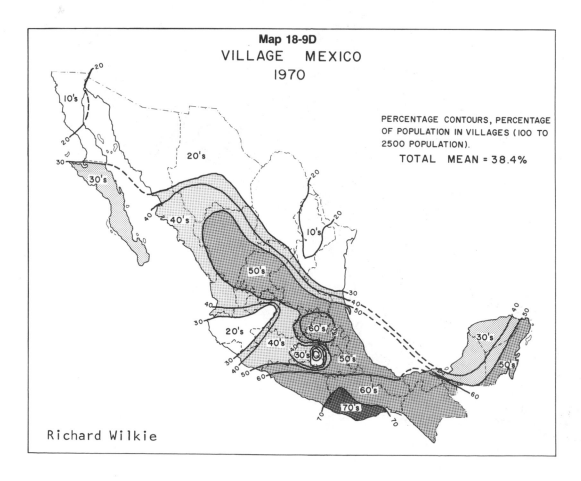

Map 18-9D
VILLAGE MEXICO
1970

PERCENTAGE CONTOURS, PERCENTAGE
OF POPULATION IN VILLAGES (100 TO
2500 POPULATION).

TOTAL   MEAN = 38.4%

Richard Wilkie

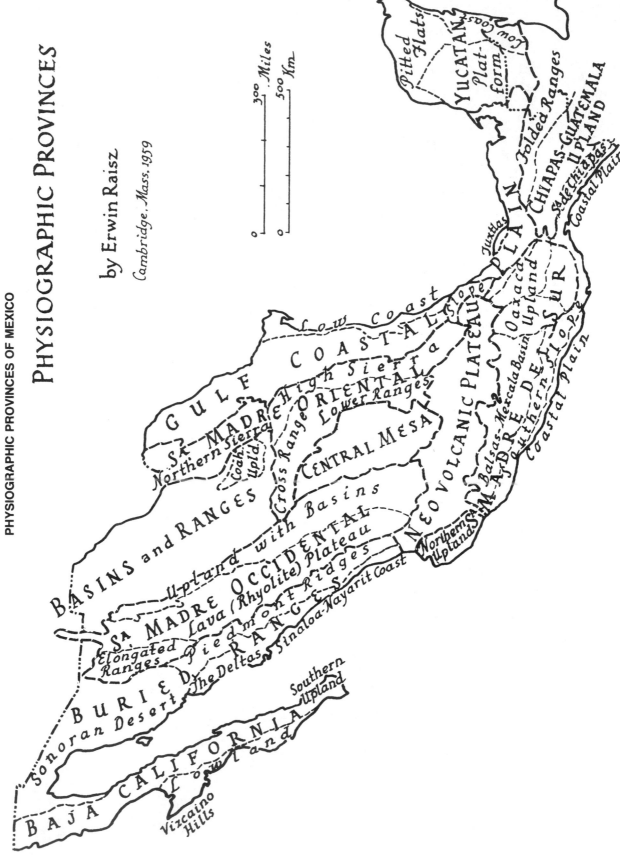

PHYSIOGRAPHIC PROVINCES OF MEXICO

Map 18-10

PHYSIOGRAPHIC PROVINCES

by Erwin Raisz

Cambridge, Mass, 1959

300 Miles

500 Km

Photo 18-1

MIDDLEMAN VENDORS SELLING DRIED FISH AT A PERIODIC
MARKET, CHIAPAS, MEXICO (1979)

Map 18-11A

PHYSIOGRAPHIC MAP OF CENTRAL MEXICO

ERWIN RAISZ

Photo 18-2

**CHURCH PLAZA IN OAXACA, MEXICO, DURING
VISIT OF POPE JOHN PAUL II (1979)**

Map 18-11B

PHYSIOGRAPHIC MAP OF NORTHWEST MEXICO

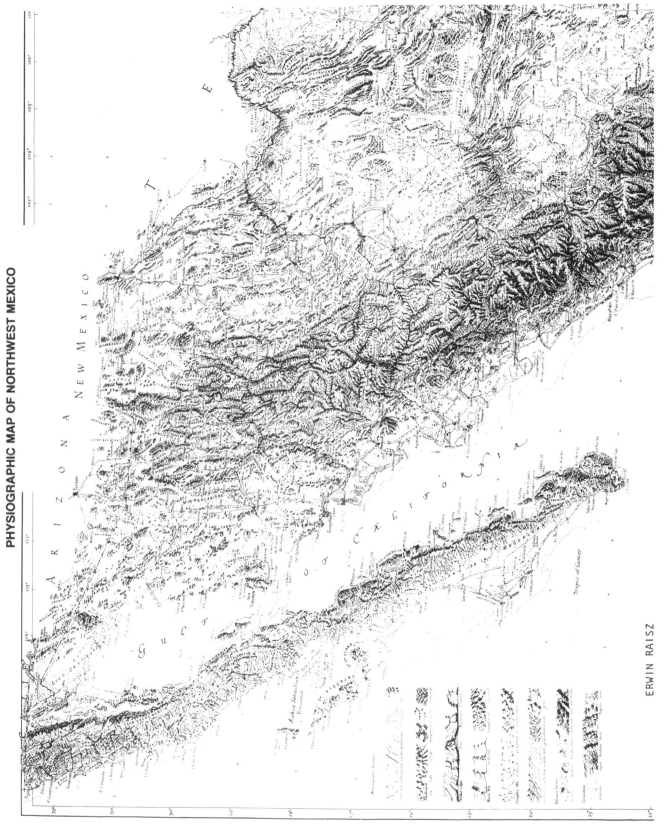

ERWIN RAISZ

Map 18-11C

PHYSIOGRAPHIC MAP OF SOUTHEAST MEXICO

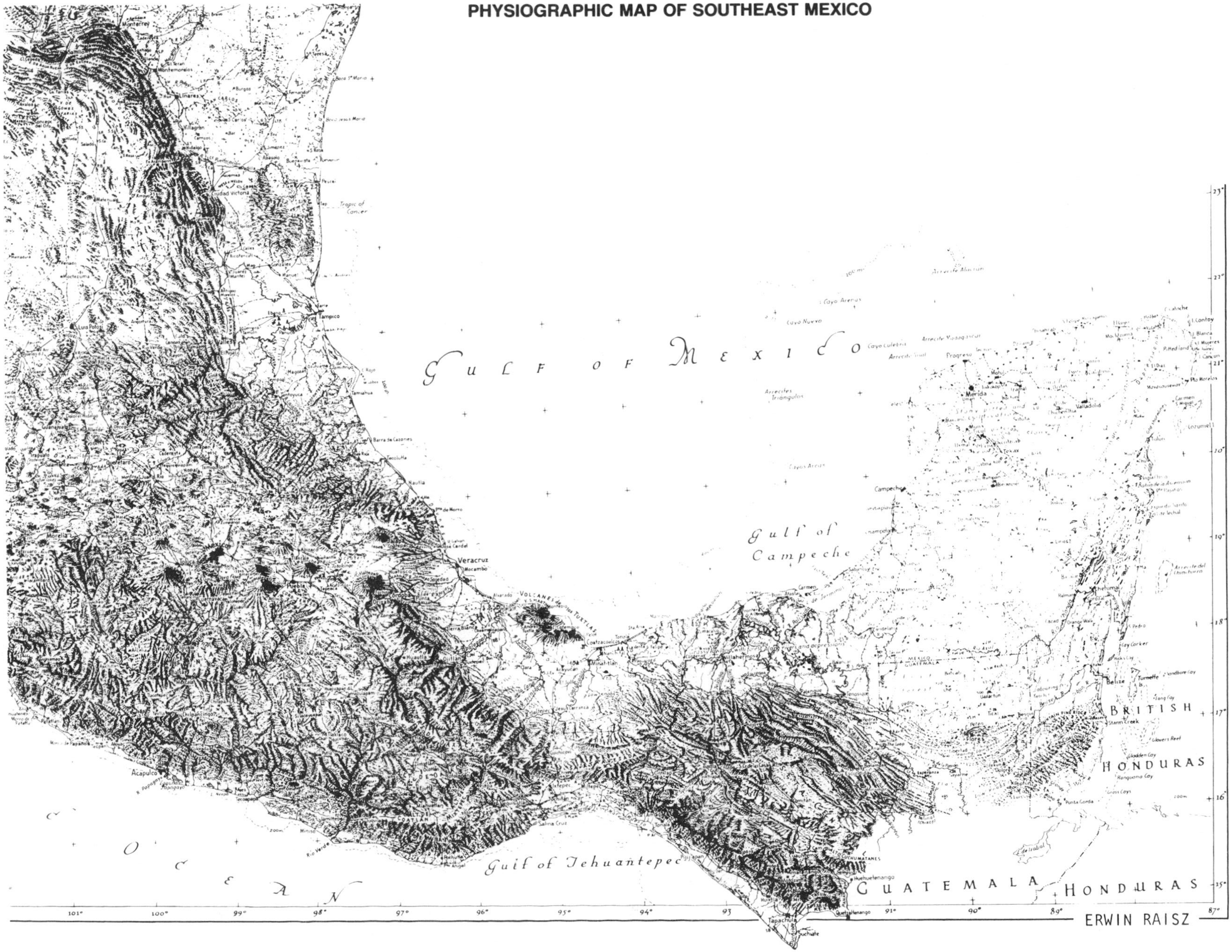
Gulf of Mexico
Gulf of Campeche
Gulf of Tehuantepec
OCEAN
GUATEMALA
BRITISH HONDURAS
HONDURAS
Veracruz
Tampico
Campeche
Merida
Acapulco
ERWIN RAISZ

Map 19-1

PHYSIOGRAPHIC MAP OF NICARAGUA

ERWIN RAISZ

19

Nicaragua

Nicaragua has had eight official censuses over a 205-year period. The first census (1778) counted 106,926 inhabitants. By the sixth census (1950), Nicaragua passed the one million mark for the first time with 1,057,023. The latest census (1971) documented a rise of 79 percent to 1,894,690 inhabitants. In 1980 the population was estimated by the Latin American Economic Commission to be 2,559,000.

The population totals, trends, and characteristics of Nicaragua are presented in six tables and six maps. Some of the findings concerning Nicaragua are outlined below.

URBAN TRENDS

There were no metropolitan centers with more than half a million population in 1971, but there were eight complex urban centers. The capital city of Managua with nearly 400,000 is the largest city in the country and it had 21 percent of the nation's inhabitants in 1971. Other large cities include León (54,800), Granada (35,400), Masaya (30,800), and Chinandega (29,900). Overall, complex urban centers with over 20,000 population accounted for 32.3 percent of the national total, while simple urban centers between 2,000 and 20,000 in size accounted for 15.2 percent.

RURAL TRENDS

Slightly more than half of all Nicaraguans (52 percent) lived in rural areas in 1971. While the percentage is down from two-thirds (65 percent) in 1959, the total number of rural dwellers was up by 307,000 to nearly one million.

SETTLEMENT HIERARCHY

Nicaragua could be classified in 1971 as a dispersed–complex urban settlement hierarchy (0–3), with between two-thirds and three-fourths of all Nicaraguans living in those two levels. There is more balance in the hierarchy of places in Nicaragua than there is in most of the neighboring countries in the Central American region.

OTHER DEMOGRAPHIC DATA

The annual rate of population growth in Nicaragua has been greater than 3 percent since the late 1950s, and it has been 3.4 percent since 1978. Life expectancy in 1982 was fifty-five years, and 48 percent of the population was under fifteen years of age. Per capita GNP in 1982 of $720 was up by only 53 percent from $470 in 1975, ranking Nicaragua number 16 among the twenty Latin American republics in that category.

Table 19-1

POPULATION DATA AND DENSITY BY DEPARTMENT IN NICARAGUA, 1971[a]

Rank	Department	Population	Percent	Percent Change 1963-1971	Population Density 1971 (km^2)
1	Managua	482,600	25.5	+15.4	133
2	Matagalpa	172,180	9.1	+.4	25
3	León	166,270	8.8	+10.8	32
4	Chinandega	158,210	8.4	+23.0	34
5	Zelaya	148,830	7.9	+67.3	3
6	Masaya	94,200	5.0	+23.0	174
7	Jinotega	92,340	4.9	+20.0	10
8	Estelí	78,630	4.2	+13.5	36
9	Rivas	75,630	4.0	+17.5	35
10	Granada	73,150	3.9	+11.4	76
11	Carazo	71,810	3.8	+9.0	70
12	Boaco	70,850	3.7	-1.1	14
13	Chontales	69,530	3.7	-8.0	14
14	Nueva Segovia	66,650	2.8	+45.2	20
15	Madriz	53,560	2.8	+6.6	31
16	Río San Juan	20,250	1.1	+29.2	3
	Total	1,894,690	100.0	+23.4	14

a. The U.S. Bureau of the Census (1978) estimated a net underenumeration of 3.8 percent, for an adjusted total of 1,953,000 inhabitants. In addition, they estimated the population on July 1, 1979, to be 2,365,000 (1981).

SOURCE: Census of April 20, 1971.

Table 19-2

MAJOR URBAN CENTERS IN NICARAGUA, 1971

Rank	Major Urban Centers	Population	Percent
1	✪ Managua (1)	398,514	21.0
2	● León (3)	54,800	2.9
3	● Granada (10)	35,400	1.9
4	Masaya (6)	30,800	1.6
5	Chinandega (4)	29,900	1.6
6	Jinotepe/Diriamba (11)	22,700	1.2
7	Matagalpa (2)	20,700	1.1
8	Estelí (8)	20,000	1.1
			32.3
9	○ Chichigalpa (4)	14,600	
10	Bluefields (5)	14,400	
11	Corinto (4)	13,400	
12	Jinotega (7)	10,200	
13	Rivas (9)	10,000	

SOURCES: Census of April 20, 1971; SALA, 20-626 and 629; Robert Fox and Jerrold Huguet, *Population and Urban Trends in Central America and Panama* (Washington, D.C.: Inter-American Development Bank, 1977), p. 168.

Photo 19-1

**MANAGUA CATHEDRAL, JULY 19, 1981, SECOND ANNIVERSARY
OF SANDINISTA VICTORY OVER SOMOZA**

Photo by James W. Wilkie

Map 19-2

BASE MAP OF DEPARTMENTS IN NICARAGUA AND LOCATION
OF MAJOR URBAN CENTERS

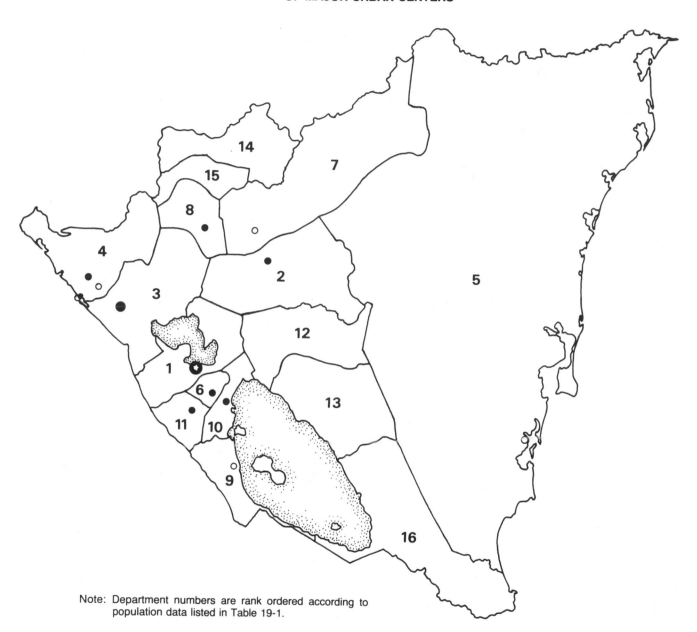

Note: Department numbers are rank ordered according to
population data listed in Table 19-1.

Map 19-3

POPULATION CARTOGRAM OF NICARAGUA, 1971

NICARAGUA
1971

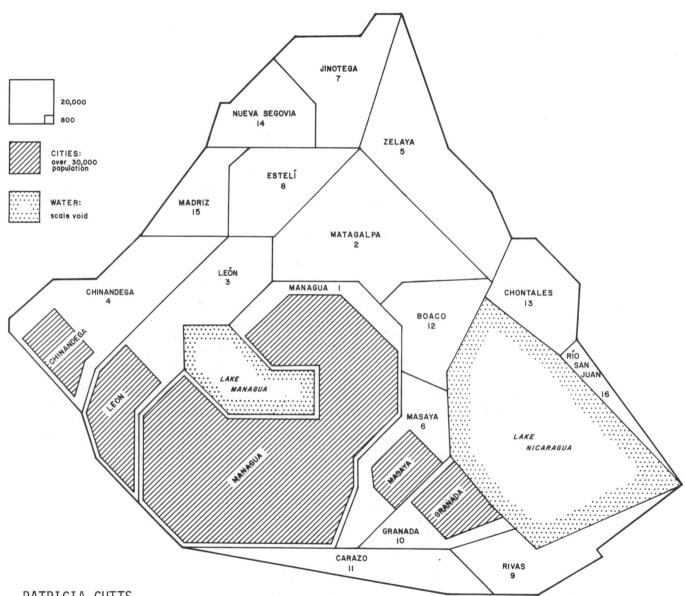

PATRICIA CUTTS
Geography Cartographic Laboratory
Univ. of Massachusetts, Amherst

Map 19-4

THREE-DIMENSIONAL CHOROPLETH MAP OF TOTAL POPULATION BY
DEPARTMENT IN NICARAGUA, 1971
(By Major Civil Division)

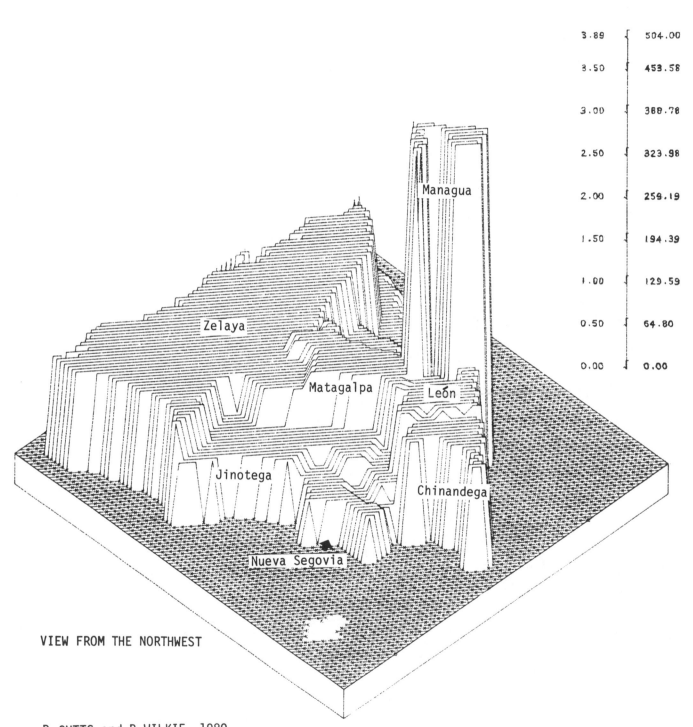

3.89	504.00
3.50	453.58
3.00	388.78
2.50	323.98
2.00	259.19
1.50	194.39
1.00	129.59
0.50	64.80
0.00	0.00

VIEW FROM THE NORTHWEST

P.CUTTS and R.WILKIE, 1980
Geography Cartographic Laboratory, University of Massachusetts, Amherst
using the SYMVU program from the Harvard Univ. Computer Graphics Center

Map 19-5

THREE-DIMENSIONAL CHOROPLETH MAP OF POPULATION DENSITY
IN NICARAGUA, 1971
(Persons per km²)

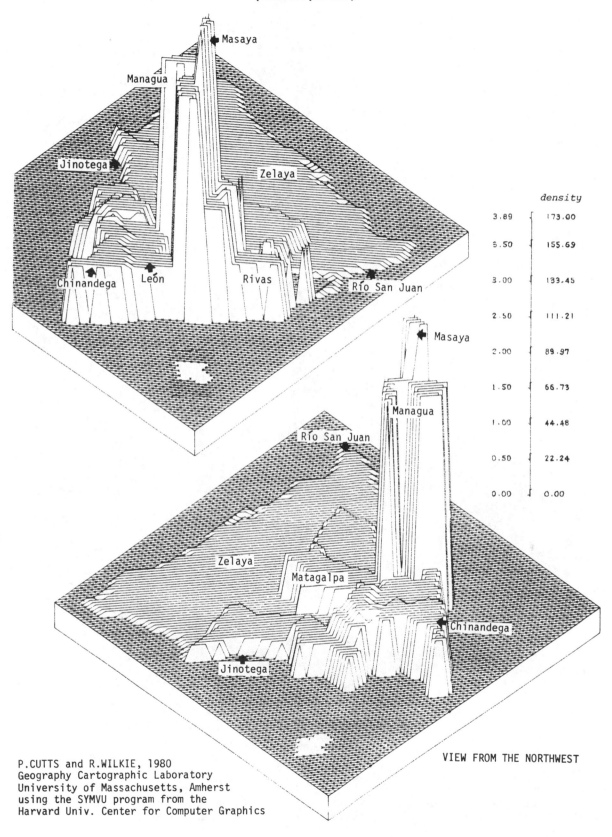

density

3.89	173.00
6.50	155.69
3.00	133.45
2.50	111.21
2.00	89.97
1.50	66.73
1.00	44.48
0.50	22.24
0.00	0.00

VIEW FROM THE NORTHWEST

P.CUTTS and R.WILKIE, 1980
Geography Cartographic Laboratory
University of Massachusetts, Amherst
using the SYMVU program from the
Harvard Univ. Center for Computer Graphics

Map 19-6

THREE-DIMENSIONAL CHOROPLETH MAP OF POPULATION CHANGE
IN NICARAGUA, 1963–1971
(%)

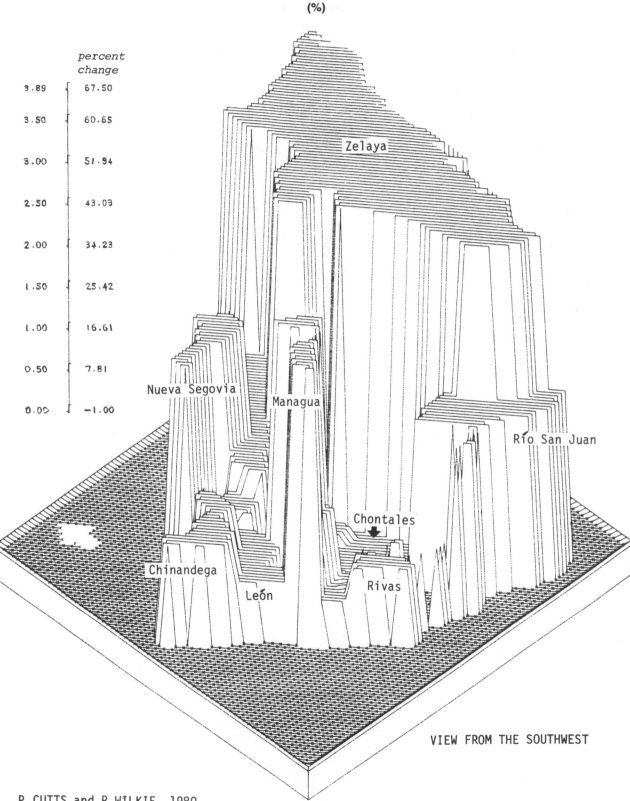

percent change	
3.89	67.50
3.50	60.65
3.00	51.94
2.50	43.03
2.00	34.23
1.50	25.42
1.00	16.61
0.50	7.81
0.00	-1.00

Zelaya

Nueva Segovia

Managua

Río San Juan

Chontales

Chinandega

Rivas

León

VIEW FROM THE SOUTHWEST

P.CUTTS and R.WILKIE, 1980
Geography Cartographic Laboratory, University of Massachusetts, Amherst
using the SYMVU program from the Harvard Univ. Computer Graphics Center

Photo 19-2

ISOLATED FAMILY DWELLING ON A DISPERSED SETTLEMENT LANDSCAPE (1979)

Table 19-3

POPULATION FOR EACH NATIONAL CENSUS IN NICARAGUA, 1778-1971

Census Year	Population
1778	106,926
1867	257,000
1906	505,377
1920	638,119
1940	983,000
1950	1,057,023
1963	1,535,588
1971	1,894,690[a]

a. Recommended adjustment of population to 1,953,000 by the U.S. Bureau of the Census (1978).

Table 19-4

TOTAL AND PERCENT POPULATION IN FIVE LEVELS OF THE URBAN-RURAL SETTLEMENT HIERARCHY OF NICARAGUA SINCE 1950

	0	1	2	3	4	SETTLEMENT HIERARCHY	
CENSUS YEAR	DISPERSED Population 1 to 99	VILLAGE 100 to 2,500	SIMPLE URBAN 2,501– 20,000	COMPLEX URBAN 20,001– 500,000	METROPOLITAN over 500,000	Classification	PERCENT in top 2 levels
TOTAL							
1950	. . . .	687,774	. . . .	208,318	160,931	- -	
1963	. . . .	905,997	. . . .	275,648	353,946	- -	
1971	. . . .	994,002	. . . .	287,874	612,814	- -	
PERCENT							
1950	. . . .	65.1	. . . .	19.7	15.2	- -	0–2	68 to 75
1963	. . . .	59.0	. . . .	18.0	23.0	- -	0–3	68 to 75
1971	. . . .	52.0	. . . .	15.2	32.3	- -	0–3	65 to 75

SOURCES: Calculated from the various Nicaraguan national censuses since 1950, and from SALA, 20-631, 632, 634, 635, 636, 637, and 638.

Table 19-5

SELECTED INDICATORS OF POPULATION CHANGE AND PER CAPITA GNP IN NICARAGUA

Years	Per 1000 Population		Rate of Natural Increase (Annual %)	Number of Years to Double Population	Percent Population Under Age 15	Life Expectancy at Birth	Per Capita GNP (US)
	Births	Deaths					
1940-45	49	17	2.3	- -	- -	- -	- -
1945-50	40	13	2.6	- -	- -	- -	- -
1950-55	43	10	2.7	- -	- -	- -	254 in 1955
1955-60	44	9	3.0	- -	- -	- -	- -
1960-65	50	9	3.1	- -	- -	- -	- -
1965-70	49	8	3.0	- -	- -	- -	- -
1970-74	48	12	3.6	24 in '70	48 in '70	- -	360 in 1970
1975	48	14	3.3	21	48	53	470
1976	48	14	3.3	21	48	53	650
1977	48	14	3.3	20	48	53	720
1978	47	13	3.4	20	48	53	750
1979	47	12	3.4	20	48	53	830
1980	47	12	3.4	20	48	55	840
1981	47	12	3.4	20	48	55	660
1982	47	12	3.4	20	48	55	720

MAJOR SOURCES:

Births: SALA, 19-204; SALA, 20-705 through 1975.

Deaths: SALA, 18-703d and 706 through 1970.

Life expectancy: SALA, 19-700 through 1970.

Per capita GNP: 1955 data from Ginsburg, *Atlas of Economic Development* (Chicago: University of Chicago Press, 1961).

Rate of natural increase: SALA, 22-626 from CELADE-BD 10 (1972) through 1970.

All other data: Population Reference Bureau, Washington, D.C., annual world population data sheets.

Table 19-6

NICARAGUAN DEPARTMENTS BY GEOGRAPHICAL SIZE AND SUBDIVISION, 1970

Department	Civil Subdivisions (N)	Area	
		km^2	%
Total	125[a]	118,358[b]	100.0
Departments			
Boaco	6	4,982	4.2
Carazo	8	1,032	.9
Chinandega	13	4,662	3.9
Chontales	8	4,947	4.2
Estelí	5	2,199	1.9
Granada	4	964	.8
Jinotega	4	9,576	8.1
León	11	5,234	4.4
Madriz	9	1,758	1.5
Managua	6	3,635	3.1
Masaya	9	543	.5
Matagalpa	10	6,794	5.7
Nueva Segovia	11	3,341	2.8
Río San Juan	4	7,448	6.3
Rivas	9	2,149	1.8
Zelaya	8	59,094	49.9

a. Municipios.

b. Excludes 9,000 km^2 in lakes.

SOURCE: SALA, 21-301.

Map 20-1

PHYSIOGRAPHIC MAP OF PANAMA

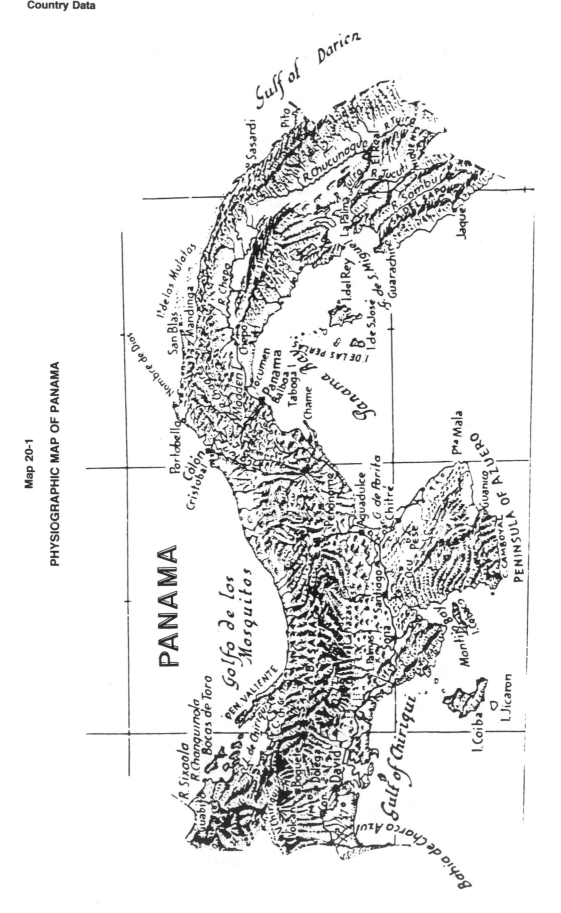

ERWIN RAISZ

20

Panama

Panama has had eight official censuses over a 72-year period. The first census (1911) counted 336,742 individuals. By the fifth census (1950) the figure had reached 805,285, an increase over thirty-nine years of 139 percent. The latest census (1980) documented a further increase of 122 percent to 1,788,748 inhabitants.

The population totals, trends, and characteristics of Panama are presented in six tables and six maps. Some of the findings concerning Panama are outlined below.

URBAN TRENDS

Greater Panama City in 1970 had slightly more than one-third of the nation's population (36.4 percent) and with 520,000 inhabitants was the only metropolitan center in the country. Three other cities had more than 20,000 population and are classified as complex urban—Greater Colón with 103,029, Greater Davíd with 40,819, and Greater Chitré–Los Santos with 22,914 inhabitants. Together these three complex urban centers account for nearly 12 percent of the total population. The simple urban level of towns between 1,500 and 20,000 population has a far smaller percentage—less than 4 percent—with only 52,177 inhabitants.

RURAL TRENDS

The rural population in 1970 was nearly 690,000 and accounted for nearly half of the population of Panama (48 percent). In both 1950 and 1960 rural villagers in units between 100 and 1,500 in size outnumbered dwellers in rural dispersed units of under 100 individuals by a three to two ratio. In 1970 the census totals did not subdivide the categories finely enough to calculate these differences, but it is likely that the ratios were similar in 1970.

SETTLEMENT HIERARCHY

Panama in 1970 could be classified as a metropolitan–village (4–1) settlement landscape, with about two out of every three Panamanians living in either Greater Panama City or in villages. In 1950 the classification was village–dispersed (1–0) and in 1960 it was village–complex urban (1–3). Clearly the flow of people from the interior to the capital city metropolitan area accounted for this transition in the classification of where people are living in the urban-rural hierarchy of places.

OTHER DEMOGRAPHIC DATA

The annual rate of population growth in Panama has been gradually declining to 2.1 percent in 1982 after peaking above 3 percent between 1955 and 1970. Life expectancy in 1982 was seventy years, and 43 percent of the population was under fifteen years of age. Per capita GNP in 1982 of $1730 was up by 97 percent from $880 in 1975, ranking Panama number 7 (tied with Costa Rica) among the twenty Latin American republics in that category.

Table 20-1

POPULATION DATA AND DENSITY BY PROVINCE IN PANAMA, 1970 AND 1980[a]

Rank	Province	1970 Population	Percent Change 1960-1970	1980 Population	1980 Percent	Percent Change 1970-1980	Population Density 1980 (km^2)
1	Panamá	576,645	+54.8	800,500	44.8	+38.8	63
2	Chiriquí	236,154	+25.4	286,416	16.0	+21.3	33
3	Veraguas	151,849	+15.3	172,868	9.7	+13.8	16
4	Colón[b]	134,286	+27.4	157,627	8.8	+17.4	21
5	Coclé	118,003	+26.7	140,524	7.8	+19.1	28
6	Herrera	72,549	+17.6	81,876	4.6	+12.9	34
7	Los Santos	72,380	+2.6	70,272	3.9	-2.9	18
8	Bocas del Toro	43,531	+33.5	52,416	2.9	+20.4	6
9	Darién	22,685	+15.1	26,247	1.5	+15.7	2
	Total	1,428,082	+32.8	1,788,748	100.0	+25.3	23
10	Canal Zone	44,198					

a. The U.S. Bureau of the Census (1978) estimated a net 1970 underenumeration of 1.3 percent, for an adjusted total of 1,447,000. In addition, they estimated the population on July 1, 1979, to be 1,876,000.

b. Includes San Blas territory.

SOURCES: Censuses of May 10, 1970, and May 11, 1980, for Panama, and April 1, 1970, for the Canal Zone.

Table 20–2

MAJOR URBAN CENTERS IN PANAMA, 1970

Rank	Major Urban Centers	City Proper	Census of May 10, 1970 Metropolitan District	Percent	July 1, 1978
1	❂ Gran Panamá (Ciudad de) (1)		519,643	36.4	
	Panamá (Ciudad) proper	349,000	386,527	27.1	439,870
	● San Miguelito		68,400	4.8	146.310
	● La Chorrera	26,000	45,269	3.2	
	Arraiján		19,347	1.4	
2	● Gran Colón (4)		103,029	7.2	
	Colón	68,000	95,421	5.7	
	Chagres		6,063		
	Portobelo		1,545		
3	● Gran Davíd (2)	40,819		2.8	
	Davíd	35,677		2.5	
	San José	5,142			
4	Gran Chitré–Los Santos (6/7)	22,914		1.6	
	Chitré (6)	12,379		.9	
	Los Santos (7)	3,939			
	Mongrillo (6)	3,832			
	La Arena (6)	2,764			
				48.1	
5	○ Santiago (3)	14,595			
6	Puerto Armuellas (2)	12,015			
7	Aguadulce/Pocrí (5)	11,354			
8	La Concepción (2)	9,200			

SOURCES: Census of May 10, 1970; SALA 20-626; Robert Fox and Jerrold Huguet, *Population and Urban Trends in Central America and Panama* (Washington, D.C.: Inter-American Development Bank, 1977), p. 193; United Nations, *Demographic Yearbook 1978*.

Map 20-2

BASE MAP OF PROVINCES IN PANAMA AND LOCATION OF MAJOR
URBAN CENTERS

Note: State numbers are rank ordered according to population
        data listed in Table 20-1.

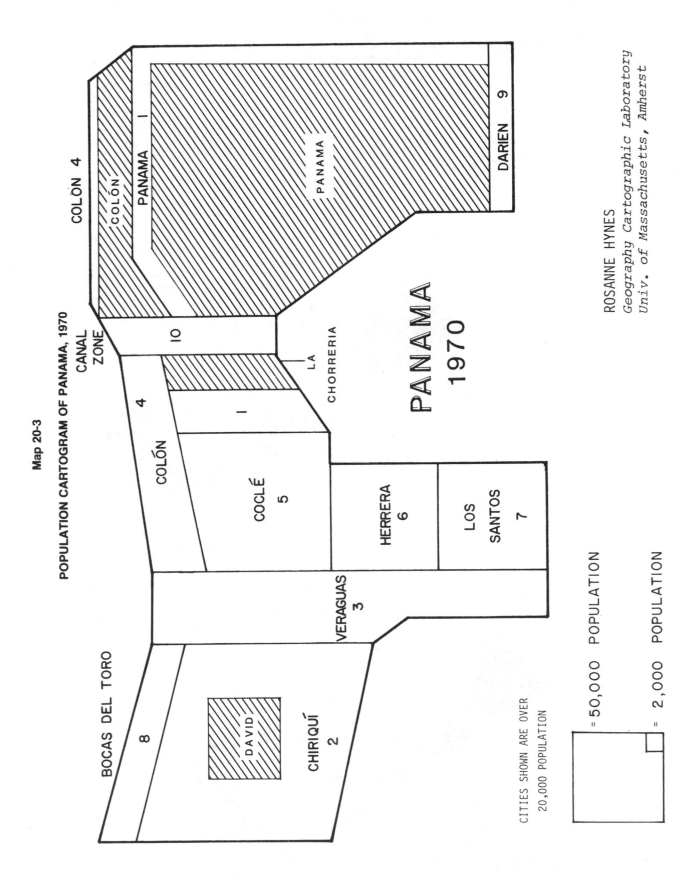

Map 20-3

POPULATION CARTOGRAM OF PANAMA, 1970

PANAMA
1970

CANAL ZONE

COLÓN 4

PANAMA 1

COLÓN

DARIEN 9

10

LA CHORRERIA

COLÓN 4

COCLÉ 5

1

HERRERA 6

LOS SANTOS 7

VERAGUAS 3

BOCAS DEL TORO 8

DAVID

CHIRIQUÍ 2

CITIES SHOWN ARE OVER 20,000 POPULATION

☐ = 50,000 POPULATION

▫ = 2,000 POPULATION

ROSANNE HYNES
Geography Cartographic Laboratory
Univ. of Massachusetts, Amherst

Map 20-4

THREE-DIMENSIONAL CHOROPLETH MAP OF TOTAL POPULATION BY
PROVINCE IN PANAMA, 1970
(By Major Civil Division)

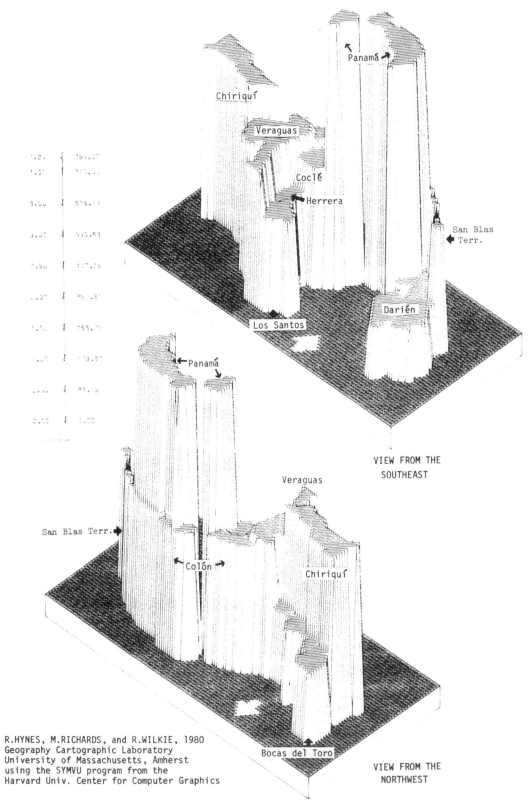

VIEW FROM THE
SOUTHEAST

VIEW FROM THE
NORTHWEST

R.HYNES, M.RICHARDS, and R.WILKIE, 1980
Geography Cartographic Laboratory
University of Massachusetts, Amherst
using the SYMVU program from the
Harvard Univ. Center for Computer Graphics

Map 20-5

THREE-DIMENSIONAL CHOROPLETH MAP OF POPULATION DENSITY
IN PANAMA, 1970
(Persons per km²)

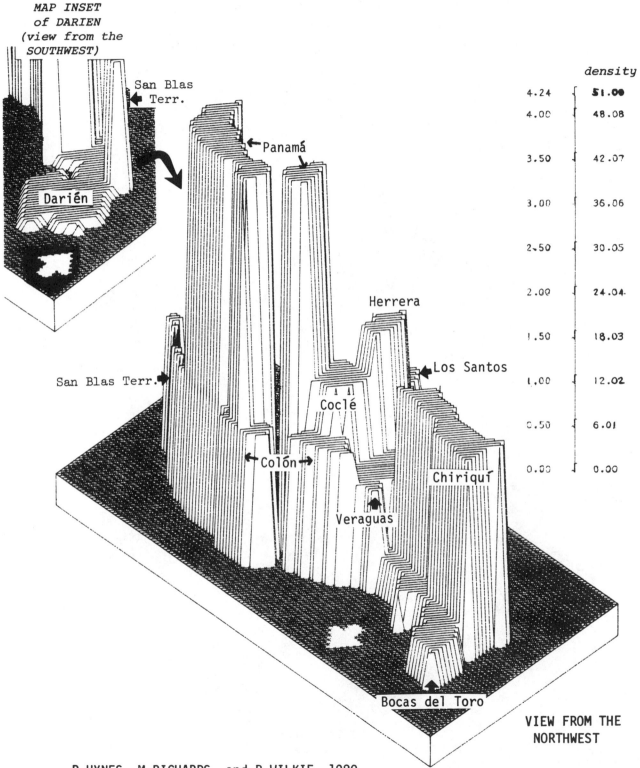

MAP INSET
of DARIEN
(view from the
SOUTHWEST)

San Blas
Terr.

Darién

density

4.24	51.00
4.00	48.08
3.50	42.07
3.00	36.06
2.50	30.05
2.00	24.04
1.50	18.03
1.00	12.02
0.50	6.01
0.00	0.00

Panamá

Herrera

San Blas Terr.

Los Santos

Coclé

Colón

Chiriquí

Veraguas

Bocas del Toro

VIEW FROM THE
NORTHWEST

R.HYNES, M.RICHARDS, and R.WILKIE, 1980
Geography Cartographic Laboratory, University of Massachusetts, Amherst
using the SYMVU program from the Harvard Univ. Center for Computer Graphics

Map 20-6

THREE-DIMENSIONAL CHOROPLETH MAP OF POPULATION CHANGE IN PANAMA, 1960–1970
(%)

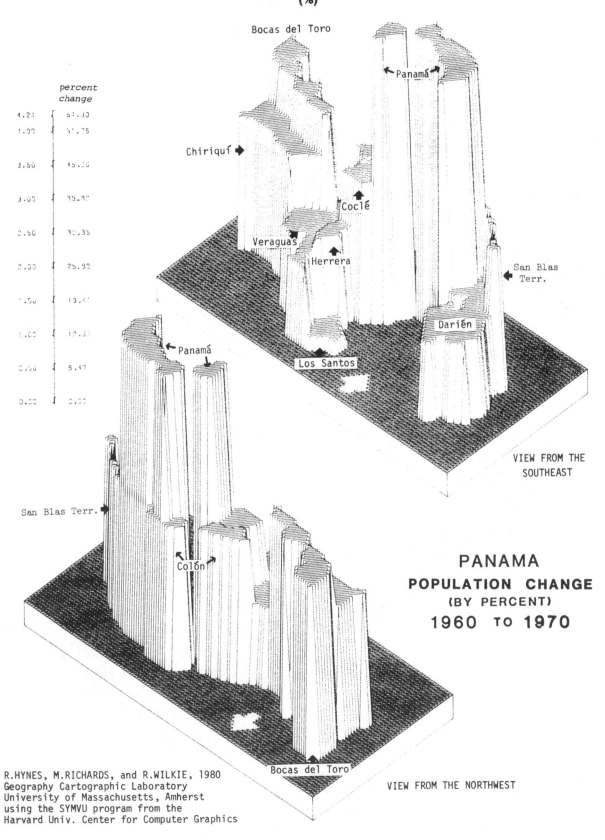

percent change

4.24	54.30
1.00	51.75
3.50	45.20
3.00	38.80
2.50	32.35
2.00	25.93
1.50	19.40
1.00	12.90
0.50	5.47
0.00	0.00

Bocas del Toro

Panamá

Chiriquí

Coclé

Veraguas

Herrera

San Blas Terr.

Darién

Los Santos

VIEW FROM THE SOUTHEAST

Panamá

San Blas Terr.

Colón

PANAMA
POPULATION CHANGE
(BY PERCENT)
1960 TO 1970

Bocas del Toro

VIEW FROM THE NORTHWEST

R.HYNES, M.RICHARDS, and R.WILKIE, 1980
Geography Cartographic Laboratory
University of Massachusetts, Amherst
using the SYMVU program from the
Harvard Univ. Center for Computer Graphics

Photo 20-1

**DOUBLE-DECK WOODEN TENEMENT FOR FOUR FAMILIES,
PANAMA CITY, PANAMA (1967)**

Table 20-3

POPULATION FOR EACH NATIONAL CENSUS IN PANAMA, 1911–1980[a]

Census Year	Population
1911	336,742
1920	446,098
1930	467,458
1940	622,576
1950	805,285
1960	1,075,541
1970	1,428,082[b]
1980	1,788,748

a. Includes the indigenous population; excludes the Canal Zone.
b. Recommended adjustment of population to 1,447,000 by the U.S. Bureau of the Census (1978).

Table 20-4

TOTAL AND PERCENT POPULATION IN FIVE LEVELS OF THE URBAN-RURAL SETTLEMENT HIERARCHY OF PANAMA SINCE 1950

	0	1	2	3	4	SETTLEMENT HIERARCHY	
CENSUS YEAR	DISPERSED Population 1 to 99	VILLAGE 100 to 2,500	SIMPLE URBAN 2,501– 20,000	COMPLEX URBAN 20,001– 500,000	METROPOLITAN over 500,000	Classification	PERCENT in top 2 levels
TOTAL							
1950	214,318	301,177	109,712	180,078	- -		
1960	255,523	373,213	90,843	355,962	- -		
1970	....	689,500	52,177	166,762	519,643		
PERCENT							
1950	26.6	37.5	13.5	22.4	- -	1-0	64.1
1960	23.8	34.7	8.4	33.1	- -	1-3	67.8
1970	....	48.3	3.6	11.7	36.4	4-1	66 to 69

SOURCES: Calculated from the various Panamanian national censuses since 1950, and from SALA, 20–631, 632, 634, 635, 636, 637, and 638. Especially useful was Robert Fox and Jerrold Huguet, *Population and Urban Trends in Central America and Panama* (Washington, D.C.: Inter-American Development Bank, 1977), pp. 193–195.

Table 20-5

SELECTED INDICATORS OF POPULATION CHANGE AND PER CAPITA GNP IN PANAMA

Years	Per 1000 Population Births	Per 1000 Population Deaths	Rate of Natural Increase (Annual %)	Number of Years to Double Population	Percent Population Under Age 15	Life Expectancy at Birth	Per Capita GNP (US)
1940–45	38	9	2.6	- -	- -	- -	- -
1945–50	36	11	2.5	- -	- -	- -	- -
1950–55	38	9	2.9	- -	- -	- -	350[a]
1955–60	40	9	3.0	- -	- -	- -	- -
1960–65	41	8	3.2	- -	- -	- -	- -
1965–70	38	7	3.3	- -	- -	- -	- -
1970–74	36	7	2.9	21[b]	43[b]	66[b]	550[b]
1975	36	7	2.8	25	43	66	880
1976	30	5	2.6	27	44	66	1,010
1977	29	5	2.6	27	43	66	1,060
1978	32	7	2.6	27	43	66	1,310
1979	29	6	2.3	30	43	68	1,220
1980	28	6	2.2	31	44	70	1,290
1981	28	6	2.2	31	43	70	1,350
1982	27	6	2.1	33	43	70	1,730

a. 1955.
b. 1970.

MAJOR SOURCE:
  Births: SALA, 19-204; SALA, 20-705 through 1977.
  Deaths: SALA, 18-703d and 706 through 1970.
  Life expectancy: SALA, 19-700 through 1970.
  Per capita GNP: 1955 data from Ginsburg, *Atlas of Economic Development* (Chicago: University of Chicago Press, 1961).
  Rate of natural increase: SALA, 22-626 from CELADE-BD 10 (1972) through 1970.
  All other data: Population Reference Bureau, Washington, D.C., annual world population data sheets.

Table 20-6

PANAMANIAN PROVINCES BY GEOGRAPHICAL SIZE AND SUBDIVISION, 1970

Province	Civil Subdivisions (N)	Area km²	Area %
Total	65[a]	77,085	
Provinces			
Bocas del Toro	3	8,917	11.8
Coclé	6	5,035	6.7
Colón	6	7,465	9.9
Chiriquí	12	8,758	11.6
Darién	2	16,803	22.2
Herrera	7	2,427	3.2
Los Santos	7	3,867	5.1
Panamá	10	11,292	14.9
Veraguas	11	11,086	14.7
Total	64	75,650	100.0
Panama Canal Zone	1	1,432	

a. Distritos.

SOURCE: SALA, 21-301.

Map 21-1

PHYSIOGRAPHIC MAP OF PARAGUAY

PARAGUAY

GUY HAROLD-SMITH

21

Paraguay

Paraguay has had only four official censuses over a 47-year period, with the first census in 1936 recording 932,000 inhabitants. By 1962 the population doubled to 1,819,000. The latest census (1972) showed a further rise of 30 percent to 2,354,071. In 1980 the population was estimated by the Latin American Economic Commission to be 2,888,000 inhabitants.

The population totals, trends, and characteristics of Paraguay are presented in six tables and six maps. Some of the findings concerning Paraguay are outlined below.

URBAN TRENDS

Rapid urbanization characterized Paraguay in the late 1960s and through the 70s. Much of the influence came from neighboring Brazil which established major transportation linkages between the two countries. Between 1962 and 1972, Greater Asunción nearly doubled in size to become a metropolitan center of 565,363 inhabitants with 24 percent of the nation's population. According to *América en Cifras* (1974), the entire urban hierarchy developed rapidly in a decade and the rural population dropped rapidly. Some of this rise can be explained by a change in classification of what the population of an urban area really is, but it is also the most striking example of urbanization that this author has seen personally. Twenty-one cities were classified in 1972 as having more than 20,000 population, including Caaguazú (58,752), Coronel Oviedo (54,690), and Pedro Juan Caballero (49,245), and together they accounted for 679,000 persons with nearly 29 percent of the population of Paraguay. Simple urban centers ranging from 2,000 to 20,000 in size also accounted for 570,000 individuals, 24 percent of the population.

RURAL TRENDS

The rural population dropped from more than 60 percent in the 1950s and early 1960s to only 23 percent in 1972, owing in part to differences in the classification of urban areas. It is clear, however, that the rural population of Paraguay has much greater access to urban services and jobs than it did previously, and the strong influence from Brazil has played an important role in this process.

SETTLEMENT HIERARCHY

Paraguay could be classified as a complex urban−simple urban (3−2) settlement landscape by 1972, with slightly more than half the nation's population living in those two middle levels in the urban-rural settlement hierarchy of places. If the figures are accurate, Paraguay has developed one of the more balanced settlement hierarchies in Latin America.

OTHER DEMOGRAPHIC DATA

The annual rate of population growth in Paraguay has been higher than 2.6 percent since the early 1950s, peaking at 3.5 between 1965 and 1970. Life expectancy in 1982 was sixty-four years, and 45 percent of the population was under fifteen years of age. Per capita GNP in 1982 of $1340 was up by 320 percent from $320 in 1975, ranking Paraguay number 10 (up from a tie for 17th in 1975) among the twenty Latin American republics in that category.

Table 21-1

POPULATION DATA AND DENSITY BY DEPARTMENT IN PARAGUAY, 1972[a]

Rank	Department	Population	Percent	Percent Change 1962-1972	Population Density 1972 (km^2)
1	Capital	392,753	16.6	+34.2	1938
2	Central	310,101	13.1	+35.3	117
3	Caaguazú	213,356	9.0	+46.0	9
4	Paraguarí	211,704	8.9	+3.7	26
5	Itapúa	201,776	8.5	+34.5	12
6	De la Cordillera	194,365	8.3	+3.6	39
7	San Pedro	138,091	5.9	+49.8	7
8	Guairá	124,843	5.3	+8.2	39
9	Concepción	108,198	4.6	+26.7	6
10	Caazapá	103,002	4.4	+11.0	11
11	Alto Paraná	78,037	3.3	+275.3	5
12	Ñeembucú	72,978	3.1	+26.1	5
13	Misiones	69,315	2.9	+16.4	9
14	Amambay	65,527	2.7	+91.8	5
15	Presidente Hayes	38,515	1.6	+26.1	1
16	Boquerón	26,142	1.1	-34.9	.2
17	Olimpo	5,368	.2	+43.4	.3
	Total	2,354,071	100.0	+28.0	6

a. The U.S. Bureau of the Census (1977) adjusted the 1972 census figure for 8.9 percent underenumeration based on the 1972 post enumeration survey to 2,588,315 inhabitants. In addition, they estimated the population on July 1, 1979, to be 3,117,000 (1981).

SOURCES: *América en Cifras 1974*; Census of July 9, 1972.

Table 21–2

MAJOR URBAN CENTERS IN PARAGUAY, 1972

Rank	Major Urban Centers	Population	Percent	December 1974
1	✪ Gran Asunción	565,363	24.0	- -
	Asunción proper (1)	392,753		434,928[a]
	Lugué (2)	40,000		
	San Lorenzo (2)	37,000		
	Fernando de la Mora (2)	37,000		
	Lambaré (2)	32,000		
	Capiatá (2)	26,000		
2	● Caaguazú (3)	58,752	2.5	
3	Coronel Oviedo (3)	54,690	2.3	
4	● Pedro Juan Caballero (14)	49,245	2.1	
5	Concepción (9)	44,681	1.9	
6	San Estanislao (7)	42,000	1.8	
7	Encarnación (5)	40,902	1.7	
8	Villarica (8)	33,553	1.4	
9	Horqueta (9)	33,000	1.4	
10	Villa Hayes (15)	32,018	1.4	
11	San Pedro del Paraná (5)	30,000	1.3	
12	Carapeguá (4)	27,176	1.1	
13	Puerto Presidente Stroessner (11)	26,545	1.1	
14	San Pedro (7)	26,000	1.1	
15	Ibicuí (4)	26,000	1.1	
16	Itá (2)	25,000	1.1	
17	Hernandarias (11)	23,000	1.0	
18	Piribebuy (6)	22,000	.9	
19	Caazapá (10)	22,000	.9	
20	Caacupé (6)	21,000	.9	
21	San Joaquín (3)	21,300	.9	
22	Itauguá (2)	20,000	.8	
			52.9%	
23	o Yaguarón (4)	19,000		
24	Arroyos y Esteros (6)	19,000		
25	General Aquino (7)	19,000		
26	Santa Rosa (13)	18,048		
27	Caraguatay (6)	18,000		
28	San Juan Nepocumeno (10)	18,000		
29	Pilar (12)	17,261		
30	Capitán Meza (5)	17,000		
31	Quiindy (4)	16,306		
32	Acahay (4)	16,000		
33	San Ignacio (13)	15,910		
34	Eusebio Ayala (6)	15,490		
35	Dr. Juan Manuel Frutos (3)	15,000		
36	San José de los Arroyos (3)	15,000		
37	Independencia (8)	15,000		

a. United Nations, *Demographic Yearbook 1978*.

SOURCES: *América en Cifras 1974*; Census of July 9, 1972.

Map 21-2

BASE MAP OF DEPARTMENTS IN PARAGUAY AND LOCATION OF
MAJOR URBAN CENTERS

Note: Department numbers are rank ordered according to
1972 population data listed in Table 21-1.

Map 21-3

POPULATION CARTOGRAM OF PARAGUAY, 1972

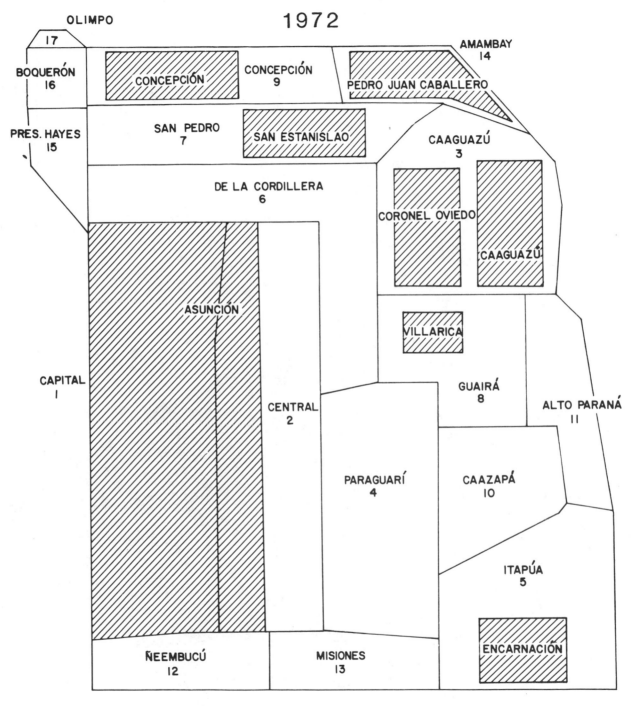

PARAGUAY
1972

OLIMPO
17

BOQUERÓN
16

CONCEPCIÓN

CONCEPCIÓN
9

AMAMBAY
14

PEDRO JUAN CABALLERO

PRES. HAYES
15

SAN PEDRO
7

SAN ESTANISLAO

CAAGUAZÚ
3

DE LA CORDILLERA
6

CORONEL OVIEDO

CAAGUAZÚ

ASUNCIÓN

VILLARICA

CAPITAL
I

CENTRAL
2

GUAIRÁ
8

ALTO PARANÁ
II

PARAGUARÍ
4

CAAZAPÁ
10

ITAPÚA
5

ÑEEMBUCÚ
12

MISIONES
13

ENCARNACIÓN

= 5,000   POPULATION

= 25,000 POPULATION

CITIES SHOWN ARE OVER
20,000 POPULATION

V.B.NII and P.CUTTS
Cartographic Laboratory
Dept. of Geology and Geography
University of Massachusetts, Amherst

Map 21-4

THREE-DIMENSIONAL CHOROPLETH MAP OF TOTAL POPULATION BY DEPARTMENT IN PARAGUAY, 1972
(By Major Civil Division)

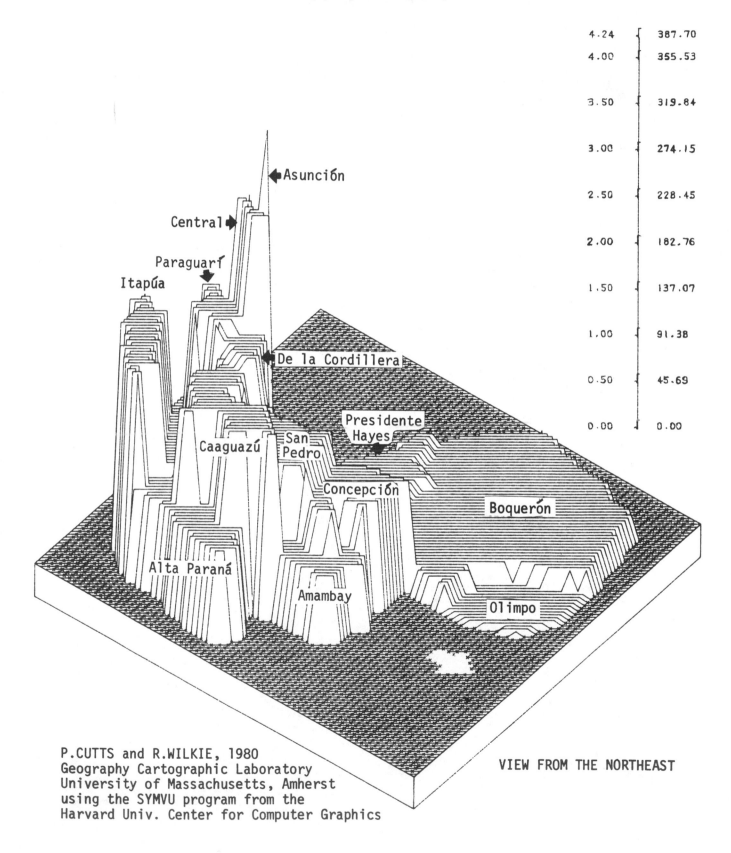

P.CUTTS and R.WILKIE, 1980
Geography Cartographic Laboratory
University of Massachusetts, Amherst
using the SYMVU program from the
Harvard Univ. Center for Computer Graphics

VIEW FROM THE NORTHEAST

Map 21-5

THREE-DIMENSIONAL CHOROPLETH MAP OF POPULATION
DENSITY IN PARAGUAY, 1972
(Persons per km²)

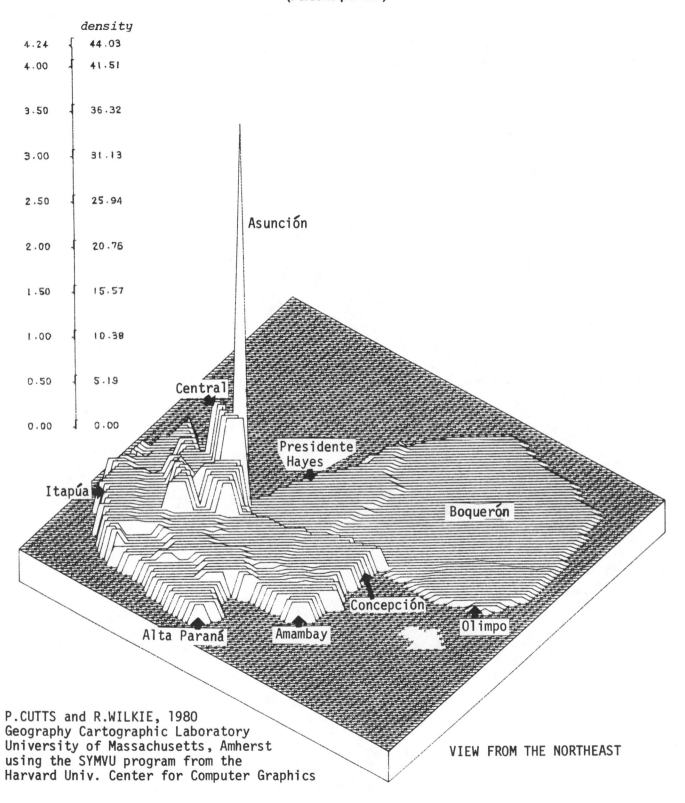

density	
4.24	44.03
4.00	41.51
3.50	36.32
3.00	31.13
2.50	25.94
2.00	20.76
1.50	15.57
1.00	10.38
0.50	5.19
0.00	0.00

Asunción

Central

Presidente Hayes

Itapúa

Boquerón

Concepción

Olimpo

Alta Paraná   Amambay

P.CUTTS and R.WILKIE, 1980
Geography Cartographic Laboratory
University of Massachusetts, Amherst
using the SYMVU program from the
Harvard Univ. Center for Computer Graphics

VIEW FROM THE NORTHEAST

Map 21-6

**THREE-DIMENSIONAL CHOROPLETH MAP OF POPULATION CHANGE
IN PARAGUAY, 1962–1972
(%)**

PARAGUAY
POPULATION CHANGE
(BY PERCENT)
1962 TO 1972

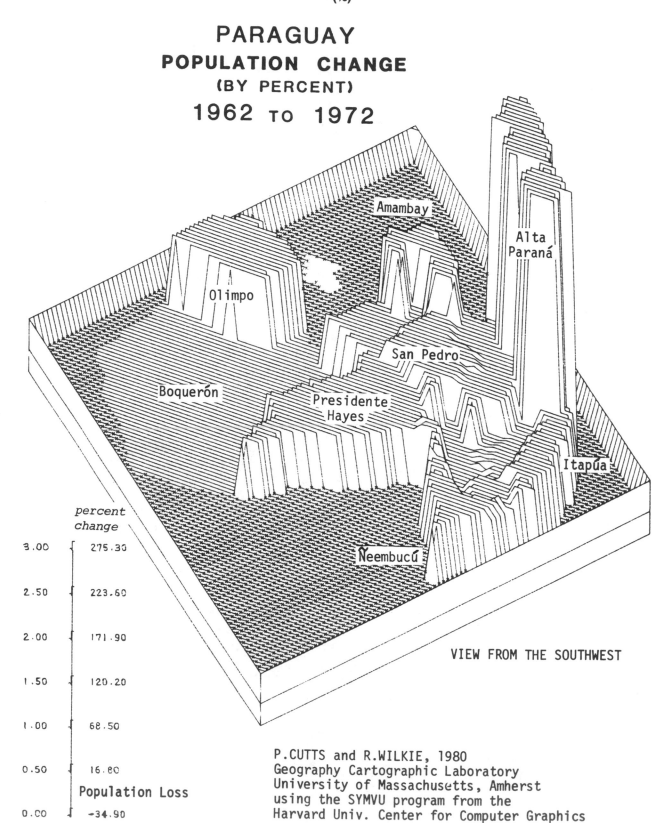

percent
change

3.00	275.30
2.50	223.60
2.00	171.90
1.50	120.20
1.00	68.50
0.50	16.80

Population Loss

| 0.00 | -34.90 |

VIEW FROM THE SOUTHWEST

P.CUTTS and R.WILKIE, 1980
Geography Cartographic Laboratory
University of Massachusetts, Amherst
using the SYMVU program from the
Harvard Univ. Center for Computer Graphics

Photo 21-1

RIVERBOAT TRAVEL ON THE RIO PARAGUAY (1966)

Photo 21-2

SQUATTER SETTLEMENT BARRIO IN ASUNCIÓN, PARAGUAY (1966)

Photo 21-3

MILITARY PARADE ON THE 450th ANNIVERSARY OF THE FOUNDING
OF ASUNCIÓN, PARAGUAY (1966)

Table 21-3

POPULATION FOR EACH NATIONAL CENSUS IN PARAGUAY, 1936–1972

Census Year	Population
1936	931,799
1950	1,328,452
1962	1,819,103
1972	2,354,071[a]

a. Recommended adjustment of population to 2,616,000 by the U.S. Bureau of the Census (1978).

Table 21-4

TOTAL AND PERCENT POPULATION IN FIVE LEVELS OF THE URBAN-RURAL SETTLEMENT HIERARCHY OF PARAGUAY SINCE 1950

	0	1	2	3	4	SETTLEMENT HIERARCHY	
CENSUS YEAR	DISPERSED Population 1 to 99	VILLAGE 100 to 2,500	SIMPLE URBAN 2,501– 20,000	COMPLEX URBAN 20,001– 500,000	METROPOLITAN over 500,000	Classification	PERCENT in top 2 levels
TOTAL							
1950	. . . . 863,494		258,324	206,634	- -		
1962	. . . . 1,164,226		349,717	305,160	- -		
1972	. . . . 540,071		569,775	678,862	565,363		
PERCENT							
1950	. . . . 65.0		19.4	15.6	- -	0–2	68 to 75
1962	. . . . 64.0		19.2	16.8	- -	0–2	68 to 75
1972	. . . . 22.9		24.2	28.9	24.0	3–2	53.1

SOURCES: Calculated from the various Paraguayan national censuses since 1950, and from SALA, 20–631, 632, 634, 635, 636, 637, and 638.

Table 21-5

SELECTED INDICATORS OF POPULATION CHANGE AND PER CAPITA GNP IN PARAGUAY

Years	Per 1000 Population		Rate of Natural Increase (Annual %)	Number of Years to Double Population	Percent Population Under Age 15	Life Expectancy at Birth	Per Capita GNP (US)
	Births	Deaths					
1940–45	43	20	1.8	- -	- -	- -	- -
1945–50	43	14	2.0	- -	- -	- -	- -
1950–55	47	13	2.6	- -	- -	- -	- -
1955–60	45	11	2.8	- -	- -	- -	108[a]
1960–65	44	11	3.2	- -	- -	- -	- -
1965–70	44	- -	3.5	- -	- -	- -	- -
1970–74	40	12[b]	3.0	21[b]	45[b]	- -	220[b]
1975	40	9	2.8	25	45	62	320
1976	40	9	2.7	26	45	62	480
1977	40	9	3.1	22	45	62	570
1978	39	8	3.1	22	45	62	640
1979	39	8	3.1	22	45	62	760
1980	39	8	3.1	22	45	64	850
1981	34	7	2.6	26	44	64	1,060
1982	34	7	2.6	26	45	64	1,340

a. 1955.
b. 1970.

MAJOR SOURCES:
   Births: SALA, 19-204; SALA, 20-705 through 1975.
   Deaths: SALA, 18-703*d* and 706 through 1970.
   Life expectancy: SALA, 19-700 through 1970.
   Per capita GNP: 1955 data from Ginsburg, *Atlas of Economic Development* (Chicago: University of Chicago Press, 1961).
   Rate of natural increase: SALA, 22-626 from CELADE-BD 10 (1972) through 1970.
   All other data: Population Reference Bureau, Washington, D.C., annual world population data sheets.

Table 21-6

PARAGUAYAN DEPARTMENTS BY GEOGRAPHICAL
SIZE AND SUBDIVISION, 1969

Department	Civil Subdivision (N)	Area km^2	%
Total	164[a]	406,752	100.0
Departamentos			
Alto Paraná	5	20,247	5.0
Amambay	3	12,933	3.2
Boquerón	2	168,030	41.3
Caaguazú	12	21,613	5.3
Caazapá	10	9,496	2.3
Capital (Asunción)	4	200	#
Central	18	2,652	.7
Concepción	6	18,051	4.4
De la Cordillera	17	4,948	1.2
Guairá	15	3,202	.8
Itapúa	17	16,525	4.1
Misiones	9	7,835	1.9
Neembucú	16	13,868	3.4
Olimpo	1	20,415	5.0
Paraguarí	17	8,255	2.0
Presidente Hayes	2	58,480	14.4
San Pedro	10	20,002	4.9

a. Distritos.

SOURCE: SALA, 21-301

Map 22-1

PHYSIOGRAPHIC MAP OF PERU

PERU

Guy-Harold Smith

22

Peru

Peru has had eight official censuses over 147 years, with the first census (1836) counting 1,373,736 individuals. By the fourth census (1876), the national total had doubled to 2,652,000. There was not another census for sixty-four years, so that by 1940 the population had grown by 134 percent to 6,208,000. The latest census (1972) showed a tabulated population of 13,568,000, but the U.S. Bureau of the Census suggested an underenumeration of 4.9 percent and recommended a figure of 14,235,000 for that year. In 1980 the number of people living in Peru was estimated by the Latin American Economic Commission to be 16,821,000 inhabitants.

The population totals, trends, and characteristics of Peru are presented in six tables and six maps. Some of the findings concerning Peru are outlined below.

URBAN TRENDS

Greater Lima in 1972 was the only metropolitan center and had 3,618,000 inhabitants, nearly 27 percent of the population. There were also thirty-seven cities that were classified as complex urban centers with between 20,000 and 500,000 population, including eight cities with more than 100,000 people. The major regional centers include the populations of greater Arequipa (302,316), Trujillo (240,322), Chiclayo (187,809), Chimbote (159,045), Huancayo (126,754), Piura (126,010), Cuzco (121,464), and Iquitos (110,242). Together, these complex urban centers account for 17.8 percent of the population. The percentage of population in simple urban centers between 2,000 and 20,000 in size accounts for an additional 15.8 percent.

RURAL TRENDS

In the twenty-two years between 1950 and 1972 the rural population declined from nearly 60 percent to 40 percent, but the real population grew by 757,000 persons.

SETTLEMENT HIERARCHY

Peru could be classified in 1972 as a dispersed—metropolitan settlement landscape (0—4), with nearly three-fifths of the population living in those two extreme ends of the urban-rural continuum.

OTHER DEMOGRAPHIC DATA

The annual rate of population growth in Peru has been higher than 2.7 percent since the late 1950s, with a peak of 3.1 percent between 1960 and 1974. Life expectancy in 1982 was fifty-seven years, and 44 percent of the population was under fifteen years of age. Per capita GNP in 1982 of $930 was up by 79 percent from $520 in 1975, ranking Peru number 15 (down from 9th in 1975) among the twenty Latin American republics in that category.

Table 22-1

POPULATION DATA AND DENSITY BY DEPARTMENT IN PERU, 1972[a]

Rank	Department	Population	Percent	Percent Change 1961-1972	Population Density 1972 (km^2)
1	Lima	3,485,411	25.7	+71.6	103
2	Cajamarca	916,331	6.8	+22.7	26
3	Piura	854,668	6.3	+27.8	26
4	La Libertad	806,368	5.9	+38.5	35
5	Puno	779,594	5.7	+13.6	12
6	Ancash	726,665	5.4	+24.7	20
7	Cuzco	708,719	5.2	+15.8	9
8	Junín	691,216	5.1	+32.6	16
9	Arequipa	530,528	3.9	+36.4	8
10	Lambayeque	515,363	3.8	+50.5	31
11	Loreto	494,935	3.7	+46.8	1
12	Ayacucho	459,747	3.4	+11.9	10
13	Huánuco	420,764	3.1	+27.9	12
14	Ica	357,973	2.6	+39.9	17
15	Huancavelica	331,155	2.4	+9.4	16
16	Callao	315,605	2.3	+47.8	4,265
17	Apurimac	307,805	2.3	+6.8	15
18	San Martín	224,310	1.7	+38.7	4
19	Amazonas	196,469	1.4	+65.9	5
20	Pasco	176,750	1.3	+27.7	8
21	Tacna	95,623	.7	+44.8	7
22	Tumbes	75,399	.6	+35.1	16
23	Moquegua	74,573	.5	+44.5	5
24	Madre de Dios	21,968	.2	+47.5	0.3
	Total	13,567,939	100.0	+37.0	11

a. The U.S. Bureau of the Census (1977) adjusted the 1972 census figure for an estimated 4.9 percent net underenumeration to 14,235,000 inhabitants. In addition, they estimated the population on July 1, 1979, to be 17,164,000 (1981).

SOURCES: *América en Cifras 1974*; Census of June 4, 1972.

Table 22-2

MAJOR URBAN CENTERS IN PERU, 1972

Rank	Major Urban Centers	Population	Percent
1	✪Gran Lima (1)	3,618,128	26.7
	Lima proper	2,833,609	20.9
	In Lima provincia	468,914	3.5
	●Callao (16)	315,605	2.3
2	●Gran Arequipa (9)	302,316	2.2
	Arequipa proper	99,000	
	Paucarpata	56,000	
	Miraflores	44,000	
	Mariano Melgar	33,000	
	Cerro Colorado	27,000	
	Socabaya	23,000	
	Others	20,316	
3	●Gran Trujillo (4)	240,322	1.8
	Trujillo proper	128,000	
	El Porvenir	59,000	
	La Esperanza	43,000	
4	Gran Chiclayo (10)	187,809	1.4
	Chiclayo proper	149,000	
	Picsi	22,000	
	Others (S. Carlos, etc.)	16,809	
5	Chimbote (6)	159,045	1.2
6	Gran Huancayo (8)	126,754	.9
	Huancayo proper	65,000	
	El Tambo	30,000	
	Chilca	21,000	
	Others	10,754	
7	Gran Piura (3)	126,010	.9
	Piura proper	60,000	
	Castilla	45,000	
	Others	21,010	
8	Gran Cuzco (7)	121,464	.9
	Cuzco proper	68,000	
	Santiago	31,000	
	Huanchac	22,000	
9	Iquitos (11)	110,242	.8
10	●Ica (14)	74,000	.5
11	Sullana (3)	60,000	.4
12	Callar]la (11)	58,000	.4
13	Tacna (21)	56,000	.4
14	Huacho/Hualmay (1)	54,000	.4
15	Pativilca/Barranca (1)	51,000	.4

Table 22-2 (Continued)

MAJOR URBAN CENTERS IN PERU, 1972

Rank	Major Urban Centers	Population	Percent
16	●Chincha Alta/Puebla Nuevo (14)	45,000	.3
17	Pisco (14)	41,000	.3
18	Huánuco (13)	41,000	.3
19	Puno (5)	41,000	.3
20	José Leonardo Ortíz (10)	41,000	.3
21	Juliaca (5)	38,000	.3
22	Cajamarca (2)	38,000	.3
23	Nazca/Marcona (14)	37,000	.3
24	Chaupimarca (20)	36,000	.3
25	Ayacucho (12)	35,000	.3
26	Tumbes (22)	33,000	.3
27	Pariñas (3)	30,000	.2
28	Huaraz (6)	30,000	.2
29	Tarma (8)	28,000	.2
30	Saña (10)	27,000	.2
31	Chulucanas (3)	26,000	.2
32	La Oroya (8)	26,000	.2
33	Chepén (4)	24,000	.2
34	Ilo (23)	22,000	.2
35	Tarapoto (18)	21,000	.2
36	Chocope (4)	21,000	.2
37	Huaral (1)	20,000	.1
38	Rupa Rupa (13)	20,000	.1
			44.2
39	○Santiago del Cao (4)	19,000	
40	Lambayeque (10)	18,000	
41	Yurimaguas (11)	17,000	
42	Moquegua (23)	17,000	
43	Ferreñafe (10)	16,000	
44	Huancavélica (15)	16,000	
45	Mollendo (9)	16,000	
46	Pascamayo (4)	15,000	

SOURCES: Census of June 4, 1972; SALA, 20–629; *United Nations, Demographic Yearbook 1978; América en Cifras 1974.*

Map 22-2

BASE MAP OF DEPARTMENTS IN PERU AND LOCATION OF MAJOR URBAN CENTERS

Note: Provincial numbers are rank ordered according to 1972
population data listed in Table 22-1.

Map 22-3

POPULATION CARTOGRAM OF PERU, 1972

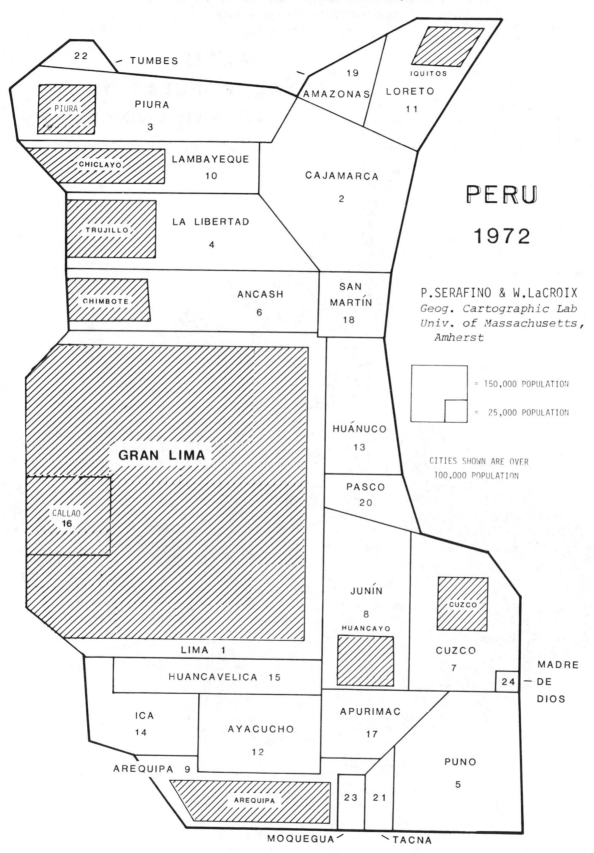

PERU

1972

P.SERAFINO & W.LaCROIX
*Geog. Cartographic Lab
Univ. of Massachusetts,
Amherst*

= 150,000 POPULATION

= 25,000 POPULATION

CITIES SHOWN ARE OVER
100,000 POPULATION

Map 22-4

THREE-DIMENSIONAL CHOROPLETH MAP OF TOTAL POPULATION
BY DEPARTMENT IN PERU, 1972
(By Major Civil Division)

PERU
TOTAL POPULATION
(BY MAJOR CIVIL DIVISION)
1972

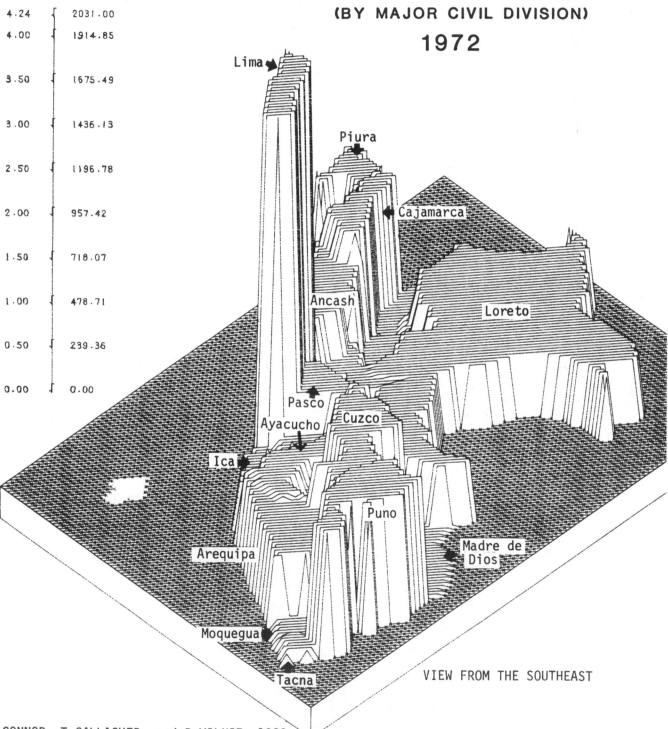

4.24	2031.00
4.00	1914.85
3.50	1675.49
3.00	1436.13
2.50	1196.78
2.00	957.42
1.50	718.07
1.00	478.71
0.50	239.36
0.00	0.00

VIEW FROM THE SOUTHEAST

S.CONNOR, T.GALLAGHER, and R.WILKIE, 1980
Geography Cartographic Laboratory, University of Massachusetts, Amherst
using the SYMVU program from the Harvard Univ. Center for Computer Graphics

Map 22-5

**THREE-DIMENSIONAL CHOROPLETH MAP OF POPULATION DENSITY
IN PERU, 1972**
(Persons per km²)

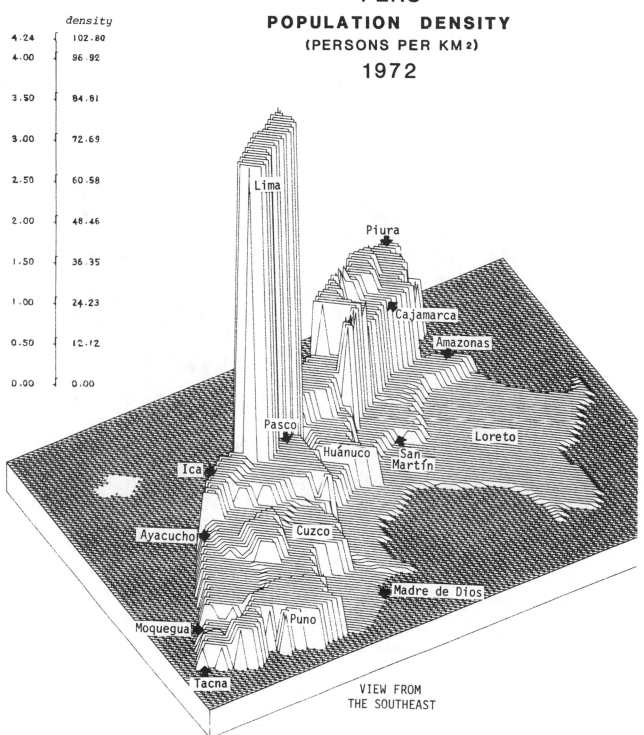

PERU
POPULATION DENSITY
(PERSONS PER KM²)
1972

density

4.24	102.80
4.00	96.92
3.50	84.81
3.00	72.69
2.50	60.58
2.00	48.46
1.50	36.35
1.00	24.23
0.50	12.12
0.00	0.00

Lima

Piura

Cajamarca

Amazonas

Pasco

Loreto

Huánuco   San Martín

Ica

Ayacucho

Cuzco

Madre de Dios

Moquegua   Puno

Tacna

VIEW FROM
THE SOUTHEAST

S.CONNOR, T.GALLAGHER, and R.WILKIE, 1980
Geography Cartographic Laboratory, University of Massachusetts, Amherst
using the SYMVU program from the Harvard Univ. Center for Computer Graphics

Map 22-6

THREE-DIMENSIONAL CHOROPLETH MAP OF POPULATION CHANGE IN PERU, 1961–1972
(%)

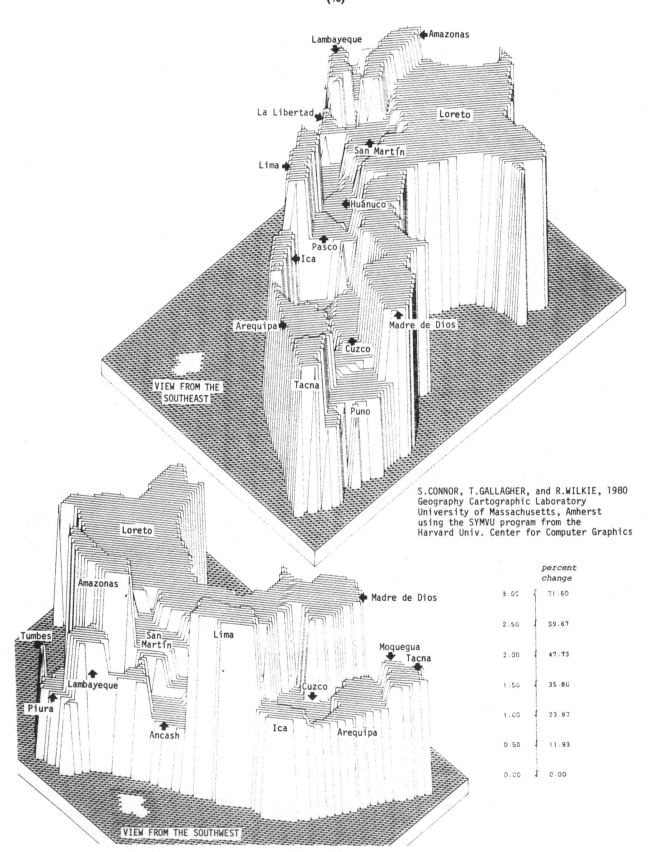

S.CONNOR, T.GALLAGHER, and R.WILKIE, 1980
Geography Cartographic Laboratory
University of Massachusetts, Amherst
using the SYMVU program from the
Harvard Univ. Center for Computer Graphics

VIEW FROM THE SOUTHEAST

VIEW FROM THE SOUTHWEST

	percent change
3.00	71.60
2.50	59.67
2.00	47.73
1.50	35.80
1.00	23.87
0.50	11.93
0.00	0.00

Photo 22-1
ALPACAS AND PERUVIAN VILLAGE NEAR PISAC (1966)

Photo 22-2
OLD TILE ROOF IN LA PAZ, PERU (1966)

Table 22-3

POPULATION FOR EACH NATIONAL CENSUS IN PERU, 1836–1972

Census Year	Population
1836	1,373,736
1850	2,001,203
1862	2,460,684[b]
1876	2,651,840[b]
1940	6,208,000
1950	7,915,000[a]
1961	9,906,746
1972	13,567,939[c]

a. Estimated.
b. Excludes the population of the province of Arica and the department of Tarapaca.
c. Recommended adjustment of population to 14,235,000 by the U.S. Bureau of the Census (1978).

Table 22-4

TOTAL AND PERCENT POPULATION IN FIVE LEVELS OF THE URBAN-RURAL SETTLEMENT HIERARCHY OF PERU SINCE 1950

	0	1	2	3	4	SETTLEMENT HIERARCHY	
CENSUS YEAR	DISPERSED Population 1 to 99	VILLAGE 100 to 2,500	SIMPLE URBAN 2,501– 20,000	COMPLEX URBAN 20,001– 500,000	METROPOLITAN over 500,000	Classification	PERCENT in top 2 levels
TOTAL							
1950	.... 4,669,850[a]		1,493,462	539,936	1,211,752		
1961	.... 5,250,575		1,582,870	1,227,391	1,845,910		
1972	.... 5,427,176		2,148,673	2,373,962	3,618,128		
PERCENT							
1950	.... 59.0[a]		18.9	6.8	15.3	0–2	60 to 68
1961	.... 53.0		16.0	12.4	18.6	0–4	58 to 64
1972	.... 40.0		15.8	17.5	26.7	0–4	54 to 60

a. Estimated

SOURCE: Calculated from the various Peruvian national censuses since 1950, and from SALA, 20–631, 632, 634, 635, 636, 637, and 638.

Table 22-5

SELECTED INDICATORS OF POPULATION CHANGE AND PER CAPITA GNP IN PERU

Years	Per 1000 Population		Rate of Natural Increase (Annual %)	Number of Years to Double Population	Percent Population Under Age 15	Life Expectancy at Birth	Per Capita GNP (US)
	Births	Deaths					
1940–45	25	14	1.8	- -	- -	- -	- -
1945–50	27	13	1.8	- -	- -	- -	- -
1950–55	32	13	2.0	- -	- -	- -	- -
1955–60	36	12	2.7	- -	- -	- -	140[a]
1960–65	43	11	3.1	- -	- -	54	- -
1965–70	43	8	3.1	- -	- -	58	- -
1970–74	41	12	3.1	23[b]	45[b]	- -	350[b]
1975	41	12	2.9	24	44	56	520
1976	41	12	2.9	24	44	56	710
1977	41	12	2.9	24	45	56	810
1978	40	11	2.9	24	45	56	800
1979	40	12	2.8	25	44	55	830
1980	40	12	2.8	25	44	56	740
1981	39	12	2.7	26	42	56	730
1982	38	11	2.8	25	44	57	930

a. 1955.
b. 1970.

MAJOR SOURCES:
   Births: SALA, 19-204; SALA, 20-705 through 1975.
   Deaths: SALA, 18-703d and 706 through 1970.
   Life expectancy: SALA, 19-700 through 1970.
   Per capita GNP: 1955 data from Ginsburg, *Atlas of Economic Development* (Chicago: University of Chicago Press, 1961).
   Rate of natural increase: SALA, 22-626 from CELADE-BD 10 (1972) through 1970.
   All other data: Population Reference Bureau, Washington, D.C., annual world population data sheets.

Table 22-6

PERUVIAN DEPARTMENTS BY GEOGRAPHICAL
SIZE AND SUBDIVISION, 1966

Department	Civil Subdivisions (N)	Area km^2	%
Total	148[a]	1,280,219[b]	100.0
Departamentos			
Amazonas	5	41,297	3.2
Ancash	16	36,308	2.8
Apurimac	6	20,654	1.6
Arequipa	8	63,528	5.0
Ayacucho	7	44,181	3.5
Cajamarca	11	35,418	2.8
Cuzco	13	76,225	6.0
Huancavelica	5	21,079	1.6
Huánuco	7	35,315	2.8
Ica	5	21,251	1.7
Junín	7	43,384	3.4
La Libertad	7	23,241	1.8
Lambayeque	3	16,586	1.3
Lima	7	33,895	2.6
Loreto	6	478,336	37.4
Madre de Dios	3	78,403	6.1
Moquequa	2	16,175	1.3
Pasco	3	21,854	1.7
Piura	7	33,067	2.6
Provincia Constitucional del Callao	- -	74	#
Puno	9	67,386	5.3
San Martíin	6	53,064	4.1
Tacna	2	14,767	1.2
Tumbes	3	4,732	.4

a. Provincias.
b. Excludes 4,966 km^2 Peruvian part of Lake Titicaca.
SOURCE: SALA, 21-301.

Photo 22-3

CARRYING HEAVY LOAD TO THE MARKET AT PISAC, PERU (1966)

Map 23-1

PHYSIOGRAPHIC MAP OF URUGUAY

URUGUAY

GUY HAROLD-SMITH

23

Uruguay

Uruguay has had six official censuses over 131 years, with the first census (1852) counting 131,969 inhabitants. By the third census (1908) the population had grown nearly eightfold to 1,043,000. The latest census (1975) enumerated a population of 2,763,964. In 1980 the number of inhabitants was estimated to be 2,886,000 by the Latin American Economic Commission.

The population totals, trends, and characteristics of Uruguay are presented in six tables and six maps. Some of the findings concerning Uruguay are outlined below.

URBAN TRENDS

Greater Montevideo has always dominated the nation as a primate city, and in 1975 its 1,388,000 inhabitants accounted for 50.1 percent of the national total. There were also fifteen complex urban centers with greater than 20,000 population, but none of them had more than 75,000. The second largest city in Uruguay—Salto—had only about one-twentieth of the population of Montevideo (71,881) and 2.6 percent of the national total. Other important cities in the interior include Paysandú (62,412), Rivera (49,013), and Melo (38,260).

RURAL TRENDS

Uruguay has gradually become one of the least rural countries in Latin America with only one out of every five inhabitants (20.3 percent) living in rural areas. Most of those individuals live in dispersed clusters with fewer than 90,000 people (3.3 percent) living in villages between 100 and 2,000 in size.

SETTLEMENT HIERARCHY

Uruguay in 1975 could be classified as a metropolitan—complex urban settlement landscape (4−3), with nearly seven out of every ten Uruguayans living in the most urban levels above 20,000 in size.

OTHER DEMOGRAPHIC DATA

The annual rate of population growth in Uruguay has slowly declined to .8 percent in 1982 from a high of 1.5 percent in the early 1950s. Life expectancy in 1982 was seventy years, and only 27 percent of the population was under fifteen years of age. Per capita GNP in 1982 of $2820 was up 271 percent from $760 in 1975, ranking Uruguay number 2 (up from 5th in 1975) among the twenty Latin American republics in that category.

Table 23-1

POPULATION DATA AND DENSITY BY PROVINCE IN URUGUAY, 1975[a]

Rank	Province	Population	Percent	Percent Change 1963-1975	Population Density 1975 (km^2)
1	Montevideo	1,229,748	44.4	+2.2	2,265
2	Canelones	321,662	11.6	+24.6	70
3	Colonia	109,889	4.0	+4.3	18
4	Salto	102,899	3.7	+11.6	7
5	Paysandú	98,895	3.6	+12.3	7
6	San José	89,410	3.2	+12.4	18
7	Tacuarembó	84,830	3.1	+10.2	5
8	Rivera	81,969	2.9	+6.3	9
9	Soriano	80,305	2.9	+3.1	8
10	Maldonado	75,633	2.7	+23.5	16
11	Cerro Largo	73,697	2.6	+3.8	5
12	Florída	66,276	2.4	+3.6	6
13	Lavalleja	65,220	2.4	-.9	6
14	Rocha	59,359	2.1	+7.7	6
15	Artigas	57,432	2.1	+8.7	5
16	Durazno	54,693	2.0	+2.0	5
17	Río Negro	49,963	1.8	+6.6	5
18	Treinta y Tres	45,680	1.6	+5.2	5
19	Flores	24,684	.9	+4.9	5
	Total	2,769,781	100.0	+6.7	16

a. The U.S. Bureau of the Census (1977) estimates a 2.1 net underenumeration for 1975, and thus a population of 2,842,000. In addition, they estimated the population on July 1, 1979, to be 2,910,000 (1981).

SOURCES: Census of October 16, 1963, and May 21, 1975; SALA, 18-602a.

Table 23-2

MAJOR URBAN CENTERS IN URUGUAY, 1975

Rank	Major Urban Centers	Population	Percent
1	✪ Gran Montevideo	1,387,198	50.1
	Montevideo proper	1,173,254	42.4
	Metropolitan area in the Departamento de Canalones	213,944	7.7
	● Las Piedras (2)	53,983	
	Pando	16,184	
	La Paz	14,402	
	Paso de Carrasco	8,557	
	Barros Blancos	8,432	
	Progreso	8,257	
	10 centers between 2,000 and 5,000	31,266	
	9 villages between 150 and 2,000	10,724	
	Unincorporated areas in the metropolitan area	62,139	
2	● Salto (4)	71,881	2.6
3	Paysandú (5)	62,412	2.3
4	● Rivera (8)	49,013	1.8
5	Melo (11)	38,260	1.4
6	Minas (13)	35,433	1.3
7	Mercedes (9)	34,667	1.3
8	Tacuarembó (7)	30,674	1.1
9	Artigas (15)	29,256	1.1
10	San José (6)	28,427	1.0
11	Durazno (16)	25,811	.9
12	Trenta y Tres (18)	25,757	.9
13	Florida (12)	25,030	.9
14	Maldonado (10)	22,159	.8
15	Rocha (14)	21,672	.8
			68.2

Source: *Uruguay, V Censo General de Población, 1975, Datos Preliminares* (Montevideo: Ministerio de Economía y Finanzas, Dirección General de Estadística y Censos, 1976).

Map 23-2

**BASE MAP OF PROVINCES IN URUGUAY AND LOCATION
OF MAJOR URBAN CENTERS**

Note: Department numbers are rank ordered according to
         population data listed in Table 23-1.

Map 23-3

POPULATION CARTOGRAM OF URUGUAY, 1975

URUGUAY
1975

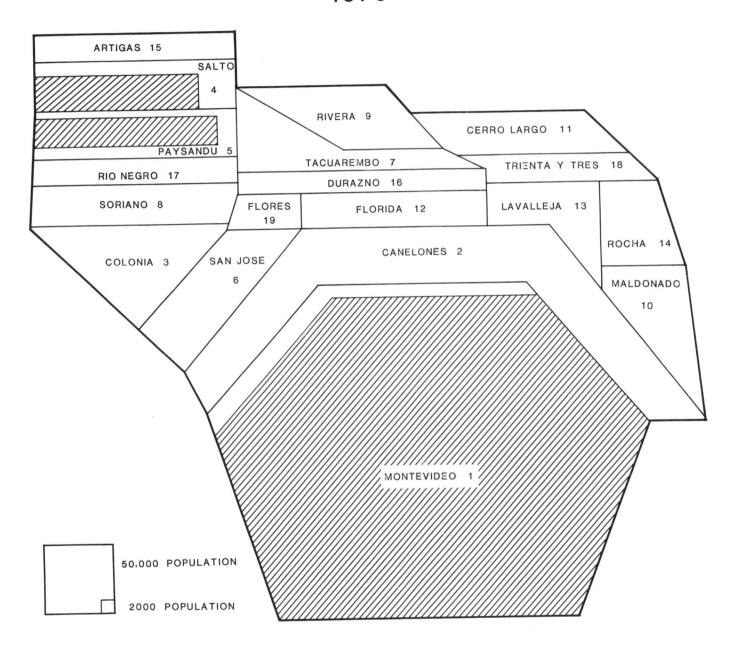

ARTIGAS 15

SALTO
4

PAYSANDU 5

RIO NEGRO 17

SORIANO 8

RIVERA 9

TACUAREMBO 7

DURAZNO 16

FLORES
19

FLORIDA 12

CERRO LARGO 11

TRIENTA Y TRES 18

LAVALLEJA 13

COLONIA 3

SAN JOSE
6

CANELONES 2

ROCHA 14

MALDONADO
10

MONTEVIDEO 1

50,000 POPULATION

2000 POPULATION

ROSANNE HYNES
Geography Cartographic Laboratory
Univ. of Massachusetts, Amherst

Map 23-4

THREE-DIMENSIONAL CHOROPLETH MAP OF TOTAL POPULATION
BY PROVINCE IN URUGUAY, 1975
(By Major Civil Division)

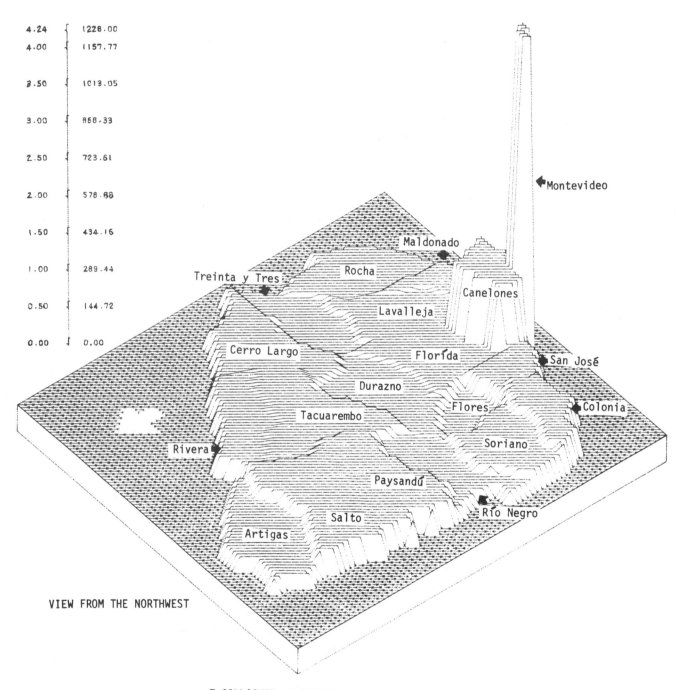

VIEW FROM THE NORTHWEST

T.GALLAGHER, M.RICHARDS, and R.WILKIE, 1980
Geography Cartographic Laboratory, University of Massachusetts, Amherst
using the SYMVU program from the Harvard Univ. Computer Graphics Center

Map 23-5

**THREE-DIMENSIONAL CHOROPLETH MAP OF POPULATION
DENSITY IN URUGUAY, 1975
(Persons per km²)**

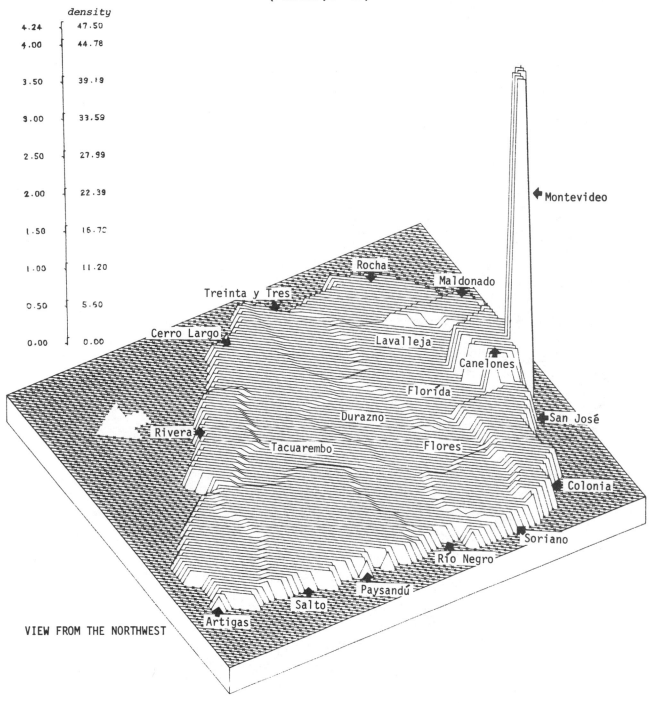

VIEW FROM THE NORTHWEST

T.GALLAGHER, M.RICHARDS, and R.WILKIE, 1980
Geography Cartographic Laboratory, University of Massachusetts, Amherst
using the SYMVU program from the Harvard Univ. Computer Graphics Center

Map 23-6

THREE-DIMENSIONAL CHOROPLETH MAP OF POPULATION CHANGE IN URUGUAY, 1963–1975

(%)

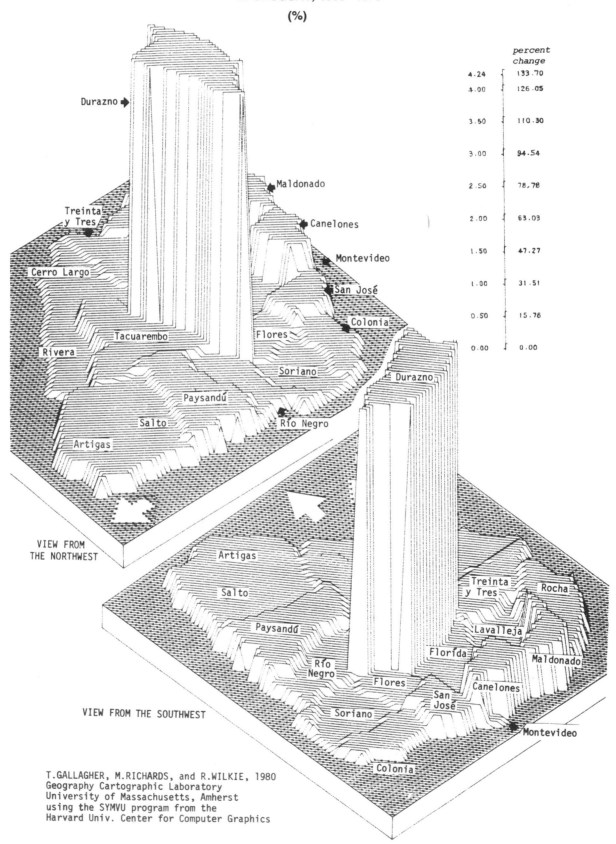

	percent change
4.24	133.70
4.00	126.05
3.50	110.30
3.00	94.54
2.50	78.78
2.00	63.03
1.50	47.27
1.00	31.51
0.50	15.76
0.00	0.00

VIEW FROM THE NORTHWEST

VIEW FROM THE SOUTHWEST

T.GALLAGHER, M.RICHARDS, and R.WILKIE, 1980
Geography Cartographic Laboratory
University of Massachusetts, Amherst
using the SYMVU program from the
Harvard Univ. Center for Computer Graphics

Photo 23-1

**QUIET SIDE STREET IN A COMPLEX URBAN CENTER,
PAYSANDÚ, URUGUAY (1975)**

Table 23-3

POPULATION FOR EACH NATIONAL CENSUS IN URUGUAY, 1852–1975

Census Year	Population
1852	131,969
1860	229,480
1908	1,042,686
1950	1,328,452[a]
1963	2,595,510
1975	2,763,964[b]

a. Estimated.
b. Recommended adjustment of population to 2,842,000 by the U.S. Bureau of the Census (1978).

Table 23-4

TOTAL AND PERCENT POPULATION IN FIVE LEVELS OF THE URBAN-RURAL SETTLEMENT HIERARCHY OF URUGUAY SINCE 1950

	0	1	2	3	4	SETTLEMENT HIERARCHY	
CENSUS YEAR	DISPERSED Population 1 to 99	VILLAGE 100 to 2,000	SIMPLE URBAN 2,001– 20,000	COMPLEX URBAN 20,001– 500,000	METROPOLITAN over 500,000	Classification	PERCENT in top 2 levels
TOTAL							
1950	....	943,420	54,038	286,923	909,619		
1963	....	726,743	274,205	435,477	1,159,085		
1975	470,066	89,970	316,278	500,452	1,387,198		
PERCENT							
1950	....	43.0[a]	2.4	13.1	41.5	4–0	67 to 73
1963	....	28.0	10.5	16.8	44.7	4–2	64.3
1975	17.0	3.3	11.5	18.1	50.1	4–3	68.2

a. Estimated.

SOURCES: Calculated from the various Uruguayan national censuses since 1950, and from SALA, 20–631, 632, 634, 635, 636, 637, and 638.

Table 23-5

SELECTED INDICATORS OF POPULATION CHANGE AND PER CAPITA GNP IN URUGUAY

Years	Per 1000 Population		Rate of Natural Increase (Annual %)	Number of Years to Double Population	Percent Population Under Age 15	Life Expectancy at Birth	Per Capita GNP (US)
	Births	Deaths					
1940–45	19	10	1.1	- -	- -	- -	- -
1945–50	20	9	1.3	- -	- -	- -	- -
1950–55	19	9	1.5	- -	- -	- -	- -
1955–60	21	9	1.4	- -	- -	- -	569[a]
1960–65	22	9	1.4	- -	- -	68	- -
1965–70	21	10	1.2	- -	28	- -	- -
1970–74	21	9	1.2	58[b]	28[b]	- -	550[b]
1975	19	9	1.0	69	28	70	760
1976	19	10	1.1	63	28	70	1,060
1977	21	10	1.1	63	28	70	1,330
1978	21	10	1.1	63	28	69	1,390
1979	21	10	1.1	63	27	69	1,450
1980	21	10	1.1	65	27	69	1,610
1981	20	10	1.0	67	27	71	2,090
1982	19	11	.8	87	27	70	2,820

a. 1955.
b. 1970.

MAJOR SOURCES:

Births: SALA, 19-204; SALA, 20-705 through 1976.

Deaths: SALA, 18-703*d* and 706 through 1970.

Life expectancy: SALA, 19-700 through 1970.

Per capita GNP: 1955 data from Ginsburg, *Atlas of Economic Development* (Chicago: University of Chicago Press, 1961).

Rate of natural increase: SALA, 22-626 from CELADE-BD 10 (1972) through 1970.

All other data: Population Reference Bureau, Washington, D.C., annual world population data sheets.

Table 23-6

URUGUAYAN PROVINCES BY GEOGRAPHICAL
SIZE AND SUBDIVISION, 1963

Province	Civil Subdivisions (N)	Area km^2	Area %
Total	227[a]	177,508	100.0
Provinces			
Artigas	9	12,145	6.8
Canelones	16	4,533	2.6
Cerro Largo	12	13,851	7.8
Colonia	14	6,114	3.4
Durazno	13	12,208	6.9
Flores	6	5,133	2.9
Florida	13	10,384	5.9
Lavalleja	13	10,149	5.7
Maldonado	9	4,705	2.7
Montevideo	24	543	.3
Paysandú	12	14,106	7.9
Río Negro	12	9,637	5.4
Rivera	9	9,099	5.1
Rocha	10	10,991	6.2
Salto	11	14,359	8.1
San José	7	4,994	2.8
Soriano	14	8,914	5.0
Tacuarembó	14	15,969	9.0
Treinta y tres	9	9,676	5.5

a. Secciones Judiciales.

SOURCE: SALA, 21-301.

Photo 23-2

**ISOLATED HOMESTEADS ON THE DAIRY AND CROP SETTLEMENT
LANDSCAPE OF SOUTHERN SOUTH AMERICA (1975)**

Map 24-1

PHYSIOGRAPHIC MAP OF VENEZUELA

VENEZUELA

GUY-HAROLD SMITH

24

Venezuela

Venezuela has had eleven official censuses over 110 years. The first census (1873) enumerated 1,784,194 inhabitants. By the fifth census (1926) the population had slightly more than doubled to 2,890,631. The eighth census (1950) counted 5,034,838 (up 74 percent in twenty-four years), and that total more than doubled by 1971 to 10,721,522. The latest census (1981) had a tabulated population of 14,602,480, for an increase of 36 percent in a decade.

The population totals, trends, and characteristics of Venezuela are presented in six tables and six maps. Some of the findings concerning Venezuela are listed below.

URBAN TRENDS

In 1971 there were two metropolitan centers with more than half a million population—Greater Caracas with 2,175,400 and Maracaibo with 651,574—and together they accounted for 26.4 percent of the nation's total. An urban census in 1976 counted 2,576,000 in Greater Caracas and 792,000 in Maracaibo. The complex urban level was the most highly developed sector in Venezuela in 1971 and there were 51 cities between 20,000 and 500,000 in size. The six cities over 150,000 at that time were Greater Valencia (402,171), Barquisimeto (330,815), Maracay (255,134), Cabimas/Ciudad Ojeda (201,037), Greater Barcelona (184,000), and San Cristóbal (151,717). All of these had between 240,000 and 481,000 in 1976. Overall, the complex urban level accounted for 34.2 percent of the population in 1971,

with the simple urban level of towns between 2,500 and 20,000 population accounting for 14.4 percent.

RURAL TRENDS

The rural population in 1971 had dropped to one-quarter of the population (25 percent) from 37 percent in 1961 and 51.4 percent in 1950. In spite of the sharp decline in the percentage, the number of rural inhabitants has remained relatively constant at about 2.6 million throughout the twenty-one years.

SETTLEMENT HIERARCHY

Venezuela could be classified as a complex urban—metropolitan (3−4) settlement landscape in 1971, with three out of five Venezuelans living in the two most urban levels in the settlement hierarchy. Previously the two most important levels had been complex urban and dispersed in 1950 and 1961.

OTHER DEMOGRAPHIC DATA

The annual rate of population growth in Venezuela has been high since the 1940s. In the early 1950s the rate reached 4 percent a year before declining to 2.8 in the early 1970s and then rising to slightly over 3 percent between 1977 and 1981. Life expectancy in 1982 was sixty-six years, and 43 percent of the population was under fifteen years of age. Per capita GNP in 1982 of $3630 was up by 193 percent from $1240 in 1975, ranking Venezuela number 1 among the twenty Latin American republics in that category.

Table 24-1

POPULATION DATA AND DENSITY BY CIVIL SUBDIVISION IN VENEZUELA, 1971[a]

Rank	State	Population	Percent	Percent Change 1961-1971	Population Density 1971 (km^2)
1	Distrito Federal	1,860,637	17.4	+48.0	964
2	Zulia	1,299,030	12.1	+41.2	26
3	Miranda	856,272	8.0	+73.9	108
4	Lara	671,410	6.3	+37.3	34
5	Carabobo	659,339	6.2	+72.8	151
6	Aragua	543,170	5.1	+73.4	79
7	Táchira	511,346	4.8	+28.1	46
8	Anzóategui	506,297	4.7	+32.5	12
9	Sucre	469,004	4.4	+16.7	40
10	Falcón	407,957	3.8	+19.8	16
11	Bolívar	391,665	3.7	+83.4	2
12	Trujillo	381,334	3.6	+16.7	52
13	Mérida	347,095	3.2	+28.2	31
14	Guárico	318,905	3.0	+30.2	5
15	Monagas	298,239	2.8	+21.1	10
16	Portuguesa	297,047	2.8	+45.8	20
17	Barinas	231,046	2.2	+65.9	7
18	Yaracuy	223,545	2.1	+27.5	32
19	Apure	164,705	1.5	+40.1	2
20	Nueva Esparta	118,830	1.1	+32.8	103
21	Cojedes	94,351	.9	+29.9	6
22	Delta Amacuro Territory	48,139	.5	+41.7	1
23	Amazonas Territory	21,696	.2	+84.5	0.1
	Dependencias Federales (Islands)	463	- -	-46.2	4
	Total	10,721,522	100.0	+42.5	12

a. The U.S. Bureau of the Census (1978) adjusted the 1974 census figure for an estimated underenumeration of 4.6 percent to 11,234,000 inhabitants. In addition, they estimated the population on July 1, 1979, to be 14,539,000 (1981).

SOURCE: Census of November 2, 1971.

Table 24-2

MAJOR URBAN CENTERS IN VENEZUELA, 1971

Rank	Major Urban Centers	1971 Population	1971 Percent	June 30, 1976
1	✪ Gran Caracas	2,175,400	20.3	2,576,000
	Caracas proper (1)	1,035,000		1,662,627
	Petare (9)	230,000		
	El Valle (1)	186,000		
	Antímano (1)	169,000		
	Baruta (9)	122,000		
	El Recreo (1)	114,000		
	La Vega (1)	107,000		
	Chacao (9)	79,000		
	Leoncio Martínez (9)	59,000		
	Macarao (1)	48,000		
	other in (1 & 9)	26,400		

TABLE 24-2 (Continued)

MAJOR URBAN CENTERS IN VENEZUELA, 1971

Rank	Major Urban Centers	1971 Population	1971 Percent	June 30, 1976
2	● Maracaibo (2)	651,574	6.1	792,000
3	● Gran Valencia (5)	402,171	3.8	481,000
	Valencia proper	367,171		439,000
	Guacara	35,000		
4	Barquisimeto (4)	330,815	3.1	430,000
5	Maracay (6)	255,134	2.4	301,000
6	● Cabimas/Ciudad Ojeda (Lagunillas) (2)	201,037	1.9	265,000
7	Gran Barcelona (8)	184,000	1.7	242,000
	Barcelona	76,000		
	Puerto La Cruz	63,000		
	Pozuelos	45,000		
8	San Cristóbal (7)	151,717	1.4	241,000
9	Ciudad Guayana (San Felix de) (11)	143,000	1.3	180,000
10	Maturín (15)	122,000	1.1	154,000
11	Cumaná (9)	120,000	1.1	148,000
12	Ciudad Bolívar (11)	104,000	1.0	130,000
13	● Acarigua/Araure (16)	84,000		109,000
14	Maiquetía/La Guaira (1)	79,000	.7	
15	Valera (12)	74,000	.7	100,000
16	Mérida (13)	74,000	.7	
17	Puerto Cabello (5)	73,000	.7	
18	Turmero/Cagua (6)	73,000	.7	
19	Coro (10)	69,000	.6	
20	Los Teques (3)	63,000	.6	
21	Catia la Mar (1)	62,000	.6	
22	Barinas (17)	56,000	.5	
23	Punto Fijo (10)	55,000	.5	105,000
24	Carúpano (9)	51,000	.5	
25	El Tigre (8)	50,000	.5	
26	● San Felipe (18)	44,000	.4	
27	La Victoria (2)	42,000	.4	
28	S. Fernando de Apure (19)	39,000	.4	
29	San Juan de los Moros (14)	38,000	.4	
30	Guanare (16)	38,000	.4	
31	Calabozo (14)	37,000	.4	
32	Valle de la Pascua (14)	37,000	.4	
33	Carona (4)	36,000	.3	
34	Guarenas (3)	33,000	.3	
35	Porlamar (20)	32,000	.3	
36	Anaco (8)	29,000	.3	
37	Villa de Cura (6)	28,000	.3	
38	S. Carlos del Zulia (2)	27,000	.3	
39	Trujillo (12)	26,000	.2	
40	Mariara (5)	24,000	.2	
41	Ocumare del Tuy (3)	24,000	.2	
42	Yaritagua (19)	24,000	.2	
43	Upata (11)	23,000	.2	
44	S. José de Guanipa (8)	22,000	.2	
45	Rubio (7)	22,000	.2	
46	Tucupido (14)	21,000	.2	
47	El Vigía (13)	21,000	.2	
48	Altagracia (2)	21,000	.2	
49	San Carlos (21)	21,000	.2	
50	Caraballeda (1)	21,000	.2	
51	Caripito (15)	21,000	.2	
52	Altagracia de Orituco (14)	21,000	.2	
53	S. Antonio de Táchira (7)	20,000	.2	
			51.0%	

SOURCES: Census of November 2, 1971; *América en Cifras 1974*; United Nations, *Demographic Yearbook 1978*. SALA, 20-629; U.S. Bureau of the Census, *World Population 1977*.

Map 24-2

BASE MAP OF CIVIL SUBDIVISIONS IN VENEZUELA AND
LOCATION OF MAJOR URBAN CENTERS

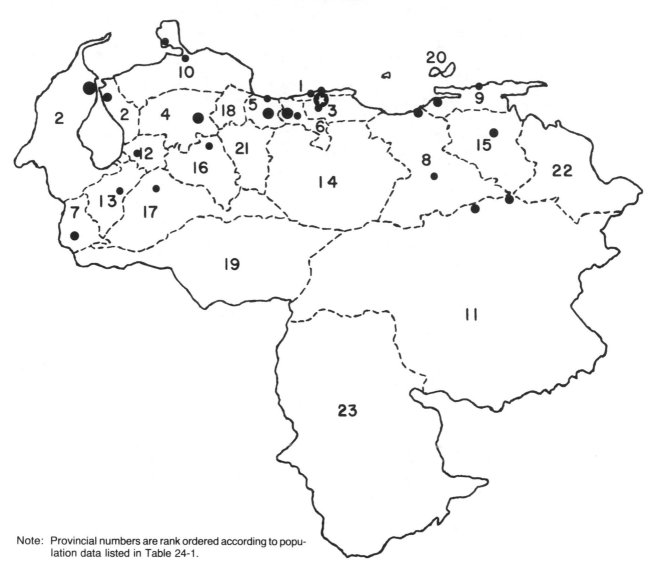

Note: Provincial numbers are rank ordered according to population data listed in Table 24-1.

Map 24-3

POPULATION CARTOGRAM OF VENEZUELA, 1971

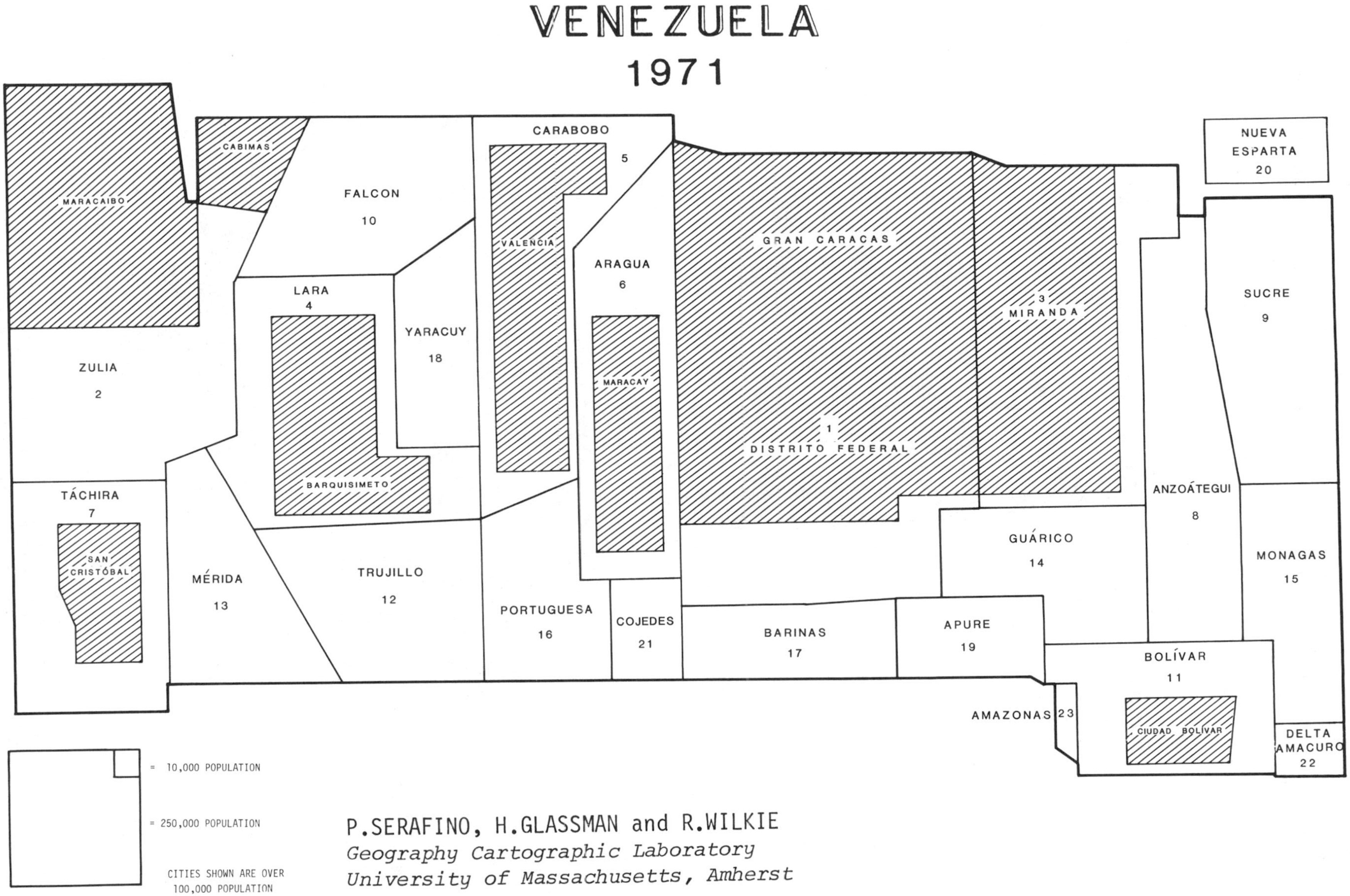

VENEZUELA
1971

P.SERAFINO, H.GLASSMAN and R.WILKIE
Geography Cartographic Laboratory
University of Massachusetts, Amherst

NUEVA ESPARTA 20

SUCRE 9

MONAGAS 15

DELTA AMACURO 22

ANZOÁTEGUI 8

BOLÍVAR 11

CIUDAD BOLÍVAR

MIRANDA 3

GUÁRICO 14

AMAZONAS 23

GRAN CARACAS

DISTRITO FEDERAL 1

APURE 19

BARINAS 17

CARABOBO 5

ARAGUA 6

MARACAY

COJEDES 21

VALENCIA

PORTUGUESA 16

FALCON 10

YARACUY 18

TRUJILLO 12

LARA 4

BARQUISIMETO

CABIMAS

MÉRIDA 13

ZULIA 2

MARACAIBO

TÁCHIRA 7

SAN CRISTÓBAL

= 10,000 POPULATION

= 250,000 POPULATION

CITIES SHOWN ARE OVER 100,000 POPULATION

Map 24-4

THREE-DIMENSIONAL CHOROPLETH MAP OF TOTAL POPULATION BY
STATE IN VENEZUELA, 1971
(By Major Civil Division)

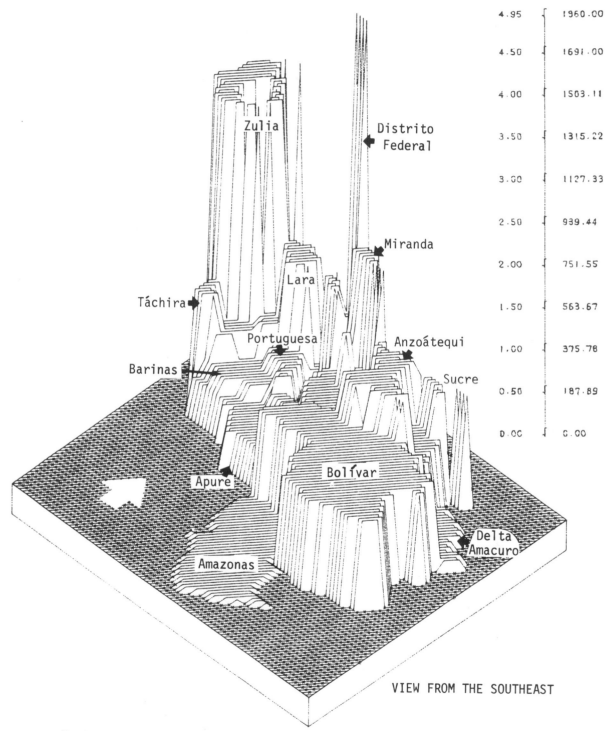

VIEW FROM THE SOUTHEAST

K.MAXWELL, T.GALLAGHER, M.RICHARDS, and R.WILKIE, 1980
Geography Cartographic Laboratory, University of Massachusetts, Amherst
using the SYMVU program from the Harvard Univ. Computer Graphics Center

Map 24-5

THREE-DIMENSIONAL CHOROPLETH MAP OF POPULATION
DENSITY IN VENEZUELA, 1971
(Persons per km²)

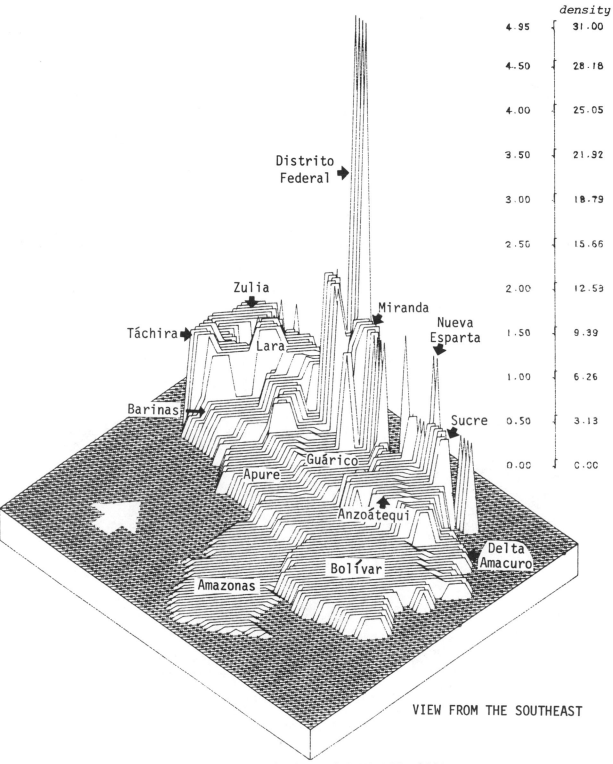

VIEW FROM THE SOUTHEAST

K.MAXWELL, T.GALLAGHER, M.RICHARDS, and R.WILKIE, 1980
Geography Cartographic Laboratory, University of Massachusetts, Amherst
using the SYMVU program from the Harvard Univ. Computer Graphics Center

Map 24-6

THREE-DIMENSIONAL CHOROPLETH MAP OF POPULATION CHANGE
IN VENEZUELA, 1961–1971
(%)

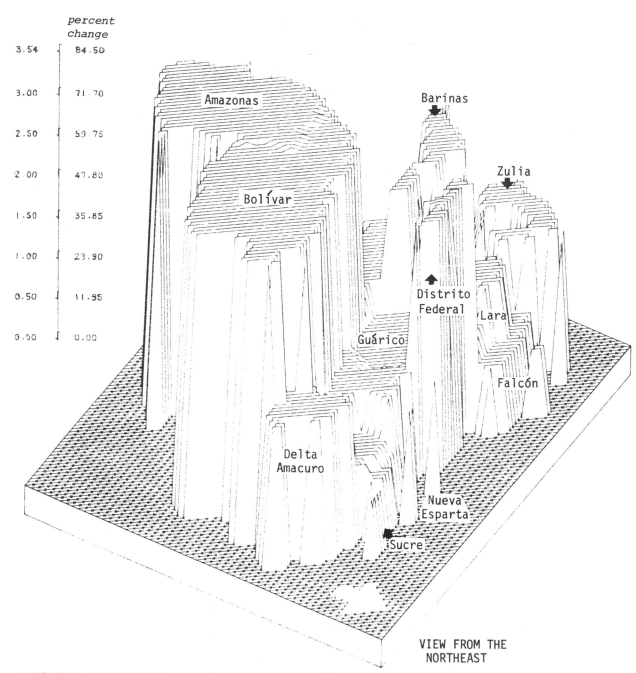

K.MAXWELL, T.GALLAGHER, M.RICHARDS, and R.WILKIE, 1980
Geography Cartographic Laboratory, University of Massachusetts, Amherst
using the SYMVU program from the Harvard Univ. Computer Graphics Center

Photo 24-1

YOUNG GIRL TENDING GOATS, EASTERN SLOPE OF THE ANDES MOUNTAINS (1966)

Table 24-3

POPULATION FOR EACH NATIONAL CENSUS
IN VENEZUELA, 1873–1981

Census Year	Population	Census Year	Population
1873	1,784,194	1941	3,850,771
1881	2,075,545	1950	5,034,838
1891	2,323,527	1961	7,523,999
1920	2,365,098	1971	10,721,522[a]
1926	2,890,631	1981	14,602,480
1936	3,491,159		

a. Recommended adjustment of population to 11,234,000 by the
U.S. Bureau of the Census (1978).

Table 24-4

TOTAL AND PERCENT POPULATION IN FIVE LEVELS OF THE URBAN-RURAL
SETTLEMENT HIERARCHY OF VENEZUELA SINCE 1950

	0	1	2	3	4	SETTLEMENT HIERARCHY	
CENSUS YEAR	DISPERSED Population 1 to 99	VILLAGE 100 to 2,500	SIMPLE URBAN 2,501– 20,000	COMPLEX URBAN 20,001– 500,000	METROPOLITAN over 500,000	Classification	PERCENT in top 2 levels
TOTAL							
1950	1,988,578	597,628	771,987	886,189	790,602		
1961	....	2,783,880	1,203,813	2,043,928	1,492,378		
1971	....	2,680,380	1,544,529	3,668,874	2,827,739		
PERCENT							
1950	39.5	11.9	15.3	17.6	15.7	0–3	57.1
1961	....	37.0	16.0	27.2	19.8	3–0	55 to 60
1971	....	25.0	14.4	34.2	26.4	3–4	60.6

SOURCES: Calculated from the various Venezuelan national censuses of the country since 1950, and from SALA, 20-631, 632, 634,
635, 636, 637, and 638.

Table 24-5

SELECTED INDICATORS OF POPULATION CHANGE AND PER CAPITA GNP IN VENEZUELA

Years	Per 1000 Population		Rate of Natural Increase (Annual %)	Number of Years to Double Population	Percent Population Under Age 15	Life Expectancy at Birth	Per Capita GNP (US)
	Births	Deaths					
1940–45	36	16	2.8	- -	- -	- -	- -
1945–50	39	14	3.1	- -	- -	- -	- -
1950–55	44	10	4.0	- -	- -	- -	762[a]
1955–60	44	9	3.9	- -	- -	- -	- -
1960–65	45	8	3.3	- -	- -	60[b]	- -
1965–70	40	7	3.4	- -	- -	- -	- -
1970–74	36	8	2.8	21[c]	46[c]	- -	880[c]
1975	36	7	2.9	24	50	65	1,240
1976	36	7	2.9	24	48	65	1,710
1977	37	6	3.1	22	45	65	2,220
1978	36	7	3.0	23	45	65	2,570
1979	36	6	3.0	23	43	65	2,820
1980	36	6	3.0	23	43	66	2,910
1981	36	6	3.0	23	42	66	3,130
1982	34	5	2.9	24	43	66	3,630

a. 1955.
b. 1961.
c. 1970.

MAJOR SOURCES:
Births: SALA, 19-204; SALA, 20-705 through 1970.
Deaths: SALA, 18-703*d* and 706 through 1970.
Life expectancy: SALA, 19-700 through 1970.
Per capita GNP: 1955 data from Ginsburg, *Atlas of Economic Development* (Chicago: University of Chicago Press, 1961).
Rate of natural increase: SALA, 22-626 from CELADE-BD 10 (1972) through 1970.
All other data: Population Reference Bureau, Washington, D.C., annual world population data sheets.

Table 24-6

VENEZUELAN STATES BY GEOGRAPHICAL
SIZE AND SUBDIVISION, 1961

State	Civil Subdivision (N)	Area	
		km^2	%
Total	174[a]	898,805[a]	100.0
Federal District	2[b]	1,930	.2
States and Territories			
Anzóategui	13	43,300	4.8
Apure	6	76,500	8.5
Aragua	8	6,920	.8
Barinas	7	35,200	3.9
Bolívar	6	238,000	26.5
Carabobo	6	4,369	.5
Cojedes	7	14,800	1.6
Falcón	12	24,800	2.8
Guárico	7	64,986	7.2
Lara	7	19,800	2.2
Mérida	11	11,300	1.3
Miranda	11	7,950	.9
Monagas	7	28,900	3.2
Nueva Esparta	6	1,150	.1
Portuguesa	8	15,200	1.7
Sucre	10	11,800	1.3
Táchira	9	11,100	1.2
Territorio Amazonas	4[b]	175,750	19.6
Territorio Delta Amacuro	3[b]	40,200	4.5
Trujillo	7	7,400	.8
Yaracuy	7	7,100	.8
Zulia	10	50,230	5.6

a. Composed of 165 districts and 9 departments.
    Excludes 13,245 km^2 for lakes Maracaibo and Valencia.
b. The Federal District and the 2 territories have the 9 departments.

SOURCE: SALA, 21-301.

Photo 24-2
SOIL EROSION IN THE ANDEAN REGION (1966)

Photo 24-3
USE OF THE OXEN-DRAWN SPANISH-STYLE PLOW IN THE ANDEAN REGION (1966)

About the Author

Richard W. Wilkie is Professor of Geography at the University of Massachusetts, Amherst, where he has taught for the last 16 years. He is the author of numerous articles, chapters, and monographs on urbanization, population change, rural to urban migration, periodic markets, and rural economic development in Latin America. His interests in Latin America began early when he spent three years as an undergraduate at Mexico City College (1956–1959), before graduating with a B.A. in geography and history from the University of Washington in 1960. He earned an M.A. in 1963 and a Ph.D. in 1968 in geography from the same institution. Professor Wilkie was a Fulbright Fellow to Argentina in 1965–1967, and he has undertaken other funded research in Argentina, Bolivia, Mexico, Guatemala, and Ecuador. His latest research in Ecuador involves rural development through the decentralization of urban functions into small market towns and the improvement of rural marketing practices.